THE KNOWLEDGE
OF STRATEGY

THE KNOWLEDGE OF STRATEGY

Foundation For An Intelligence of Strategy

by

NATHAN D. GRUNDSTEIN
Professor (Em.) Management Policy
Weatherhead School of Management

Foreword by Ronald G. Smart

A Zeus Book

Weatherhead School of Management
Case Western Reserve University

FIRST EDITION

Library of Congress Cataloging-in-Publication Data

Grundstein, Nathan D.
    The knowledge of strategy : foundation for an intelligence of strategy / Nathan D. Grundstein.
        p.   cm.
    Continues: The managerial Kant; The futures of prudence.
    Includes bibliographical references and index.
    ISBN 0-930305-01-9
    1. Strategic planning—Philosophy. 2. Knowledge, Theory of.
HD30.28.G78   1992
658.4'012—dc20   92-47479
                                                                                                         CIP

    Copyright retained by the author. All rights reserved. No part of this book may be reproduced or transmitted in any form, or by any means, electronic or mechanical, including photocopying, recording, or by any information storage and retrieval system, without permission in writing from the author.

    Copyright © book cover design by N. D. Grundstein

DEDICATED TO THE STAFF

AT THE

SCHOOL OF ADMINISTRATIVE STUDIES,

CANBERRA COLLEGE OF

ADVANCED EDUCATION, AUSTRALIA

(NOW FACULTY OF MANAGEMENT,
UNIVERSITY OF CANBERRA)

WHO TREATED ME AS A MATE

Sam S. Richardson
(Founding Principal of the College)

Cecil Carr	Alexander Kouzmin
Anne McMahon	Roger Wettenhall
Geoffrey Hawker	Alan Jarman

A Trilogy on the Foundation for an Intelligence of Strategy

THE KNOWLEDGE OF STRATEGY (1992)
THE FUTURES OF PRUDENCE (1984)
THE MANAGERIAL KANT (1982)

With this, the third volume, the trilogy is now complete. The title of this final volume declares the subject matter of the entire trilogy, *The Knowledge of Strategy*. It is a subject matter as to which each volume of the trilogy stands by itself with its own theme and path of development. To think strategically, the strategist must invest an idea of strategy with an intelligibility such that a course of strategizing can be said to be known. An explanation of strategic thinking, then, searches for those underlying cognitions in which understanding and knowledge are grounded and also for how they become the stuff for strategy by the strategist.

CONTENTS

PERMISSION TO REPRINT	xxi
ACKNOWLEDGEMENT	xix
FORWARD	xxi
PROLOGUE	xxix

PART I—COMMAND COGNITION
THE KNOWLEDGE OF STRATEGY:
THREE QUESTIONS

Knowledge of strategy exists as a knowledge for whom?	1
CHAPTER I: Towards Knowledge Based Strategizing	5
CHAPTER II: Command Cognition and Strategic Knowledge	14
1. The Business of Telephony	14
The Knowlege of Command Cognition	15
The Business of Telephony	16
Strategy and Telephony: Strategist and Strategizing	18
Command Cognition and Grand Strategy	22
NOTE: The Information Business	24
2. The Business of Entrepreneurial Capitalism	26
Financial Entrepreneurship	26
Fitted Knowledge: Structure Without Strategy	26
Possibilities Knowledge: The Knowledge Strategy	28

Command Cognition: From "Finance Capitalism" to Entrepreneurial Capitalism	29
Strategizing the Business of Entrepreneurial Capitalism	30
NOTE	33
3. The Business of Electronics	34
Possibilities Knowledge and the Knowledge of Strategy	34
Possibilities Knowledge: European and Japanese Technologies	37
Diffusion/Application of Technology	38
The Technology/Product and Product/Technology Relation	39
"Mechatronics" and the Technology/Product Interrelation	40
Hegemonic Industrialization	41
The Vision of Strategy	41
The Foundation of a Base Technology	42
Hegemonic Industrialization As Grand Strategy	44
The Knowledge of Grand Strategy	44
Focused Industrialization As Grand Strategy	47
NOTE: Grand Strategy: Japan, The Take-off Years	49
CHAPTER III: Command Cognition: Power, Agency and Experience	57
1. Command Cognition	57
Power and Cognition	57
The Person as Agent	58
Strategy as Engagement	59
Strategic Knowledge and Micro-Capitalism	59
"Real Capitalism" and Command Cognition	61
2. Experience as Rule Cognition	62
The Rule as Cognitive Knowledge	62
The Idea of Power	63
Real Existence and Command Cognition	63
Rule Cognition	64
3. The Rules of Command Cognition	65
Experience, Rules and Cognition	65
The Discipline of Command Cognition	66
4. The Rule Categories of Command Cognition	67
Category I:	67
Rules of Place	67

Investment Rules	67
Money Market Rules	68
Category II:	68
Rules of the Trading Deal	68
Rules of the Trading Profit	68
Rules of Market Identity	69
Rules of the Networks	69
Rules of Information	69
5. Negative Experience and Rule Cognition	69
Significance of Negative Experience	69
Land—Agriculture	70
Production—Pre-Industry	71
6. Cognition of the Rules of Negative Experience	73
Seven Rules	

PART II (A)—STRATEGIC KNOWLEDGE AS KNOWLEDGE OF VARIETY

	75
NOTE: External Variety and Internal Variety	75
CHAPTER IV: The Knowledge of External Variety	79
1. Variety as Knowledge	79
The Knowledge of Variety	79
Ordinary Experience and the Knowledge of Variety	80
The Category of External Variety	82
Varietal Discernment	83
Variety, Utility and "Fitted Knowledge"	83
The Category of Internal Variety	85
CHAPTER V: Knowledge, The Physical World and External Variety	87
The Knowledge of Materiality: Creation I	87
The Knowledge of Materiality ("Physica")	87
Essence and Substance	89
The Boundary of Thought	90
Finite Intelligence and the Physical Surrounding	90
Thought as Nominal Knowing: Physica	90
The Idea of Substance	91
Ideas and Knowledge	92
The Use Differentiation Between Ideas	93
The Way to Knowledge	94
CHAPTER VI: Strategy and the Domination of External Variety	97

Three Centuries of Domination	97
External Variety as Invention	98
The New Industrial System	100
Stage Two: The New Industrial System	101
Stage Three: The Linkage to Capital	103
Strategic Knowledge and the Knowledge of External Variety	104

CHAPTER VII: The Knowledge of Internal (Inward) Variety: Physics as Possibilities	108
Experience and the Inwardness of Physical Reality	108
Internal (Inward) Variety: Physics	109
Realm of Space	111
The Knowledge of Autonomous Variety	112
Inward Variety and Strategic Knowledge	113
The New Possibilities	113

PART II (B)—STRATEGIC KNOWLEDGE AS KNOWLEDGE OF VARIETY: VARIETAL DOMAINS: 115

Considered by itself, what is strategic knowledge? 115

CHAPTER VIII: Relational Variety: The Knowledge of Relation	117
1. Relation and Knowledge	117
Relational Knowledge	118
Relation as Knowledge	118
The Classes of Relation	120
2. Strategic Knowledge as Relational Knowledge	
Mind Passive and Mind Active	120
The Relational Knowledge of Creation I	120
The Fitted Knowledge of Creation I	122
The Relational Knowledge of Creation II	123

CHAPTER IX: The Knowledge of Invisible Variety Strategizing Flight	130
Possibilities and the Way of Strategic Knowledge	130
Pre-Industrialized Flight Knowledge	131
Industrialization of Military Flight	132
Industrialization of Private, Non-Commercial Flight	134
Industrialization of Commercial Flight	134
Radical Technological Innovation and World Competitive Air Transport	136

CHAPTER X: Strategizing Flight for Commercial Aviation 139
  1. The Emergence of Commercial Aviation 139
  2. Commercial Aviation as an Industry (Appendix) 156
  NOTE: USAir 154

CHAPTER XI: The Knowledge of Internal (Inward)
    Variety: Industrialized Biology:
    The Life Phenomena 170
  1. The Industrialization of Biological Knowledge 170
    The Empty Person of Biology 170
    Materiality and the Knowledge of Life Phenomena 171
    Industrial Microbiology and "Real Capitalism" 172
      Pharmaceuticals 173
      Industrial Microorganisms 174
      Food, Drink, and Microbiological Production 175
  2. The Knowledge of Regulation: The Life
    Phenomena Market 175
    Regulative Cognition, Biological Knowledge and
      Varietal Regulation of the Life Phenomena
      Market 175
    Regulative Cognition 176
    Regulative Capability, Regulative Intelligence and
      Strategic Knowledge 177
    Strategic Knowledge and the Knowledge of
      Variety 177
  3. From Empty Person to the Person as Product
    Reservoir 179
    NOTE: The Path of Recombinant DNA 180

CHAPTER XII: Strategizing Biotechnology 182
  1. The Biotechnological Scene 182
  2. The Path From Antibiotics to Strategized
    Biotechnology 183
  3. Strategizing Biotechnology 184
    The Dream Knowledge of Strategy: "Bioriches" 184
    The Product Knowledge of Strategy 185
    The Chain of Strategy: The Deterministic Chain 188
    The Duality of the Chain of Strategy 190
      The Investment Expectations Strand 191
      The Product Expectations Strand 191
  4. Counter Strategy to Venture Capital Startups 193
    Command Cognition and the Will to Strategize 193
    Strategizing at the Level of Command Cognition 195

Command Cognition: The Strategy of
   Domination   196
NOTE 1., NOTE 2.   198

PART III: THE FOUNDATION KNOWLEDGE OF STRATEGIC KNOWLEDGE   203

CHAPTER XIII: The Knowledge of Persons as Idea   205
  1. The Person as Material Entity   205
     Cognitative and Incognitative Existants   205
     Consciousness and Identity   206
     That Conscious Thinking Thing   207
     The Nominal Person   208
  2. Genuine and Facsimile Persons   209
     Locke on Understanding Persons   209
     The Natural and the Metaphysical Person   210
     Facsimile Being and Genuine Being   211
     Genuine Being   213
     Genuine Being and the Knowledge of
        Personal Identity   214
     Genuine Being: The Monad as World Mind   215
     Genuine Being: The End of Knowledge   217

CHAPTER XIV: Knowledge of the Person:
           Pre-Industrialized Biology   220
  1. The Empty Person of Locke   220
  2. Locke's Legacy of Biological Variety   221
  3. The Post-Lockean Legacy of Biological Variety   225
  4. Biological Research   227
     Experimental Biological Research   227
     Research in Microscopy and in Cytology   228
     Organic Chemistry and Experimental Biological
        Research   230
     Microbiology and Bacteriology   231
     Biochemistry   232
     NOTE: The Foundation of Knowledge   234

CHAPTER XV: Knowledge Foundation I:
           The "Fitted Knowledge" of John Locke   236
  1. The Foundation of "Fitted Knowledge"   236
  2. The Knowledge of Intelligibility   239
  3. The Knowledge of Finite Intelligence   242
     Finite Intelligence   242
     Being in Time and Place   242

The World as Idea	243
The Knowledge Categories	244
The Knowledge of Finite Intelligence	245
Knowledge of Materiality ("Physics")	246
Ideas and Knowledge	247
The Use Differentiation Between Ideas	248
The Way to Knowledge	249
4. The Knowledge of Knowledge Itself	250
5. The Architecture of Knowledge	253
Simple Ideas Queried	253
Quasi-Autonomous Mind: Complex Ideas	254
Complex Ideas as Real Ideas	255
Complex Ideas as Inadequate Ideas	255
6. The Knowledge of Simple Ideas: (Real Ideas as Knowledge)	256
The Material Surround as Simple Idea	256
The Simple Idea of Thinking	257
The Simple Ideas of Pleasure and Pain	257
Power, Volition and Freedom as Simple Ideas	258
7. The Knowledge of Reason	260
The Knowable and Deficiencies in Knowing	260
The Knowledge of Reason (A)	261
The Limits of Rational Knowledge	262
The Knowledge of Reason (B)	263
8. The Knowledge of Choice and Action	264
The Idea of Power	264
The Volitional Determinant	264
Time and the Volitional Determinant	265
Judgement: The Interrogative State of Command Cognition	266
The Knowledge of Choice	266
The Pursuit of Happiness	267
9. The Language of Knowledge	267
Language and Simple Ideas	268
Language and the Idea of Substance	268
Language and the Idea of "Man"	269
CHAPTER XVI: Knowledge Foundation II: The "Possibilities Knowledge" of Gottfried Leibniz	274
1. Finite Intelligence	278
Post- and Pre-Operative Knowing	278
Critique of Post-Operative Knowing	279

The Material Fundament of Thinking	280
An Internal Knowledge Structure	280
The Function of the Senses	281
Necessary Truths and Truths of Fact	282
The Black Box of Human Understanding	282
Virtual (Pre-Formative) Knowledge	283
Cognitive Variety	285
2. Command Cognition	285
Thought and Action	285
Power and Action: Locke	285
Power and Action: Leibniz	286
Thought and Action	287
Action as Command Cognition: Perceptions and Action	288
Thought and Decision	289
Decision as Command Cognition	289
Decision as "The Art of Consequences"	291
Decision as "The Final Determination"	292
The Determinative Reason of Command Cognition	293
Decision: The Final Determination as Judgment	294
Freedom and Command Cognition: Volition and the Understanding	295
NOTE: Deals	296
3. The Field of Knowledge	297
The Idea Itself	297
Beyond Idea as Knowledge	298
Sensibilized Knowledge	300
4. The Knowledge of Reason	301
Reason and Its Knowledge	301
The Knowledge of Truth	301
Reason and Analysis	303
Reason and Knowledge of the Possible	303
Reason and and Knowledge of Matter	305
CHAPTER XVII: Knowledge Foundation III: Moral Knowledge. Motivational Knowledge and the Knowledge of Morality	308
NOTE: Moral Knowledge and the Knowledge of Strategy	308
The Moral As Idea	311
The Moral As Judgment	312
Prudence as the Morality of Strategy	313

1. The Knowledge of Motivation 322
     The Separation of Motivation from Morality 322
     Motivation, Desire and Volition 322
     Motivational Knowledge 323
     Motivational Judgment 324
  2. Morality and Motivation 325
     Morality as Knowledge 325
     Morality Not Innate Knowledge 326
     Virtue and Conscience Non-Motivational 327
  3. Moral Knowledge 328
     The "True Ground" of Morality 328
     Positive Moral Knowledge 328
     Accessible Inwardness for Moral Knowledge 329
     Moral Relations 330
     Rule Basis of Moral Relations 330
     Morality as Relation 331

CHAPTER XVIII: Knowledge Foundation III: Moral Knowledge and the Art of Consequences 334
Locke and Leibniz 334
Comparative Impotence of the Moral 335
Beyond Desire 335
The Art of Consequences 336
False Judgments of Morality 337
True Judgments of Morality 338
The Foundation of Virtue 338
The Advancement of Moral Knowledge 339
"Moral Relations" and the Judgment of Others 340
Moral Judgments and Motivated Actions 341

BIBLIOGRAPHY 343

INDEX 349

PERMISSION TO REPRINT

Excerpt from *Mechanization Takes Command*. Reprinted with the permission of Oxford University Press from *Mechanization Takes Command* by Sigfried Giedion. Copyright 1948.

Excerpts from *The Wheels of Commerce* by Fernand Braudel. Copyright 1982 by Librarie Armand Colin. English translation copyright 1982, by William Collins Ltd. and Harper & Row, Publishers, Inc. Reprinted by permission of Harper Collins Publishers.

Excerpts from *The Structures of Everyday Life* by Fernand Braudel. Copyright 1979, by Librarie Armand Colin. English translation copyright 1981, by William Collins Sons & Co. Ltd. and Harper & Row, Publishers, Inc. Reprinted by permission of Harper Collins Publishers.

Excerpts from *The Sky's the Limit*. Reprinted with the permission of Macmillan Publishing Company from *The Sky's the Limit," A History of U.S. Airlines* by Arch Whitehouse, McMillian, N.Y. 1971.

Excerpts from *The Story of Quantum Mechanics*. Reprinted with the permission of Charles Scribner's Sons, an imprint of Macmillan Publishing Company from *The Story of Quantum Mechanics* by Victor Guillemin. Copyright 1986, Victor Guillemin.

Excerpts from a *Military History of the Western World*. Reprinted with permission from *A Military History of the Western World*, Volume III, by J.F.C. Fuller. Copyright (c) 1956, by J.F.C. Fuller. Copyright renewed 1984 by Lloyds PLC Ltd.. Reprinted by permission of Harold Ober Associates Incorporated.

Excerpts from *Elements of Economics of Industry*, Vol. I. Reprinted with permission of the Macmillan Press Ltd. from *Elements of Economics of Industry*, Vol. I by Alfred Marshall. Copyright 1892.

Excerpts from *Dialogues of Alfred North Whitehead*. Reprinted with permission of Little, Brown and Company from *Dialogues of Alfred North Whitehead* by Lucien Price. Copyright 1954.

Excerpts from *New Essays Concerning Human Understanding*. Reprinted with permission of Open Court Publishing Company from *New Essays Concerning Human Understanding* by Gottfried Wilhelm von Leibniz. (Translation by Alfred G. Langley, 1896)

Excerpts from *Discourse on Metaphysics*. Reprinted with permission of Open Court Publishing Company from *Discourse on Metaphysics: Correspondence with Arnould* and *Monadology*, by Gottfried Wilhelm von Leibniz, introduction by Paul Janet; translation by George R. Montgomery. Copyright 1916.

Excerpts from *Biotechnology: The University-Industrial Complex*. Reprinted with permission of Yale University Press from *Biotechnol-*

ogy: *The University-Industrial Complex* by Martin Kenney. Copyright 1986.
Excerpts from *Ideas and Opinions*. Reprinted with permission of Random House, Inc. from *Ideas and Opinions* by Albert Einstein. (Translation by Sanja Bargmann, Crown Publishers, Inc., copyright 1954.)
Excerpts from *A History of the Sciences*. Reprinted with permission of Blackie and Son Ltd., from *A History of the Sciences* by Stephen J. Mason. (Rev. 1962, Collier Books, New York.)
Excerpts from *The Industrial Revolution in the Eighteenth Century*. Reprinted with permission of Harcourt Brace Jovanovich from *The Industrial Revolution in the Eighteenth Century* by Paul Mantoux. (Translation by Marjorie Vernon. Revised edition 1928.)
Excerpts from *The Metaphysical Foundations of Logic* Reprinted with permission of Indiana University Press from *The Metaphysical Foundations of Logic* by Martin Heidegger. (Translation by Michael Hein. Copyright 1984.)
Excerpts from *The General Theory of Employment Interest and Money* Reprinted with permission of Harcourt Brace Jovanovich, Inc. from *The General Theory of Employment Interest and Money* by John Maynard Keynes. Copyright 1936.
Excerpts from *Great Britain in the World Economy*, Alfred E. Kahn 1946. Reprinted by permission from the publisher, Columbia University Press, New York.

PERMISSION TO REPRINT PERIODICALS AND NEWSPAPERS

Excerpts from interview with Takimochi Ishi of the Sumitomo Corp. Reprinted with permission of Takemochi Ishi from the *Sumitomo Quarterly*. Spring 1989.
Excerpts from "Limited Knowledge and Economic Analysis". Reprinted with permission of the American Economic Association from the article by Kenneth J. Arrow in *The American Economic Review*, March 1974, Volume 64.
Excerpts from *The Institutional Investor*. Reprinted with permission of Institutional Investors, Inc. from the 20th Anniversary Issue of *The Institutional Investor: The Way It Was; An Oral History* (June, 1987).
Excerpts from "Wall Street: Disguising the Risks of Research" Reprinted from the article by Diana B. Henriques, The New York Times, February 3, 1991. Copyright (c) 1991 by The New York Times Company. Reprinted by permission.

Excerpts from "The Microbiological Production of Pharmeceuticals", p.140, by Yair Aharonowitz and Gerald Cohen, and from "The Microbiological Production of Industrial Chemicals", p.154, by Douglas Eveleigh.
Reprinted with permission of Scientific American from these two articles as published in *The Scientific American*, Volume 245, Number 3, September, 1981. Bracketed information inserted by the writer.

Excerpts from *Software Magazine*, September 1991 " 'Potential' Still Describes AI-Rooted Knowledge Tools," Howard Millman and Elizabeth Harding. Reprinted with the Permission of *Software Magazine*, Sentry Publishing Co., Inc., Westborough, Mass.

ACKNOWLEDGMENTS

In the performance of an extended endeavor such as this, one is buoyed by the supportive interest of others and also helped in its execution by the assistance that is timely provided by those with special practical talents.

Richard Osborne has long been friend, colleague and confidante. As might be expected then, Richard has maintained an interested, active support of the trilogy from the time of its inception. Richard is Executive Dean and Director of the George S. Dively Center, whose function for the Weatherhead School of Management is development of the capabilities of the executive level of enterprise. No stranger to pragmatic and operative concerns of enterprise direction, Richard is yet quite aware that executive thinking should reach out to include still other domains of capability.

The support of Ronald G. Smart emerged from its own unique source. Ron, for many years has been Director of Management Research for the Digital Equipment Corporation. Our acquaintance was renewed after a lapse of years. What followed thereon was a disclosure of mutual concerns in the realm of ideas and theory. Given all that, Ron took a special interest in this, the final volume of the trilogy. He has his own pages on which to make his own statement. But the nub of the matter is that we enjoyed dueling over these concerns and the pleasures of spirited dialogue ripened into the calm discourse and trust of friendship.

Putting the several versions of the manuscript into a finished and complete work made necessary the timely assistance of several competent persons with a tolerance for author eccentricities.

Terri Pryatel took on the large job of putting the first manuscript draft into its initial computerized and printed form. For further improvement there was a lot of niche typing that had to be done and Bonnie Reynolds picked up on these tasks. Retta Holdorf took time out from her departmental administrative position to provide special assistance with essential correspondence. Efficient liaison with the office of Ron Smart relied on the talents of Margaret Rand. If there were a Day-Glo font, it would go to Shirley Pitman, on whom rested the ultimate burden of putting it all together as a corrected, ordered, inclusive, finished manuscript.

FOREWORD

Dr. Ronald Smart
Management Systems Technology Research Center
(Monash University and Mt. Eliza: Australia Management College)
Australia

This is a fascinating and very important work having special relevance to enterprise management in today's dynamic, globally connected world. It associates the operations in the minds of senior executives with successes and failures in their organizations' business operations.

My experience with DIGITAL Equipment Corp. as manager of the General International Area, as staff consultant and then as Director of their Management Systems Research program brought me to a very similar field of study. My work became focussed on the immediate research questions that we faced in designing organisational decision-making systems that were robust enough to deal effectively with multi-dimensional forms of organisation which were composed of networks of interdependent yet autonomous business units. To understand the problem adequately enough to identify the new management systems designs that were needed, we had to develop models describing executives' mental structures and behaviours, and then link these models by way of the organisational decision-making systems, to business performance expectations. This provided hypotheses for how the manager's knowledge and beliefs could be expected to impact the actual business results. Late in this research program Professor Grundstein and I met again and began the process of debating the efficacy of our respective theories and of their application to actual business management situations.

This book is Professor Grundstein's intellectual platform from which our debates and combined research is expected to move forward. He makes reference to the possibilities that computers may become key tools for supporting manager's mental processes. It became apparent to us early in our research program that the massive amount of manager development required to make our management systems designs function effectively required the computerisation of knowledge development, exchange and application. This development is yet another intersection between our research and application interests.

Making headway with our investigation, the way we posed the questions, meant developing models for human information and knowledge processing that could be represented in the supporting "Knowledge Processors." To make these developments possible we needed to create or discover new models for mental structures and functioning that could become useful representations of the executive behaviours in their decision-making contexts. Much of the book deals with these matters and is, therefore, a very relevant platform with which to engage Professor Grundstein in the debate that needs to accompany our current prototyping of designs for Knowledge Processor Networks.

The book accepts the reality of continuing technological invention and shows how executive strategists make successful enterprises from the better product, service and process opportunities. What is implied but not emphasised in the book is that increasingly, strategising has to do with how the enterprise is structured and managed and with how knowledge is developed, exchanged and applied by the organisation. This is strategy beyond the product, service, market, production and other functional strategies. It is the strategy for developing human systems which are capable of creating and then implementing strategies that exploit new technological possibilities for enterprise. It is the strategy for developing new forms of organisation that are consciously driven by opportunities in new knowledge; organisations (or business networks) that are closely linked to research organisations and which see their rate of knowledge development, exchange and application as their competitive advantage. However, note that the competitor here is obsolete knowledge rather than some other competing organisation.

This book is especially relevant today. Enterprises are floundering in the confusion of their senior executives. The enterprise opportunities that are inherent in the dynamics of global business interconnections are a threat to executives who cannot project their own organisation's interests into thrusts that really exist in the future possibilities. Instead of being buoyed up by the excitement of using their humanness to create successful enterprises, organisation members, especially managers, are today often disappointed by the seeming impossibility of again multiplying their capital and other assets at historical rates. Seeing these diminishing returns, they focus on cost cutting tactics. They have given up as strategists and have become victims of their own obsolete knowledge. The natural human excitement experienced by those who are deliberately discovering, creating and testing the possibilities for future enterprise can be propogated through their organisations by the strategists. This book has the potential to make the process of creating strategically important enterprise a much more conscious one.

I found Grundstein's descriptions of what it meant to create a "grand strategy" extremely useful. He converted my intuitive knowledge about strategy into explicit knowledge which I could then incorporate cleanly and elegantly into my own models. I could, for example, improve an algorithm, or a logic, which I had been using to explain how to prioritize among competing investment opportunities. The examples he gives for the different industries rivet his theory together to give it the excitement of finding a new, systematic approach to strategizing. This is a new knowledge of strategy.

Grundstein gives lucid, fascinating descriptions of grand strategies developed by some senior executives in partnership with their creative technology contributors. The emergence of several modern industries is described in terms of the human achievements of leading strategists. These strategists built whole new enterprises from their perceptions of the business opportunities that were exposed by their collaborating new technology contributors. Professor Grundstein offers important contrasts between the thinking of Western and Japanese strategists in this domain of new enterprise creation.

Senior executives who, on realising the possibility that strategising can become consciously manageable, may want to study the theoretical sections of the book. Students of effective enterprise management who want to follow the history of human thought as it led towards the possibilities for conscious creation of enterprise strategy, will find in this book a fascinating account of a still incomplete journey. There is a framework here for further exploration and application of the models which Professor Grundstein provides as tools for thinking about and doing strategy development.

The book could be characterised as a research source. Students and teachers who wish to understand the management malaise, for example in America but not only there, will have to understand the confusion in the executives' minds. To be helpful, they will need to show how the problems and opportunities of executive management today can only be understood in terms of the Psychological as well as the Social changes that are abroad in the world. Some of us believe that the management of global enterprises in our complex and dynamic world environment can become simple again while dealing effectively with all the situational complexity which we see growing worse. But this return to simplicity can only occur after executives learn new truths about who we humans are and can become in the world.

It is interesting to read Grundstein's account of the historical journey by which knowledge has become an object in mental space. As such, knowledge has become an object with which to discipline the possibilities that we can imagine and thus to develop useful and empowering strategies for times and spaces which do not yet exist. Locke had limited his attention to the everyday world, and his mental objects to those generated by immediate sensation. The strategist has to go into the unknown and prepare a model of what could be and then to select among competing alternatives. Each choice has its projected possible outcomes, based on our knowledge of the probabilities and of the importances of gaining or avoiding these outcomes. Leibnitz aptly used the term "the Art of Consequences" for this process whereby we make managerial judgements in this kind of anticipatory mental space.

From my own research experience, the way to create a useful model to represent this mental space was to put the individuals into their business organizations, to have them making agreements about their roles and performance commitments, and then to have them planning and managing their way into the future. What evolved was a methodology for issue recognition and resolution, called the MIRR model. This model provided a structure for mental space that included knowledge as an explicit kind of mental object. This led to a systematic approach to understanding belief and behaviour change. This approach continues to be tested in managerial and other contexts.

Having developed a model for representing the individual person's mental space, we were able to go on to model the mental space for a whole organisation in terms of an Enterprise Management System Architecture (EMS-A). The MIRR model was but one of five design parameters in this architecture. The architecture facilitated the diagnosis and the redesign of more effective management decision-making systems for networked business organizations. Again, as with Grundstein's exposition, our models relate the operations in the executive's mental space to the effectiveness of their enterprise in the marketplace.

My continuing collaboration with Professor Grundstein will be aimed at introducing material from this book along with my models, into a new Australian Management Systems Technology Research program now under development. I expect we can move forward on the platform constructed by Locke and Leibnitz, towards a further understanding of mental space. Doing so will include a valid supporting role for networks of Knowledge Processors. We are aiming at a situation where new knowledge development, exchange and application becomes a business enterprise in its own right. This new business will support an explicit and critical knowledge management role for executives in our modern knowledge driven enterprises.

The immense scope of content in this book is impressive. I

anticipate many interesting and fruitful discussions about the application of our respective models. As we continue our research explorations, we will be aiming at the goal of improving managers' knowledge about creating effective strategies, both for particular businesses, and for designs of enterprises which produce and modify their strategies in response to the unfolding reality of their executive's incompletely understood enterprise opportunities.

Peter Drucker calls him "The Grundstein." ("The foundation stone") His colleagues call him Grundy. Both are right.

Nathan Grundstein is a philosopher prince of management strategy. He is master of the grand idea. He sees connections that others miss. His concepts transcend models and measurements. They are a bold flirtation with wisdom.

Grundstein's life is testament to the power of intelligence and decency. The privately-funded publication of this volume by friends and admirers who continue to benefit from his wisdom is a fitting tribute to the quality of his life and the importance of his ideas.

Richard L. Osborne
Professor for the
Practice of Management
Weatherhead School
of Management

"Thinking, in the propriety of the English tongue, signifies that sort of operation of the mind about its ideas wherein the mind is active; where it, with some degree of voluntary attention, considers anything . . ."[1]

"It is astonishing what foolish things one can temporarily believe if one thinks too long alone, particularly in economics (along with the other moral sciences), where it is often impossible to bring one's ideas to a conclusive test either formal or experimental."[2]

"The past is relevant because it contains information which changes the image of the future; the probabilites which govern future actions as modified by observation on the past. It follows that present decisions with implications for the future are functions of past values of variables as well a present values."[3]

"If thinking . . . stands under laws, then the questions must be asked: What are the fundamental laws belonging to thinking as such? What is, in general, the character of lawfulness and regulation?"[4]

---

1. Locke, John, *An Essay Concerning Human Understanding*, (6th edition, BK II, Ch. IX, Sec. 1, p. 92), with the notes and illustrations of the author, and an analysis of his doctrine of ideas. Also, Questions on Locke's Essay, by A. M., Ethical Moderator in Trinity College, Dublin. (New Edition, The World Library, Ward, Lock & Co., London, undated) The original edition of Locke's *Essay* is 1689.
2. Keynes, John Maynard, *The General Theory of Employment Interest and Money*, Preface pp. vii-viii (Harcourt, Brace ed. 1936).
3. Arrow, Kenneth J., "Limited Knowledge and Economic Analysis," 64 Amer. Econ. Rev. No.1 (March 1974) 1,6.
4. Heidegger, Martin, *The Metaphysical Foundations of Logic* (Michael Hein, trans., Indiana University Press 1984, with Translator's Introduction, Bloomington, IN, p. 19).

PROLOGUE

There is a base reference for a work such as this. It is Locke's *Essay Concerning Human Understanding*.[1] Between that work of John Locke and the goals established for the (Japan's) Sixth Generation Computer Project are significant linkages. The dominating and enduring explanation of empirically based knowing is that provided by Locke. The Sixth Generation Computer Project appears on the scene as both a challenge to his explanation of knowing and, perhaps, also as a continuation of it.

Within statements formally defining the Project goals are language references to "humanlike," and to "brain processes," and to "the human brain" as a model for advanced computer information-processing systems. As set forth by the Japanese research Committee on New Information Processing Technologies (the NIPT Committee), the overall goal of the Sixth Generation Computer Project, and one of its listed broad goals, are as follows:[2]

> "*Goals*—The overall goal is to produce humanlike, flexible information-processing technologies that can form the basis of advanced computers in the next century. The key paradigm is what the NIPT Committee calls the 'micro- macro information loop,' which describes how information is passed back and forth continuously between an advanced computer (a micro network of components) and the real world (the macro level). In essence the micro network processes information received from the macro level, then feeds the result back to the macro level where some kind of change is effected; this change is then transmitted back to the micro level in a continous cycle."
>
> . . . .

[one of "four broad goals"]
"—Understanding how the human brain processes information. The human brain was chosen as a model for advanced computing functions for several reasons: it is a massively parallel neural network; it processes all types of pattern information; it handles incomplete or incorrect information; and it is able to learn. Understanding how the brain performs these functions is no small task, however; delays here could delay work in other areas. The brain also is not a perfect model; mimicking its operation may lead to unforseen complications."

[A strategic area of project inquiry]
"—Research as flexible understanding and flexible inference mechanisms. This work would focus on understanding how the human brain (the most massively parallel distributed processing system recognized on earth) organizes information, distributes processing work, learns, filters information and interacts with external motor systems (for example, arms and legs). This effort would bring together researchers from biology, mathematics, neurology and cognitive/behavioral psychology."

The Sixth Generation Computer Project has an ancestry of earlier projects: (1) The High Performance Computer Project (fiscal years 1966-1971); (2) The Pattern Information Processing System (ficsal years 1971-1980); and (3) The Fifth Generation Computer Project (fiscal years 1979-1992 mid year). The last was the most ambitious and, technologically the most revolutionary. It incorporated a vision of friendly interface between humans and their computers, with reciprocities of understanding and response utilizing everyday language. "Computers of the future would play a larger role in creative and decision making processes, aiding or even replacing human intelligence." So the Fifth Generation Computer would have the goals of (a) problem solving and inference (deductive and inductive) functions, (b) knowledge based management, (c) modalities of intelligent man-machine interfacing, and (d) automatic problem conversion into a computer program.

There is a 300 year separation between the Essay on Human Understanding (1689) and the period of The Fifth Generation Comnputer (1979-1992). What unites the two is that they are each into their own exploration of the same subject—entities with attributes of intelligence. It was however, artificial intelligence—the intelligence designed into an information—language-logic processing artifact that was the identified aspiration of the Fifth Generation Project.[4]

"Intelligence" as a term of meaning giving significant identity to the artifact has been said to be traceable to the Latin terms *legere* and *intelligere*. The requisites for intelligence on the part of the artifact are therefore listed as the capability to "collect, assemble, choose among, understand, perceive and know."[3] There are however several other Latin terms that are also applicable to the definition of intelligence: *intelligo, inter-lego, intellectus, intelligens,* and *intelligentia*. That which has the understanding of a something is an *intelligense*. *Intellectus* and *intelligo* cover both sensory perception and discernment, as well as mental understanding. There is an additional meaning for *intelligo*, namely, accurate knowledge of or a skill in the same thing. As for *intelligentia*, it is a power of discernment or understanding.[5]

Not suprisingly, then, an English definition of intelligence could have several meanings:

"Intelligence (in-telli-jens), n. [L. *intelligentia*, from *intelligo*, to understand—inter, between, and *lego*, to choose out, to select; to observe] 1. The act of knowing; the exercise for the understanding. 2. The capacity to know, understand, or comprehend. 3. The capacity for the higher functions of the intellect. 4. Knowledge imparted or acquired by study, research or experience; general information; as, a person of *intelligence*. 5. Notice; information communicated by any means or contrivance; an account of things distant or before unknown. 6. Familiar terms of acquaintance; intercourse; as, there is a good *intelligence* between persons when they have the same views or are free from discord."[6]

Interestingly, the term "know" has Anglo Saxon and Icelandic origins. The original meaning in which it is rooted is that of being able to produce; that is, to be able (know how) to do a thing. From this comes the derivative conception of a clear, certain and convincing perception or understanding of the truth or reality of something. One can know by being informed—as by information—assuming that one has been assured of its credibility.[7] The intelligent artifact requires knowledge—"lots of it"—problem specific knowledge, factual and experiential knowledge—without which there cannot be intelligent behavior.[8]

The expectation is that The Fifth Generation of intelligent computers will introduce a much magnified reasoning power into the design of the ultimate intelligent artifact, which is an expert system into which has been incorporated the VLSI (very large system integration) chip. Tantalizing claims of thinking powers are made on behalf of these VLSI intelligent artifacts as against the mental powers of human understanding. The first claim is that there is a pre-program and a post-program smartness of the intelligemt artifact. While initially it may not be the equal of human smartness, it quickly becomes smarter. The second claim is that intelligent artifacts will displace human intelligence in that the former will assume the "burden of producing the future knowledge of the world." The third claim is that extensions of human intelligence follow from mental networks of users of these artifacts, who both enrich and draw upon large and elastic knowledge bases in their networking.[9]

Human understanding was investigated by Locke within a frame of inquiry not confined to work focused behavior, and not confined to behavior that was subsumed within the complex task structures of specialized, performance oriented business entities. The fundamentals of knowing by humans was not, for Locke, the applied intelligence of task focused performance. And this holds, even though Locke explained human understanding as that of an intelligence adequate for the acquisition of fitted knowledge, meaning a knowledge fitted to practical concerns and useful duties of persons. Knowledgeable as he was about the scientific endeavors of Frances Bacon, he nevertheless specifically ruled out restricting understanding to the data and inferences of technical experiment.

The respective differences between the human understanding of Locke and the artificial intelligence (AI) and knowledge information processing system (KIPS) represented by the Fifth Generation can be placed side by side:

Human Understanding (Locke)	Fifth Generation (AI and KIPS)
1. Finite intelligence	1. Intelligent artifact
2. Mental operations	2. Mechanism of mind
3. Individual outside of organization context	3. Individual within organized enterprise context
4. Individual knowing	4. Networked knowing
5. Uninstrumented senses	5. Instrumentally enhanced senses
6. Knowing unconstrained by technical experiment	6. Knowing that is problem/technology constrained
7. Improvement and discovering capability	7. New magnitudes of improvement and discovery
8. Infra-structure of cognition	8. Knowledge information processing
9. Fitted knowledge	9. Engineered knowledge

Contemporary knowledge based approaches as signified by artificial intelligence, and of which the Fifth Generation Computer Project aspired to be the most advanced, intend to knowledge engineer a system of understanding. They intend to design an intelligent artifact that can successfully manipulate task specific knowledge. A problem focus, problem related inference, a managed data base, and artifact-user interaction are the system design components of the intelligent artifact. An expert system is a form of experience based but instrumented intelligence, another turtle shell of technology (as Heisenberg put it) that now fits onto the backs of investigatory scientists.[10]

Strategy, whatever it is, is not task specific. It may be preceded by task specifics and, as consequence, it may be followed by specific tasks. More commonly, strategy is taken to be recourse to a teleological category of behavioral acts. Thus merger, or acquisition, or leveraged buyout are categorized as strategic actions, True enough, a specific catageory of strategizing actions such as merger, or acquisition, or leveraged buyout can build from an immense data base. There is, to illustrate, a computer program—"1 2 3 Plan/Merge"—which permits transfers of information from a computerized data base—Data C.D. Corporate Data base—which, in turn, contains the equivalent of "one million printed pages on 10,000 companies." Moreover, "1 2 3 Plan/Merge" as a program contains all that is needed by way of financial data, company valuations, factor projections, sensitivity analyses, graphics, and report generation power. No doubt it could be knowledge engineered, as the judgment about the program is that for an investigative analyst it contains almost everything he could want.[11]

Why, then, given the foregoing, may it still be asserted that strategy is not task specific, or a set of defined and specified operarant acts and decisions, in the sense that strategizing might not be transformed into an expert system as the knowing of an intelligent artifact? The "why" of this assertion is that strategy is domain creation. One has only to bring to mind biotechnology and genetic engineering, and transistor and chip technology to make obvious that domain creation establishes the identity of strategy. And even mergers and acquisitions and buyouts—once done as an informal back-of-the-envelope kind of analysis (see p. 31)—were converted into a new domain for the entrepreneurial stategizing of capital investment. Base technologies provide the primal ground for domain creation. The knowledge of domain creation is a knowledge of strategy. The created domain is the reality from which and within which all else has existence—the industry, the enterprise, the wealth, the capital, the economic values, the dynamics of opportunity, the product utility, and so on.

Though the matter may be pushed aside by optimistic literature about knowledge engineering and artificial intelligence, it is important to be cognizant that Locke was impressed with the finiteness of human intelligence. Human understanding was limited to being within that finiteness. The knowledge of strategy as the knowledge of domain creation—the knowledge of another knowledge—challenges the boundaries of whatever the finiteness of human intelligence are pressumed to be. Strategy as the knowledge of domain creation brings the knowledge of strategy closer to human understanding of possibilities, even while conceeding the finiteness of the underlying intelligence.

Foundational grounds of knowing enter into human understanding. What these might be were the object of inquiry by Locke. The summit model of the Sixth Generation Computer Project is the human brain, and the "key paradigm" is the " 'micro [computer component network] macro [real world] information loop' " of change effectuating (or producing) information processing. Given the brain as the model, the impish suggestion that designed computers might dream of intelligent humans even as the latter dream of intelligent computers has a great deal of point to it.[12] The model chosen as the brain model is one which accepts human intelligence as "a culturally-determined, experientially-driven attribute of high-level cognitive functions."[13] The choice of this brain model will guide the architecture of the Sixth Generation Project. The current stalking horse of this brain model for computer design is the biological model (molecular computer) and its ideal goal of an artificial brain.[14]

These kinds of considerations aside, however, what might be lost sight of is the important element of change—change in the real world. Not just cleverness in information processing, but real world change. "In essence, the micro network processes information received from the macro level, then feeds the result back to the macro level where some kind of change is effected; this change is then transmitted back to the micro level in a continuous cycle."[15] What is the macro-level as the actuality of the real world? What is the micro level as the processing subjectivity of the strategist? What is the processed information as the knowledge of strategy? What is the knowledge of strategy as change effectuating knowledge?[16]

REFERENCES

1. Locke, John, *An Essay Concerning Human Understanding*, (6th edition), with the notes and illustrations of the author, and an analysis of his doctrine of ideas. Also, Questions on Locke's Essay, by A. M., Ethical Moderator in Trinity College, Dublin. (New Edition, The World Library, Ward, Lock & Co., London, undated) The original edition of Locke's *Essay* is 1689.

2. "Advanced Computing in Japan: The Next Generation?," Japan Economic Institute Report, No. 42A, November 8, 1991, 9.

3. Ibid., 3.
4. Feigenbaum, Edward A. and McCorduch, Pamela, *The Fifth Generation:* Artificial Intelligence and Japan's Computer Challenge To The World, (Signet Edition 1984, New American Library, New York, N.Y.).
5. *The White Latin Dictionary,* (New Edition, White, John T., 1958, The Follett Foreign Language Series, Follett Publishing Company, Chicago, Illinois), 303.
6. *Imperial Dictionary,* (Oglivie, John, ed., New Edition. Annadale Charles, ed. (London, The Century Co., New York, 1883), Vol II, p. 625.
7. Ibid., Vol. II, p. 629.
8. Feigenbaum and McCorduch, 37.
9. Ibid., 39.
10. Ibid., 55,66.
11. Sandberg—Diment, Erik, "The Executive Computer," *New York Times,* November 23, 1986, p. 18F.

The strategy of the experimental biosphere has generated an expert system (Artificial Intelligence) by which to monitor biosphere processes in real time. Rifkin, Glenn, "Keeping Track of a Hermetic Universe," February 10, 1991, p. 8F, Sec. 3.

12. Cross, Michael, "Do Computers Dream of Intelligent Humans?," *The New Scientist,* November 26, 1988, 42.
13. Anderson, Mike, "Intelligence and the Development of Intellect," *British Science News,* No. 222/1990 SPECTRUM/2.
14. Connor, Steve, "Why Can't a Computer Be More Like a Brain," *The New Scientist,* January 21, 1989, Forum, 69; "Clever Molecules for Thinking Computers," *The New Scientist,* December 24, 1988, 29.
15. "Advanced Computing in Japan: The Next Generation?," Japan Economic Institute Report, No. 42A, November 8, 1991, 9.
16. Alexander, Tom, "Teaching Computers the Art of Reason," Fortune, May 17, 1982, 82. (Why do humans do anything as a requisite for computer understanding of human events, 91).

NOTE

The judgement of an experienced management information systems preactitioner—one who has surveyed efforts to develop, build and apply knowledge based systems (KBS)—is that these KBS of artificial intelligence are still (1991) less than proven and more a potential, despite scattered successful applications.

One aspect of their being so is already quite clear, and that is their incapacity for "creative thought." Another aspect is the consequence of hyping by technological evangelists that expect system-based applications could achieve a high level of processing efficiency independently of what the user had by way of experience and skills. It is simply that the user and interface with the user cannot be done away with. A further aspect is the weakness in embedding or integrating the expert system into the databases or information respositories of the organization. Here there is an absence of prototype applications. Finally, there is the matter of human experience with linear logic in information systems, and the absence of such experience with inference based information sytstems. Experience has proven that linear logic application can be validated prior to network installations. But for inference based structures of data, such experience is absent. The latter is logic based and the former is data based.

User and knowledge engineer and designer of an expert system must be joined.

> "Just as expert systems seek to emulate the human thought process, they must expect input in a form patterned after that process. Thus, the knowledge engineer who designs the software must possess a complete underrstanding of the user's needs, expectations and level of expertise.

. . . .

> "Problems associated with getting the 'doc in a box' demand new ways of organizing and transferring the expert's knowledge into the KBS."

Millman, Howard and Harding, Elizabeth U.—" 'Potential' Still Describes AI-Rooted Knowledge Tools," Vol. II *Software Magazine* No. 11 (September 1991), pp. 40, 47, 50, 51. The authors provide a list of "Representative Knowledge-Base Development Systems." They suggest that expert systems be separated out from the broad umbrella of artificial intelligence, as these systems have their own recognized design, method, logic, validity, programming, and technological and maintenance options.

Expert system development and application has its own special knowledge domains, including cooperation essentials between users, experts and knowledge engineers. As to this knowledge, see Lenz, N.G. and Saelens, S.F.L.—"A Knowledge-Based System for MVS Dump Analysis," 30 *IBM Systems Journal*, No. 3, p. 336 (1991).

With respect to the suggestion that Artificial Intelligence be separated from Expert Systems, the following contain relevant ideas and expositions:

1. Feinstein, Jerald; Awad Elias; Medsker, Larry and Turban, Efraini (eds.), *Proceedings, IEEE/ACM International Programs* (September 30—October 2, 1991), IEEE Computer Society Press, Los Alamitos, CA 1991.

2. Liebowitz, Jay; Feinstein, Jerald and Shumaker, Randall (eds.), *Proceedings, IEEE Conference on Managing Expert System Programs and Projects* (September 10-12, 1990), IEE Computer Society Press, Los Alamitos, CA 1990.

3. Addis, T.R. and Muir (eds.), *Research and Development in Expert Systems VII* (Tenth Annual Technical Conference of the British Computer Society Specialist Group on Expert Systems, London, Septemberr 1990) Cambridge U. Press, New York, 1990.

4. Ellis, Charlie (ed.), Expert Knowledge and Explanation (Ellis Harwood Ltd., (Hals Ltd. Press, Dist.) West Sussex, England 1989.

PART I

Command Cognition

The knowledge of strategy exists as a knowledge for whom?

The Knowledge of Strategy: Three Questions

B<small>Y THE KNOWLEDGE OF</small> strategy is meant that which undergirds the understanding of strategy as an activity sourced in human knowing and directed by it. Three questions about this knowledge are addressed in this work. Query into these questions is query into the foundation of the intelligence of strategy.

The first question: What is the knowledge by reason of which it may be asserted that there can be a knowledge of strategy?

The second question: Considered by itself, what is strategic knowledge?

The third question: The knowledge of strategy exists as a knowledge for whom?

In relation to the first question, strategic knowledge is derivative knowledge. It is derived from a more foundational knowledge, one which is identified with human understanding itself. The latter is the knowledge by which posited consciousness critically structures an understanding both of its own knowing and of what knowledge it can have of the material world in which it exists as agent. Controverted from the time of its formulation, but still dominant, nevertheless, Locke's template of knowing operates as a limitation on the knowledge of strategy.

The second question is addressed to strategy as a particular ordering of a body of knowledge particulars. In the face of a variety of events, actions, processes, actors and phenomena, strategy as knowledge searches for patterns of relation and significance: What is constructed is the cognitive ordering of a domain of knowledge that serves as the knowledge of the domain for strategizing. As knowledge, strategy then exists as varietal knowledge that has been subordinated to the directives of domain focused teleonomic knowing. It is these directives that particularize the knowledge of strategy.

The third question addresses the matter of the strategic knowers. The knowledge of strategy is knowledge to whom and for whom? The economist Alfred Marshall associated a business organization component with the command of capital (see pp. 3–4). It consisted of a power of organizing the application of machinery and other fixed capital and of raw material of goods. Here, however, the strategic knowers are taken to be those in actual command of capital, rather than those who are engaged in the organized activity of auxiliary capital management. So it is that here the knowledge of strategy is the knowledge of command cognition—the knowledge of a category of strategic actors.

Within that category they are those who, by reason of their place and function within an economy, are in a position to be strategists. In the final judgment of Braudel they are the actors who are, and who have historically always been, the embodiment of "a superior force," namely, of capitalism itself. Theirs is the place and the function to link an economy to capital investment and "a high rate of capital formation." The historical context of the movement of capital into different spheres of an economy provides the ground for the judgment.

> "Capitalism did not take up all the possibilities for investment and progress that economic life offered. It was constantly watching developments in order to intervene in certain preferred areas—in other words, it was both *sufficiently informed* and *materially* able to choose the sphere of its action. And more than the actual

> choices made—which might vary from century to century with changing circumstances—the very fact that it had the means to create its own strategy or to alter that strategy if necessary, defines capitalism as a superior force."[1]

The reach towards the knowledge of strategy puts to one side the organizational task operations associated with strategy formulation, along with the organized procedures, group processes, structural coordination, and the documentation of plans, forecasts, profit margins and market penetration. Its reach towards the knowledge foundation of strategy is also a reach that stretches beyond the instrumented and technologized apparatus that may be incorporated into protocols for rational strategic decision—data files, information systems, computerized programs. All this is here put to one side.

Instead, throughout the pages of this work will be a different connectedness. It is a connectedness between (1) the thinking that constitutes the operation of the understanding itself as an ordering of experience; between (2) the applicability of the knowledge of understanding to strategic cognition; and between (3) the activity of a special category of agents for whom a knowledge of strategy is critical for the allocation and commitment and raising of capital. It is because of their economic function with respect to capital that they constitute a critical category of strategic agents. They are driven to create and to alter strategies for the generation of capital and for capital utilization. Capital driven strategies quest for preferred strategic paths for the entry of capital by investment or otherwise.

What constitutes the knowledge of strategy is unfolded and disclosed through their connectedness, as manifested over durations of time, which are sometimes of long duration and sometimes of relatively short duration.

> "The conception of capital involves . . . two fundamental attributes, that of 'productiveness' and that of 'prospectiveness,' or the subordination of present desires to future enjoyments."

* * *

". . . the supply of business power in command of capital may be regarded as consisting of three elements, the supply of capital, the supply of the business power to manage it, and the supply of the organization by which the two are brought together and made effective for production."[2]

REFERENCES

1. Braudel, Fernand, *The Wheels of Commerce* (Vol. 2 of *Civilization and Capitalism 15th-18th Century*; transl. from the French by Siam Reynolds, Harper and Row, 1982 ed., 400).

2. Marshall, Alfred, *Elements of Economics of Industry* (Macmillan and Co., 1892 Vol., I, 63, 299).

CHAPTER I

Towards Knowledge Based Strategizing

STRATEGY AS BOTH knowledge structured knowing and a structure of knowledge is the core concern of this work. There are indications that inquiry itself and computer technology are each now about to progress along parallel (and possibly converging) paths with respect to the knowledge of strategy. The Fifth Generation Computer architecture aimed at achieving knowledge processing capability.[1] It has been succeeded by a Sixth Generation, which selects as the ground for design human engagement with the surround that is the world about.

To strategize is to engage with the manifold of the world. To engage is to bring into play on the part of the strategist those of his powers by which to bring a something into existence; to introduce a particular directionality or relation into events; to utilize his powers so as to drive desired possibilities of a perspective about the manifold to their consummation as actualities. Engagement requires that the strategist be capable of exercising powers of perceiving and understanding through ideas which seize or take hold of the manifold of the world as a knowing of it. These are the mind's powers of apprehension. It is these powers, expressed as the mental activity of thought, imagination, conceptualization, supposition and so on, that are the activity which undergirds strategy comprehended as an activity both sourced in and directed by human knowing.

One would be brought to a different conception of the knowledge of strategy were one to turn towards the pageant of operative actions by which the structural complexity of an organization is brought to a strategy. One would be brought to confront an overwhelming array of processes, procedures, data requisites, participant roles, operations practices, profitability calculations, product planning, market analyses, and much more. The knowledge of practices in complex organizations for arriving at a strategy for the enterprise are apt to be accepted as the equivalent of strategic knowledge. That is to say, the knowledge of strategy becomes the derivative of these practices. A structurally constrained mode for consensually arriving at a strategy casts a cloak over matters addressed to the cognition by which strategy becomes intelligible knowing.

What such a mode cloaks over are the formative cognitions by which a strategy becomes apprehended by thought; cognitions that are indigenous to the mind of the strategizing knower; cognitions through which a strategy is seized upon by that person. So understood, the knowledge of strategy is a knowledge subsumed within the formative cognitions.

A look at contemporary strategic engagements could be illustrative. The distinctive attribute of these engagements is the centrality of base technologies. Discovery and application of base technologies precipitate the strategic engagements. By base technologies is meant those technologies which have developed as an outgrowth from the formal, disciplined knowledge of the newer basic research. The traditional macro-physical metal working, iron making, machinery tooling, power and product mechanics of applied technologies that were rooted in the then base technologies of the late 18th—early 19th centuries had played themselves out as fundamental product manufacture and market strategies by the mid-twentieth century.

By mid-century the transistor had made its appearance as an expression of the base technology of solid state physics. What followed in electronics was micro-electronics and integrated circuit technology. The transition from microbiology to molecular biology began at mid-twentieth centurry and was formalized by Watson-Crick in 1963. Microbiology itself (sourced in the discovery of infectious disease) evolved out of virology. The progression was a path from cellular viruses to cellular genetics.

Then genetics itself progressed from orientation at a cellular level to one at the molecular level.[5]

"Molecular biology has been called the greatest development in scientific thought since Darwin's Theory." The discovery and construction of a model of the molecular structure of DNA—"The giant self-replicating molecule at the core of all living cells that controls the hereditary shaping of life"—marked the start of disciplined investigation into the basis of life phenomena, even to genetic modification of organic life. A base technology (bio-technology) of life phenomena emerged.[2]

Biotic and pre-biotic chemistry then entered upon molecular syntheses, an achievement of vast significance for the pharmaceutical industry. Partial and total molecular syntheses were experimantally achieved. The path to base technology is one of progression from experimental laboratory synthesis to industrial pharmaceutical processes. Synthesized life phenomena had begun to emerge as base technology in its own right.[3,4]

What is actually taking place is a proliferation of base technologies—medical imaging, high performance liquid chromatography, satellite communications, supersonic transport, genetic engineering, organ transplant, liquid robotics. It is this array of proliferating base technologies that now comprise the terrains for strategic engagement with command cognition. Moreover, it is in the working through of these novel and knowledge generative engagements that another intelligence of strategy is in the making. Thus proliferating base technologies also generate the reality for those who are in actual command of capital. They, in the words of Braudel, watch "developments in order to intervene in certain preferred areas."

The complex of constitutive elements that make up base technologies is such that they can elicit and sustain other than stand-alone, single product strategizing—the now familiar interfirm, product competitive, market share and product niche strategies. The comparative consequences of the difference between American and Japanese cognition of the possibilities of electronics serves as historical proof of the foregoing. Base technologies include the engineering concept of technomorphology ("The way engineering component and systems appear, grow, become obsolete, change, and are replaced") and extend beyond it.[6] Base technologies are potentially knowledge generating. What base technologies do is to introduce a kinetics into knowledge pools. The kinetics is manifested in applications of the technological dynamics that are implicit within them. It is the kinetics of knowledge generated by managed discovery at the places of application, upstream and downstream. Knowledge generated is incited by upstream and downstream applications sustaining each other in further discovery.

Base technologies contain possibilities of radical (or discontinuous) innovations in product, equipment design, manufacturing process, and market. These are innovations as to which the knowledge structure and knowledge content can be quite different from that which constitutes the knowledge that is relied on for perturbating market share, single product, competitive strategizing. The latter are apt to be patterned in terms of a different logic of reasoning, absent the radical innovations developed from the new base technologies. Their product market is then likely to be known, to be there as a disclosed market, and to remain in place despite incremental adaptations in relationships to market elements by the firm.

With the heightened awareness of the possibilities consequent on conscious development of the dynamics of the new base technologies—novel foundations of knowledge respecting utility, production, product, value and market—the radical innovations become social, structural, technological and developmental (economic). We are not without historical knowledge of earlier technological experiences with radical product innovations "invading stable businesses"—automobiles, photography, refrigeration, calculators, aircraft engines, and more. Viewed historically, however, the judgment is that the similarity between the old and the new, products allowed manufacturers "to a large extent, [to] apply their established techniques and facilities in making the new product."[7]

Suppose, however, that we select a new base technology, one that is without historical similarity and with no historical precedent; in this case, cell farming in space using NASA's Rotating Wall Bioreactor adapted to work in prolonged weightlessness in orbit. Utopian technologists project the Rotating Wall Bioreactor as a weightless chamber in which conditions could exist for living cells to develop into actual body parts and organs. For the present there is only an orbiting bio-body shop from which an unpredented space-based industry could emerge.[8]

The standard quartet of (1) base technology, (2) drive, (3) possibilities, (4) change, is here. Possibles are the imagined "can be" of the actual. All "can be" has its source in a viewpoint respecting the manifold of the world (existence). If that viewpoint is an opportunity for capital investment, then we are in the stage of the pre-utilitarian. There is an inert pre-utilitarian (no potential for possibilities) and a latent pre-utilitarian (potential for possibilities). The stage of the utilitarian (realized possibilities) can be constrained, unconstrained, and faulted (including latent fault, as in the case of the vegetable fungicide Benlate). As for the drive, what *is* the drive? That is, the tendency toward, the reaching toward, the striving as a technological force of change?[9]

In sum, where are the formative cognitions? Not only for cell forming in space, but also with respect to globally dispersing high-technology capabilities—R&D, acquisitions, joint ventures, transnational alliances. Where are the formative cognitions? They may and do exist for individual firms, but not for an American economic strategy.[10] At the level of the firm there is a plentifulness of engagement with the requisite capabilities for strategizing sourced in and directed by human knowing. It is a knowledge subsumed within the path of understanding marked out by the formative cognitions.

Formative cognitions function as a cognitive domination. They may not yet constitute a strategic knowing. Yet they could pre-figure what it might be, by providing beforehand a certain pre-hensive sense or awareness of fitness with respect to that knowing. They are cognitions that contain the dynamics of the logic of the understanding. They are also a ground for thought consciously reflecting about what these cognitions are as a knowing.[11] In this work cognitive domination is expressed in the form of command cognition.

The newer base technologies are without historical precedent. Command cognition faces radical innovations without precedent, not only in manufacture and materials but also in biologicals and pharmaceuticals. Increasingly demand and desire coalesce in quest for pre-operative knowledge—knowing the goal of which is to anticipate experiencing and thus antecedently to introduce the desired directionality and tendency and limits into its cognized possibilities.

NOTE

The Knowledge Focus of Knowledge Based Strategizing

Marshall has set forth (see pages 3–4) the factors that will constitute a base reference for appraising the focus of knowledge for knowledge based strategizing. The first of these is time. Capital is, in fact, conceptualized by Marshall in terms of time. Capital is understood, has meaning and significance, imposes a logic of action and an expectation of outcome within a framework of time. The framework is the time of the present and the time of the future. The second of these is the conception of power, of a specific kind of power, namely, business power. As Marshall put it, business power has a supply side. It is only to this supply side that he refers. His reference consists of an enumeration of its elements as supply: capital, management, and organization. The last enables the first two to be conjoined; the second subordinates the first to the managerial element of business power. By unstated implication, business power would also have its demand side, as there is a criterion of effectiveness introduced by Marshall.

It is by reason of this joinder of capital with the command capability of business power that it posseses what Braudel has described (see pp. 2–3) as a power to create and alter strategy as a "superior force." Through strategizing it quests for possibilities. Selecting preferences from among possibilities emerging from development is the mode by which business power places itself in time. The time of the present technology and the time of future technology; the time of hi-tech and the time of metatechnology; the time of present enterprise structure and the time of future enterprise structure; the time of domestic, national markets and the time of global markets; the time of present competiveness and the time of future competiveness; the time of present products and time of future product families; the time of present capabilities as manifestations of business power and time of future capabilities.

Thus it is that knowledge based strategizing becomes focused on the knowledge demand side of business power. The knowledge demand side, in its relation to business power, may be envisioned as an indisputable feedstock. For business power there are both possible and aspired to achievement levels of strategizing capabilities, which are expressions of placement in a framework of time. The Penelope project is just such a delineation of demand side knowledge. Building from the time of present conjunction of high technology and global competiveness, it delineates the knowledge requisites for a possible strategy whereby the unified European communities could become part of a global triad with Japan and the United States.[12]

Encompassing an enterprise is a nation; beyond the nation is a potential continental community of nations; beyond even that unified community is the dominating oligarchic but competitive global structure of the markets of world trade. Weaving within and through and over and between this global structure is the global network of technology and invention and technologically focused research.[13] To be globally competitive, a high technology Europe must satisfy the threshhold condition—potential unity with a common market. This knowledge is self-knowledge; knowledge of its perdurable and persisting national and ethnic hostilities and antagonisms and divisiveness.[14]

The demand knowledge for business power is the knowledge whereby European enterprise would acquire the capabilities for participating in the dynamics of global scale capital generation, international capital investment, global hi-technology research, the development of global technological futures, and global R&D innovation. In short, the demand knowledge (1) whereby to achieve an efficient high-tech capability within European enterprise, and (2) whereby to achieve in international markets for that enterprise equality of competitive advantage with enterprise in Japan and the United States in the high-tech sector. Taken in the details of their focus, they are the issues of knowledge based strategizing.[15]

REFERENCES

1. Cross, Micheal, "Do Computers Dream of Intelligent Humans?," *New Scientist*, November 26, 1988, 42; "Japan Shares Its Fifth Generation Dream," New Scientist, December 10, 1988, 26; Cross, Michael, "Japan's Quest For The Brainy Computer," *New Scientist*, January 26, 1991, 51.

2. Lessing, Laurence, "Into The Core of Life and Self," *Fortune*, March 1966, 146; Lessing, Laurence, "Inside The Molecules of The Mind," *Fortune* July 1, 1966, 100; Lessing, Laurence, "The Life-Saving Promise of Enzymes," *Fortune*, March 1969, 119; Monmane, Terence, "Complex Window on Life's Most Basic Molecules" (Molecular Graphics), 16 *Smithsonian*, No. 4, July 1985.

3. Browne, Malcolm, "Chemists Make Synthetic Molecules With a Hint of Life," *New York Times*, October 30, 1990, 135; Interview by ED. Regis of Christopher Langton "Concerning Artificial Life, Cell Simulation, Computer Simulation of a Complete Biological Cell," *Omni*, Vol. 14, No. 1 (October 1991) p. 98.

4. Angier, Natalie, "Biologists Unravel Key Link of Cell Division," *New York Times*, November 6, 1990, 86; Shulins, Nancy, "What In Creation" (Producing Artificial Life), *Cleveland Plain Dealer*, January 13, 1991, p. 1G; Browne, Malcolm W., "Computer Creature Shows Signs of Life," *Cleveland Plain Dealer*, August 29, 1991, p. 12E.

5. Watson, James, *Molecular Biology of The Gene*, 3rd (ed.) Preface. (W. A. Benjamin, Inc., Menlo Park, Ca. 1976).

6. Duffy, M.C., "Techmorphology and the Stephenson Traction System," 54 *Newcomen Society Transactions* (1982-83) 55, p. 56.

7. Utter, James M. and Kim, Leusre, "Invasion of a Stable Business By Radical Innovation," Ch. 10 of Kleindorfer, Paul, R. (ed.). *The Management of Productivity and Technology in Manufacturing* (Plenum Press, New York, 1985), p. 137. Avoiding technological determinism, and placing the new "core technologies" (micro-electronics, biotechnology and new materials) in a context of dynamic historical, societal and institutional influences. Roobeek provides a full and critical explanation of differences in competitive capability between seven countries in relation to applications of these core technologies. Roobeek, Annemieke J. M.—*Beyond The Technology Race:* An Analysis of Technology Policy In Seven Industrial Countries. (Elsevier, New York, 1990). See, too, "The Theater of High Tech," New York Times, February 10, 1991, Sec. 3-1.

8. Sawyer, Kathy, "People Parts: Growing Cells in Orbit Called a Possibility," *Cleveland Plain Dealer*, December 20, 1991, p. 6G.

9. Stipp, David, "Nasty Blight: Bad Acting Pesticide is Giving DuPont a Costly Headache," *Wall Street Journal*, December 16, 1991, p. A1.

10. Pollack, Andrew, "Technology Transcends Borders, Raising Tough Questions in U.S.," *New York Times*, January 1, 1992, p. 20; Markoff, John, "A Network of Networks That Keeps Scientists Plugged In," Ibid., p. 21.

11. The Zaibatsu-Kereitsu structure of Japan is an epitome of what can be the place in strategic apprehension of formative cognitions.

12. Woot, Philippe de, *High Technology Europe:* Strategic Issues for Global Competiveness (Blackwell, Oxford GB 1990). The volume is a report from the FAST Programme (Forecasting and Assessment in Science and Technology) of the Commission of the European Communities.

13. Pollack, Andrew, "Technology Transcends Borders, Raising Tough Questions in U.S.," Markhoff, John, "A Network of Networks That Keeps Scientists Plugged In." Both *The New York Times*, January 1, 1992, pp. 1A, 20 and p. 21A.

14. Riding, Alan, "At East-West Crossroads, Western Europe Hesitates," *The New York Times*, March 25, 1992, pp. 1A and A6.

15. In addition to the volume by de Woot, above, see: Starr, Martin K., *Global Corporate Alliances and the Competitive Edge:* Strategies and Tactics for Management (Quorum Books, Westport, CT 1991); Ferdous, Kasra (ed), *Managing International Manufacturing* (North Holland, NY 1989); Roberts, Edward B., *Entrepreneurs In High Technology* (Oxford U. Press 1991); Omahi, Kenichi, *The Mind of the Strategist* (Penguin Books—ed. NY 1983); Oster, Sharon, *Modern Competitiveness Analysis* (Oxford U. Press 1990).

CHAPTER II

Command Cognition and Strategic Knowledge

1.
THE BUSINESS OF TELEPHONY

THE INVENTION IS KNOWN, but what is the business? Given the telephone (or the transistor), what is the business? The technology is known, but what is the business? Given anti-body and recombinant DNA technology (or integrated circuit technology), what is the business? The investment function is known, but what is the business? Given institutional investment finance, what is the business of the capital market?

Command Cognition

Command cognition refers to dominating strategic cognitions. It refers to a knowledge of strategy that is cognition directed. Its attribute of command joins both psychological domination of the understanding and the freedom possessed by capital with respect to choice of strategy. Being cognition directed, command cognition refers to a strategic knowledge that is not focused on or confined to a problem decision point. What is the dominating cognition, rather than what is at hand as a problem.

Command cognition introduces a dominating intelligibility

into the world that is there, but which has to be understood as an object of strategy. It is not the thinking of adaptive strategizing.

The knowledge of strategy assumes a state of events and conditions as sufficiently initiating or driving of an order of things for strategizing activity to be worthwhile. Suppose, however, as in the case of mergers and acquisitions, the outcomes of tendencies in corporate finance were—as in the 70's, coming into fruition—but they were as yet without ground or foundation of intelligibility as a business. Then the understanding of cognitive knowledge—command cognition—became critical for infusing strategy with a directive power.

Teleonomic knowing is part of the strategic knowing of command cognition. It is part of the logic of an order of comprehension of possibilities that constitutes the knowledge of strategy. Teleonomic knowledge, given the pre-figured logic of choice between strategic possibilities, is knowledge of the dynamics of the operative mode through which the logic will be realized. It is a logic of understanding which, although it is prior in time to strategic experiencing, is intended to ferret out determinative factors regarding what that strategizing experience might be like. Teleonomic knowing is focused on what is thought to be demanded by the strategy itself as a logic of the possible performance activity that will achieve it.

Command Cognition and the Knowledge of Strategy

The knowledge of strategy consists of the knowledge of a logic of the directionality, the choices, and the acts which, taken together, are judged to constitute a determinate basis for belief sufficient for the commitment of the will to do, the power to do, and the resources for doing. But from wherein comes that logic which is the knowledge of strategy? It comes from command cognitions, which are its source. Command cognitions are the pre-logic of thinking: They are, nonetheless, thinking. Their function as thought is that they are logic enabling. Being logic enabling, command cognitions presage the possibility of a strategizing logic. They constitute an order of comprehension, and the logic of that order of comprehension is the knowledge of strategy.

Command cognition is knowing without being directed by a program for knowing. It is pre-program knowledge. It is not, like consciousness, or psychological awareness, a pre-condition for knowing; for it is, in itself, a knowing. It is a knowing that is not divorced from experience, but it is not a formally derived inference from experience. Nor is it necessarily determined by it. It is not a complex of mental operations like programmed problem solving. It is a knowing apart from, yet not without relevance for problem solving.

Strategy, and the Business of Telephony

Given Bell's patented invention of the telephone in 1876, a patent contested on the very day of its filing by another American inventor (Elisha Gray), what was the telephone business to be like?[1] It quickly began as the Bell Patent Association, which was financed by what today would be considered venture capital, although the two persons who were the first and main sources of capital were personal acquaintances. The already in-place competitor of the telephone was the telegraph. The telegraph was a station based, geographically distributed, message sending—and—receiving system organized as Western Union and capitalized at $40 million. While convinced of the superiority of the telephone to the telegraph (in terms of ease of use, rapidity of message delivery, and technical simplicity) neither the inventor nor his lead venture capitalist (Gardiner G. Hubbard) had cognized what the telephone business should be. Hubbard took his cognitive reference points from his legal experience within the shoe industry, being acquainted with royalty arrangements in the leasing of shoe machinery. Bell was without understanding of both finance and management. He cognized an ideal vision of telephone lines enabling any two persons anywhere in America to speak to one another whenever they desired to do so. What overwhelmed or frightened Hubbard was the imagined (i.e.

forecast) capital requirements (with only the challenged Bell patents as the security foundation) for bringing into existence what Bell had visioned. So uncertain then were both of them about even getting started as a precondition to survival itself that the Bell patents were offered to Western Union for $100,000. But Western Union declined the offer.[2]

Despite corporate restructurings in 1877 and 1878, formation of the Bell Telephone Company, which broadened the investor base to bring in a group of "Boston Aristocrats," and formation of The New England Telephone Company, (focused on a regional service), the situation worsened. Royalty based territorial franchises were being sold to local companies, but the franchises were without experience, without adequate capital, and without essential capabilities. The telephone itself remained more a technical curiosity than a utilitarian product. Even though individual subscribers were renting telephones, two party lines were increasing, and the first stirrings of growth of public exchange installations were now apparent.

What had worsened the situation to the very edge of insolvency was the revival of interest on the part of Western Union in the telephone. It was an interest revived because of the loss of business to the telephone. Western Union confronted the dual spectre of a fatal competitive advantage and exclusion from entry into a new domain of business. Check and checkmate? In a straight forward response to this cognition Western Union purchased the challenging telephone patents of Elisha Gray and several others in telephony. It organized The American speaking Telephone Company. It used its financial resources to establish rival telephone exchanges and to inaugurate a program of territorial expansion into unfranchised areas. It embarked on a technological research and product development effort to build a superior telephonic type product, financing Thomas A. Edison for this project.

From the standpoint of strategic knowledge, the knowledge of a strategy that would extricate Bell Telephone from the looming end or death in the market place, Hubbard, as company president and general manager, recognized that in his own thinking he lacked whatever intelligible ground that might be essential for this knowledge. The cognitions that would undergird a strategic knowledge were not within his understanding. Serious problems aplenty, to be sure, but no cognitive foundation for a strategy.

The Strategist

The strategist for Bell Telephone was the successor to Hubbard. He was a person whom Hubbard had chosen, with whom he had earlier become friendly, with whom he knew he could work, and who had had a great variety of work interests and experience, including telegraphy. It was Theodore N. Vail.[3] He entered his position in a company that had just been again reorganized. It was a reorganization initiated by the Boston group that had provided the capital to finance Bell Telephone. That firm was now merged with New England Telephone to form National Bell Telephone. In recognition of their increased investment in the recapitalized company, the Boston banks who had invested the new money elected their choice as company president and, by 1880, controlled the administration of National Bell Telephone.

The Sticks and Stones for Strategizing

What was there for Vail to strategize with? What he had were some sticks and stones for strategizing. Not a strategy, but the sticks and stones from which there might be possibilities for devising one. These were his sticks and stones:

1. An entity -
    Essentially a receptacle for investment of capital and for stashing/asserting the legal claims of proprietary ownership, but also a control base.
2. An instrument -
    The telephone equipment.
3. A technology -
    Wire based voice transmission.

4. A pool of captital -
   The prime mover of choice of strategy and that which neither sleeps nor slumbers with respect to investment performance.
5. Operations theaters -
   Territories of activity.
6. Utility -
   The service value of wire based voice transmission.
7. Markets -
   Not a market, but devisable markets according to criteria of divisibility and connectibility.
8. An alternative technology -
   Wire based signal transmission.
9. Players of the game -
   Known present players only.
10. An existential state -
    The circumstances of time and place.
11. Time -
    A conception of the past (the standing of the Bell patent); a conception of the present (theaters of operations); and a conception of the future (the period after expiration of the Bell patent).

The Strategizing

As matters turned out, the existential state—the circumstances of time and place—provided the expedients for much of the early strategizing. The expedients were a spillover from the struggle in the capital market between Jay Gould and the Vanderbilts for control of the telegraph industry through attack, replacement, or control of Western Union. The struggle had begun two months before Vail formally took office July 1, 1879. The work of Sobel on American entrepreneurs (from Francis Cabot Lowell through Royal Little, with a separate chapter on Thedore N. Vail) discloses the essentials of the conflict between the two. The Vanderbilts controlled Western Union. Gould intended to merge National Bell and Western Union into a single firm, The American Union Telegraph Company, which he had organized for this purpose. Gould had also embarked on a related program of stock purchases in the companies that were a part of National

Bell. The Vanderbilts then submitted an offer to Forbes, Hubbard and Vail which was accepted by them in November 1879.

> ". . . Western Union agreed to withdraw from the telephone business and sell its properties in that area to National Bell. In return, Western Union would receive 20 percent of Bell's license fees. It would pay 20 percent of the costs of developing new Bell patents as well, and Bell promised not to enter the telegraph business, a clear blow to Gould."
>
> ". . . But the agreement seemed minor at the time, a sideline to the greater Vanderbilt-Gould struggle for telegraphs, one that Gould won in 1880 when he took control of the Western Union."[4]

Vail as a game player was not part of the "inner circle" of the Boston group of investors who exercised domimant control of the company. He would not be selected as company president. There was an interval of years from September 1887 to May 1907, which began when Vail resigned his position and withdrew from affiliation with the reorganized National Bell (American Bell Telephone 1880) and from its long-distance subsidiary (American Telephone and Telegraph 1885). His return in 1907 to the business of telephony was an outcome of changes that had taken place among the players of the game. In terms of dividends, return on investment, capital gains, revenue stream growth—the success of telephony, whatever it might be as a business—had become more than evident. Enter, then, another group of "major capitalists," but a New York group this time. Originally it was an investment syndicate, with J.P. Morgan as one of the players of the game. The original plan was to use the capital ($30 million) of a newly incorporated firm to finance acquisitions among the independents and then build on the base of a major (7 state) independent telegraph and telephone company to where it would be possible either to (1) absorb American Bell or (2) replace it as the dominant firm within the industry. The syndicate disintegrated when J.P. Morgan chose to go it alone. Morgan also chose to go it with Vail as president of Amerrican Telephone and Telegraph when the time would come that control of the Board would be his. In the end, Morgan forced out the

Boston group, who, wrote Sobel, were judged by him to have mismanaged the company, who were always capital short, and who had diluted their stock control to where it amounted to only 5 percent.

The Strategy: 1

Early experience with strategizing the business of telephone/telegraphy opens the door to strategic knowledge as the knowledge of command cognition. There is the command cognition sourcing the strategy of domination and control within an industry. There is the command cognition in which is sourced the enterprise teleonomics of strategic knowledge. The first is preeminently the strategic knowledge of players of the game in the capital markets. The second is particularly associated with executive/managerial game players within the firm. They need not be disconnected. The experience of Vail had intersected with both.

J.P. Morgan had cognized not a firm, but an industry; not rivalry between competitors, but industry dominating consolidations; not dispersion of business power, but its oligarchic/monopolistic concentration. It was a cognitive pre-logic of strategy about which Vail and Morgan were as one. For Vail the obligation of the Bell system with respect to the field of telephone/telegraph services was " 'to occupy and develop the whole field.' " He meant both vertical and horizontal occupation, both the field of customer services and the field of equipment manufacture. Working control of Western Union was achieved (30 percent share interest) and Western Electric, as the manufacturing arm, was subordinated to centralized control as well as almost total share control.[5]

So it was a strategy the logic of which had been prefigured. In its execution there was a logic of prudential concerns. In its execution it was aggressive and unyielding in tactics for the acquisition of control over the independent telephone companies. Yet a certain conciliatory morality in post-acquisition, local community relationships, together with dividend steadiness in stockholder relationships, enabled Vail to avoid both anti-trust dissolution and European style nationalization of the telephone system.

Strategy with and without Command Cognition

To return to telephony and Vail in 1879, the dominant logic of possibilities was that exercised by Hubbard (Company President) and not by Vail (General Manager). The teleonomical element of the strategy then in force for a start-up company like Bell Telephone was directed at resolving the dilemma of expansion without adequate capital with which to finance it. Given the shortage of capital, how would the possibilities for expansion of service territories be cognized? Hubbard thought in terms of problem limited possibilities—operating within an inescapable financial constraint on possibilities. There could not be any possibility of a national telephone system. Instead, from his legal experience with royalty based licensing of shoe machinery, he borrowed the logic for a strategy whose operative mode would be royalty based franchising of independent local telephone companies who would raise their own capital and purchase equipment from Bell Telephone.

The re-entry of Vail into the Bell system, (now A.T. and T.) was in a command position (President) and as the agent of J.P. Morgan, who had a pre-figured logic of strategy with respect to the entire industry. Command cognition was now fixed on possibilities with repect to the entire industry. As to these possibilities the firm would itself be the teleonomic intelligence and operative mode. A.T. and T. would be directed to become not just a national telephone system, but a dominating and integrated service, manufacturing monopoly in communications. A universal system that would "occupy and develop the whole field."[6]

Command Cognition and Grand Strategy

The course of an interconnected, universal, monopolistic, industry dominating, acquisitions and share control of independent's strategy so successfully followed by Vail brought A.T. and T. to the point where there was a confrontation with national economic policy as expressed by the Sherman Anti-Trust Act. He had brought A.T.&T. to where a grand strategy was essential. The concept of grand strategy is more familiar to the literature of military strategy than to the strategy of capital with repect to enterprise. In particular, Luttwak has exposited grand strategy as the final and ultimate encounter level of strategy.[7] For Luttwak, all strategy is the logic of parties in contention. They are in contention at different but interrelated levels of encounter, and additionally, each level of encounter contains its own dynamic of relationships. The ascending levels of encounter begin with (1) the technical (weapons), and then (2) the tactical (the "craft of war"), with the next higher levels (3) the operational (command conceptions of methods of war) and (4) theater (territory), and, finally, (5) grand strategy. The last is an encounter level that exists within the definitive context of governance, politics and economics.

Vail was searching for an escape from the unacceptable alternatives of dissolution of A.T.&T. by Anti-Trust Action and nationalization of the industry. The opportunity to do so was provided by the reluctance of the Attorney General of President Taft to prosecute for violation of the Anti-Trust laws. Vail initiated the working out of a settlement between the Attorney General and a vice president of A.T.&T. (the Kingsbury Commitment) in which the company "would dispose of its holdings in Western Union, restrict its acquisition of independent telephone companies that competed with its licenses, and cooperate with independents in connecting them to the Bell lines."[8]

There had been a research component of Western Electric which, in 1924, was sufficiently important in its own right to be spun off in 1924 as the Bell Telephone Labooratories. It was a source of basic inventions in advanced technologies. They were inventions that could have brought A.T.&T. into new fields of communications, but they were licensed for commercial purposes to other firms. In 1924, in terms of asset values, A.T.&T. became the largest company in the U.S., with assets larger than those of the Pennsylvania Railroad and of U.S. Steel.

Grand Strategy: Restructuring and Redefining Business

In 1949, the Justice Department commenced an anti-trust suit against Western Electric. The object of the suit was both to restructure the company and to separate it from the Bell system. The legal action terminated in a 1956 Consent Decree that defined the business of A.T.&T. as that of a regulated common carrier of communications. Hindsight would judge that Bell had not only been confined by the Consent Decree to a business position that was obsolete, but also that there was a developing convergence of computer and communications technologies that would now lie outside the business of the company. In 1982, there was a Consent Decree divesting A.T.&T. of local exchange companies. There was obvious need for another vision of the business of the company and its market. It was time for command cognition to know other possibilities. Certainly telephony was no longer an appropriate limitation of the business. Nor was telecommunication. Both were rejected by the President of A.T.&T. who, in the 1980 annual report to shareholders, wrote that its business would be "the business of information-handling. The knowledge business. And the market we seek to serve is global."[9]

NOTE

The Information Business

What is the information business? In 1980, the President of AT&T had placed the future of the Bell System in the business of information-handling. But ("handling" aside) what is the business of information?

The business of information has been conceptualized to include relevant technological developments. That is, the stream of information technologies; to include device, equipment and machine innovations; to include novel applications of the foregoing; to include the structures and the media modes and the disciplines for information utilization. The business of information has been conceptualized so as to encompass both the expansion and the fusion of all that it includes. So conceptualized, the name for the business of information is Teleinformatics.[10]

In terms of prospective markets for Teleinformatics, they consist of a variety of submarkets for components, fields of equipment, special devices, programs, network systems, use innovations, licensing and joint venture agreements. Market goals are directed at national, and international, and Pan-European, and global markets. Both positive and negative factors are operative with respect to open markets, market competition, market cooperation, closed national markets, market expansion, and market penetration.

There are individual company strategies, integrated strategies for company Groups (the STET Group), National Government strategies, and strategies of multinational firms. Pacific Telesis, a Baby Bell company that was created in 1984 by the breakup of AT&T, has begun to strategize about entering the domain of Teleinformatics.[11] Its core business is that of providing local telephone services. The disadvantages of this core business are that it is a regulated business; that phone competition is increasing, offering phone services at lower prices and thus skimming off the high volume corporate trade; that outside the regulated business are other present and future opportunities which might require a restructuring of the enterprise. There are seven regional Baby Bells.

The strategic transformation of Pacific Telesis would be from the utility domain into the domain of Teleinformatics as a non-regulated telecommunications company. A Teleinformatics strategy is focused on (1) the businesses that are unregulated and (2) those businesses with a large potential down the road, the former include (a) wireless communications (cellular, paging and vehicle tracking), (b) home entertainment via cable TV, and (c) a variety of international information services (phone viewing, entertainment, medical, etc.). The quest is for prospects with more rapid growth possibilities.

2.
ENTREPRENEURIAL CAPITALISM

Financial Entrepreneurship

The transformation of the business of American finance capitalism took place within the twenty year period of change that started in the 1960's. One of the key players in that transformation has characterized it as the introduction of "financial entrepreneurship" or entrepreneurial capitalism into the business economy of America.[12] It suffers not in comparison with other great transformations of business in American history. Indeed, only a generation earlier, finance capitalism in America had entropied to where, in retrospective appraisal, it was judged to have been in a state of failure.[13]

What is of compelling interest about the introduction of "entrepreneurial capitalism" is that it can be brought forward in terms of a knowledge of strategy that existed on line with the undergirding events and actions and synchronicity of driving forces that were operative in its own time frame. The knowledge of strategy, as the knowledge of living strategists, functioned as the transformational intelligence of capitalism. True enough, one might confirm the historically grounded conclusion of Braudel that capitalism, by virtue of its capability to choose whatever it would as its course of strategy, existed as a superior force in the history of civilization. In the experience and memory of those living, however, it had foundered and lay quiescent. How could—how would—capitalism emerge from its quiescence and again enter into a state of vigorous strategizing capability?

Fitted Knowledge:
Structure Without Strategy

American finance capitalism had gradually organized itself into a structure for the performance of function with respect to the capital/financial markets. It was, however, organization for function, but without any knowledge of strategy. The knowledge of function is fitted knowledge. It is knowledge of task operations that fit with a schema of function. Function itself, in relation to the capital/financial markets, had taken the form of a generally understood and accepted structure of activity for the performance of which traditional firms with traditional operating practices were in place.

> "It seems to me that the securities business used to be, with a few exceptions, a gentleman's game. People had pretty good manners and followed standard rules of behavior . . .
> ". . . In the old days certain investment bankers had long and friendly relationships with certain companies, and these companies had confidence in the bankers."[14]

Of the traditional practices of syndicated underwritings of capital offerings:

> "In the late '60's the syndicate man had the responsibility to commit capital all by himself . . .
> "Syndicates then were, in today's terms, sort of naked positions. When you took down 450 million, it was a big event . . . Syndicate business actually meant putting on your hat and going to meetings. Syndicates, too, were stylized affairs, all wrapped around a registration statement, all done with long-standing habits of client relationship . . .
> "What you got paid for in Wall Street in those days was your origination. And origination was a relationship business."[15]

Of the vulnerable capitalization base of many of the older partnerships on Wall Street, it could finance function, but not strategy.

> "Most of the companies that we bought in the early '70's were not doing poorly in the business; they were just not capitalized properly . . . These old partnerships really didn't have permanent capital: When a partner retired, that money went out. Not many young people came into this industry from the 1929 crash until after the Korean War, so firms didn't have enough money to replace what left, so the capital structures were really crazy; they created capital with mirrors, not with cash."[16]

Mergers and acquisitions were taking place, but they were not leveraged deals.

> "In the '60's when mergers were made, they were made with stock mostly. There were not so many cash deals, so that didn't add debt. The leverage came in the '70's, when the stocks were undervalued and managements didn't want to use undervalued stock, so they started to borrow money."[15]

Possibilities Knowledge: The Knowledge of Strategy

Putting aside the fitted knowledge of function, therefore, what is the knowledge by reason of which it may be asserted that a knowledge of strategy exists? The knowledge that constitutes the knowledge of strategy is sourced in possibilities knowledge. Command cognition introduces an order of comprehension into possibilties. What is the mode by which things might be made to be what they can become, or what they give signs of coming to be? Nothing that exists has a sufficient reason for its existence within itself. The persistence of its existence is not necessity, but some contingent state of things. Another cognition of phenomena perceived as indicative of the state of things (temporal, material, relational, technological, etc.) leads the understanding to knowledge of possibilities for the existence of other possible states of things. Command cognition is the thought that constructs the pre-logical ground on which to base strategic thinking. In relation to strategic knowledge it is logic enabling. Being logic enabling, command cognition presages the possibility of a strategizing logic.

Command cognition, as knowledge, constitutes an order of comprehension regarding, the phenomena of existence—time, action, place, practice, circumstances, events and the like. It is not, like consciousness or psychological awareness, a pre-condition for knowing. It is, in itself, a knowing. It is neither divorced from experience, nor determined by it. It is knowing in which possibilities are understood in terms of whatever tendencies they possess towards entering and becoming real existence. In relation to the reason of strategic knowledge, command cognition provides an order of comprehension that is the infra-logic or underlying knowledge of strategy. Through command cognition, knowledge becomes strategic in the sense of constituting sufficient reason for selection of a course of strategy.

Command Cognition: From "Finance Capitalism" to "Entrepreneurial Capitalism"

The novel act by Citibank of issuing negotiable CD's, an initiative taken in 1962, was cognized by a major player in the financial markets as "the birth of the restructuring of the financial markets, because it was then that the banks started gradually to bid for funds; previously people just went into the bank to deposit."[18] He "sensed" (a mode of pre-knowing) that a new environment was in the making. The impediments to interest rates were being removed. Market constraints were also being removed. Financial institutions were no longer limited to their traditional type of business. The interest braking function of financial institutions within the credit mechanism had disappeared. "The financial institution had become part of the mechanism that was pushing credit and would allow the system to operate at a higher level of interest rates."[19] Finally, the progress of a changeover in generations was filling the positions that had decision power with persons who had not experienced the depression and who did not recoil from high interest credit. It was indeed, and Kaufman understood the significance of it, "a more aggressive group."

There was yet more for command cognition to comprehend. Traditional trading practices in stocks were being altered by the emergence of large block trading as a new standard of practice. They were also being changed by the rise to dominance of institutional investing as against the individual (retail) stock investor. Research would be forced out of its independent "boutique" structure and into the large investment houses. The weakness in the capital structure of the traditional trading partnerships of Wall Street was exposed. Block trading required levels of capital beyond what the traditional trading partnerships could raise.

What was also increasingly taking place in the '60's was the emergence of the "growth" stocks of fledgling hi-tech enterprises that had begun with research in electronics technology in makeshift quarters. Very large pension funds had been accumulated by a few large firms, but they remained as moneys held without specialized management.

Strategizing the Business of Entrpreneurial Capitalism

By itself "entrepreneurial capitalism" is a term of a cognition. Its utility is not solely that, for it is also a term that invests phenomena with intelligibility. There was a period of time during which the phenomena indicative of the reality of capital/financial market activity was concurrently coming to be as a novel reality while passing away as an established reality. Possibilities concerning the capital/financial markets were disclosing themselves as rethought or as re-cognized knowledge of the business of capital. This re-cognition of the business of capital—the construction of different schemata of its logic and by which to guide action—is strategizing knowledge. Command cognition dominates the understanding of the strategic.

Money management was one of the strategic business innovations of entrepreneurial capitalism. It began with an insight that corporations with pension funds were possibly in need of money managers for those funds.[20] And also what was money management as a business?

> "The $64 billion question that haunts me most is whether money management is really a business at all. Or is it like other strange things that have come and gone . . .
> "After all there isn't much history yet. 'Money management' didn't really exist until the late '60's; it was all custodianship, really. The big banks had all the money, and their charge was to be careful and produce an income. They didn't have to beat the S & P 500 or anything else. I blame the creation of this whole business on Jack Dreyfuss, because he was the first guy who publicized investment returns—known today as 'performance'."[21]

But money management of pension funds turned out to be a business, with corporations as its clients. Performance information became both a necessity to the business itself, but also a saleable product. The R&D end built upon "intelligence base and data base" that could be self-financing. Money management of the pension funds developed into a business with "just a hell of a lot of information". Risk modification—if not risk control—and the improvement of returns was understood to be the responsibility of the money management business. The schema of its logic as a business (its strategizing knowledge) has been clearly stated by the founder of the industry:

> "We really introduced, I think, the concept of getting away from the balanced—bank—manager theory that one organization has all the answers. Over a period of three or four years, we persuaded all of our clients to get to a multimanager mix, diversified by style, which makes sense in an efficient market, where it's quite important to spread your bets."[22]

Mergers and acquisitions. They were a standard activity of traditional finance capitalism. Here again it was recognized as a straight-forward, rather simply calculated, established function—all done witthin a certain context of understanding, method, and expectation. Mergers and acquisitions nested in a slot of fitted knowledge. Function without strategy. Entrepreneurial capitalism strategized function; re-cognized the possibilities of M&A as and object of strategy, thereby investing them with a formative content and a directive power.

> ". . . what we saw was an opportunity to professionalize the M&A business. We said we will be more knowledgeable as to the conceptualization of transactions, the analyses of transactions and the implementation of transactions.
> "That was our strategy. What we next needed was to develop tactics to implement it and make ourselves competitive . . .
> "On the analysis side . . . [the obligation] . . . was to professionalize our whole system. At the time, people worked out mergers on the back of envelopes rather than through the management—consulting—type, by-the-pound analysis that's fairly stan-

dard now. We tried to go beyond computer printouts to get a qualitative analysis of companies, and that differentiated us."[23]

The early stages of the period of transformation from finance to entrepreneurial capitalism was a time when conceptions of what was the business of the capital market were fluid imaginings and undergoing conjectural transformations. It was a time when it was a matter of feeling (also a mode of pre-knowing) one's way around a variety of things: Block Trading, Negotiated Rates, Financial Services, Takeover Leveraging, Money Management. It was a time when the outcomes of new tendencies in the capital/financial markets were coming into fruition, but they were as yet without ground or foundation of intelligibility as a business. The formative knowledge still had a certain inchoateness about it. There was a search for teleonomic knowing, which is part of strategic knowing. Teleoonomic knowing is concerned with the design and dynamics of a business as an operative mode through which strategic possibilities will be realized. Although prior in time to the actual experiencing of perceived strategic possibilities, it is knowing that expresses an understanding of what it is that might be determinative performance factors for that experience. The business is organized with reference to this teleonomic knowing:

> "Twenty years ago we made our first acquisition—the money management concern . . . We felt it was important to have a recurring source of income, and not just income related to the exchange volume or the direction of the markets, but the kind of income you can earn at night and Saturday and Sunday. That acquisition started a thrust for our company into the area of money management.
> "But most of our acquisitions were within the brokerage business, because that gave us the outreach to consumers, and through those consumers we were able to bring in additional accounts for money management. They all really fed off each other. Plus, in the brokerage industry you can make money on Saturdays and Sundays also, through margin account and, with enough accounts, by lending out securities. And you also needed enough business to be able to just expand that back office, through overtime, without big

fixed costs. We really didn't have layoffs. We ran lean in good times."[24]

The worth of expert knowledge to money management investors? Expert in comparison with whom? Those who stayed with the markets throughout the period of transformation of capitalism regarded themselves as having become knowledgeable, and acquainted with the variety of developments in the market, and confident in their judgments. The low estimate of experts has been explained as due to their inability to identify what was of most importance for the money management investor. Successes were not because of experts. Successes could otherwise be explained as "the result of strategic decisions" rather than by investment in "hot stock." There was also, by the founder of one of the first of the money management firms, recognition of a decision mode in which:

1. Stock purchase judgment was related to a valuation model rather than to intuition.
2. Knowledge that some market pools (e.g., a low price-earnings ratio pool), present more advantages than others.
3. "A decision doesn't have to be made every minute." No frantic decision.[25]

Traditional performance of the traditional back office function of the Wall Street firms was destroyed by developments in entrepreneurial capitalism. A large number of firms were unable to manage the surprise surge in the volume of stock trading that took place in the late '60's. More advanced capability in both data processing and operations knowledge had become essential. Failure to achieve it and to integrate it into the business, could be and, as measured by forced mergers, was often, fatal to the existence of firms.[26]

NOTE

Entrepreneurial Capitalism as both a strategized time space, marked off by a beginning and an ending, and as a strategized social space, containing its own content of structural events, personalities, perceptions of opportunity, and activity patterns, is well and informatively described in the following: (1) Brooks, John, "The Go-Go Years," a series of articles starting in the June 23, 1973 issue of *The New Yorker Magazine*, at p. 40; and (2) Bruck, Connie, "Undoing the Eighties," *The New Yorker Magazine*, July 23, 1990, at p. 56.

As late as 1988, an article in Forbes about the firm of Brown Brothers Harriman & Co. centered on the theme of its "Living in the Past", *Forbes* (Vol. 142, No. 1, July 11, 1988, pp. 64-72). The transformation within of the House of Morgan, starting with the 1960's, to match the new creed of modern finance ("The Postwar Casino Age" of banking) is told in detail by Ron Chernow, *The House of Morgan* (Atlantic Monthly Press, NY 1990).

What tends to be lost sight of is the proliferation of financial product innovations that has its origins in the period of financial entrepreneurship, see Smith, Clifford W., Jr., and Smithson, Charles W., *The Handbook of Financial Engineering* (Harper Business Books, NY 1990). The strategy of financial entrepreneurship created a fertile domain of financial product innovations.

3.
THE BUSINESS OF ELECTRONICS

Possibilities Knowledge and the Knowledge of Strategy

A differentiation between knowledge possibilities and possibilities knowledge will provide a useful reference base for getting at the knowledge of strategy with which this chapter is concerned. Knowledge possibilities are the possibilities within or of a frame of knowledge. Possibilities knowledge are the possibilities for another knowledge frame. The difference is such as between possibilities within the germ theory as a frame of knowledge, and possibilitites for a viral theory or a DNA theory as a knowledge frame. Physics has its classical and non-classical knowledge frames. The distinction is not to be confused with differential perception, wherein the knowers know within the same frame of knowledge, but from different spatial/functional points of perception.

Knowledge of the experience of Great Britain with globalized strategy provides a particular frame of knowledge and experience with industry possibilities for strategizing. Knowledge of the post World War II experience of Japan with globalized strategy provides experience with possibilities as knowledge—possibilities for other knowledge frames for strategizing. Perception, in the meaning assigned to it by Locke, is understanding, and not just object representation. The unblindering of perception is the disclosure of that which has been concealed from understanding. The globalized strategic knowledge of Japan and the Asian Rim countries is the understanding of new and repositioned players. The globalized strategic knowledge of the nineteenth century was predominantly the understanding of the economic circumstances of the Atlantic countries (England and the nations of Continental Europe) and of the United States. Rostow has brought together a chronological enumeration of industrialization take-offs (growth economies) by countries of the world. The only Far East country listed for "take-off" in the period 1870-1901 is Japan. However, within the period starting in 1933, the Asian Rim countries of China (mainland), Taiwan and South Korea are listed for modern economic growth take-offs.[27] Gregory has listed the scope of Asian Rim economic industrialization as now including the economies of Hong Knog and Singapore. Additionally, he noted a present and future broadening of the base of the electronic industry into the East Asian countries of Malaysia, Thailand and Philippines.[28]

What was the cognition from whose core of comprehension emerged a fertile logic of possibilities, one that initiated chains of causality by which Japanese/Asian capital markets, and enterprise, and entrepreneurship, and technological innovation would succeed in upending the structure of established world industry? It was a cognition the generative sources of which are traceable to blindered perceptions of the transistor radio by the American retail chains who function as mass merchandisers of consumer products to the United States. The transistor radio embodied a new technology, but was nevertheless still perceived within the structure of the knowledge of mass marketing for the domestic market—production costs, profit margins, market share, competitive advantage. The elements for explanation of what took place have been brought together by Gregory:

1. Semi-conductor technology (the demise of vacuum tube technology), the basis of the transistor radio, was freely licensed by Bell Laboratories in 1952.
2. The American manufacturers of transistor radios
   a) did not come to terms with the domestic mass merchandisers who dominated the United States retail market for these radios.
   b) were absent a strategy focused on export markets.
   c) the result was a separation in the domestic market of a union between production and marketing.
3. The American mass merchandisers, pursuing an aggressive low cost purchase policy, joined marketing to production by linking up with cost-efficient Japanese radio manufacturers, who, in the 1950's, then had no overseas marketing organization.
4. The success of the American mass merchandisers in their domestic marketing of Japanese transistor radios persuaded manufacturers, both in the United States and in Europe, to choose to abandon radio production, rather than invest in technological innovation in radio design. In effect, a default of the respective markets to Japanese manufacturers took place.
5. American industry had functioned within a framework of "prewar international cartel arrangements governing manufacturing," and, in consequence, had established our industrial base "structured along national lines with essentially domestic manufacturing and market strategies."
6. A strategy of relying upon overseas suppliers to provide the consumer products for domestic marketing by American mass merchandisers provided the former with " 'instant access' to the vast American market without significant investment in marketing organizations and operations."
7. In the beginning, the technology for the manufacture of transistor radios was supplied from abroad, including the designs, specifications and quality control standards that were included in the purchase contracts with American retail chains.[29]

Command Cognition:
Possibilities Knowledge as Unconcealment

What had begun with Japanese manufacture of transistor radios is not fully comprehensible in terms of the knowledge frame of enterprise decisions for electronic based consumer products. True enough, there were larger new product opportunities in the domestic market. These opportunities for sales of television products would support, as rational choice, the decision of American manufacturers to produce T.V. sets incorporating the new electronics technology. What had begun, however, was but the first stride along an hitherto untrod step-path of learning with respect to the inter-relationships between manufacturing, production, technological innovation, product generation, product concepts, and the economies of nations.

The calculation of capital investment incorporates a taught logic. It is reflected in the calculative logic of enterprise, which is the logic of profit maximaization, cost efficiencies, and profit margins. While a logic of investment calculation, it is not necessarily the knowledge of understanding. What the reason of understanding has as its concern is the perception or disclosing of that which is concealed in the circumstances of events. Perceptual disclosure—the disclosure of intelligible seeing—is the fundament of the knowledge of strategy. The calculation of capital investment simply as the calculative logic of capital management is a heavily blindered perception.[30] It is not a logic that unconceals.

Possibilities Knowledge:
European and Japanese Technologies

Aristotle's cardinal descriptive principle of change—"coming-to-be and passing-away"—is exemplified here by the passing-away of vacuum tube technology.[30] An enumeration of what it is that has been unconcealed within the circumstances of events since the innovation of semi-conductor technology can be gleaned from Gregory's study of electronics enterprise in Japan and the Asian Rim countries.

That gleaning, however, would best be done within a comparative perspective. The reference base for that perspective would be supplied by the original national experience with unprecedented technological innovation (Great Britain), and the consequent of competitive economic industrialization that ensued from the diffusion among European nations of economic applications of those technologies.

Diffusion/Application of Technology

In the case of the technology that undergirded the first Atlantic/European industrial revolution, its diffusion among the nations of the Continent was relatively unhindered by ineffectual regulatory controls on both the inventors and the inventions. The real and effective hindrances were those of application of technology. These were hindrances that were sourced in the political, the class, craft and occupational, the geo-physical and resource infra-structures in which were contained biases that were adverse to the expansion and growth of technology driven industrialized economies. There occurred, then a period of relatively long duration between the time of the origins of the undergirding technology and competition for markets between national economies.

In the case of the technology that undergirds the contemporary Japan/Asian Rim industrial revolution, it begins as borrowed technology, freely disclosed by its foreign (American) originators. It is also a borrowed technology on whose application within the host country no hindrances were placed and no adverse infra-structure bias laid waste to the conditions for expansion and growth at an industry level. There occurred, then a period of relatively short duration between the time of the origins of the undergirding technology and its offshore availability; also between the time when, following its availability, the levels of its utilization and improvement, in both knowledge base and in application, by the borrowers of that technology introduced competition for markets between national economies. The point has been stressed that so long as catch-up technology is accessible through purchase, and that there exists a commitment of national capabilities for its adaptation to flexible globalized market strategies, the origins of a technology are absent decisive effect in the competition for globalized markets.[31]

The Technology/Product and Product/Technlogy Relation

"Staples" is the descriptive term applied to those products the output of which was the intended consequent of the eighteenth century technology of mechanical invention. The staple products were basic iron and steel, textile machinery, coal and steam powered engines, and iron machinery. The technology of mechanical invention is the technology suited and adapted to the category of external variety. This external variety is the diversified and multiplicitous physical properties of the sensibilized things of the material world. The technological inventions of the industrial revolution that expanded outward from Great Britain established that the accessible, sensible, macro-physical properties exhibited by material things could be altered and reduced to the utilitarian purposes of manufacture by application of the technology of mechanical invention.

It was a technology that could and did expand the variety and quantity of invented products for manufacture. It was, however, not a technology that could itself be radically transformed either by its own product inventions or by its own technological base. It was a practical knowledge that had its possibilities within its frame of knowing, but it did not contain within itself the possiblities for another knowledge frame. It remained one as to which the state of its practical arts could be improved through the learning consequent to its applications. There could and did ensue a succession of "rising" industries to meet expanded and additional product demands. The appearance and entry of "new" industries into the economy was another matter.

There could be "new" industries without "new" technologies. Their newness would be that they were not technologies focused on iron-working and the engineering of mechanical inventions to be coupled to primary (coal, water, steam) energy sources. Those new industries that emerged in the opening decades of the twentieth century were based on the applications of radically new technologies. Technological innovation had shifted its ground, shifted from the earlier foundation in mechanics and external variety. It was a shift in the cognitive terrain of innovation and technology. The shift was now to foundations of knowledge that supplied structures of manageable empirical content to the internal variety of matter (physics and chemistry) and to invisible variety (Atmospheric space). The cognitive terrain had moved away from sole concern with the products of a physical materiality that had been accepted (within Locke's knowledge frame) as an unalterable given because of its inaccessibility. It was moving to the conditions under which, the constituent micro-materiality of matter itself could be accessed, recombined and altered by production technologies.

The new industries of Great Britain that emerged in the opening decades of the twentieth century were ". . . in the fields of power (electricity), transportation (automobiles, airplanes), engineering (electrical machinery), metal manufacture (aluminum), textiles (rayon), and chemistry (synthetic nitrogen and dyes, coal hydrogenation . . ."[32]

"Mechatronics" and the Technology/Product Interrelation

The technology of the electro-mechanical as a basic technology surpassed and displaced the purely mechanical. It was itself surpassed and displaced as a basic technology by the semi-conductor and integrated circuit technologies. Of the Japanese application of these technologies to machinery, Gregory has written that it has resulted (by building on integrated circuit developments) in yet another technological spin-off, termed "mechatronics," in which mechanics and electronics are combined in optimum joinder of the two technologies.[33]

A double interaction between technology and product has thereby been set in motion—technology drives product innovation and the latter drives technological development. There is a particular dynamics to the process of deliberate replacement, practical substitution, and addition of electronic devices to the conventionally mechanical in either design, function, or operation. The growth of market demand for integrated circuits is stimulated. There is also a stimulation of demand for the total product.

Gregory refers to an even more fundamental effect on the macrodynamics of industry—"structurally-induced efficiency in the application of new semi-conductor technology." He has put it as an inevitable consequence of "an immutable law of techno-economic behavior." The thrust of that law is that basic technology, while originally dominated by the place of its initial development, will yield to development domination at the place where it is most efficiently applied and produced. There are, in other words, stages of development in basic technology; leadership in each stage is contingent on the presence of conditions "necessary for continuing innovation."[34]

Hegemonic Industrialization

The Vision of Strategy

The original strategic vision spawned by the industrial revolution of Great Britain was that of hegemonic industrialization. The most that could be achieved in those earlier periods, when it was long distance trade (product exchanges) that were the focus of merchant capitalism, were contingent and shifting durations of national and ethnic influences with respect to commercial networks and geographic catchments of trade.[35] Hegemonic industrialization is a stragegic vision. It is a vision of competitive domination of globalized markets; a vision of hegemony achieved through the preponderant influence of a market controlling industrialization. The technologies of mechatronics, of semiconductors, and of integrated circuits have reinvigorated the strategic vision of hegemonic industrialization. It is the box of strategy revisited.

HEGEMONIC INDUSTRIALIZATION

The Time Frames	The Players	The Dynamics
1750	ENGLAND TECH.	INNOVATION

HEGEMONIC INDUSTRIALIZATION (Continued)

The Time Frames	The Players	The Dynamics
1850	CONTINENTAL EUROPE	TECH. TRANSFER
1870	UNITED STATES	MANUFACTURING AND THE NATIONAL MARKET
1873	JAPAN	MODERNIZATION AND INDUSTRIALIZATION
1900	UNITED STATES/ GERMANY ENGLAND	INDUSTRIALIZATION
1910/20/30	UNITED STATES ENGLAND	NEW PRODUCT TECHNOLOGIES
1946	UNITED STATES	HIGH-TECHNOLOGY INNOVATION
1950-55	JAPAN	INDUSTRIAL RECOVERY & EXPANSION
1960	JAPAN	TECHNOLOGICAL TRANSFER
1974	JAPAN	HI-TECH INDUSTRIALIZATION
1970	ASIAN (PACIFIC) RIM	DIFFUSION OF HIGH TECHNOLOGY
1980	ASIAN (PACIFIC) RIM	HI-TECH INDUSTRIALIZATION
1980	UNITED STATES AND JAPAN	COMPETITIVE HI-TECH INDUSTRIALIZAION

The Foundation of a Base Technology

A concentration of thought upon staples and non-staples, upon traditional products and new products, upon consumer goods and capital goods diverts thought away from hegemonic industrialization. The focus is then upon product competitive industrialization and the world markets. It is a focus upon comparative portions and relative share of country industrial output and world product markets within the strategic box of product competitive industrialization. Hegemonic industrialization is a strategic box of different design.

The staple products with which the hegemony of Great Britain over the industrialization of Western Europe was associated were not the real foundation upon which rested that hegemony. The foundation was always a basic technology and the knowledge indispensable for its application in production and manufacture. That knowledge came to be entwined with the knowledge of capital investment and with the knowledge of demand in domestic and overseas markets for manufactured products. Competitive industrialization followed upon the diffusion of the knowledge of the basic technologies.

The newer and subsequent modern products of the later nineteenth century were not the product derivatives of those first "paleotechnologic" technologies. They were the derivative innovations of new basic technologies. They required structural innovations in marketing, production, management, manufacture, and investment that were not always forthcoming within the economy of Great Britain. Still, these later technological advances and their utilization for renewed ventures into overseas markets were so managed as to be contained within the strategic frame work of product competitive industrialization.

The possibility of ascendency of a strategy of hegemonic industrialization reemerges with the discoveries of solid state and micro-electronics. The possibility was one that lay dormant within the product competitive strategy that permeates the mass marketing of comsumer goods. It was a possibility concealed by a perception of strategy that seizes upon and leverages an inter-firm competitive advantage to achieve a targeted goal of product market share. (In this case, the advantage of lower manufacturing costs). The perception of a strategy of focused country industrialization in and of itself (the historical example of Germany) has a focus different and apart from that of perceptions of inter-firm competitive advantage in product marketing. At its most optimistic level of strategic aspiration, it is a focus of industrial preeminence, or hegemonic industrialization.

Hegemonic Industrialization As Grand Strategy

The difference between the two foci of strategy is the difference between product strategy and grand strategy. The one (product strategy) is enveloped by the other (grand strategy). The one takes its direction from and feeds back into the other. The grand strategy of Japan is focused industrialization in and of itself. It was enunciated by statute in 1957 with respect to an industry without production in quantity, without significant magnitude of product export, and with little more than minimum existence as enterprise. Between its formal enunciation (in the 1957 law of "Extraordinary measures for the promotion of the Electronics Industry") and the time interval till the 1980's (1) Japan took over world leadership in the production of a wide brand of electronic products; (2) Japan discovered and developed new electronics technology fields whose harvest was new product lines; (3) the value of production of the Japanese electronics industry multiplied to where it was second only to that of the United States, and the electronics industry became an established major industrial sector of Japan.[36]

The Knowledge of Grand Strategy

Simply as knowledge, what is the knowledge of strategy? There is a strategic choice, to be sure, but what is the knowledge of the choice? The assumption is that it is not an arbitrary choice, that it is sustained by more than mere justification. So what is the knowledge of the act of choosing? These are queries that take the querist back to the idea of knowledge as expanded by Locke. Knowledge is the understanding of a relation. And the relation for this choice of strategy would be what? By itself, the high technology of electronics and semiconductors is without relation. Standing by itself it would be a stand-alone product technology. So it was perceived and understood in the United States. There the developments in microelectronics—particularly integrated circuits—brought the firms comprising the industry (microcircuit producers and component makers) to a state of "uneasiness" because of the uncertainties consequent upon the very changes that these technological developments would bring about. Visions of impressive new product opportunities, but also very high manufacture entry cost, an intensely competitive market, the need for a new mix of personnel capabilities to be engineered and managed, research and development charges, and a variety of other relevant concerns. Its expanding product future notwithstanding, for American enterprise electronics was weighed and considered in terms of the logic of inter-firm product competition; and the industry future was the likelihood of known patterns of "mergers and concentrations" characteristic of "maturing industries."[37]

The Japanese, by way of contrast, cognized the new technology of electronics in relation to an established Japanese tradition of modernization as the determinative knowledge of strategy. The term "modernization" signifies a commitment, as technology is an integral part of industrialization. The processes and events and institutions of modernization incorporate the technological changes that necessarily accompany industrialization. The history of modernization discloses national experiencing with both engrafted technologizing and institutionalized industrialization. The two are quite different. The former stops short of industrialization. The latter necessitates a reconstruction of all institutions, cultural revisions, and changes in the social character of populations. It is not that engrafted technologizing does not have its "drivers." It is that technology utilization by itself still leaves it unrooted in the primary structures and processes and directional forces of the using society.

Japanese modernization begins with technological engrafting and ends with institutionalized industrialization. Muramatsu has put together an informative history of the technologies introduced into Japan over the period of four centuries, beginning with its pre-western, indigenous mathematics.[38] But, modernization in the history of Japan has a long, continuous history of association with Anit-Westernism. It is because of this "driver" that Japanese modernization also has a long association with Japanese foreign policy. The "driver" itself emerged as a response to the aggressively invasive actions of the Western Powers, leading Japan to embark as a policy which was—as Beasley has put it—one of "Western technology for anti-Western ends."[39]

He cites the initiatives taken in the early period of the 19th century: Nariaki, who introduced those Western technologies of military significance—cannon foundries, iron making, shipbuilding technology. Others, (like Hizen and Satsuma) turned to solving the problems of producing the quality of iron essential for modern cannon and also to Western Style shipbuilding. A small steamship was completed in 1865. Hizen had built a reverberatory furnace (the first in Japan) as well as blast furnaces. These furnaces were used to produce the modern weaponry of the West. The Western techniques of gun making had been introduced into Japan in 1846.

The discomfiture and fears of the Japanese that were roused by the arrival of Commodore Perry in 1853, and by his return visit in 1854, stimulated further technological modernization. It was all to be done with the assistance of foreign technicians—shipbuilding (1855-56) and iron foundry (1857). A full commercial treaty with the United States was reluctantly signed on July 29, 1858. There was also a later commercial treaty between Japan and the United States which was signed in June, 1866. This latter treaty signing, however, had been preceded by a joint (British, French, Dutch and United States) naval bombardment of Japanese shore batteries in the straits of Shimarosiki, (Sep. 1864). It was in this latter treaty that imports into Japan and foreign trade with Japan were freed from practically all of the regulative restrictions that Japan had imposed.[40]

The foregoing characterizes the modernization of Japan that preceded the Meiji period. It was the modernization that accompanies engrafted technologizing. There followed, under the Emperor/Meiji (February 1867), a course of modernization in which Japan was committed to institutionalized industrialization. It was focused on bringing a new Japan into existence. It was the work of the seasoned leadership that governed Japan under a new and young emperor. The way for the reforms of modernization had been opened by the removal of institutional and political obstacles.

The underlying beliefs of the Meiji leadership were two: 1) to save Japan from the danger of foreign attack, "strong rule and an efficient military machine" were necessary; 2) "trade and industry were the foundations [of] Western greatness."[41] It was with considerable symbolic significance that the Gregorian (Western) calendar displaced the lunar (Chinese) calendar on January 1, 1873. Furthermore, the failure of efforts at treaty revision demonstrated that Japan was not in a position of equality with either England or Germany. The conclusion drawn from this experience was more rapid, more coherent, more focused, and more modernization. Japanese industrialization would require interlocking, complementary, synergizing, reinforcing, reforming, disciplinary, spillover and tradition-breaking measures. The place and role for the technological innovation and change—indeed, for the structure of industry itself in a national economy—would be provided by these measures.

The breadth of the Meiji modernization ranged from the inauguration of compulsory primary school education (1872) to providing state capital to finance large enterprise in those newer manufacturing sectors of the economy absent an inflow of adequate private investment. (As in the case of the European merchants at the start of the Industrial Revolution, banking, land, finance, and commercial ventures were preferred as fields of investment.) The period of development of the manufacturing industry by a pattern of state initiative followed by private investment ended in 1881, with a sell-off of the factories operated and owned by the government.

The economic policy that followed was one of state subsidies and contracts to encourage the expansion of heavy industries. New shipyards, the manufacturing of electrical equipment and machinery, the modernization of mining, and domestic production of locomotives were encouraged.[42]

Focused Industrialization as Grand Strategy

The experientially selected and learned cognition that was determinative of Japanese modernization was one of focused industrialization and the enfolding of the firm into a strategy of industrialization of the economy. Command cognition for Japanese modernization was—and is—one of grand strategy. It is a strategy that constructs for itself a structural state of the economy within which are generated chains of causality infused with a directionality that will initiate a transformation of the industrial economy. An un-material frame of cognition exists wherein there takes place the formation and emergence of strategic first cause. Understanding, thought and activity within the complex of industrial structures takes on the character of efficient cause. Command cognition is super-positioned as the dominating cognition, but not as the operational control of the organized empirics of efficient cause.

The firms of an industry make available for grand strategy an array of diversified, self-organizing, autonomous, performance capable, intelligent systems. What is essential for the effectiveness of grand strategy are autonomic contributions, rather than the pattern of mobilized production that distinguished wartime industrial mobilization. The contributions of the firms, as organized enterprise are threefold. They have been identified by Gregory as three in number: first, research and product development; second, cooperative multifirm research projects; third, intra-industry competition within the economy. The first included both imported and exported technology, and patent protection of Japanese discoveries. The second was intended to discourage stand-alone innovation on the one hand, and to effect a joinder of applied with basic research on the other. The third was a striving for synergism and dynamics in a structure of inter-firm relationships that cut across costs, product and process innovations, efficiencies in production, and marketing.

Grand strategy places the firm within a field of energy sourced in human cognition. It is an energy field driven by the cognition that possibilities in time, while presently imperceptible, can be nonetheless real, cognized as ultimate achievement. The business of electronics began with a ready cognition of present possibilities, but without any driver for cognition of another—a different—knowledge of possibilities. It began as a strategy for the products, the product technology, and the product markets which was that of the American mass merchandisers of consumer goods to their domestic markets. It was the present knowledge of a strategy in quest of the present possibility of high profit margins and comparative advantage in manufacturing costs. It was absent any imperative to acquire utilizable knowledge of the possibilities concealed within the base technology itself. The opportunity for Japan to begin acquisition of that possibilities knowledge was presented by commerical arrangements for the manufacture in Japan of certain electronic products—the transistor radio, the hand calculator, and the TV—commercial arrangements wherein the expectation was that the Japanese would manufacture specific electronic products, but without their having any cognized strategy respecting either the products or the solution and application of base technology.

NOTE

Grand Strategy: Japan, The Take-off Years

In 1980, and again in 1981, the Japanese firm of Matsushita placed two long articles in the form of advertisements in the Scientific American Journal. Their titles were "Japanese Technology Today."[43] Their lead authors were internationally known experts on the economy of Japan and the Japanese achievement of world class technological development. James G. Abegglen is the lead author of the first article. Gene Adrian Gregory is the lead author of the second article. The prestigious Akio Etori, also a professor in Japan, cooperated as a joint author of each of the two articles. Their interviews with Japanese executives, as well as their first hand knowledge, supplied the substance of what Matsushita viewed as in depth reports on the foundations and the state of Japanese technology at the start of the 80's decade.

From the content of the report by Abegglen and Etori, the following can be extracted:

   1. Seen in a long term prospective, starting from the period of the Meiji reforms, the path of the Japanese economy has proceeded from domestic handicraft industry to import sub-

stitution, to industrial competence, to foreign (import) basic technology, to technology advancement and application innovations, to technologically focused re-industrialization of production, to closure of the technological gap between Japan and The United States and key nations of Europe.
2. Japan's acquisition by purchase of foreign (import) technologies, starting in the mid-40's, proceeded to rise to a massive scale. In the years 1950 through 1978 the total of purchases reached $9 billion and included 32,000 purchase contracts.
3. While the sellers of the foreign technology might congratulate themselves on R&D windfall income, the purchasing Japanese understood what they were really acquiring: (a) the foundation for a competitive competence in a diversity of world markets; (b) the loss by foreign firms of their possible leverage for direct investment in Japan.
4. Starting in the later 60's, the Japanese stressed two courses of conduct respecting technological advancement: the first—improvements of the purchased basic technology, as evidenced by patent registration increase; the second—innovations in production technology.
5. Consciousness among the leadership levels of Japan that the realization for Japan of the possible benefits from import technology was dependent on these being a synchronous culture and structure and design and policy dynamic on the part of government, business and financial institutions, labor and management.
6. The Japanese concept of their government. It is not possessed of any special insight, or foresight, or prescience, or cleverness respecting the future. It is not possessed of any special capability for doing good. Nevertheless, government had a role to play. It had licensing and regulative powers; it was a vehicle for public sector instruments; it could be a repository of particular policies. But that role had to be indirect rather than direct; facilitating rather than controlling; specific to particulars rather than general; and focused on avoidance of doing harm in the transformation of the economy through import technology and technological development.
7. As for Japanese corporate enterprise: the culture, the structure, the ethnic homogeneity, the values entering into incentives and rewards, the reciprocities of relationships among and between managers and production labor—all these combined into a multiplicity of coherent systems of enterprise engaged in technology gap reductive activity.
8. All industrial policy and all trade policy and all investment pol-

icy took its reference from the directness of its relevance to technology, particularly high technology. The new and emergent industries (computers and telecommunication) were protected. High technology meant high growth potential and high value added. Dying industry (such as ship building) was closed down, but by a process that kept the high efficiency firms and that also raised the level of technology utilization in these retained firms. As for the purchase of foreign technology, Japanese companies made a global search for the best technologies and the goverment approved the price of the purchase and the length of purchase agreements. An educated labor force, particularly at the shop level, and one that was also fairly young, could be brought to accept and adapt to the introduction and diffusion of automated production technology. Tax policies supported high investment levels. Within Japan, competitive investment was linked to competitive market economy. Export competitiveness was a derivative of competitive investment.

The second report, the article by Gregory and Etori, concentrates on changes which had already taken place—the benchmark date being 1957, when the electronics industry was marked by policy as the priority development sector,—and on changes which they predict will continue to take place. These are the changes in the structure of the "global and industrial and technological order" that are the consequence of Japanese innovations in high technology electronics. They are consequences of the innovations in advanced semi-conductor technology and also consequences of the diffusion within Japanese enterprise of applied high technology innovations among the components, the equipment and products, and the concepts and methods of industrial design and production.

High technology electronics was the shining star of the grand strategy of closing the technological gap between Japan and the West. Gregory and Etori take special note of the long range vision of possibilities in electronics technology that dominated Japanese thinking, and they also take special note of the suitability of Japanese business structures for these visioned possibilities. Through quoted interviews there is a sampling of executive psychologies of explanation of Japanese business performance.

There are also projections of further stages of technological progress and utilization of electronics technologies. They put forth grounds to substantiate their judgemnt of the comparative advantage of Japanese over American manufacturers in marketing and production.

After Grand Strategy What?

For all parties, however, for authors as well as for these Japanese executives who were interviewed and quoted, the big question for the 80's was: After the closing of the technological gap, what then? The take-off stage had been driven by a grand strategy that both introduced and sustained a technololgical initiative. That initiative could be extended to other technologies compatible with electronics—i.e. optical technologies. There were also domains other than electronics—i.e. space. As of then, there was no reference to biotechnology. There was also a demand for another initiative—Japan, on its own, to develop its own basic science. Japan, therefore, to undertake to restrucutre graduate science education and the structures and relation of research in science to the institutions of university and business.

The decade of the 90's marks the end of a base period of forty years, a period that extends back to the Japanese vision of the future of the electronics industry in the 1950's. It has been forty years of an investment oriented, growth oriented, export oriented, market share oriented, and business structures oriented to institutional linkages tied to cooperative and stable relationships. A general strategy so durable accomplishes more than only its targeted achievements. It opens the way for changes in the foundational ground from which originally its cognitions were drawn. In the case of general strategy of Japan, the foundational grounds are in the roots of the social economy itself, and recognized as the ultimate cause. What has occured is another cognition of transformed foundational grounds. An extensive and pervasive re-cognizing of these grounds has surfaced in national consciousness and is being diffused within it. A "new mentality", so to speak; "an erosion in the previous fundamental templates of the long-term view of Japanese management."[44]

The new factors in the transformed foundational grounds of Japan are factors for which cognitive templates are in dispute and, while identified, are not yet formative strategic cognitions. These non-traditional factors include formation of a new social character within the population's personal lifestyle changes, the rise of inter-firm career flexibility, the increase in graduate university education, increased deregulation, and the protective restrictions of hard pressed foreign competitors. Nothing in this list of factors—which impinge on competivie style and intensity—diminish the technological initiative that long has been the driving force of Japan's grand strategy, and which searches still for new domains of technology.

REFERENCES

1. The story, in detail, of the invention of "Bell's Telephone" is related in Chapter 1 of Fagan, M.D. (ed.), *A History of Engineering and Science in the Bell System: The Early Years (1875–1925)*, Bell Telephone Laboratories, Inc., 1975.

2. "The Early Corporate History" of Bell Telephone and its successor companies will be found in Chapter 2 of the Bell Labs history edited by Fagan, above, note 1. There is considerable detail of organizational and managerial innovation. A primary innovation was to link scientific research and applied research with technological progress in telephony.

3. Sobel, Robert, *The Entrepreneurs: Explorations Within the American Business Tradition* (Weybright and Talley, N.Y. 1974), Ch. VI. An informative work. The author has drawn from the material contained in Ch. VI, which is focused on Theodore N. Vail, who Sobel states to be a "neglected" and "ignored" figure in American economic and business history.

Documented homage to Vail's cognition of the business of telephony will also be found in Chapter 2, "A Perennial Question," of the work by Auw, Alvin von, *Heritage and Destiny: Reflections on the Bell System in Transition* (Praeger, N.Y. 1983). A brief conspectus of the tribulations that have afflicted Western Union is set forth by Janet Guyon in *The Wall Street Journal*, October 13, 1989, p. A 1.

4. Ibid., 214.

5. Hinterhuber, Hans and Wofgang, Papp, "Strategy as a System of Expedients," 21 *Long Range Planning* No. 4 (1988), 107-120.

6. Sobel, *Entrepreneurs*, 232.

7. Luttwak, Edward N., *Strategy: The Logic of War and Peace*, (Harv. U., Belknap Press, Cambridge, MA, 1987).

8. Sobel, *Entrepreneurs*, 240.

9. Auw, Pt. 1, Ch. 2, p. 30. Relevant also is Bernstein, Jeremy, *Three Degrees Above Zero: The Bell Labs in the Information Age* (Scribners, N.Y. 1984). Criticism of the stifling of innovative developments in telecommunications since the 1984 splitup of AT&T has been directed at Federal and State regulatory policies as the cause. Mary Lu Carnevale, "Phone Servce Shows Only Minor Advances 5 Years After Breakup," *Wall Street Journal*, January 6. 1989, p. 1 A.

10. "European Teleinformatics," special report by Joel Stratte-McClure, 245 *Scientific American* No. 4, p. E1 (October 1981).

11. Groves, M. and Flanagan, J., "PacTel to Study Spinoff of Core Phone Forms," *Los Angeles Times*, Sec. D, p. 1, April 17, 1992. For a survey of some coming teleinformatics products in terms of their projected user applications, see Schwartz, John, "The Next Revolution," *Newsweek*, April 6, 1992, 42-48.

Generally, see the study, *The Economics of Innovation in the Telecommunications Industry* by John R. McNamara (Quorum Books 1991)

A brief conspectus of the tribulations that have afflicted Western Union is set forth by Janet Guyon in *The Wall Street Journal*, October 13, 1989, p. A1.

Note

The breakup of AT&T has produced a special literature about that event:

[1] Sterling, Christopher H., Kasle, Jill F., and Glakas, Katherine T., (eds.), *Decision to Divest: Major Documents in U.S. v. AT&T, 1974-1984* (3 Vols. Communications Press, Inc., Washington D.C. 1986)

[2] Evans, David S. (ed.), *Breaking Up Bell: Essays on Industrial Organization and Regulation* (ERA Research Study, North Holland, NY 1983)

[3] Temin, Geter and Galambos, Louis, *The Fall of the Bell System* (Cambridge U. Press, NY 1987)

[4] Stone, Alan, *Wrong Number: The Breakup of AT&T* (Basic Books, NY 1989)

[5] Kraus, Constantine R. and Duerig, Alfred W., *The Rape of Ma Bell: The Criminal Wrecking of the Best Telephone System in the World* (Lyle Stuart, Secaucus, NJ 1988)

12. Kaufman, Henry, Chief Economist, Soloman Brothers, 21 *Institutional Investor* No. 6, (June 1987), p. 223, 227. This is the twentieth anniversary (oral history) issue.

13. Sobel, Robert, *The Age of Giant Corporations: A Microeconomic History of American Business 1914—1984* (2nd ed, 1984, Greenwood Press, Westport, CT), Ch. 4.

14. Loeb, John, Former Senior Partner, Loeb, Rhoades & Co., *Institutional Investor*, above, Note 12, p. 339.

15. Whittemore, Frederick, Managing Director, Morgan Stanley & Co., *Institutional Investor*, above, Note 12, pp. 47-48.

16. Weill, Sanford, Chairman, Commercial Credit Co., *Institutional Investor*, above, Note 12, p. 83, 84.

17. Steinberg, Saul, Chairman, Reliance Group Holdings, *Institutional Investor*, above, Note 1, p. 43, 45.

18. Kaufman, 224.

19. Ibid.
20. Russell, Jr., George, President, Frank Russell Co., *Institutional Investor*, above, Note 12, at pp. 295-299.
21. Kirby, Robert, Chairman, Capital Guardian Trust Co., *Institutional Investor*, above, Note 12, p. 35. A severely critical view of the business value of the pension fund money (investment) management consultants is stated by Ellis, Charles, Partner, Greenwich Associates, *Institutional Investor*, above, note 12, pp. 435-436.
22. Russell, 296.
23. Wasserstein, Bruce, Co-Head, Investment Banking, First Boston Corp., *Institutional Investor*, above, Note 12, p. 414.
24. Weill, 83-84.
25. Miller, Paul, Partner, Miller, Andersen & Sherrerd, *Institutional Investor*, above, Note 1, p. 228, 230.
26. Tuite, William, Senior Vice President for Data Processing, Drexel Burnham Lambert, *Institutional Investor*, above, Note 12, pp. 283-284.
27. Rostow, W.W., *The World Economy: History and Prospect* (University of Texas Press, Austin 1978).
28. Gregory, Gene, *Japanese Electronics Technology: Enterprise and Innovation* (John Wiley and Sons, 2nd ed. 1986, New York), p. 414.
29. Gregory, Ch. 30.
30. An informative article by Max Ways, "Why Japan's Growth Is Different" (*Fortune*, November 1967, p. 127) provides a cultural qualification to Aristotle's principle of change. In effect it can function as a principle of high social cost, because it is one which "might be called progress by substitution." The preference of the Japanese was for a principle that minimized the cost of change. "Advance is the margin between what is created and what is destroyed." Thus a slower, limited policy of institutional destruction was practiced. "Japan . . . proceeded by accumulation, by placing a new pattern on top of an older layer, retaining the latter in full vigor." (p. 257).
31. Gregory, Ch. 30.
32. Kahn, Alfred E.—*Great Britain in the Word Economy* (Columbia, U. Press, NY 1946), p. 105.
33. Gregory, p. 32.
34. Ibid., p. 204.
35. Braudel, Fernand—*The Wheels of Commerce* (Vol. 2 of *Civilization and Capitalism, 15th-18th Century*, translated from the French by Sian Reynolds, Harper and Row, 1982 ed.).
36. Gregory, p. 206.
37. Siekman, Philip—"In Electronics, The Big Stakes Ride on Tiny Chips," (*Fortune*, June 1966), p. 120.
38. Muramatsu, Teijiro—*Industrial Technology in Japan: A Historical Review* (Hitachi, Ltd., Tokyo, Japan 1968).
39. Beasley, W.S.—*The Modern History of Japan* (Prager, NY, 2nd ed., 1974), p. 53.
40. Ibid., Ch. 5, pp. 54-55.
41. Ibid., Ch. 8.

42. Ibid.

43. *Scientific American*, Vol. 243, No. 4 (October 1980); Vol. 245, No. 4 (October 1981).

44. "Japanese Corporate Management: Does It Need To Be Changed?", *Japan Economic Institute Report*, No. 15A, April 17, 1992.

CHAPTER III

Command Cognition: Power, Agency and Experience

1.
COMMAND COGNITION

The Cognitive As Power

THINKING-MIND ACTIVE, as Locke had put it—in active operation about its ideas when considering anything, but thought alone? Separated from will? From power? From action? From relations?

Locke never disconnected mind from the idea of power. Mind established the directive preferences to which actions were subordinated. They were the outcome of mental operations. They were directive, a cognition of command. They were directive in that, to use a phrase of Locke, "barely by a thought or preference of the mind" the exercise (or forbearance therof) of action was ordered as commanded. Locke had reference to the linkages between perceptual acts of the understanding and will and volition as a power of the mind.

Power for Locke, was an idea; in particular an idea that included "a relation to action or change." By change, however, was meant observable change in that which was sensibly perceived. Power, as idea, thus connected to objects of "perceivable ideas," was thereby rooted in cognition. It was traced by Locke to the reference by mind to alterations in its own perceived ideas of sensible things. He could have chosen an external explanation of power through the observation of the sensible qualities of bodies. "But yet," he wrote, "if we will consider it attentively, bodies, by our senses, do not afford us so clear and distinct an idea of active power, as we have from reflection on the operations of our minds."[1]

The Person as Agent

External phenomena—the phenomena of things to be known through sensibilization—provide the perceptual materials for cognizing by the person as an agent of action. Attention is centered on the person or individual as agent who is endowed with a power to engage in particular actions (or to forbear doing them) "according to the determination or thought of the mind."[2] Locke had conjoined the cognition of command (of will and volition) and the preference of choice with respect to action, in the context of the individual as an agent of change-inducing action (active power).

Nonetheless, in the context of agency and active power, cognition and directive preference cannot be explained entirely as individual psychology, which is where they had been left by Locke. There needs to be a certain extrication of cognition and choice from the explanatory confines of individual psychology. The active power of the acting person intrudes into the external world as an exercise of agency. In response to this intrusion the bodies and the substances and the others of the external world exhibit sensible evidence of their own powers. "I confess power includes in it some kind of relation—a relation to action or changes; as, indeed, which of our ideas, of what kind soever, when attentively considered, does not?"[3]

Strategy as Engagement

In consequence of that relation, it is not action or behavior as such that is the object of consideration by mind active. The object of consideration is the power in the agent of action to conclude upon that course of action which will effect whatever change or outcome is preferred to any other. Necessity is excluded. It is the knowledge for exercise of directive preference that is included. This is the knowledge that is strategic knowledge; that is, the knowledge of the possibilities consequent to power exercised in pursuance of preferred action or change.

As to this strategic knowledge, the agents of strategic change enter into an active-relation with the external world, with "the bodies and the substances and the others of" that world. Exhibiting as they do their own powers, as Locke has noted, there are engagements with identifiable strategizing agents who are acting so as to acquire the knowledge for strategizing, to understand it as a specialized cognitive capability, and to apply it in directing their respective ventures.

It is with reference to these engagements between strategists with their powers and the external world with its powers that the extensive researches of Braudel are especially informative. Strategic activity is located in time, by geographical place, by venture activity, and linked to economic differentiation within a society as well as to stages in the historical development of capitalism.

Strategic Knowledge and Micro-Capitalism

The findings of Braudel join the personal psychology undergirding strategic knowledge to structural locus, to institutional place where strategy as a differentiated knowledge can be recognized, acquired, understood, mastered, and applied. Those who exercised strategic choice emerge from an historical frame of typological and hierarchical economic differentiation. At ground level is the base economy, the economy of "material life." Here there are no opportunities for strategic choice. It is very elementary as an economy; more an infra-economy. It is "routine bound," and its very self-sufficiency imprisons it within situation, within locality and by participants.[4]

At the next higher level is the typological model for "economic life." It is a model in which micro-capitalism emerges and in which there is also a tendency to merge with the economy of the competitive market. The latter introduces the economy of trade based processes of exchange. Here, writes Braudel:

> "The economy, in the sense in which I wish to use the word, was a world of transparence and regularity, in which everyone could be sure in advance, with the benefit of common experience, how the processes of exchange would operate. This was always the case on the town market-place . . . And it was the case too, even if the distance was greater, for any *regular* trade of which the origins, conditions, routes and market were fixed: . . . Such trade links were innumerable and usually long-established; their itinerary, calendar and price differentials were known by everyone—and as a result regularly open to free competition."[5]

What of the micro-capitalism of this typological model in the three step hierarchy of structural differentiation? It emerged in connection with the sphere of trade that had to do with the transactions of the private, as against the public or supervised market. These micro-capitalists stood "outside the regular market price system, by means of advance payments and elementary forms of credit: they bought grain before it was harvested, wool before it was sheared, wine before the grapes were picked. And they controlled prices by hoarding foodstuffs; in the end they had the producer at their mercy."[6]

It was hardly possible for micro-capitalism to emerge in the period of pre-industry workshops and manufactories. Within these production structures there was absent the differentiation of tasks from the activity of the ordinary work of the wage earners. There were, however, instances of merchant capitalism connected with pre-industry production, particularly with the system of putting out work (advancing materials and wages and contracting for production) by trading merchants.[7] But it was never a whole hearted commitment to production. The commitment of the merchant of wealth and importance was to marketing—the sector in which premium profits could be made.[8]

"Real Capitalism" and Command Cognition

Placed by Braudel at the hierarchical summit of his structural typology is capitalism. It is, to him, categorically different from the economy of the market. The latter is that "transparent economy" of the regularized processes of market exchange. Capitalism, as a super-structure, is not a necessary outcome of the underlying market economy. As against the natural or exchange economy (the economy for the circulation of goods), Braudel characterizes capitalism as a superior and sophisticated artificial economy. Real captalism is differentiated from the market economy by very "tangible" distinctions of agents, of participants, of actions, of mentalities, of "calculations and speculation," and of power accumulation.[9]

> ". . . The distinction of sectors between what I have called the 'economy' (or the market economy) and 'capitalism' does not seem to me to be anything new, but rather a constant in Europe since the Middle Ages."[10]

Looked at historically, that is, capitalism, looked at for a term of 500 years and in relation to periods of economic life during which non-capitalism would occupy by far most of the sectors of current economic life, then it might be concluded that:

1. Capitalism exhibited new and emergent forms.
2. Capitalism preceded the industrial revolution, which "was above all a transformation of *fixed capital*," improving its quality, extending its durability, adding to its cost, and altering "radically" rates of productivity.
3. The nineteenth century does not mark the advent of "true" capitalism.
4. The capitalism of the past would reach out from its limited and narrow sectors of economic life to exhibit a very deliberate selectivity in searching out those new areas in which capital reproduction was favored.
5. In some economic sectors, capitalism "was really at home"; but in others there was only oblique and very limited penetration.
6. The experience of capitalism before the end of the sixteenth

century was such that it could be concluded: "The hunt for and maximization of profits were already implicit rules of capitalism, even then."
7. What within societies of the past contained capitalism? What, that is, barred it from unlimited expansion and domination? "Perhaps in this fact was the condition of its survival, since in yesterday's societies a significant rate of capital formation was possible only in certain sectors and not in the whole market economy of the time."[11]

2.
EXPERIENCE AS A RULE COGNITION

The Rule As Cognitive Knowledge

Accepting the thesis of Locke that experience is a precondition of knowing, how is it that the idea of a rule becomes cognitive knowledge? His only explicit analysis of rule cognition is in his dissection of moral relations. Moral rules exist as a cognitive reference norm (laws) for judgement of the rectitude or pravity of actions, and as to which reward and punishment attach.[12]

With command cognition, however, the dominant focus of concern is with power and not with moral relations. The idea of power is a something that mind "comes by" or "concludes" from information provided by the senses from everyday experience. For Locke, sensation is dependent on notice being taken thereof in the understanding. It is by this "notice" that there is imprinted an idea on the mind. So power, as idea, is not the product of raw sensory data. Power, as idea, is something that the mind has taken "notice" of from that which it has constantly observed. At bottom, then, is the perceptive power of mind.

> "The power of perception," wrote Locke, "is that which we call the understanding. Perception, which we make the act of the understanding, is of three sorts: 1) the perception of ideas in our minds. 2) The perception of the signification of signs. 3) The perception of the connexion or repugnancy, agreement or disagreement, that there is between any of our ideas. All these are attributed to the understanding, or perceptive power, though it be the two latter only that use allows us to say we understand."[13]

What is it that the understanding concludes, and from what kind of sensory information is that conclusion derived? Locke puts it that the sensory information is about things that once were, and then being not; about things that once were not, and then coming into existence; about that which was changed, and about that which effected the observed change; about the ceaseless continuation from past into future of changes, of agents of change, and the ways of effectuating change.

The Idea of Power

What it is that the understanding concludes?

1. The idea of "power includes in it some kind of relation,—a relation to action or change."
2. The idea of power encompasses that which is able to make change (active power), and that which is able to receive change (passive power).
3. Persons as human beings are "created spirits." As to them, it "may be worth consideration," with reference to the idea of power, "whether the intermediate state of created spirits be not that alone which is capable of both active and passive power."
4. All power is a relation to action, and therefore includes the reflective activity of thinking and the activity of movement, or the production of motion. It is reflection on its own operations of thought and preference that provides mind with its clearest idea of active power.
5. The idea of power is one that reaches into the sensible ideas of things. It does so by a) introducing a possiblity of change in those ideas, and b) power itself being considered by reference to the changes of perceivable ideas about sensible things.
6. The idea of an agency, either capable of volition or bound by necessity, and by which change and action are conjoined to preference and command.

Real Existence and Command Cognition

The idea of power confronts command cognition with lemmas of reflection, preference, action, and agency of action with respect to the manifold of sensible things that constitue the material world. The need is for knowledge of real existence, for knowledge of the substance of things, for knowledge of voluntary and necessary relationships. The source of their knowledge lies in experience, not in reason. It is from thought reflecting on experience that rule cognition emerges.

The knowledge of real existence consists of sensory particulars (excepting the intuitive knowledge of one's own existence). It is not knowledge of universals and it is not knowledge of abstractions. Nor is there any necessary connection of real existence with any idea about it. The path of knowledge is a quest for knowledge of co-existence—"the qualities of things co-existing with my complex ideas of them." It was a path which, for Locke, went from our own thoughts "to the things themselves as they exist." It was the path of experience.

> "Where our inquiry is concerning co-existence, or repugnancy to co-exist, which by contemplation of our ideas we cannot discover, there experience, observation, and natural history must give us, by our senses and by retail, an insight into corporeal substances."[14]

Rule Cognition

What then of rule cognition and experience in all this? What is it in the way of knowledge that is disclosed by experience? It is not just knowledge of the observable qualities of things. It is not simply knowledge of their exterior causes. The knowledge of power in question is the knowledge of the actuality of its being experienced (its experiencing), as against only the mere idea of it. Hence it involves an agent reflecting on his own power by virtue of his own actions.

With the experience of acting power there is disclosed the knowledge of connections between actions. Rule cognition is the knowledge of the understanding reflecting on the connections between "perceivable ideas" and actions in the exercise of power by an acting agent. These connections between actions are the content of the relation of action to change—their causality in relation to an outcome. Cognition invests them with the modal form of a rule. A rule is not a universal. A rule is not an abstraction. A rule is not an intuitive knowing. A rule is a modal form for expressing the sensory particulars of "perceivalbe ideas" in their connected and co-existing relationship to the attainment of an action effectuated outcome.

3.
THE RULES OF COMMAND COGNITION
Experience, Rules and Cognition

The acting agent whose experience is here the substance of concern is the capitalist. Braudel provides a richly detailed source (a "topology of capitalism") from which can be drawn the information of three hundred years of their experience with capital investment and capital reproduction, and from which are derivable the rules of command cognition. The realm within which the capitalist has functioned is "the realm of investment and of a high rate of capital formation." It is a realm that has been identified by Braudel as the realm of capitalism itself.

Experience in these three centuries discloses no one, no single, no invariant form and structure of capitalism. At different historical periods each form and structure of capitalism has its "strategic position *par* excellence." It is as to this strategic position about which there is a striving for preferred access and domination. In the period of merchant capitalism that position was long distance trade, conferring as it did "legal or actual monopoly and the possibility of price manipulation." In the period of industrial capitalism, that position was industrial production.[15]

The realm that is capitalism contains within it "the means to create its own strategy or to alter that strategy if necessary."[16] There is a search for the preferred profit making areas of the economy for possible intervention and investment. It is within these areas that there exists the opportunity of preferred choice and action. That is to say, they are as foci for agents who, exercising a liberty of selective choice, have a power to introduce, or to withhold the introduction of, particular relations into the economies of societies. They are, in the sense in which Locke has given content to the terms of agency, agents of liberty and not agents of necessity. Capitalism, as a realm of agents with liberty to choose and to engage in actions of investment, is, by Braudel, differentiated from the market economy (competitive necessities) because it "does not seem to me to be anything new, but rather a constant in Europe since "The Middle Ages."[17]

The Discipline of Command Cognition

Choice in and of itself is not a strategy. Moreover, choice in and of itself is a contingent preference. The appropriateness of capitalist choice lay in its linkages to the creation, to the maintenance and to the alteration of a strategic course regarding a preferred sphere of action. The experience of history does not disclose an "unerring perception of the right path." Nor does it reveal a pre-disposing mentality. As was the case among the general population, so did individual capitalists, throughout the three hundred years that Braudel investigated, exhibit the characteristic variety of temperaments and attitudes toward risk.[18]

There yet remains to be taken into account the important factor of competency education and apprenticeship, and practical training for those who would become merchant capitalists. It was important enough to earn the tribute of being singled out as one of the contributing pre-conditions to the creation of merchant capitalism. So it has been appraised by Braudel in his review of the uneven spread throughout Europe of practical and technical education for those who would be young merchants. From the fourteenth century, organized and specialized merchant apprentice education in Florence, Italy, was of a technical content such that a graduate from the apprentice high school "was already able to keep the registers of accounts we can inspect today, which reliably recorded details of sales on credit, commission, compensatory payments between different centers, or the distribution of profits among the partners in companies.[19] As for the competency level of attainment required of the young merchant apprentices, it was not to be underestimated:

". . . The young merchant had to be able to establish buying and selling prices, to calculate costs and exchange rates, to convert weights and measures, to work out simple and compound interest, to be able to cast up a 'simulated balance sheet' for an operation, and to handle the various instruments of credit . . . And when one looks at the masterpieces of bookkeeping that have survived in the great ledgers from the fourteenth century onwards, one is overcome with retrospective admiration."[6]

In sum, the evidentiary content of capitalist experience of a long duration establishes clearly enough that they proceeded as disciplined agents of action. Disciplined in their tactical activity and disciplined in their strategic actions. Disciplined action is rule based action. The rules involved become known through formal education, through practical training, through apprenticeships, and through actual experience with commercial networks and trade circuits. These are the rules of command cognition.

4.
THE RULE CATEGORIES OF COMMAND COGNITION*

Category I
    1. Cognition of the Rules of Place
    2. Cognition of Investment Rules
    3. Cognition of Money Market Rules

Category I   1. Cognition of the Rules of Place
    1.1 The Rule of Retention of Command Initiative
    1.2 The Rule of Leveraging the Perquisites of Capital
    1.3 The Rule of Locus in the Commercial Structure of Domination and Inequality
    1.4 The Rule of Inside Information Sources, Channels of Communication, and Information Content

Category I   2. Cognition of Investment Rules
    2.1 The Rule of Sufficient Information in Relation to Risk

*The rule categories have been extracted by the author from the extensive historical materials reviewed and evaluated in Braudel, Vol. 2, Ch. 3.

2.2   The Rule of Super-Profitability
2.3   The Rule of Payback and Recovery of Capital
2.4   The Rule of Material (Capital/Asset) Capability for a Preferred Sphere of Strategic Action

Category I   3. Cognition of Money Market Rules
3.1   The Rule of Money Supply/Investment Opportunity Relationship
3.2   The Rule of Augmentation of Capital with Credit
   3.2.1   The Rule of Capital from Interest Free Credit Internal to the Structure of the Commercial System.
   3.2.2   The Rule of Capital from Interest Bearing Credit Sourced in External Financial Structures.
3.3   The Rule of Negotiable Exchange

Category II
1.   Cognition of the Rules of the Trading Deal
2.   Cognition of the Rules of Trading Profit
3.   Cognition of the Rules of Market Identity
4.   Cognition of the Rules of the Networks
5.   Cognition of the Rules of Information

Category II   1. Cognition of the Rules of the Trading Deal
1.1   The Rules of the Supply/Demand Deal Components of the Trade Circuit
1.2   The Rules of the Monetary Exchange Market
1.3   The Rule of Access to Financial Conversion Services
1.4   The Rule of Fiscal Closure

Category II   2. Cognition of the Rules of Trading Profit
2.1   The Rules of Cost Calculation
2.2   The Rules of Profit Calculation
2.3   The Rules of Commodity Profitability Differentiation
   2.3.1   The Rule Regarding Commodities of Assured Profitable Demand
   2.3.2   The Rule Regarding Contingently Profitable Commodities
   2.3.3   The Rule Regarding Primary Commodities

Category II   3. Cognition of the Rules of Market Identity
  3.1 The Rule of Catchment Area Identification
  3.2 The Rule of Leveraging Catchment Area Growth
  3.3 The Rule of Market Differentiation by Commodities

Category II   4. Cognition of Network Rules
  4.1 The Rule of Joinder of Networks and Circuits
  4.2 The Rules of Network Interaction and Relationship
    4.2.1 Coexistence
    4.2.2 Competition
    4.2.3 Conflict
  4.3 The Rules of Structural Choice of Network Agencies
    4.3.1 The Family Firm
    4.3.2 Local Subsidiaries
    4.3.3 Factors
    4.3.4 Branches with Flexible Status
    4.3.5 Commission System with Reciprocal Services
  4.4 The Rule of States of Network Domination, Appropriation and Exclusion
    4.4.1 The Rule of Territorially Identifiable Ethnic and Nationality Solidarity and Control of Networks

Category II   5. Cognition of Information Rules
  5.1 The Rule of Information Monitoring
    5.1.1 The Rule of Structural Information Sources
    5.1.2 The Rule of Poly-Modal Information Sources
    5.1.3 The Rule of Inclusion in Communications Networks
  5.2 The Rule of Information Advantage

5.
NEGATIVE EXPERIENCE AND RULE COGNITION

Significance of Negative Experience

Negative experience is adversative experience. Its adverse qualities constitute the experiential ground for the ideas by which there is an understanding that there has been a misperception of the favorable possibilities to be expected from a selected course of action.

In the case of capitalists, it would be the misperception of the possibilities of investment opportunities. Capitalism had negative experiences with certain economic sectors of past societies.

> ". . . in yesterday's societies a significant rate of capital formation was possible only in certain sectors and not in the whole market economy of the time. Capital which was adventurously invested outside this favoured zone bore little fruit, when it was not simply swallowed without trace."[21]

Negative experience was often followed by quick withdrawal from the capital adverse sector.

The relation between rule cognition and negative experience has not to do with knowledge rules regarding negative experience. There is no motivation for such knowledge. Rather, rule cognition and negative experience has to do with knowledge rules regarding the preconditions for highly profitable investment opportunity. It made more accurate the cognition of the rules of favorability for capital investment. The primary economic sectors for illustrating these precondition rules were 1) Land—Agriculture and 2) Production—Pre-Industry.

Land—Agriculture

Here the profitability failures of investment in European agriculture was the inability of investors of capital to introduce a structure of agrarian investment. They were unable to do this because they could not establish the necessary preconditions for doing it. They could not, for one thing, demolish stable, long-lived feudal superstructures that dominated agricultural production and that were resistant to innovation. And because they could not do this, they could not reshape the management for the cultivation of land within an organization framework of economic rationalization.[22] The pattern of the English tenant who managed a leased farm provided the model that accounted for exceptions, both by way of social and technological innovations and by rationalized methods of farm production.

Across the Atlantic, in the sugar plantations set up in Brazil and in the offshore West Indies islands of St. Dominique and Jamaica, where rationalized production was wealth creating, the investment returns of settlers, nonetheless, was severely limited. The limiting actors were oceanic transport strategems, exchange systems, high debt structures, and market subordination to the European merchants and traders who commanded export production and overseas output. It was the home country traders, bankers and merchants who made the high rates of profit.[23]

Production—Pre-Industry

Pre-industry is the period prior to that in which the industrial revolution took hold. How is it that the industrial revolution itself can be characterized, as was done by Mantoux, "as essentially a commercial phenomenon . . . connected with the gradual hold obtained by merchants over industry?"[24]

Between the fifteenth and the eighteenth centuries there were four overlapping structural forms of industrial activity. These four were: 1) Artisan family workshops; 2) Distributed manufacturing; 3) Concentrated manufacture; and 4) Energy sourced machine manufacture. In terms of industry product, the dominant industry was textiles (comparable in its dominance to that of the modern steel industry). In relation to the progress of the general economy, pre-industry was neither growth driving nor growth driven. In short, pre-industry was of uncertain value "as a cradle of change." Moreover, its possibilities for profitability presented "too stuffy" an appearance to capital investors.

There was a stout resistance to innovations on the part of the Artisan Family Workshops. Distributed Manufacturing was the geographical dispersion of the sequences of operations in the production of a finished product. Here it was the merchant entrepreneurs who coordinated the operations and took over the marketing of the finished product. With Concentrated Manufacture, because the labor force was brought together at one place in one physical structure, "this made possible supervision of the work, an advanced division of labour—in short increased productivity and an improvement in the quality of products."[25] Energy (hydraulic) based manufacture with machinery was a significant pre-industrial innovation in mining, in Dutch naval shipyards, and in a variety of small specialty product manufacture.

Starting with "The boom of the thirteenth century," the urban merchants, who became both traders (importers and exporters) and entrepreneurs, existed within a money economy that was expanding, markets that were developing, external trade that was growing, and the practice of wealth accumulation—with its recognized and established inequalities. What remained outside of the control of wealthy merchants was the productive labor force. That labor force, until "the putting-out system" became dominant, was guild controlled. The "putting-out system" is one in which the merchant—as middleman—puts out the work for production, supplies the raw materials, and provides partial wage advances until the finished product is delivered to him for final sale. It was a system that spelled the fate of the guilds. What ensured their downfall were the introduction of labor dependency (including, often, that of the guildmaster); the imposition of choice of production activity; the alternative available to the merchant of resort to a rural cottage industry to hold wages in check; and the domination of the marketing organization.[26]

Even the entry into a putting-out venture was not an unequivocal commitment to production. It was but a corollary of being a commanding link in the trading chain of commercial networks, distribution channels and markets. The conditions of pre-industry production made it still less profitable than trading. "The balance sheet of pre-industrial capitalism is pretty negative." Trading profits dwarfed all else. In a relatively brief venture into mining (the fifteenth century) merchant capitalism chose to pull out when the costs of deep mining and of mining equipment technologies posed large financial problems. The alternative choice was the distribution of products that had their origins in mining and metallurgy as less risky. It was not until the industrial revolution that industry as a sector of the economy became quite profitable.

> "Capitalism would then be profoundly modified and above all extended. It did not however abandon its habit of oscillating ac-

cording to the circumstances of the day, for over the years other options besides industry became open to it, in the nineteenth and twentieth centuries. Capitalsim, even in the industrial era, was not exclusively attached to the world of industrial production, far from it."[27]

6.
COGNITION OF THE RULES OF NEGATIVE EXPERIENCE*

1. The Rule of the Value of an Industry as a "Cradle of Change."
2. The Rule of the Relation of the Growth of the General Economy to the Growth of the Industry.
    A. A Growth Driving Industry Drives the Economy to Growth.
    B. A Growth Driven Industry is Driven to Growth by a Growth Economy.
3. The Rule of Stages in the Pragmatics of Capital Accumulation and Capital Investment.
    A. The Knowledge of Stages are State Cognitions.
    B. State Cognitions are Knowledge of the Elements Constituting a Stage in Time.
    C. In Any Time Period the Power of Capital is the Pragmatic Derivative of the Understanding that is the Knowledge of the State.
4. The Rule of Progressive Enlargements of Fixed Capital Demands.
5. The Rule of Capital Driven Innovations in the Foundation of Property Relationships.
6. The Rule of Primary Committment to Expectations Regarding Capital Accumulation.
    A. The Rule of Secondary Committment to an Industry or to a Product.
    B. The Rule of Comparative Profitability of Products within an Industry.
    C. The Rule of Negative Context Factors as Lurks that Stalk Expectations.
7. The Rule of Control Stability with Flexibility for Alternative

---

*The rules of negative experience of capitalism have been extracted from the extensive historical materials reviewed in Braudel, Vol. 2, Ch.3, pp. 249 *et seq.*

Rationalization of all and each of the Components of an Industry or Market.
A. The Rule of Innovation Requirements and the Preconditions of Human Tractability for Structural, Social and Technological Change.

REFERENCES

1. Locke, John, *An Essay Concerning Human Understanding*, (6th edition, BK II, Ch. XXI, Sec. 4, p. 165), with the notes and illustrations of the author, and an analysis of his doctrine of ideas. Also, Questions on Locke's Essay, by A. M., Ethical Moderator in Trinity College, Dublin. (New Edition, The World Library, Ward, Lock & Co., London, undated) The original edition of Locke's *Essay* is 1689.
2. Ibid., BK II, Ch. XXI, Sec. 8, p. 167.
3. Ibid., BK II, Ch. XXI, Sec. 3, p. 164.
4. Braudel, Fernard, *The Wheels of Commerce*, (Vol. 2 of *Civilization and Capitalism, 15th-18th Century*; translated from the French by Sian Reynolds, Harper and Row, 1982 ed.), Foreword.
5. Ibid., Vol. 2, p. 455.
6. Ibid., Vol. 2, p. 413.
7. Ibid., Vol. 2, p. 312, *et seq*.
8. Ibid., Vol. 2, p. 372.
9. Ibid., Vol. 2, p. 22, 600.
10. Ibid., Vol. 2, p. 229.
11. Ibid., Vol. 2, p. 231, *et seq*.
12. Locke, BK II, Ch. XXVIII, Sec. 6, p. 279.
13. Ibid., BK II, Ch. XXI, Sec. 5, p. 166.
14. Ibid., BK IV, Ch. XII, Sec. 12, p. 550.
15. Braudel, Ch. 4, p. 403.
16. Ibid., Vol. 2, Ch. 4, p. 400.
17. Ibid., Vol. 2, Ch. 2, p. 229.
18. Ibid., Vol. 2, Ch. 4, p. 402.
19. Ibid., p. 408.
20. Ibid., p. 409.
21. Braudel, Vol. 2, p. 248.
22. Ibid., Vol. 2, p. 249, *et seq*.
23. Ibid., Vol. 2, pp. 272 *et seq*.
24. Mantoux, Paul, *The Industrial Revolution in the Eighteenth Century*, (Revised 1928, Harcourt, Brace & Co., New York).
25. Braudel, Vol. 2, p. 300.
26. Ibid., Vol. 2, pp. 314 *et seq*.
27. Ibid., Vol. 2, p. 373.

PART II. (A)

Strategic Knowledge as Knowledge of Variety

Considered by itself, what is strategic knowledge?

A Note on External Variety and Internal (Inward) Variety
1. The Knowledge of External Variety
2. Strategy and the Domination of External Variety
3. The Knowledge of Internal (Inward) Variety
   The Knowledge of Physics

NOTE

External Variety and Internal (Inward) Variety

The differentiation has been made between "Fitted Knowledge" and "Possibilities Knowledge." It is a differentiation that has its parallel in the distinction made within this section between *external variety* and *internal (inward) variety* with respect to strategic knowledge. The utility of the distinction is in its worth for ascertaining the knowledge underlying the varietal ways or paths of strategy. Once theoretical physics had passed beyond Newton's mechanics and perceived bodily objects as material points positioned in a concept of space—passed beyond, that is to say, an explanatory theory of physics which is a theory "directly connected with complexes of sense experiences"—and had moved on through "constructive speculation" to achieve a progressively unfolding theoretical exploration for "the interior of matter,"[1] then the category of "Possibilities Knowledge" attained ascendency over that of "Fitted Knowledge." Then it was that the strategic way or path of high technology could become the preferred possible variety of strategic thought as against strategic knowledge of the other and earlier variety of low technology.

Locke had built his descriptive explanation of human understanding on the unqualified fundament of sensibilized experience. There was both a directness and a mediateness between thinking and the perceptually grounded experience. It supported the inductive inference of sensibly finite knowledge of matter, and thereby set a limit to knowledge of the reality that is the physical world.

For Locke, persons exist in the world in a way such that their finite intelligence is excluded from all understanding of the primary qualities of their material surround. Matter, material things and objects, the material world itself—it was all there, and all there as a pre-supposition of thinking, but it was not a reality accessible to human thought. Locke, for one thing, has excluded without qualification all human possibility of either creating new matter or destroying existing matter.[2] Additionally, Locke had also excluded all knowledge of substance, whether material (matter) or immaterial (spirit), for here there was a failure of sensory knowing. The senses fail "us in the discovery of the bulk, texture, and figure of the minute parts of bodies, on which their real constitutions and differences depend."[3]

REFERENCES

1. Einstein, Albert, "Physics and Reality," No. 13 in *Out of My Later Years* (The Wisdom Library of Philosophical Library, New York 1950).
2. Locke, John, *An Essay Concerning Human Understanding*, (6th edition, p. 445), with the notes and illustrations of the author, and an analysis of his doctrine of ideas. Also, Questions on Locke's Essay, by A. M., Ethical Moderator in Trinity College, Dublin. (New Edition, The World Library, Ward, Lock & Co., London, undated) The original edition of Locke's *Essay* is 1689.
3 Ibid., BK II, Ch. XXXIII, Sec. 8, p. 212.

Interview; New Materials

Q: What do you foresee in the field of new materials?

A: In the past we were unable to design materials by manipulation at the level of molecules or atoms. When we created a crystal, for example, we just had to wait until the crystal was formed naturally. Recently, though, it has become possible to arrange atoms artificially in rows, so that crystals can be formed by human means.

As a consequence, it is now possible to design molecules by using computer graphics and to create experimentally entirely new materials that do not exist in nature. I think that new possibilities will emerge in the field of materials.

A.E. Cullison, "How New Technologies
will Change Society," Interview of
Takimochi Ishi, 36 *Sumitomo Quarterly* 8
(Spring, 1989, Tokoyo, Japan).

Pre-biotic Chemistry

"Laboratory synthesis of self-replicating molecules whose structure and chemical behavior are analogous to living processes in biological molecules."

New York Times, October 30, 1990,
pp. 85,8.

"Scientists at American Telephone & Telegraph Corp.'s Bell Laboratories say they have created a new form of matter consisting of between 100 and 10,000 atoms in a crystalline pattern, that could lead to smaller electronic devices. The size of the stable semiconducting atomic clusters of the material are described as well below the several billion atoms currently required in the smallest microelectonic devices. Clusters made so far are composed of materials from the second and sixth columns of the periodic table of elements, including zinc, cadmium, sulfur and selenium.

"AT&T Bell Lab Scientists Cite New Form
of Matter," *Metal Working News*,
February 6, 1989, p. 10.

CHAPTER IV

The Knowledge of External Variety

1.
VARIETY AS KNOWLEDGE

No Strategy Without Variety
No Knowledge of Strategy Without a Knowledge of Variety
What is the Knowledge of Variety?

The Knowledge of Variety

In terms of its significance for strategy, the knowledge of variety cannot be understood simply as an outgrowth of the progressive and cumulative development of the knowledge of science. While unquestionably related to that other knowledge, the knowledge of variety exists apart from it as a something that is differently cognized. It is this different cognizing of variety that infuses it with significance for the knowledge of strategy.

How is it that the knowledge of variety became part of the stuff of strategic knowledge, rather than remaining part of the stuff of scientific knowledge? The historian of science, Sarton[1], separated science from technology, even though parts of the history of the latter were includable in the history of the former. The genesis of the great technical inventions—likened by Sarton to seeds of gigantic trees—lie in science, but their elaboration and ramification into life's business lie in technology. Another historian of science, Mason[2], separated out the origins of the craft tradition and the origins of the scholarly tradition as part of the development of science. He so termed these two traditions so as to provide historical designations by which to refer to the empirical and the rational-analytic as practical and intellectual (or cognitive) faculties whereby to make inventions and discoveries about nature.

However, whether it be in terms of the history of science, or of the history of technology, or in terms of the historical juxtapositions of the two, the contributions to the understanding of human knowledge itself by Locke and Leibniz were parts of that historical progression. Not only matter being conquered by mind (Sarton), but from then on mind turned in upon itself to understand both its own knowing of matter and the mind's knowledge of its own thinking—Aristotle's "thinking of thinking" resumed as post-Renaissance Science.

Sarton took the period of the Scientific Renaissance as extending from 1450 (marked by the discovery of printing in the West) to 1600 (marked either by the death of Giordano Bruno, an excommunicated Copernican cosmologist who was burnt at the stake), or by the appearance of the work *Concerning the Magnet* by William Gilbert, (who was court physician to Queen Elizabeth). It was his judgement that to extend the terminal year of the Renaissance to 1632, so as to take in the publication of Galileo's *Dialogue Concerning the Two Chief Systems of the World, The Ptolemaic and the Copernican*, would be to include too large a portion of the seventeenth century.

Ordinary Experience and the Knowledge of Variety

The year 1632 also marked the birth of John Locke. Of Locke it has been written that he was a person of "religious disposition"; that he nevertheless dreaded the imposition of impediments to free inquiry by churchmen; that he had a "sharp inclination for scientific investigation"; that as a member of the Royal

Society he experimented in chemistry and also in meteorology; that he was inclined "to politics, as well as to theology and medicine"; that his reading of Descartes gave him a relish for philosophy; and that his *Essay Concerning Human Understanding*, which was begun by chance through discussions at the Exeter House reunions, and which was subjected to long intervals of neglect, written in bits on intermittent occasions, and was completed nearly twenty years after it was begun in 1670.[3]

The relevance of all this is that although John Locke was himself a participant in scientific investigation and educated in Medical Science, his treatment in the *Essay* of such of the legacy of the scientific Renaissance as he appropriated for consideration by his non-dogmatic, inquisitive temperament was a treatment not only "in the Baconian Spirit", but also not confined to technical criticism. Consequently human understanding was not by him placed within a technological context, nor was it by him explained as empirical inference from data of technical experiment.

It is because of this that Locke provides the initial answer to the question previously put: How is it that the knowledge of variety became part of the stuff of strategic knowledge, rather than remaining part of the stuff of scientific knowledge? Locke's inquiry into human understanding was an inquiry into the human understanding of experience in relation to the manifold of the world as a material given of human existence. His juncture of the ordinary sensiblilized attributes of humans with the acquisition of knowledge about that given world is taken by him to be obviously demonstrable. It would look to be especially so in the light of certain discoveries in the period of the Scientific Renaissance. To take just the sensibilized attribute of sight, for illustration, Sir Oliver Lodge has linked it thus to discoveries in astronomy:

> "Our whole direct knowledge of the planetary and stellar universe, from the early observations of the ancients down to the magnificent discoveries of a Herschel, depends entirely upon our happening to possess a sense of sight. To no other of our senses do any other worlds than our own in the slightest degree appeal. We touch them or hear them never. Consequently, if the human race

had happened to be blind, no other world but the one it groped its way upon could ever have been known or imagined by it. The outside universe would have existed, but man would have been entirely and hopelessly ignorant of it. The bare idea of an outside universe beyond the world would have been inconceivable, and might have been scouted as absurd."[5]

Moreover, as Mason has commented, a certain craft based empirics of scientific inquiry carried over from the Middle Ages into the sixteenth and seventeenth centuries. "In mechanics, as in magnetism, we find that craftsmen and engineers could develop the scientific method and new experiments, but not new bodies of theory."[6] His reference is to discoverers in the science of mechanics like Tartaglia (1500-57) and Stein (1548-1620), but culminating in the founding of modern mechanics by Galileo Galilei (1564-1642) and his publication in 1638 of his *Discourses on Two New Sciences*.

The Category of External Variety

We now have the foundation for comprehending the category of strategic knowledge that is the knowledge of Lockean variety. It is variety derived from the knowledge of external givens. That knowledge is the variety of external things in terms of ordinary human relationships to their accessible attributes. External variety is the sensory, experiential outcome with accessible givens of the external things of the universe. It is an accessibility which, for Locke, excluded their being instrumentally accessible. That exclusion of instrumented accessibility was Locke's mark of commitment to ordinary human experience. Locke's understanding through experience is the knowledge of ordinary experience. The senses thereby become varietal postulates for the category of external variety. ". . . the mode in which the universe strikes us, our view of the universe, our whole idea of matter and force, and other worlds, and even of consciousness, depends upon the particular set of sense organs with which we, as men, happen to be endowed."[7]

Varietal Discernment

The category of external variety that has its source in Locke provides strategy with a principle of intelligibility. It is one by which persons can intelligibly relate these senses to the things and objects that are part of the manifold of the world. While that world exists apart from persons, it presents objects that have within them qualities that produce various variety. The organs of sensation exist as an unalterable given for humans, no matter what, conceivably, "other and different intelligible beings" possible somewhere within the universe may be endowed with.

The knowledge of variety presumes a capability of the mind to discern and distinguish between the ideas generated by the perception of different objects and their qualities.[8] There is both varietal discernment and varietal utility. The knowledge of varietal discernment precedes the knowledge of varietal utility. The latter is a further knowledge of strategy. In the thinking of Locke, however, the two were connected.

> "The infinite wise Contriver of us and all things about us hath fitted our senses, faculties, and organs to the conveniences of life, and the business we have to do here. We are able by our senses to know and distinguish things, and to examine them so far as to apply them to our uses, and several ways to accomodate the exigencies of this life. We have insight enough into their admirable contrivances and wonderful effects to admire and magnify the wisdom, power, and goodness of their Author. . . . we are furnished with faculties (dull and weak as they are) to discover enough in the creatures to lead us to the knowledge of the Creator, and the knowledge of our duty; and we are fitted well enough with abilities to provide for the conveniences of living" These are our business in 'this' world."[9]

Variety, Utility and "Fitted Knowledge"

Locke had merged the knowledge of external variety with the utility of sensory based knowledge itself. The merger was all of a piece with Locke's "fitted knowledge." By so doing, he confined the knowledge of variety to the knowledge of ordinary experience. The latter knowledge is a practical, utilitarian knowledge. It is also a fore-ordained given of all human experience. As such, it will be the knowledge common to the experience of all. Locke rejected, on utilitarian grounds, the extension of this knowledge of ordinary experience by the introduction of instrumentation.

> "Nay, if that most instructive of our senses, seeing, were in any man a thousand or a hundred thousand times more acute than it is now by the best microscope, things several millions of times less than the smallest object of his sight now would then be visible to his naked eyes, . . . but then he would be in a quite different world from other people" nothing would appear the same to him and others: the visible ideas of everything would be different. So that I doubt whether he and the rest of men could discourse concerning the objects of sight, . . . and if by the help of such microscopical eyes (if I may so call them), a man could penetrate farther than ordinary into the secret composition and radical texture of bodies, he would not make any great advantage by the change, if such an acute sight would not serve to conduct him to the market and exchange; if he could not see things he was to avoid at a convenient distance, nor distinguish things he had to do with by those sensible qualities others do."[10]

What about non-ordinary experience and the variety of non-ordinary experience? Non-ordinary experience could be attained by alteration of the sense themselves. That is to say, divinely fitted "senses, faculties, and organs" would no longer be postulational requisites for the simple ideas of perception. Another face of experience, wrote Locke, would then be put upon "appearances and the seeming scheme of things." He conceded, as "an extravagant conjecture" that among spirits or angels "one great advantage some of them have over us may not lie in this, that they can so frame and shape to themselves organs of sensation or perception as to suit them to their present design, and the circumstances of the object they would consider." Ordinary humans necessarily presented a different case.

> "But to us, in our present state, unalterable organs, so contrived as to discover the figure and notion of the minute parts of

them, would perhaps be of no advantage. God has, no doubt, made them so as is best for us in our present condition. He hath fitted us for the neighborhood of the bodies that surround us, and we have to do with; and though we cannot, by the faculties we have, attain to a perfect knowledge of things; yet they will serve us well enough for those ends above mentioned, which are our great concernment."[11]

The Category of Internal Variety

In addition to external variety, there is internal variety. Locke recognized and considered the former in terms of its linkage to sensory-based cognition. Internal variety, however, he put to one side. It was not an essential of knowledge about the great, practical concerns of ordinary living. Apart from its not being a part of "fitted knowledge", it was not within the comprehension of what Locke accepted as finite intelligence. Understanding fell short of knowledge because the sensory faculties of that finite intelligence could not access the composition of texture or minute particles or structures or movement within the matter of which bodies and things were composed. It is the sensible secondary qualities, then, rather than the primary qualities of matter, that provide an adequate sensory foundation for the ideas of utilitarian knowledge.

REFERENCES

1. Sarton, George, *Six Wings: Men of Science in the Renaissance.*, (Meridian ed. 1966, World Publishing Company, Cleveland, OH).
2. Mason, Stephen F., *A History of the Sciences*, (Collier Books, Revised, 1962, New York).
3. The Enclyclopedia Britannica (11th ed., Vol. 16, p. 845, 1911 New York, The Encyclopedia Britannica Company).
4. It was the kind of intellectual frame that is advocated by Sarton for the study of the history of Renaissance Science.
5. Lodge, Sir Oliver, *Pioneers of Science*, (MacMillan and Company, Ltd., London 1926), Secutre X, p. 235).
6. Mason, p. 153.
7. Lodge, p. 235.

8. Locke, John, *An Essay Concerning Human Understanding*, (6th edition, Bk. II, Ch. XI, Sec. 1, p. 10), with the notes and illustrations of the author, and an analysis of his doctrine of ideas. Also, Questions on Locke's Essay, by A. M., Ethical Moderator in Trinity College, Dublin. (New Edition, The World Library, Ward, Lock & Co., London, undated) The original edition of Locke's *Essay* is 1689.

9. Ibid., BK II, Ch. XXIII, Sec. 12, pp. 213-14.

10. Ibid., p. 214.

11. Ibid., Sec. 13, p. 215.

CHAPTER V

Knowledge, the Physical World and External Variety

Material Reality and the Boundary of Thought: Creation I

There was, however, a strictly empirical (non-ontological) ground on the basis of which Locke set limits to knowledge of the physical world. That ground exists in the relation between the knowledge of material reality and the boundary of thought.

The Knowledge of Materiality ("Physica")

The knowledge of materiality is the knowledge of matter and of substance. Locke, taking his cue from the history of philosophy, designated the knowledge of materiality as "natural philosophy." But, for Locke, it was classified as "physica." He made it one of the three divisions of the sciences that he placed "within the compass of human understanding."[1] Included within the division of the science of "physica" was:

> "The knowledge of things as they are in their own proper beings, their constitutions, properties, and operations, whereby I mean not only matter and body, but spirits also, which have their proper natures, constitutions, and operations, as well as bodies."[2]

Locke came to the conclusion that the end of the knowledge of "physica" was not material reality. Rather, its end was "bare speculative truth."[3]

What was the fundament on which Locke grounded his conclusion that the knowledge of matter and substance could end only in speculative knowing? It had its source in the separation he made between ideas and the qualities of matter. While the former might be caused by the latter, the latter were independent of the former. An idea was that "which the mind perceives in itself, or is the immediate object of perception, thought, or understanding."[4] The qualitites of matter are not in the ideas, but are produced by a power in the things of matter. Between that which becomes the object of the idea, and that which is in the things of matter, is an unknown something concerning materiality itself.

There was contact with the things of matter, but there was not access to materiality itself. Hence the knowledge of "physica" could only be of a speculative character. The knowledge of "physica," that is to say, was not directly knowable as experiential knowledge. Not surprisingly, then as between idea/perceptions and the matter of bodies.

> ". . . we may not think (as perhaps usually is done) that they are exactly the images and resemblances of something inherent in the subject; most of those of sensation being in the mind no more the likeness of something existing without us than the names that stand for them are the alikeness of our ideas, which yet upon hearing they are apt to excite in us."[5]

Still, despite the inability to access materiality itself, the "original or primary qualities" of matter in bodies were known and knowable as the simple ideas of sensation and reflection. These are the simple ideas of solidity, extension, figure, motion/rest, and number. They are, Locke wrote, the "real qualitites of bodies, which are always in them," so that as to them ideas are "resemblances of something really existing" in bodies.[6]

Beyond the ideas, however, there is only mediate knowledge of the qualities of matter. Such knowledge is mediate because what appears to be qualities are but the secondary effects of the "powers" of those original or primary qualities, "viz., by the operation of insensible particles on our senses."[7] Here again the inability to access materiality itself prevents direct experiential knowledge of that which affects the senses. And here, too, "the ideas produced in us by these secondary qualities have no resemblance of them at all. There is nothing like our ideas existing in the bodies themselves . . . only a power to produce those sensations in us. . . ."[8]

Essence and Substance

Hence the stance taken by Locke that the "real essence" of things was not a knowable. And for Locke, also, substance was not a knowable. Locke had taken his stance in the classic dispute as to whether universals, as mental abstractions, were real, or whether external objects existed only as particulars. Locke, as a nominalist, held that in the knowledge of matter there are no universals, only particulars. Therefore substance, as an abstract idea, fell short of being real knowledge. The abstract idea of pure substance was an obscure general idea, an "invention of the understanding" to account for an unknown and supposed something by which qualities of material objects are so sustained as they exist together. The co-existence of these qualities, each of which constituted a "simple idea" of the understanding, wanted explanation.

Substance, as idea, (or notion) illustrated what Locke termed a "mixed mode" category of ideas. It was a category whereby mind made (generated) combinations of compositions of simple ideas into "complex ideas," but without considering whether, as such, they had any real being.[9]

The essence of things was defensible as knowledge only as "nominal essence," not as real essence. Locke took it that "essence" refers to that whereby anything is what it is, or its being as an existant. It was only because of the "real internal constitution of things" that they had particular, discoverable qualities. The difference between real and nominal essence was that the latter consisted only of the name attached to an abstract idea of the supposed internal reality. Hence the "nominal essence," as a "complex idea," was an artifice, "nominal essence" becomes separated from material particularities and their mutations.[10]

Locke placed the idea of matter in the class of "confused ideas." Matter, as a term of reference for an idea of that having real existence, was a cloak by which to cover ignorance of the real properties of bodies.

> "In matter, we have no clear ideas of the smallness of parts much beyond the smallest that occur to any of our senses, and therefore when we talk of the divisibility of matter *in infinitum*, though we have clear ideas of division and divisiblity, and have also clear ideas of parts made out of a whole by division; yet we have but very obscure and confused ideas of corpuscles, or minute bodies, so to be divided, when by former divisions they are reduced to a smallness much exceeding the perception of any of our senses and so all that we have clear and distinct ideas of, is of what division in general or abstractly is, and the relation of *totum* and pars: . . ."[11]

The Boundary of Thought

Finite Intelligence and the Physical Surrounding

For Locke, Persons exist in the world in a way such that their finite intelligence is excluded from all understanding of the primary qualities of their material surround. Matter, material things and objects, the material world itself—it was all there, and all there as a pre-supposition of thinking, but it was not a reality accessible to human thought. Locke, for one thing, has excluded without qualification all human possibility of either creating new matter or destroying existing matter.[12] Additionally, Locke had also excluded all knowledge of substance, whether material (matter) or immaterial (spirit), for here there was a failure of sensory knowing. The senses fail "us in the discovery of the bulk, texture, and figure of the minute parts of bodies, on which their real constitutions and differences depend."[13]

Thought as Nominal Knowing: Physica

Material reality is thereby experienced and understood at one level removed from its primary properties as matter. What becomes visible and observable to the senses about the bodies and things of matter are the manifestations of their "secondary qualities" or powers. What are taken to be the inherent qualities of matter are "active powers," that is, to "change some sensible qualities in other subjects." Activity as a power, and passivity as a capacity in matter, are at the foundation of ideas that differentiate between matter. Material change is the path to "mediate discovery of [active] powers."[14]

These "powers" of matter provide the basis for the experiential knowledge of matter. It is these experienced "secondary qualities," the powers of matter, that are the source of ideas. Hence the ideas of sensibilized knowing enter into the provision of knowledge, but provide only ideas of the nominal attributes of matter. Beyond the nominal of matter is the primary reality of matter. Mind, however, cannot get beyond the simple ideas of the nominal. It could not, expounded Locke, because "the mind, whatever efforts it would make, is not able to advance one jot; nor can it make any discoveries, when it would pry into the nature and hidden causes of those ideas."[15] Such is the boundary of thought, leaving undiscovered and undiscoverable by human faculties in just what the ideas belonging to the body and those belonging to spirit consist.

The Idea of Substance

Is there, however, a substatum of materiality, or a something which sustains the adhesion of the several qualities of a thing, so that they are observed to exist together? A something termed the idea of pure substance? Is there, furthermore, both in immaterial and material (corporeal) substance, that which makes each distinctively different as substances? Locke answers in the negative to each of these questions. The error of the first question lies in the substitution of supposition for explanation. It is a substitution that is done (as a fashion of speaking) in order to account for the existence of particular sorts of corporeal things, which would otherwise be inconceivable. Nonetheless, there is no clear idea of substance ("we know not what it is" and it is confusing to suppose a something there "besides the extension, figure, solidity, motion, thinking, or other observable ideas."[16] A like error pervades the second question, which concerns "the operations of the mind," and supposes a substatum (a spiritual substance or spirit) to those operations, but again without knowing what it is.[17] Nothing can be either affirmed or denied about either substance.

As to whether the idea of the one (body) is clearer than the idea of the other (spirit), each is composed of "the simple ideas . . . received from sensation"; ideas of the primary qualities or properties of each are known; and each is encumbered with difficulties of explanation or understanding. Consequently, there is as much reason to be satisfied with the one as with the other.

For Locke, then, the "two primary qualities or properties of spirit, viz, thinking and a power of action; i.e., a power of beginning or stopping several thoughts or motions," present no more difficulty than the ideas of those qualities inherent in bodies.[18] As to how far "sensible qualities" could be taken to be knowledge of body (material substance), it was Locke's conclusion that they leave us "as far from the substance of body as if we knew nothing at all."[19] Spirit—in material substance—is "finite spirit"; "soul" is a "real being," and "spirits and bodies cannot operate but where they are."[20]

Ideas and Knowledge

Nevertheless, the world of materiality though only mediately known and knowable, is one whose materiality can be made intelligible. It is a world in which there are things of real existence, things that intrude upon human consciousness. It is a world made intelligible by operations of the mind or ideas. Simple ideas enable the understanding to recognize "marks of distinction of things, whereby we may be able to discern one thing from another, and so choose any of them for over uses as we have occasion."[21]

The color blue, for example, is a simple idea. Was it in the mind only (subjective), or in the power of visual texture of the external thing itself to so alter light as to produce that color (objective)? No matter, wrote Locke, it is there, a constant, regular in its operation, discernable by sight, distinguishing itself, and "beyond our capacities distinctly to know." Suppose, however, that this color blue in the mind of one person was, in the mind of another, the yellow color of a marigold? Again, no matter, reasoned Locke. Each person would know and understand and regularly "distinguish things for his use by those apperances." To each person they would be marks of distinction, with the assumption by each that in the minds of other persons there would be exactly the same simple ideas of these appearances. At bottom, Locke regarded the foregoing suppostition as untenable. "I am," he wrote, "nevertheless very apt to think that the sensible ideas produced by any object in different men's minds are most commonly very near and undiscernibly alike."[22]

The Use Differentiation between Ideas

In terms of their utility as knowledge, Locke differentiated between ideas that were real and those that were chimerical; between ideas that were adequate and those that were inadequate; between those that were true and those that were false.

Real ideas involve the concept of an archetype, or "the real being and existence of things." The reality of simple ideas is that they conform to or agree with "the reality of things"; that is, with "those powers of things which produce them in our minds." Real ideas are not necessarily "fully imagic" or representational of that which exists in reality. They can only represent the primary qualitites of things, the "utterly inseparable" qualities of solidity, extension, figure and mobility. Nonetheless, they are real ideas, because they are ideas of appearances "designed to be the marks whereby we are to know and distinguish things which we have to do with." There is a "steady correspondence" with that which is "constantly produced." That the causes or constituent elements underlying the appearances of things remain apart from and inevident to the sensory ideas "matters not."[23]

When an idea is a complete representation of that which the mind takes to be, and fixes upon as the referent archetype, there is an adequate idea. All simple ideas are adequate ideas. The foundation of such ideas is a sensory response to whatever is the power in external things that operates, or excites, the senses. In ordinary speech these powers of things are spoken of as "qualities," a term which Locke assessed as but a "vulgar notion" of common understanding.

However, all ideas of substance as a referent for the real essences of things are inadequate ideas. They are inadequate as to the archetypes of which they purport to stand. Hence, they "cannot be supposed to be any representation of them at all." No known sensible quality (simple idea) can be a basis from which to deduce any other sensible quality of a natural substance. Consequently, the idea of substance is without an archetype of real essence, and therefore inadequate as a copy or representation of it. "For since the powers or qualities that are observable by us are not the real essence of that substance, but depend on it, and flow from it, any collection whatsoever of these qualities cannot be the real essence of that thing."[24]

Ideas *qua* ideas are neither true nor false. They are "but bare appearances or perceptions in our minds" and nothing more. As appearances, they are what they are—the mental phenomena attending perception. What is necessary for any idea to be judged true or false is a referent that is exogenous or "extraneous to" the ideas of mind. "For, truth or falsehood lying always in some affirmation or negation, mental or verbal, our ideas are not capable, any of them, of being false, till the mind passes some judgment on them; that is affirms or denies something of them.[25]

The Way to Knowledge

What were these exogenous referents, and why? Locke enumerated the most frequent as ideas in the minds of others, the assumption of some real existence confirming to the idea itself, and the idea of substance or essence of anything. What interested Locke was an explanation for why the true/false referent selected by mind "is chiefly, if not only, concerning its abstract complex ideas." His explanation followed the path or course that mind "usually takes in its way to knowledge."

Mind comes to know only by reflecting upon the particulars of sensation. But mind has a "natural tendency . . . towards knowledge." There is, in consequence, a drive to know beyond "only particular things," to hasten knowing, "therefore to shorten its way to knowledge." The way of this drive to the enlargement of knowledge is for mind to take its perceptions and "bind them into bundles and rank them so into sorts," thereby transforming perceptions into comprehensive ideas as a way of extending knowledge. The way to knowledge becomes the way of taking the ideas of nominal qualities and then abstracting a collation of them and assigning a name to the bundled abstraction, thus building a memory bank of nominal essences for purposes of differentiating things. So it is that abstract ideas come to stand mediately between perception/idea and the things of existence, and that the names of identification become confused with actual knowledge. But simple ideas—because they are verifiable by the senses of each person in everyday observation—are most easily rectified and least likely to be judged false.

REFERENCES

1. Ibid., BK IV, Ch. XXI, Sec. 1-2, p. 607.
2. Ibid.
3. Ibid.
4. Ibid., BK II, Ch. VIII, Sec. 9, p. 85.
5. Ibid., BK II, Ch. VIII, Sec. 7, p. 85.
6. Ibid., Sec. 22, p. 89.
7. Ibid., Sec. 13, p. 86.
8. Ibid., Sec. 15, p. 87.
9. Ibid., BK II, Ch. XXII and Ch. XXIII, pp. 202 et seq.
10. Ibid., BK II, Ch. III, pp. 326 et seq.
11. Ibid., BK II, Ch. XXVIII, Sec. 15, p. 295.
12. Ibid., BK IV, Ch. III, Sec. 11, p. 444.
13. Ibid., BK II, Ch. XXXIII, Sec. 8, p. 212.
14. Ibid., BK II, Ch. XXXIII, Sec. 7, p. 211.
15. Ibid., BK II, Ch. XXIII, Sec. 29, p. 22.
16. Ibid., Sec. 4, p. 210.
17. Ibid., Sec. 5, p. 210.
18. Ibid., Sec. 31, pp. 222-23.
19. Ibid., Sec. 16, p. 217.
20. Ibid., Sec. 19, p. 217. Chapter XXIII of Book II is titled "Of Our Complex Ideas of Substance." The utility of ordinary knowing and the limits of knowing by "any finite being" are expounded in this chapter of Locke's *Essay Concerning Human Understanding*.
21. Ibid., BK II, Ch. XXXII, Sec. 14, p. 310.

22. Ibid., BK II, Ch. XXXII, Sec. 15, pp. 310-11.
23. Ibid., BK II, Ch. XXX, Sec. 1-2, pp. 296-97.
24. Ibid., BK II, Ch. XXXI, Sec. 13, p. 306.
25. Ibid., BK II, Ch. XXXII, Sec. 3, p. 307.

CHAPTER VI

Strategy and the Domination of External Variety

Three Centuries of Domination

As BETWEEN EXTERNAL VARIETY and internal variety, it would be external variety that would dominate the knowledge of strategy for a period of three hundred years[1]: Three centuries of domination, starting with the publication of Locke's *Essay* (1690) and terminating with the two "accidental discoveries" of X-rays (1895—Roentgen) and "Uranic rays" (1896—Becquerel). It is these two discoveries that are marked by Pais as the start of the "Inward Bound" path of the Craft/Science of the physics of matter.[2]

A number of developments merged to sustain the domination of external variety. Galileo's *Discourses on Two New Sciences* (1638) founded the modern science of mechanics, applying mathmetics to physical objects (nature), and interrelating demonstration, experiment, prediction and verification.

"During the seventeenth century," writes Mason, "the mathematical-deductive method received the wider application: Indeed it was made into a philosophy. The non-measurable properties of matter, which the mathematical sciences ignored, came to be regarded as unreal. A clear distinction was down between the measurable primary qualities of matter, and the secondary qualities which were non-measurable. The measurable primary qualities, mass, motion, and magnitude, were regarded as real, objective properties of matter, whilst the non-measurable secondary qualities, colours, smells, tastes, were regarded as subjective products of the sense organs, possessing no reality as such in the external world."[3]

Much in the way of further development followed in the wake of the rise of classicl mechanics. There was a growth of supportive instrumentation for the measurement of natural phenomena. In chemistry, chemical change was explained by the introduction of a somewhat useful mechanical theory. It was a theory, the assumption of which was that matter was inert and without life. It underwent change from being subjected to external mechanical forces, Boyle had applied the philosophy of mechanics to his work in the physics of gases, but he stuck at acceptance of the generalized principles of mechanics as an explanation of observed variations in the chemical properties of bodies. The philosopher Descartes had subordinated all of nature's operations to reasoning of a mathematical-mechanical character for their explanation. Subsequently (1686) Newton extended explanation in mechanical terms from terrestrial phenomena to the phenomena of the solar system.

The century before was distinguished by considerable applications of science in surveying, in map making, in compass improvement, in navigation aids, in ocean charts, in the reform of the calendar, in arithmetic computation. In England the Royal Society was founded in 1660. The proposed statutory documents for the charter of the Royal Society included, as drafted by Robert Hooke, in 1663, that its " 'business and design' " was " 'to improve the knowledge of natural things, and all useful art, manufactures, mechanics practices, Engynes, and Inventions by experiments . . .' "[4] Of all its specialist committees, the most popular by far was that which studied questions of mechanics.

External Variety as Invention

Industry and the crafts had now become the beneficiaries of applied science. The drainage of deep coal mines had come to the fore as an industrial problem, coal having displaced wood as the predominant fuel used by, what Mason has termed, "the pyro-technical trades." The need was for an effective, dependable, ecomonical and utilizable water-raising device; specifically, one that could produce mechanical power from heat. The industry problem was solved by 1710 by the Newcomen (he was a blacksmith) engine.

The path of technological invention leads from the Newcomen engine ("the first effective machine to convert heat into mechanical energy on a large scale"), through scientifically designed experimental engine improvements by John Smeaton, and to the manufacture of the large scale steam engine by James Watt, starting in 1776. In this way were the tin miners, and the textile mills, and the iron masters provided with an essential prime mover—the steam engine—judged by Mason to be "perhaps the most important single application [of Science] prior to the nineteenth century."[5]

The knowledge of external variety as inventions is knowledge that has a special relevance for strategic cognition. It is not itself the knowledge of strategy, but contained within it is information about the origins and application of inventions that is significant for a knowledge of strategy. The knowledge of strategy is the discernment of this significance. Thus Locke's discerning capability of mind, because it involves more than perceptual differentiation, is at the core of the knowledge of strategy.

Discerned within an historic context, as they have been, all these inventions can be understood as pre-strategic knowledge. Their significance for the knowledge of strategy is that they were the generative beginnings of a new industrial system. It is there, in that new industrial system, that pre-strategic knowledge was transformed into, and matured, as the knowledge of strategy.

It is Paul Mantoux who has brought together the comparative industry frame within which the detail of system emergence, the sustaining fabric of its component structures, the interactive dynamics, and the character, the econonic function and the system contributions of those persons who were their dominant actors—all so conjoined in the web of events that the new industrial system is invested with a special relevance for strategic cognition.[6]

The New Industrial System

1. The industries compared by Mantoux are the textile industry and the metal industries. As to the former, "the cause of the capital changes and developments was indisputably the invention of the spinning machine." As to the latter, "the turning point was the use of coal in the smelting of iron ore."[7]
2. Mantoux made still a further comparison, one in terms of the "decisive stage" in the development of the two industries.

"The evolution of the textile industry is due to mechanical inventions, that of the metal-working industry to chemical inventions. In the one case, machinery replaced manual work, whilst, in the other, processes were introduced which increased the quantity or improved the quality of the output without appreciably diminishing the part played by labour."[8]

3. The interdependence of certain industries is illustrated by the interdependence of the iron and steel industry with the machine industry. The early machines, until late in the 18th century were made of wood. "With the reign of iron and steel came also that of machinery, one being the indispensable condition of the other." The building of machinery was one of the important new uses to which iron was put.[9]
4. From the standpoint of invention, the new industrial revolution is a two-stage development. One stage was empirical invention, the second stage was scientific invention. Mantoux refers to the steam engine as marking the start of the scientific period of invention. Thus he, like Mason, later, took particular note of the interplay of the scientific and the empirical in the historical role of inventions. But unlike Mason, the perspective of Mantoux was a different one. It was that inventions should be considered as economic phenomena.[10] The empirically based technical inventions were specially illustrative of their economic character.

"Every technical question is first and foremost a practical question. Before ever it becomes a problem to be solved by men with theoretic knowledge, it forces itself upon the men in the trades as a difficulty to be overcome, or a material advantage to be gained. There is, as it were, an instinctive effort, which not only precedes, but is a necessary condition to, the appearance of conscious effort . . ."

"... The history of inventions is not only that of inventors, but that of collective experience, which gradually solves the problems set by collective needs."[11]

5. Further illustrating that inventions should be considered as economic phenomena is that those persons whose inventions had started the new industrial revolutions were not able to found great industrial concerns. They are not listed among the "first generation of great manufacturers." The explanation of Mantoux has its sources in genealogical stock, related personal aptitudes, and the social character of those persons who did successfully transform localized and domestic production into the great industries of the new industrial system.

"Their distinguishing feature was not inventiveness, but a gift for turning other people's inventions to practical results. They were not all, like Arkwright, lucky or audacious enough to take complete possession of them and to secure a monopoly protected by patent rights. But, following the dictates of self-interest, they worked untiringly to reduce the inventor's legitimate rights to nothing. This conduct, questionable, though human enough, is abundantly illustrated . . . We must, however, not exaggerate the incompetence of these manufacturers in technical matters, since it was by no means general. Even though they were not the originators of any important invention, yet several of them introduced improvements of great practical value."[12]

Stage Two: The New Industrial System

The first stage was marked by the shift from the empirical to the scientific as the basis for the inventions that underlay the new industrial system. The second stage was marked by the shift from water to steam as the primary energy source. And here it is not the Newcomen engine that was the key invention. Rather than being a steam engine, the Newcomen invention was classified as really an "atmospheric engine," and one that was never turned to any practical use beyond that for the pumping of water, which was then used to turn a water wheel.[13]

It was the steam engine of Watt's invention (1769) that opened the "final and most decisive stage of the industrial revolution." Watt had worked through, after a thorough critical study of

Newcomen's engine, how to remedy its loss of energy. Watt had also solved how to link his invention directly to all kinds of machinery performing all kinds of operations. What was it that was decisive for the new industrial system by reason of the invention of the steam engine? First, it freed industrial location from the geographical shackles imposed by water power. The juxtaposition of coal and a steam engine meant factories could be brought closer to their product markets and to the labor supply of population centers. Second, steam lent the factory system which had already begun its growth—

> ". . . its power, and gave it a force of expansion as irresistible as itself. Above all, it gave it unity. Up till that time the various industries were much less interdependent than they are now. From the technical point of view they had little in common, and they developed separately along their own lines. The use of a common motive power, and especially of an artificial one, thenceforward imposed general laws upon the development of all industries. The successive improvements in the steam engine reacted equally on the working of mines and of metals, on weaving and on transport. The industrial world came to resemble one huge factory . . ."[14]

Stage Three: The Linkage to Capital

There were no large amounts of capital ready and available for investment in the early stages of machine manufacture. Thus capital was not at hand to give impetus to the growth of the new industrial system. Indeed, the term "manufacture: did not them exist in the English language, nor were the functions of traders, of entrepreneur, of plant owner, of workman and of production organizer really differentiated. Mantoux, providing illustrations dated as late as 1785 and 1791, describes industrialization without capital as follows:

> "The manufacturer's distinctive quality was that of an organizer. He had first to raise the necessary capital . . . But investors were not easy to find, especially at first, while machinery and factories were still looked upon unfavorably, as novelties with no certain future. Arkwright knew extermely well how to bring off these

difficult negotiations: But those men who had neither patents nor capital were in a much worse position. They had to begin in a very small way, with no capital lost their own savings . . . In the textile industry, these very modest beginnings were not at all uncommon. For they were made easy by the simplicity of the equipment then required. It cost little to set up, in any house, a few mules or ponies worked by hand. The more elaborate machines, the water frames or power looms, came later, as soon as profits had made it possible. And with those machines came water power or steam. The use of the heavy and high-power plant of the factory proper."[15]

The gound advanced for the absence of capital for industrialization was that historically capital had never been based on industrialization. The base for capital had been associated with landed property, with merchant trading, and with a limited and specialized group of financiers who functioned as bankers, money dealers and brokers.

It was not machine invention, but the factory system that supplied a new lease for capital. The use of machinery, while indubitably the determinative and "leading fact" of the industrial revolution, machine invention, in itself, is assessed by Mantoux as no more than a succession of the "technical improvements" in production, providing the substance of "technical history" and nothing more. It was, as Mantoux has noted in detail, the synthesis of machine invention and production processes in the factory system that changed the relation of capital to production.

The growth of the importance of capital marked the growth of the importance of mechanical equipment. "Joint capitalist enterprises [not joint stock companies] increased, especially in the earlier period, before great individual fortunes had been made in the [textile] industry." Machine invention had made possible concentration of the means of production and large undertakings. It followed, then, that "the hold of commercial capital was riveted on industry."[16] In sum, wrote Mantoux:

> "What is characteristic of the factory system is the use of capital in the production of goods. The creation of capital by means of industrial production, and the existence of a class of Capitalists whose interests are identified with those of industrial development."[17]

Strategic Knowledge and the Knowledge of External Variety

What is the knowledge of external variety as a knowledge of strategy? It is certainly a knowledge of technology in the context of economic history. But technology as history, if only to refer to the history of mechanical inventions,[18] is as wide and as broad as history itself. It is also, clearly, the delineation of a factor within society that enters into the structural formation and alteration of itself as a civilization. There is an historical juncture between technology and civilization.[19]

Still, conceding that it is a determinative factor in an historical dynamics, what is its significance for the knowledge of strategy? Put that question in the context not just of technology and civilization. Put it, rather, up against the chronological, comparative and thematic schema of Braudel's civilization and capitalism.[20] The stance of Braudel is that technology, while as wide and as broad as history, is nevertheless, without a satisfactory correlation with historical movement. The point of the matter is then in its relation to society and civilization. Technology is both a ceiling on human achievement and a representation of achievement possibilities.[21]

However, technological innovation, confined more narrowly and specifically to its relation to the beginnings of the industrial revolution, was dominated by, rather than dominating, the economy of that century. Experience with delayed market introduction of innovations in textiles, in iron-smelting, and in metal working confirm this early subordination of technology to the economy. The attainment of a technologically driven economy would be a later achievement.[22]

How, then, is a breaking through the ceiling an achievement to be explained? How, then, is the push to attainment and utilization of technical possibility to be explained? Not simply by developments in science or in technology, concludes Braudel. It is a conclusion to which he adheres, even while he details the advances from the 15th to the 18th century that amount to "an often imperceptible or unrecognized industrial pre-revolution in an accumulation of discoveries and technical advances, some of them spectacular, others almost invisible."[23]

The explanation is derived from the distinction put forth by Braudel between micro-capitalism and "real capitalism." The latter exists on the top floor of the structure of economic life. In economic life it is these "upper structures" that are:

> "The only ones with the capacity to move. For capitalism alone had comparative freedom of movement. As the moment dictated, it could swing to one side or the other, turn simultaneously or alternately to the profits of trade or those of manufacture, perhaps to income from real estate, loans to the State or usury. In a context where other structures were inflexible (Those of material life and, no less, those of ordinary economic life) capitalism could choose the areas where it wished and was able to intervene, and the areas it would leave to their fate, rebuilding as it went its own structures from these components, and gradually in the process transforming the structures of others."[24]

The knowledge of external variety, then—which is the knowledge of the variety of the material manifold that is the physical surround ready to hand, and reducible or transformable into fitted knowledge for the economic life of society—is the knowledge which, as the object of thinking, constitutes the understanding of capitalism. It is by virtue of its understanding of this knowledge that choice is presented to a level of economic structure that has a freedom and capacity for choice.

The first two stages of the New Industrial system (as described by Mantoux) originated, grew and developed in the period of pre-industrial capitalism. Braudel, for Europe, like for England, records that pre-industrial capitalism was merchant capitalism. In Central Europe the system of merchant capitalism had taken over mining production at the end of the 15th century. Rich merchants, as owners of capital, could mesh ownership with investment by financing the installation and maintenance of mining equipment. However, they had withdrawn from mining after the middle of the 16th century, remaining only in the manufacture of partly furnished iron products and their distribution.

Pre-industrial capitalism made no firm commitments to production. It preferred, as Braudel explains, the distribution/marketing sector or trade and commerce.

> "Capitalism did not invade the production sector until the industrial revolution, when machines had so transformed the conditions of production that industry had become a profit-making sector. Capitalism would then be profoundly modified and above all extended. It did not however abandon its habit of oscillating according to the circumstances of the day, for over the years other options besides industry became open to it, in the nineteenth and twentieth centuries. Capitalism, even in the industrial era, was not exclusively attached to the world of industrial production, far from it."[25]

The fact was that in the early stages of English industrial capitalism, the large scale manufacturer had to consider the problem of markets. Micro-capitalism, with its small manufacturers could function with local markets. Trading, marketing, the negotiation of business agreements, the entry through the activity of commerce into a commercial system—all this became an essential adjunct of industrial production. Those early manufacturers of "The New Industrial System," as Mantoux noted, were capitalists, work managers and merchants at one and the same time.

REFERENCES

1. See note on "distinction" on page 75 note, and pp. 85, 97, no. 8. and pp. 85, 97, 108.
2. Pais, Abraham, *Inward Bound: Of Matter and Forces in the Physical World* (Oxford, New York 1986) p. 8.
3. Mason, Stephen F., *A History of the Sciences* (Collier Books,Revised, 1962, New York).
4. Ibid., p. 259.
5. Ibid., Ch. 23.
6. Mantoux, Paul, *The Industrial Revolution in the Eighteenth Century* (Revised 1928, Harcourt, Brace & Co., New York).
7. Ibid., p. 40.
8. Ibid., p. 8.
9. Ibid., p. 316.
10. Ibid., p. 318.

11. Ibid., pp. 210-11.
12. Ibid., pp. 382-83.
13. Ibid., p. 325.
14. Ibid., pp. 345-46.
15. Ibid., pp. 383-84.
16. Ibid., pp. 255-56.
17. Ibid., p. 374.
18. Usher, Abbott Payson, *A History of Mechanical Inventions* (McGraw-Hill, New York 1929).
19. Mumford, Lewis, *Technics and Civilization* (Harcourt Brace, New York, 1934).
20. Braudel, Fernand, *Civilization and Capitalism: 15th—18th Century* (3 Vols. English Transl. Ed. 1982, Harper and Row, New York).
21. Ibid., 1:334-35.
22. Ibid., 3:566 *et seq*.
23. Ibid., 1:371.
24. Ibid., 1:562.
25. Ibid., 2:372-73 and Ch. 3, which is a "topology of capital."

CHAPTER VII

The Knowledge of Internal (Inward) Variety: Physics as Possibilities

Experience and the Inwardness of Physical Reality

INTERNAL VARIETY crosses both physics and biology. As an aspect of physics, it has to do with the material reality of matter as physical mass. As an aspect of biology, it has to do with the material reality of organic matter—the matter that exists in human, animal, plant and insect forms.

Neither Locke nor Newton had focused on internal attributes or properties of ponderable matter. The perceptible matter that constituted the mass of the physical objects of the external world is ponderable matter. For Locke, the internal qualities of matter could not be accessed. He took it for granted that such (whatever they might be) existed, and that they were the primary qualities of matter. But not being accessible, they were not experientially knowable. Matter could be known experientially only by its secondary or mediate qualities. Because of the invention of the microscope, Locke was familiar with the magnification of gross matter, but that still left the inwardness of physical reality inaccessible to experience. Nominal (secondary) knowledge of physical reality was all that was disclosed by experience.

Internal (Inward) Variety: Physics

The ponderable matter of Newton's system of mechanics is inert mass. Newton's mass, however, as explained by Einstein, was only a mass point. Physical reality was represented by material points in so far as it represented change through motion ("distance between mass points") as physical events in nature.

> "Perceptible bodies are obviously responsible for the concept of the material point; people conceived it as an analogue of immobile bodies, stripping these of the characteristics of extension, form, orientation in space, and all 'inward' qualities, leaving only inertia and translation and adding the concept of force. The material bodies, which had led psychologically to our formation of the concepts of the 'material point' had now themselves to be regarded as systems of material points."[1]

That matter might not be inert, and that it might, as physical reality, be something other than material points in "absolute space," was the contribution of Faraday and Maxwell. Faraday introduced the "field" as the concept of physical reality. Maxwell, to whom Einstein assigned "the lions share" of the revolution in conceptions of the structure of reality, formulated the equations for the electric and the magnetic fields ("electromagnetic field"). He thereby establishing the foundation for field theory in theoretical physics. Subsequently H. Hertz stripped the field concept of all residue of mechanics, and Lorentz formulated the theory of electrons. Then, still following the chronology of Einstein, there followed quantum—mechanics, which he described as "the last and most successful creation of theoretical physics."[2] However, physical reality as the atomic structure of matter was left without a model by which to represent it. There was only a "sort of indirect description of the real," one that was in terms of the probabilities of its occurrence as an atomic structure.[3]

Guillemin has marked the year 1932, the year of the discovery of an hitherto unknown elementary particle—the neutron—as the year in which physics branched out into "particle research or high energy research." Between 1932 and 1957 there was a discovery of thirty new kinds of elementary particles. These discoveries of experimental physics established that there were considerably more "elementary entities" of matter than the electrons and protons of Thompson and Rutherford. Nor could Mendeleeffs' table of atomic elements any longer be accepted "as the ultimate description of all material elements."[4]

As between atoms and particles as differents reference bases for the conception of matter, Guillemin has written:

> "Atoms are a half-way stopover between the things of every day experience and the weird realm of particles. They could still be treated to some extent in terms of familiar concepts. Thus, the Bohr atom model is frankly a mechanism operating in a familiar ableit altered, manner. Particles are, however, conceptually more remote from atoms than are atoms from sticks and stones."[5]
>
> "The actual march of events has shown that particle research, though it has been concerned largely with the study of matter in its rarer and more evanescent forms, has profoundly altered all previous conceptions about the nature of all material substance. It has demonstrated that matter is not, in general, as solid and enduring as it has seemed to be. Rather, it must be thought of as energy in a highly concentrated state, prone to explode into massless particles flying off with the speed of light."[6]

Physics, theoretical and experimental, by introducing new concepts of physical reality, was both drawing away from experience and, at the same time, enlarging the possibilities for experiencing a nature that was differently comprehended. Locke's knowledge of ordinary sensory experience did not account for the individual mind in quest of its own autonomous comprehension of the material fundament of the physical world. In the case of the discoveries of Newton, it was the appraisal of Einstein that he endeavored "to represent his system as necessarily conditioned by experience," and that Newton derived his law of "gravitational interaction . . . by induction from experience."[7] Classical mechanics did, indeed, "to a large extent do justice to experience."[8] But the point was that as respects the physical world there was much more about its primary constituents that wanted understanding.

Particle physics introduced conservation laws to explain the order and control of "the violent activity among particles." These conservation laws, according to Guillemin, can be stated and understood in simple non-mathematical terms.

"These laws merely impose certain broad restrictions. Within their bounds the rule is" whatever can happen will happen . . . Some happenings are more probable and occur more frequently the others."[9]

"Most importantly, conservation laws account for the existence of our material universe. Only because of them is matter constrained from exploding into nothing but photons and neutrinos."[10]

Realm of Space

Attention is now turned from conceptions of matter since classical mechanics and directed to developments in the concepts of space. Here, too, will also be found the same departure from ordinary sense experience to provide the point of view from which to understand space. Locke had explained the knowledge of space as the knowledge of a simple idea. Simple ideas were, for Locke, "truly the materials of all our knowledge." Space was a perceived distance between two bodies. It was a self-evident idea, since "we get the idea of space both by our sight and touch."[11]

Solid bodies were real, but not space. No space without a presupposition of solid bodies. Space was the relation between solid bodies. All events were contained in space. But space itself remained uninfluenced by physical events (the absolute space posited by Newton). Euclidean mathematics as a conceptual system confined itself to spatial relations between "idealized solid objects, but without any concept of the reality of space."[12]

Einstein has noted that the reconceptualization of the space-time relation followed upon the achievements of Riemann (achievements that had preceded the field theories of Faraday and Maxwell). These achievements, in turn, were followed by the special theory of relativity. Then it was that "a new conception of space, in which space was deprived of its rigidity and the possibility of its partaking in physical events was recognized."[13] The previous separability of time and space became the inseparability of the two.

> "Hitherto it had been silently assumed that the four dimensional continuum of events could be split up into time and space in an objective manner—i.e. that an absolute significance attached to the 'now' in the world of events. With the discovery of the relativity of simultaneity, space and time were merged in a single continuum in a way similar to that in which the three dimensions of space had previously been merged into a single continuum. Physical space was thus extended to a four-dimensional space which also included the dimension of time. The four-dimensional space of the special theory of relativity is first as rigid and absolute as Newton's space."[14]

The Knowledge of Autonomous Variety

Physics had altered the connection between variety and empirics. Locke had put forth a mediate or secondary materialism. Variety would be the functional derviative of the empirics of sensory experience with the secondary attributes of matter. Increasingly, the developments of theoretical and experimental physics began to establish the remoteness of experience from the primary attributes of matter. The directness of physical experience displayed a waning utility for the understanding of matter. It became necessary to go beyond the inductions of physical experience to get to the highest abstractions about the physical cosmos.

The variety of ordinary experience with matter is nominal variety. It is the ordinary variety of nominal knowledge, the empirics of which can be tested by the verifiable consequences of trains of thought. The variety not contingent on human physical experiencing is autonomous variety. It is an outcome of theoretical science, with the search for theory increasingly guided "by purely mathematical, formal considerations."[15] Additional to the nominal empirics of physical experience, and the speculative empirics of the theoretical science, are the experimental empirics of direct and indirect experiment. Each of these empirics has its own distance from sense experiences. Each of these different empirics discloses a different variety within the physical manifold that is the cosmos. The nominal variety of ordinary experience is but one of the varieties of the knowledge of strategy.

Inward Variety and Strategic Knowledge

Physics, then, as knowledge of the inward variety of matter introduces another knowledge of strategy. It is a knowledge of other possibilities—of the other possibilities contained within matter itself. Strategy is the knowledge by which the transformation of possibilities into varieties of human experience is achievable. It is the knowledge by which the transformation of thought itself takes place as other possibilities for cognitive intelligibility of the physical world (e.g. matter, space and time, field theory). It is also the knowledge by which the transformation of matter itself takes place as avenues of escape from the experience constraining limits of Locke's fitted knowledge.

The New Possibilities

So, to illustrate from specific instances supplied by Guillemin in his account of quantum mechanics, the theory of which he equated as equal in importance with that of relativity:

> "Through the use of quantum mechanics metalurgy has been transformed from a craft to an exact technology . . . Various improved magnetic materials have been developed, in particular new alloys for the construction of *superconducting electromagnets* which do not require a constant supply of power to maintain the magnetizing electric current."
>
> "The greater understanding of solids has contributed to the development of the *laser*, a device which can produce light beams of enormous intensity capable of burning instantly through the most refractory materials. Of greater significance is [the property of beam *coherence*—light waves oscillating in unison]. This property gives laser light beams unique and valuable properties for example, the ability to carry messages like radio waves that are just beginning to be explored."
>
> "But the one new advance in the physics of solids which has

had the most far-reaching consequences in science, in technology and industry, and indeed in society as a whole, is in the field of *semi-conductors,* crystalline materials whose electrical conductivity lies between that of metals, which are excellent conductors, and substances such as glass and porcelain, which do not conduct the current at all. These are the materials used to produce *transistors* and other electronic devices which are essential for the construction of miniature electonic circuits. Without *solid-state* circuits the program of space exploration beyond the earth's atmosphere would be well-nigh impossible."

"Of far greater import has been the development of *electronic computers,* whose rapid improvement in efficiency and sophistication has depended entirely on the use of solid-state electronic devices . . ."[16]

REFERENCES

1. Einstein, Albert, Ideas and Opinions, (Transl. Sanja Bargmann, Crown Publishers, Inc. NY 1954), p. 267.
2. Ibid., pp. 259, 269.
3. Ibid., p. 272.
4. Guillemin, Victor, *The Story of Quantum Mechanics,* (Scribners Sons 1968) photo caption, after p. 142. Guillemin has commented that because he changed the concept of light (from mechanical waves to an electromagnetic theory of light) James Clark Maxwell (1831-1879) is considered to be the one who made "the first important break from the materialistic-mechanistic views of Newtonian physics." p. 126.
5. Ibid., p. 174.
6. Ibid., p. 170.
7. Einstein, p. 258.
8. Ibid., p. 274.
9. Guillemin, p. 170.
10. Ibid., p. 171.
11. Locke, John, *An Essay Concerning Human Understanding,* (6th edition, Bk. II, Ch. XIII, Sec. 1,2, pp. 110-11), with the notes and illustrations of the author, and an analysis of his doctrine of ideas. Also, Questions on Locke's Essay, by A. M., Ethical Moderator in Trinity College, Dublin. (New Edition, The World Library, Ward, Lock & Co., London, undated) The original edition of Locke's *Essay* is 1689.
12. Einstein, pp. 278-80.
13. Ibid., p. 281.
14. Ibid., pp. 281-82.
15. Ibid., p. 282.
16. Guillemin, p. 116.

PART II. (B)

Strategic Knowledge as Knowledge of Variety: Varietal Domains

Considered by itself, what is strategic knowledge?

CHAPTER VIII

Relational Variety: The Knowledge of Relation

1.
RELATION AND KNOWLEDGE

"When we turn from sea to land, we find that the first practicable locomotive was designed by Richard Trevithick in England in 1801, and the first true railway was built by George Stephenson between Stockton and Darlington in 1825. Although the locomotive was wholly of British origin, it is not coincidence that the nation which produced Clausewitz was the first to grasp the supreme importance of the railway in war. Thus, in 1833, F.W. Harkort pointed out that a railway between Cologne and Minden and another between Mainz and Wesel would add enormously to the defence of the Rhineland, and C.E. Ponitz urged the general building of railways to protect Prussia against France, Austria, and Russia. Simultaneously, Friedrich List, an economist of unique genius, pointed out that from the position of a secondary military Power, whose weakness was that she was centrally placed between powerful potential enemies, Prussia could be raised by the railway into a formidable State . . .

"In 1833, before a single rail had been laid, this remarkable man projected a network of railways for Germany which is substantially that of to-day, and 13 years later, the year of his death, the first extensive troop movement by rail was made by a Prussian army corps 12,000 strong with horses and guns to Cracow. After this experiment the Prussian General Staff made a comprehensive survey of the military value of railways . . . Thus it came about that the genius of George Stephenson gave life to the Clausewitzian theory of the nation in arms, for without the railway the mass-armies of the second half of the nineteenth century could not have been supplied."[1]

Relational Knowledge

The Idea of Relation

Locke assigns The Idea of Relation a distinctive and critical place in human understanding. The idea of relation can also be assigned a distinctive and critical place in the knowledge of strategy.

What is that place for the knowledge of human understanding?

What is that place as the knowledge of strategy?

Locke places relation within the capability of mind to discern or to differentiate between its own ideas, and thus, "by distinguishing one thing from another," to arrive at a distinct perception of different things. Discernment is the requirement not just of certainty of knowledge, but also of high level of knowledge. Without the capability discernment, neither would be attainable, even if "the mind were continually employed in thinking." What Locke includes within relation he himself judges it to be "vast" in extent. As a mental operation he describes it as follows:

> "The comparing theme one with another, in respect of extent, degrees, time, place, or any other circumstances, is another operation of the mind about its ideas, and is that upon which depends all that large tribe of ideas, comprehended under relation."[2]

Relation as Knowledge

Of Locke's two categories of ideas—the simple and the complex—relation, as knowledge, belongs in the category of complex ideas. Relation, that is to say, is not an idea that is the product of mind passive. The passive knowledge of the simple idea is the knowing of an object from the simple sensation of its appearance (nominal knowing). It is not a knowledge that the mind can make up of itself. Nor is it an idea that can exist apart from its sensory origin and fundament.

Relation, as a complex idea, is a product of mind active, an idea that is a result of acts of the mind. It is the cognitive outcome of mind "bringing two ideas, whether simple or complex, together, and setting them by one another, so as to take a view at once, without uniting them into one; by which it gets all its ideas of relations."[3] Mind is exerting "acts of its own" with ideas of relation. It is not limited to what is supplied by sensation and by reflection or the sensory attributes of things themselves.

If mind passive is non-autonomous mind, mind active is quasi-autonomous mind. Not completely free of the observed materiality in the world without, but sufficiently free to engage in acts of the intellect whereby ideas may be related independently of that which may have been observed. The mind of the person is not confined "barely to observation, and what offers itself from without." Understanding is not confined to the precise object observed. Thoughts can be led beyond the idea of a thing, "beyond the subject itself denominated to something distinct from it."[4] It may be done by any idea, and so any idea can be the occasion and foundation of relation.

There is separation between the things that are related—the subject matter of relation—and the complex idea that is the idea of the relation itself. Consequently, the ideas of relation held by two separate persons may be the same, even though each may have a different idea of what is the subject matter that gives rise to the idea of relation. For each, the idea of relation is the product of mind active. The ideas (simple or complex) in the mind of each provide the foundation and the occasion for each mind to bring forth its own ideas of relation.[5] Moreover, all things are capable of being related, i.e. are "capable of almost an infinite number of considerations in reference to other things." The only requisites for relation are: "There must always be in relation two ideas, or things, either in themselves really separate, or considered as distinct, and then a ground or occasion for their comparison."[6]

The Classes of Relation

As the material of all knowledge, for Locke, consists of the simple ideas either of sensation or reflection, so too are all ideas of relation, despite the capability of their being so multitudenous. Locke resorted to four major classes of relation to illustrate this point.

1. Relations of Cause and Effect
   Derived from sensory observations of the operations of bodies of one another to produce that which did not hitherto exist.
2. Relations of Time
   Derived from ideas of length of duration.
3. Relations of Distance, Place and Extension
   Derived from ideas of length and points at rest, and from ideas of the bulk and size.
4. Moral Relations
   Derived from conformity or non-conformity to a rule of reference by which judge and measure voluntary actions.

2.
STRATEGIC KNOWLEDGE AS RELATIONAL KNOWLEDGE

Mind Passive and Mind Active

The knowledge of strategy encompasses the knowledge of variety. This knowledge of variety must be placed in a relational context. Strategic knowledge is the knowledge whereby this relational placement is to be done and what relational context to choose.

Locke's foundation for the complex idea of relation in the simple ideas of sensation and reflection is the perceptual mode by which an internalization of the external takes place in thought. But thinking alone focused on these simple ideas as the object of thought will not relate the internal to the external. Ideas of relation are the cognition whereby there is achieved an externalization of the internal. And these ideas do it by "serving as marks to lead the thoughts beyond the subject itself denominated to something distinct from it."⁷ The external enters into the internal through mind passive, perceptual receptivity. The internal re-enters into the external through mind active, mental acts that are not focused on things as they are in themselves.

The perceptual receptivity of mind passive has the effect of totally encompassing the percipient person in the time and place and object context constituting the materiality of the perceptual present. For Locke there is perceptual receptivity only of that which is present-in-the-world, of that which has being as an existent in the time of perception. Nor is there any escape from perceptual appearance, from nominal reality, although unsupportable ideas of substance are put forth as an understanding of the reality of things as they are in themselves.⁸

In ideas of relation mind active opens an avenue of cognition to a different reality focus. It is a reality focus constituted by mind itself through its own mortal acts. The reality of that focus is a reality of human significance, one infused with the understanding of its significance to human beings. The ascription of significance proceeds from the internal to an investiture of the external with significance. Reality leaves off being the subject of things that are the objects of perceptual understanding. Mind active replaces it with the knowledge through ideas of relation. Knowledge as a constituted and signified reality is a material expression of quasi-autonomous cognition.

The Knowledge of Creation I

The ideas of making, of generation, of alteration, and of creation are explained by Locke as distinct ideas that are understandable in relation to the ideas of cause and effect. It is from sensory observation that what we term cause is that which conduces or operates to produce what did not before exist, "For, to have the idea of cause and effect, it suffices to consider any simple idea or substance as beginning to exist by the operation of some other, without knowing the manner of that operation."⁹

The idea of *making* Locke illustrated by reference to all artificial things, which come into existence through the effect produced by a cause extrinsic to the product itself. The idea of *generation* refers "to a substance produced in the ordinary course of nature by an internal principle, but set on work by and received from some external agent or cause and working by insensible ways which we perceive not."[10] Here the reference by Locke is to organic entities, whether human, animal or botanical.

The idea of creation is reserved for

> ". . . When the thing is wholly made new, so that no part thereof did ever exist before; as when a new particle of matter both begin to exist, in *rerum nature*, which had before no being."[11]

However, the matter of special relevance here is not creation as a definite and particular idea of the causal relation. Locke had not only dealt with creation as a complex idea of relation, but also to designate the actuality of world creation by "the bountiful author of our being."[12] In that latter context of creation Locke, who was a Deist, placed the knowledge of persons within a constrained relationship to the world as a divine creation.

Locke intended deliberately to limit the pupose of his inquiry. It was to be limited to making the understanding its own object, and therefore the inquiry would only "consider the discerning faculties of a man as they are employed about the objects which they have to do with."[13] He also deliberately shied away from "an affectation of an universal."

The Fitted Knowledge of Creation I

But that state of limited understanding to which Locke assigned human comprehension is not simply one of finite intelligence. That is to say, finite intelligence is not simply a phenomenon of nature, a naturalistic state. It is also an ontological state of being that originates in divine creation. Finite intelligence is thus the divine mark on human understanding of that ontological state. The limited understanding and imperfect comprehension indigenous to that state of being "yet secures their great concernments that they have light enough to lead them to the knowledge of their maker, and the sight of their own duties."[14] Narrow though the human mind might be, it was still capable of acquiring whatever knowledge might be of use in providing for and improving the conditions of life. "Our business here is not to know all things, but those which concern our conduct."[15] Locke's human understanding is the understanding of finite intelligence that is adequate for the acquisition of this fitted knowledge. It is knowledge of "a rational creature," but none-the-less knowledge fitted to "that state which man is in this world."[16]

The Relational Knowledge of Creation II

Strategically, the knowledge of Creation II is the knowledge of domain creation. As domain knowledge it is both a newly differentiated field of knowing and also a new field of knowledge based possibilities in the form of utilitarian opportunities. Time stages in the knowledge of Creation II are divisible into the pre-utilitarian, the utilitarian, and the post-utilitarian. In its utilitarian stage, strategy transforms knowledge application possibilities into opportunity for capital investment. In its post-utilitarian stage, strategic thought weighs capital disinvestment. The experience of the steel industry with capital investment and disinvestment is illustrative of the inter-levels between stages of knowledge and capital strategies.[17]

The idea that something not materially present—not already there in the existing world could, through the finite intelligence of humans, by them be created from out of the material of the world as it was given, was rejected by Locke. His reasoning about human understanding excluded any further or additional or alternative creation of matter. It would be both futile and impossible. There could be no sensory based knowledge of the primary qualities of matter. The idea of a substance, of an essence of matter, was erroneous. Both access to the interior (what was not appearance) of matter, and the capability to create new matter stood outside of human knowing. Thus human thinking and understanding were grounded in and limited to the empirical phenomena of the experience sensory world. However, these could not be the existing phenomena of domain creation.

Everything that appears presents itself in the form of sensiblilized phenomena. Nonetheless, everything that so presents itself does not represent an anterior reality in which are contained what Leibniz identified as "the inclination or tendency of possibilities to become in existence." Their reality—as real though contained possibilities—is the reality of being a part of the mechanism of the already constituted world (Creation I).

Analysis of that mechanism could provide one explanation of the world as it exists, and of the non-existing world, and also of the world as it might otherwise have existed. The explanation, wrote Leibniz, would be

> ". . . as knowledge of the ultimate reason of things, which was a knowledge of them as both essences and existences. We see, by a wonderful plan in all nature, the metaphysical laws of cause, power, action, have place, and these prevail over the purely geometrical laws themselves of matter."[18]

The ultimate reason is that everything which exists in its present state has within itself the force for its own change into a future state. "The rest is only phenomena and relations."[19]

What is expressed within this foregoing reasoning is the logic for another and alternative materialization of a world (a cosmos) as a material order. It is the logic for Creation II from Creation I. It is the logic underlying the possibility of cosmoplastics, the possibility whereby causal agency, from matter that is already part of an existing material reality, produces other matter by which another cosmological reality is constituted, "Cosmoplastics refers to an independent and operative power by which a cosmos as a material order is originated and brought into being."[20] The operative power to bring into existence and the mode whereby it accompanies emergence are joined.

Strategically, domain knowledge is focused on the relations between emergence and bringing into existence. It is knowledge focused on the something which is encased in an anterior reality, but which also might be brought into existence as a separate something. Knowledge facilitative of the domain creating something, that brings it into the form of an actual existant, is the knowledge of Creation II. It is knowledge disclosing the ground for another and separate reality of possibilities.

The knowledge insight for all of the foregoing has its fundament in the pure thought of Leibniz: the possibilities of reality and the reality of possibilities exist in their being part of the mechanism of some constituted world. It is the bedrock for the knowledge of Creation II. It is reflected in Whitehead's philosophy of Organic Mechanism[21, 22];it appears prominently in the development of theoretical physics; and it enters into the advances of modern medicine, and into the advances of biology.[23]

In the frame of the union of biological with atmospheric reality, what there is as the material reality, and its possible alternative, is the biosphere.[24] Space research early marked biology in space (a Biosatellite Program) as a direction for the future.[25] The construction of a terrestrial facsimile biosphere already exists as an alternative biosphere for experimental possibilities.[26] Still, biospheric knowledge possibilities do not exist as either the ultimate or the ultimately limiting knowledge of space research. Beyond biospheric knowledge is Exobiology, which is focused on the "investigation of possible extraterrestrial life" and its "significance to fundamental biology."[27]

Note, however, that the explanation of exobiology is given in terms of possible biological mechanism.

> "In planning the biological exploration of other planets, the question, 'Is life present?' should be broadened to the question 'Is any stage of biological evolution observable?' This question covers the search for evidence of early stages in the evolution toward organisms (the prebiotic stage) as well as for living organisms and for the remains of extinct life . . . where such [prebiotic organic processes] bodies can reproduce themselves more or less perfectly and can sustain their reproduction, they may be regarded as living cells."[28]

By his "wonderful plan of nature" Leibniz had coupled the deterministic metaphysical mechanism with the deterministic physical mechanism. It was a coupling that was congruent with Newton's "modern synthesis of the physical world, a logical explanation of the universe," one through which planets and stars, men and animals, the smallest particles of matter, and even the particles of which light was deemed to consist, moved in accordance with the same mathematical laws."[29] Absolute time and absolute space were the bedrock of Newton's mechanics of the universe.

But the bedrock began first to crack and then to split under the attack first, that they were not things of fact but constructs of pure thought (MACH); and second, that universal laws of nature were but mental creations (Poincare); and third, the scientific consequences of the elctromagnetic field discovered by Maxwell. The developments of pure science with respect to the physical world culminated in the call for " 'a whole new mechanics' " (Poincare) at the 1904 Universal exposition.[30] What followed in 1905 was the Special Theory of Relativity in a paper devoid of supporting evidence by an author (Einstein) who had said of his way of thinking " 'that the gift of fantasy has meant more to me than my talent for absorbing positive knowledge.' "[31]

Einstein, in addition to transforming the objective "now" of the concept of simultaneous events into a subjective "now" that was dependent for its validity on the specific frame of reference an observer, had also introduced mass as a third yardstick by which "to measure the nature of the physical world."[32] The yardstick was the relation between mass and energy, and the transformation of one into the other. "All mass was merely congealed energy; all energy merely liberated [through the velocity of mass in motion] matter."[33]

What of the knowledge of Creation II at this point? At the outset, the introduction of actors into the physical universe generates the truth of their own physical frame of reference for their actions. This is the truth of their experienced knowledge. Second, the physical truths of the universe of Creation I could be beyond experience based knowledge, simply because some of them cannot be accessed within the range of what are the sensory capabilities of human experience. Because of the Special Theory, the hitherto existing concordance between the factual data of observation and Newton's absolutes of time and space was no more. Clark, who traced these knowledge developments in physics within the framework of a biography of Einstein, succinctly put their significance for scientific knowing:

> "For it underlined, more strongly than had previously been the case, that science might really be a search not for absolute truths but for a succession of theories that would progressivly approach the truth. It suggested, furthermore, that the best path to be followed might not be that of observation followed by the induction of general laws, but the totally different process of postulating a theory and then discovering whether or not the facts fitted it. Thus a theory should start with more scientific and philosophical assumptions than the facts alone warranted. A decade later the method was to provide the startling results of the General Theory."[34]

What was knowledge in pursuit of the knowledge of Creation I? Of the General Theory of Relativity, it was said by Born (whom Clark quotes) that it had only " 'slender' " connections with experience, while admiring it as " 'the greatest feat of human thinking about nature.' "[35] It was the coming of subatomic physics and quantum theory that upended the earlier idea, grounded in Newtonian physics, that the laws of nature were such that knowledge of causally deterministic and predictable events in the universe was possible. "Statistical physics" had now made its appearance. What was this as knowledge? Was it less than knowledge of objective facts—of an objective physical reality that was not contingent on observation? Such was the contention of Einstein, but indeterminancy and statistical physics won out.

The strategy in Creation II is to be in at the beginning, to be there at the creation. The objective of managed discovery is the advantage of starting with nothing hidden, to start without the burden of unrevealed knowledge, something which variety in organization arrangements for joint and cooperative investigation makes feasible. Strategy—given expected payoffs of domain creation knowledge—favors managed discovery at both the pre-utilitarian and utilitarian stages (e.g. genetics, biotechnology, space and atomic science domains). Parity in the structure and processes of knowledge discovery and/or no diminution of practical domain advantage in consequence of knowledge discovery become strategic objectives. What remains undetermined are the modes and the extent by which speculative knowing can/ will remain beyond the reach of managed discovery; that is, remain outside a system of controlled discovery of its own future knowledge.

REFERENCES

1. Fuller, J.F.C. (Major General), *A Military History of The Western World*, Vol. III, (Minerva Press, Funk & Wagnalls, N.Y. 1967 ed.) pp. 4-5.

2. Locke, John, *An Essay Concerning Human Understanding*, (6th edition, p. 103), with the notes and illustrations of the author, and an analysis of his doctrine of ideas. Also, Questions on Locke's Essay, by A. M., Ethical Moderator in Trinity College, Dublin. (New Edition, The World Library, Ward, Lock & Co., London, undated) The original edition of Locke's *Essay* is 1689.

3. Ibid., 108.
4. Ibid., 234.
5. Ibid., Bk. II, Ch. XXV.
6. Ibid., 235.
7. Ibid., 234.
8. Ibid., Bk. III, Ch. VI.
9. Ibid., 239.
10. Ibid., 239-39.
11. Ibid., 238.
12. Ibid., 3.
13. Ibid., 1.
14. Ibid., 3.
15. Ibid., 4.
16. Ibid.

17. Scheuerman, William, *The Steel Crisis*: The Economics and Politics of A Declining Industry (Praeger, N.Y., 1986); Tiffany, Paul A., *The Decline of American Steel*: How Management, Labor and Government Went Wrong (Oxford, N.Y., 1988); Etsuo Abe and Yoshitaka Suzuki (Eds.), *Changing Patterns of International Rivalry*: Some Lessons from the Steel Industry (U. of Tokyo, 1991).

18. Leibniz, Gottfried Wilhelm, *New Essays Concerning Human Understanding*: Together with an appendix consisting of some of his shorter pieces (Langley, Alfred G., Transl., with notes) (The MacMillan Co. 1986, reprinted 1916, 1949 by Open Court, Chicago).

19. Ibid., 712.

20. Grundstein, Nathan D., *The Futures of Prudence: Pure Strategy and Aristotelian and Hobbesian Strategies* (EEA, Hudson, Ohio 1984).

21. Angyal, Andras, *Foundations for a Science of Personality* (Viking, N.Y. 1972 ed.) Ch. 4, Organism and Environment; Ch. 5, Biospheric Dynamics.

22. Kimble, Daniel P., *Psychology as a Biological Science* (Goodyear Pub-

lishing Co., Pacific Palisades, CA, 1973). The work by Angyal introduces empirical concept and theoretical context into Whitehead's philosophy of Organic Mechanism. According to this philosphy the universe is only knowable and understandable when regarded as a succession "of organization levels." Freedman, Paul, *The Principles of Scientific Research* (Public Affairs Press, Washington, D.C. 1950), p. 71.

23. The work by Kimble, while transforming psychology into biological knowledge, still leaves the individual in "what Whitehead has criticized as "simple location" (i.e. ignores its relations as matter to indefinite spatio temporal relations) Freedman, pp. 72-73. Angyal accepts this view of Whitehead and introduces the concept of homonony (integration with superindividual units) as a non-contradictory developmental factor functioning concurrently with individual autonomy, Ch. 6. However, whether cosmologically the world is a "meaningful organization" is not considered by Angyal to be material" for a science of personality." The comparison to be made, of course, is with the material relevance of the cosmology of Einstein for the science of physics. (see text pp. 109 et seq.—and the cited biography by Clark.

24. "Eight Will Spend Next Two Years In Big Terrarium," *Cleveland Plain Dealer*, September 13, 1990, p. 16B; Stevens, William K., "Evolving Theory Views Earth as a Living Organism," *New York Times*, August 29, 1989, p. 17; Rifkin, Glenn, "Keeping Track of a Hermetic Universe," New York Times, February 10, 1991, Sec. 3-8.

25. Space Science Board, National Academy of Sciences—National Research Council—*Space Research: Directions from the Future, Part Three* (Washington, D.C., February 1966). Also relevant is Sagan, Carl, *The Cosmic Connection: An Extraterrestrial Perspective* (Anchor Press/Doubleday, Garden City, NY, 1973).

26. *Cleveland Plain Dealer*, Stevens, Rifkin, Above, Note 24.

27. Space Science Board (Above, Note 25), 146.

28. Ibid., 147.

29. Clark, Ronald W., *Einstein: The Life and Times* (World Publishing, New York 1971), p. 74.

30. Ibid., 76-83.

31. Ibid., 85-87.

32. Ibid., 88, 98.

33. Ibid., 99.

34. Ibid., 94.

35. Ibid., 20.

CHAPTER IX

The Knowledge of Invisible Variety: Strategizing Flight

Possibilities and the Way of Strategic Knowledge

FLIGHT AS THE CONQUEST of air refers to air borne flight as a possible path of human exit from the limiting condition of being earthbound. Air borne flight as idea originates as an imaginative expression of being-in-the-universe. As an aspirational idea, flight has its origins in an ontological drive within humans, one that provides the ground for a perspective about the world in which they exist as beings-in-the-world. It is a perspective that is not experience dependent. Rather, it can function as a driver of experience. As such it drives for the acquisition of knowledge and understanding.

As regards air borne flight, what was the path, from the imaginative expression of that which exists within humans as an autonomous driver of experience with flight, to the actual achievement of an air transport industry catchment for capital? Before recreating that path as an event stream in time, consider the following:

> A pre-experiential imperative drives the empirical vision
> Imagination precedes possibilities
> Aspiration imagines possibilities
> Desire drives inquiry
> Inquiry discloses empirics
> Empirics discloses relations

Invisible Variety: Strategizing Flight   131

Relations unveil possible order
Utility sieves possibilities
Possibilities shape understanding
Understanding defines knowledge
Knowledge defines possibilities
Possibilities unveil the way to strategy
The way of strategy points to directive paths
A directive path is one of causal engagement with events in the world.

The foregoing is not a problem list. It is not a sequential listing of determined steps or stages of strategic knowledge. It is not a statement of operations or an operations guide. It does not express a theoretical formulation of inter-relationships. What, then, is it? It is a conspectus or mental survey put forth in the garment of an heuretic. It is an inventive mental survey. Its function is to point towards a logic of discovery concerning the connectiveness between possibilities knowledge and the way of the knowledge of strategy.

Air borne flight, the conquest of air,

1. Begins as aspiration without a product
2. Begins as endeavor without capital
3. Begins as vision without a market
4. Begins with private inventors who were independent of one another
5. Begins without any comprehension of limits
6. Begins with European initiative

Pre-Industrial Flight Knowledge

Once the earlier visions of flight, once the ancient myths of flight, once the idea of man-powered flight, once the flapping wings of birds as a design model, once the "soft machines" (balloons, parachutes, and "non-rigid dirigibles of the aerostatic era")—once all these were abandoned, then what was left to be done by way of aeronautical advance was (1) the invention of an appropriate "prime mover," and (2) the selection of the technical problems of aerodynamics necessary to sustain heavier than air flight, and (3) fixed wing aircraft design. The bridging from air borne flight without mechanical power (gliders) to powered flight of heavier-than-air aerodynes took fifty years—from 1850 to 1900—but it was a period distinguished by practical work, equipment based research, model making, experimental testing and theoretical study. In 1903 the Wright brothers, who had been building, designing and flying gliders, had come to a decision to include a motor linked to propellers in their next glider. They were not, however, the pioneer developers of the early light-weight prime movers.

It seems odd to think of "steam aero-engines" as the prime movers, but designers did succeed in meeting the requisite free flight power to weight ratios. Still, what took place was rapid, early and total eclipse of the steam engines. It was displaced by a four-stroke internal combustion engine that would burn petrol. The inventive pioneers in the design of the aero-engine were Frenchmen. Air cooled rotary engines were built and were particularly suitable for the "period when the *achievement* of free flight and then the *preliminary development* of free flight depended upon the power unit more than upon anything else."[1] Through the airscrew, rotary motion could be converted into linear thrust, and the aero-engine as prime mover could be linked with the wing system in the propulsion of aircraft. All was now in place, and the flight truimphs in the years 1903-1908 proved the practicality of flight "in a winged, powered, controllable machine." What followed?

> "Aviation, still untainted by war, entered its most joyous and uninhibited period—perhaps its finest period. It became an inexhaustible source of interest and entertainment. It seized the attention of scientists and engineers, of sportsmen and rich dilettantes, of artists, aristocrats and inventors and, above all, of ambitious and daring adventurers and men of action."[2]

Industrialization of Military Flight

That period ended with the approach of World War I. Then, too, the construction, design and testing of aircraft by independent pioneers also ended. Increasingly there had been testing of armed aircraft and of bombing tests from aircraft starting in 1910. In England, France and Germany pilot training was inaugurated, military flying schools established, and a proliferation of aircraft producing companies in preparation for large-scale aircraft production. Industrialization had now taken command in the service of military strategies that transformed the machines of flight into military weapons.

There was no comparable industrialization in the United States. Three companies dominated aircraft production. That of Glen Curtiss, who had started to produce aircraft in 1908. Originally a racing cyclist, Curtiss had used his prize money to start up a bicycle business, then gone on to build engines for motorcycles. It was through his light-weight engine designs that he was brought into aircraft production. That of Glenn Martin, who had begun with gliders but who had moved into powered aircraft in 1909, using a Ford Model T engine to build the first one. In 1912 he established a factory in Los Angeles. There he employed "three engineers whose names were later to become famous—Donald W. Douglas, Lawrence D. Bell and James S. McDonnell."[3] What of the Wrights'? The Wright brothers had formed a company back in 1909, financed by one million dollars of venture capital from several bankers. Never a large enterprise, it was sold by Orville after the death of Wilbur. But the company was reorganized as Dayton-Wright by a group of businessmen from Dayton and Detroit when the United States entered the war. It then progressed (after it had obtained representation on the Aircraft Production Board) to become the largest wartime producer of aircraft. By the way of final note, however, it should be remembered that "no American aeronautical engineer knew how to design an up-to-date combat machine. The Americans therefore selected Allied aircraft for production."[4]

What were the consequences of the war for aerodynes?

1. Industrialization of aircraft production.
2. Especially in France, Germany and England, the existence of large aircraft industries.
3. Mass production of airframes, engines and finished aircraft.
4. A large labor force knowledgeable about aircraft production.

134   THE KNOWLEDGE OF STRATEGY

5. Dissemination among large numbers of persons of the knowledge of how to fly.
6. Absence of radical progress in technological and aerodynamic advances.
7. Unutilized advances in aircraft design.

Industrialization of Private, Non-Commercial Flight

Shifting the question somewhat, what were the consequences of the end of World War I for aerodynes?

1. The answer, in gross, was a return to the pre-war objectives of air borne flight—"The objectives of convenient, pleasurable and rapid personal transport."[5]
2. In terms of the diffusion of the experience of air borne flight, there was "uninhibited exploration of all forms of flying machine and every manner of flying attained apeal. It was flying's golden age."[6]
3. The appearance of a market for aircraft suitable for private transport. "There was a widespread belief that flying was to become the universally accepted form of personal transportation."[7]
4. The market demand was supplied by the private and individual purchaser of the small private airplane. Cost became a significant factor.
5. Private flying did not reach popularity in the United States until the 1930's.
6. Pioneering distance and endurance flights, along with trailblazing flights in light aircraft, raised public confidence in aircraft capabilities.
7. The 1930's—also known as The Flying Thirties—was dominated by the popular view that flying was a kind of sport.

Industrialization of Commercial Flight

"United States airlines in the early 1920's were non-existent. Cars, buses and trains handled virtually all the passenger traffic, and there was no transcontinental air service of any sort until July 1929 when an air/rail service was opened in which passengers flew by day and travelled in rail pullman cars by night."[8]

Commercial aviation—airline commercial transport—began from almost a clean slate after 1918, when the war formally ended. The engine factories returned to civilian production. Military aircraft were not suited for civil transport. Civil transport aircraft were in need of technical development. The British airliners of the 1920's "were a grand expression of the sailing ship translated into a new medium."[9] There was a reluctance to invest capital in the design of commercial aircraft. Passenger traffic was quite scarce. What did take place as a matter of necessity were mergers between small operators of airlines.

What supplied the foundation for the future of commercial aviation in the United States was the U.S. AirMail. It served as the funnel for a stream of captial to the private (contractual) enterprise that had, in 1926, taken over the operation of flying the mail. Prior to then, in the years since 1918, the Federal Government, as part of its responsibility for the mail routes, had "established airfields, radio systems and the other supporting services needed."[10]

In the United States the step from design of mail planes to a genuinely innovative design of commercial aircraft—which extended from 1927 to 1930—was achieved by a design team within the Boeing Airplane Company. Starting from May 1930, when a commercial aircraft with "stressed-skin construction and retractable under-carriage" was designed, within another three years the Boeing 247 was developed, an airline that "at last signalled the demise of the fabric-covered biplane and ushered in the new age of the smooth, unbraced monoplane."[11] The modern era of modern commercial airliners had begun. What followed was a period of rapid technological improvements in airframes, engines and airplane instruments. They gave promise of huge improvements in the range, speed, regularity of performance, and safety of commercial aircraft.

By 1935, the evident possibilities of commercial aviation as a mode of transportation were such that the capital for private investment in airline generation on a sustained basis was now forthcoming. The year 1927 had marked the first inter-city (New York and Boston) commercial passenger service by Colonial Airlines. There had been a marriage between the newly designed Boeing

247D and United Airlines, which flew coast to coast. It could climb even if one engine failed; it featured an automatic pilot, which reduced the stress of long distance flight; and it incorporated de-icing and other technical advances. Airframes, engines and instrumentation had progressed to where commercial airlines could enter a new era of flight safety, flight distance, airspeed, and scheduled regularity of flight.

There was now a new and growing American market for the manufacture of commercial aircraft. It was a competitive market of privately owned air carriers. Trans-World-Airlines (originally Transcontinental and Western Air) was formed in 1930 by a merger of four airlines, and it looked to the Douglas company "to build a completely new 12 passenger transport." This was the start of the DC commercial aircraft line, beginning with DC-1 and extending to the DC-3 (21 passengers/195 MPH) which, in its military versions, transported "roughly 70 per cent of the total allied air traffic throughout the war."[12] It was the Lockheed company that pioneered pressurized cabins for high altitude flight, but the first commercial airliner with pressurized cabins was built by Boeing—the 307 stratoliner (4 engines) that was built for service with TWA and Pan American (which had begun operations in October 1927).

> "But even in 1939 airliners were limited in their ability. They carried small loads. They could not fly very far and they wallowed through the bumpy air and clouds quite close to the Earth so that air sickness was taken for granted on a long flight (long in time rather than distance). To fly from New York to Los Angeles, for example, meant a succession of exhausting four to six hour flights spread over two or three days, with a total journey time not very much faster than the crack streamlined trains. Air transport was still small business."[13]

Radical Technological Innovation and World Competitive Transport

Radical technological innovation in aircraft development consisted of (1) the jet propulsion engine and (2) flight at a speed faster than sound (supersonic flight). The latter had been initiated in 1955 as a collaborative project between a group of seven American and British aircraft manufacturers. In 1960, however, the Government of Britain decided that a joint technological program with French engineers was a preferable alternative. The more ultimate goal was British entry into the European Common Market. The successful outcome of the British-French collaborative project was the Concorde. It was an aircraft that seated 130, had a range of 4,500 miles, and its cruising speed was 1,400 miles per hour. The Concorde was also distinguished by the largest launch cost in the entire history of aviation.

Both as idea and as a patentable invention the jet engine has a long history. Patents for a variety of jet engines go back to 1791. The functioning of a modern turbo-jet engine was described by inventors in 1911 and 1917. As to why, nevertheless, no jet engine was actually built, the explanation was the "the basic technology did not exist."[14] Neither the air compressor, nor the combustion chambers, nor the turbine rotor blades with requisite mechanical, metallic, heat resistance, load, weight and size qualities existed. Intense, focused research, development, and testing activity was essential. The pioneer British inventors and theorists of jet propulsion were not supported by their own institutions. The consequence was that a working turbo-jet engine fighter plane did not have a place in the RAF until 1941. Developments of this engine were introduced into the American Air Force in 1942.

It was the Germans who first flew a jet aircraft (August 27, 1939), who were first in large scale production of jet engines, and whose designers were "creating astonishingly advanced new aircraft—and even pilotless guided missiles with turboojet and rocket propulsion."[15] It was those "amazing" developments—"giant turbojet, turbofan and turboprop engines, transonic fighters with swept wings, research aircraft that were all wing, or that had delta (triangular) wings"—that were available to the allies after the end of the war in Europe.[16]

Early utilization of the knowledge built up by advances in engine and aircraft development supplied the foundation for a world dominating civil air transport strategy by the American airlines. It was a matter of now having in hand all the knowledge and technology that was needed in order to make aircraft design, engine design, and long and medium and short range air transport, performance stability, operations regularity, equipment reliability, maintenance capability, support facilities, market growth—all were now either known or sufficiently meshed into unified, consistent, profitable, and attainable strategic expectations within defined time frames.

The DC-3 was replaced by the more capacious 1947 Convair. The DC-4 was succeeded by the DC-6 in 1948. The DC-6B then took over as the operations yardstick of the long range civil aircraft. It was *the* aircraft that proved "beyond all doubt that civil airlines could make money year after year as a matter of course, with no government subsidy or hidden financial aid."[17] North Atlantic jet flight service was begun in 1958 by Pan Am, using the Boeing 707. The rival plane was the DC-8. These two aircraft came to dominate world air transport. Passenger traffic on the North Atlantic route underwent an unprecedented rise.

REFERENCES

1. Howard, Frank and Gunston, Bill, *The Conquest of the Air* (Random House, First American Edition 1972, New York), 55.
2. Ibid., 67.
3. Ibid., 99.
4. Ibid.
5. Ibid., 132.
6. Ibid.
7. Ibid.
8. Ibid., 166.
9. Ibid., 164.
10. Ibid., 166.
11. Ibid., 169.
12. Ibid., 174.
13. Ibid., 177.
14. Ibid., 195.
15. Ibid., 197.
16. Ibid., 198.
17. Ibid., 203.

CHAPTER X

Strategizing Flight for Commercial Aviation

The Emergence of Commercial Aviation

THE EMERGENCE of commercial aviation in the United States was associated with an expanding and diversified host of technological advances, including but not limited to those in engine technology and the technology of airplane design. The expansion was in the form of a rippling outward of support technologies which would sustain the commercial possibilities that were opened by engine and design innovations. Flight passengers were not a particular interest of the operators of the early private airlines, who were struggling carriers of airmail. It was not only that passenger demand was negligible, but that there was not engine reliability, that heavy pay loads were beyond engine capabilities, and that travel comforts were lacking.[1] It was also that radio communications were inadequate, weather reports were inadequate, and the mode of lighting landing fields was inadequate. Finally, air transport service for the mail had excluded carrying passengers and had relied, therefore, on single engined (rather than multi-engined) cargo planes.

Whitehouse has identified the matching of an awakened American demand for passenger air-transport with advances in the design of safe commercial aircraft and flight safety technology as the work of the Daniel Guggenheim Fund for the Promotion of Aeronautics.[2] It was now 1926. Flight safety was the problem of flight without visibility, flight that was safe despite fog and bad weather. The search was for a system of blind flying, and the investigation was done through a Full Flight Laboratory headed by Lieutenant James H. Doolittle. After more than a year of experimental flight tests the solution was achieved through the synchronized use of an in-plane instrumented artificial horizon, a landing field direction finding radio beacon tuned to a visual radio receiver on the instrument panel of the plane, and a sensitive altimeter.[3] The Guggenheim Fund was also the leader in getting airplane designers and manufacturers of aircraft to enter a world wide safe Aircraft Competition. The object of the Competition was to encourage innovations in aerodynamic design that would ensure flight safety at low plane speeds. In fact the Competition laid "the foundation for the development of high-lift devices and sound aerodynamic methods of improving the longitudinal and lateral stability of airplanes . . . [including] . . . the giant land and sea transports that were to come."[4]

Improvements in the form of technological advances both in airplane design and aircraft engines were critical for the start-ups of the early air transport ventures. The monoplane displaced the bi-plane. The monoplane was internally braced, the bi-plane was externally braced. Pacific Air Transport—a mail carrier linking Seattle to Los Angeles—relied on the newly designed Ryan monoplane powered with the Wright Whirlwind engine.[5] The Ford Air Transport relied on the monoplane developed by the Stout Engineering Laboratories. At first a single engine monoplane, it was redesigned to take on three Wright whirlwind radial engines.[6] The redesigned plane was the Ford Trimotor, also known as The Tin Goose. Unprecedented traveler conveniences were built into the Ford Trimotors flown by Maddux Air Lines between Los Angeles and San Diego: "besides the wicker seats and windows that opened for air conditioning, there were overhead luggage racks, individual reading lights—and a lavatory!"[7] Maddux Air Lines offered a popular round trip flight service, its territory of service in the southwest expanded, and in November 1929 it became part of TWA (Transcontinental and Western Air).

It was the Guggenheim Fund that pushed for the commercial adoption of multi-engined planes. An equipment loan fund was established for their purchase and use on approved passenger carrying routes. The condition of purchase was that the multi-engined planes be so designed as not to be forced to land in the event of the disablement of any one of the engines. In May 1928, Western Air Express purchased three aircraft designed by the Dutch engineer and manufacturer, Anthony Fokker. They were "Fokker F-10 three-engined transport, powered by Pratt & Whitney 400-hp Wasp engines."[8] The Aviation Corporation of America, a complex of mail-contract carriers first organized by Juan Trippe in 1928 and then reorganized into the Pan American Airways Corporation as the operating organization, began (mail) scheduled flights to Cuba in October 1929, and scheduled passenger flights in 1928. Fokker's new F-7 tri-motor planes were used.[9]

The introduction of the amphibious monoplane as a commercial aircraft was the first contribution of Donald W. Douglas to the business of commercial aviation transport. The 1928 plane was the "Douglas Dolphin, a high-winged amphibious monoplane, powered by two 300-hp—Wright Whirlwind Engines." The rumor is that William E. Boeing purchased a Dolphin in 1934 to use as a prototype for the flying boats his Seattle based aircraft company later produced—in 1935 the 314 Clipper and, in 1940, the XPBB-1 Sea Ranger.[10] Boeing had become interested in airplane manufacture from the day of his first flight in a Curtiss hydroplane on July 4, 1914. Together with his then partner, Conrad Westervelt, a former Navy pilot, they designed two models of float planes. Neither of these were up to military requirements. But the Boeing Model C did do the first (1919) international mail run—Vancouver to Seattle.[11] Boeing Aircraft continued to produce float planes, on their own and under government contract.

In 1933, Douglas introduced a twin-engined DC series of planes for TWA that transformed commercial air transport. A summation of that transformation was done by Whitehouse, who wrote:

> "Until the advent of the Douglas DC series, passenger carrying, generally regarded as a rash venture, was far from a comfortable experience. Those who tried it either as a novelty or for reasons

of emergency were subjected to periods of deafness, gastric distress, cold feet, and long hours of teeth-rattling vibration. The aircraft being used prior to 1935 were Ford Tri-Motors, Fairchilds, Boeing 40As, tri-motor Fokkers, Sibersky and amphibians, and a few single-engined mail planes which had been modified to take four or five passengers. The comparative comfort, luxury, and speed factors of the DC planes raised commercial passenger-carrying to a new level of transport operations. It was obvious other major manufacturers would have to face up to this advance in commercial air progress."[12]

What was driving the unflagging sequence of progressive innovations in airplane design and the design of aircraft engines? The immediate driver was the policy of the United States government to introduce the service of delivering mail by air. There had been unauthorized mail carrying flights in 1910 and 1911, and by 1913 stunt flights were carrying some pieces of mail between towns; but an officially authorized and government sponsored investigatory and experimental annual route was first suggested in 1910 in The House Bill sponsored by Representative Sheppard. Subsequently funded, the first flight of the official mail carrying service took off from New York's Polo Grounds via North Philadelphia to Washington, D.C. on May 15, 1918. The dominant flight personnel for carrying the mail were pilots trained by the military for World War I Combat. The start-up Chief Executive Officer in charge of flight scheduling and flight operations was an experienced and very capable lubrication and mechanical engineer with Captain status in the Army—Captain Benjamin B. Lipsner. It was Lipsner who persuasively demonstrated the feasibility of an air mail service to the Assistant Postmaster General, who had early seen its possibilities but not its feasibility.[13]

Out of the experiencing of this tentative investigatory and experimental determination concerning delivery of mail by aeroplane, there emerged two convictions. The First: Nation-wide delivery of mail by aeroplane would require a transcontinental system for air mail delivery. The Second: The success of commercial (passenger carrying) flight was dependent upon aircraft engine development—efficiency, reliability, power.

As to the first, the transcontinental system evolved from the original 1917 Woodrow Wilson Airway transcontinental route map drawn up by the Board of Governors of the Aero Club of America, "It comprised a zone eighty miles wide which, cutting through the states of New York, New Jersey, Pennsylvania, Ohio, Michigan, Indiana, Illinois, Iowa, Nebraska, Wyoming, Colorado, Utah, Nevada, and California, linked New York with San Francisco. . . . A number of similar airways were linked into the main route, setting up a network of aerial routes.' "[14] The airmail service began as a series of short air hauls, then larger inter-city stretches were added, and the lengthening of the linkages towards a transcontinental network proceeded step by step. In the ten years between December 1918 and December 1928, air mail routes had grown from 218 miles and 2 station stops to 17,890 miles and 101 station stops.[15] It was September 8, 1920 when the completed daytime transcontinental network of flight laps for airmail was in operation. Nighttime flying of the mail began in 1921, using specially improved aircraft for night flying, a set-up of beacon lights over the main flight routes, and special lighting on the main landing fields.

As for the second, the success of commercial (passenger carrying) flight, that success could be explained by the following:

1. It was in part a derivative of supportive contributions made by the Air Mail Service, particularly by its development of a scheduled transcontinental airmail route.
2. The spill-over benefits from the experience with private flight operations that were based on postal contact awards for the delivery of mail by air.
3. Entrepreneurial ventures in passenger aviation.

The Air Commerce Act of 1926 formulated a governmental policy of fostering the development of commercial aviation in the United States. It authorized the Secretary of Commerce to designate, establish, operate and maintain airways. It also authorized that official and the Postmaster General to transfer all airways under their jurisdiction to municipal control. A year earlier, in 1925, the Kelly Bill had authorized the operation of the Air Mail Service to be turned over to private contractors. Actually,

144 THE KNOWLEDGE OF STRATEGY

short-haul mail runs had for several years been contracted out to small operators. And the first contracts under the Kelly Bill were limited to twelve short air mail routes. They have been listed by Whitehouse as follows:

1. New York to Boston—Colonial Air Lines
2. Chicago to St. Louis—Robertson Aircraft Corporation
3. Chicago-Dallas-Fort Worth—National Air Transport
4. Los Angeles to Salt Lake City—Western Air Express
5. Elko, Nevada to Pasco, Washington—Varney Speed Lines
6. Detroit to Cleveland—Ford Air Transport
7. Los Angeles to Seattle—Pacific Air Transport
8. Chicago to Twin Cities—Charles Dickinson
9. Atlanta to Jacksonville—Florida Airways Corporation
10. Pueblo, Colorado to Cheyenne—Western Air Express
11. Cleveland to Pittsburgh—Clifford Ball, Inc.
12. Atlanta to Miami—Pitcairn Aviation[16]

What is of considerably more strategic interest than the contracted out route list is the condition of the carriers awarded contracts and how they responded to the opportunities provided them by the route contracts.

"Most [other than Ford Transport] were small companies, precariously financed and using equipment that at best promised only a wild adventure. Most of these operators had made their bids with doubtful aircraft, a few ex-barnstormers, and a slatternly air base. Few had any experience in carrying out scheduled runs or discipline of day-by-day operations. There was very little passenger carrying, except by hit-and-miss charter flights. There was no orderly ground organization or efficient maintenance. Few of the pilots had flown at night, and by the opening of the Kelly Bill era, there were few lighted airways to guide the airmen to their destinations."[17]

Ford Air Transport (a venture of Henry Ford) had built on the technology of an all-metal, internally braced monoplane adapted by William B. Stout from Hugo Junker's metal bomber for the German air force. Ford had purchased the Stout Engineering Laboratories, and had been using Stout's monoplane for scheduled transport of Ford's executives between cities.[18] The modern Northwest Orient Airlines had its origins in the company formed by Charles Dickinson—Northwest Airways—to perform the Chicago—Twin Cities mail contract, which then went on in July 1928 to start a passenger carrying service. The completely inexperienced small shop builder of country fair aircraft—Pitcairn Aviation—transformed itself to become Eastern Airlines, and was soon sold (July 1929) for two and one half million to North American Aviation, Inc. However, the point stressed by Whitehouse is that passenger carrying was nowhere near being a real interest for these early contract operators. It was not just that travel comforts and conveniences were non-existent. It was that "the planes available lacked reliable engines. They were not capable of heavy pay loads."[18]

Pacific Air Transport, from which emerged United Air Lines, represents a saga of visionary capitalism driven by a gutsy and prescient personality with unflagging will—Vern C. Gorst. Boeing Aircraft is still another saga of visionary capitalism driven by William E. Boeing, whose beginnings in the industry encompassed both "float plane" production and short haul mail carrying flights in the Puget Sound area between Canada and Seattle. In 1927, Boeing Air Transport began fulfilling the scheduled air mail contract flight between San Francisco and Chicago. Whitehouse, who recounts briefly several of these sagas, makes special note that Boeing, through an old friendship with the CEO of Pratt & Whitney, was priviledged to obtain twenty-five new air-cooled, radial engines "that produced 410 hp and had a cruising speed of 125 mph, carrying 1,200 pounds of mail, two passengers, and the pilot."[20] Although they were being built for Navy fighting planes, the engines were diverted to his 40-A biplanes, which allowed for redesign to increase their payload sufficiently to add $400 extra income from each try, and also for two passengers to be seated in a between-the-wings cabin.

The entrepreneurial stage of expansion of the airline industry now becomes vigorous, and there ensued a flourishing of industry structuring activities consequent to a diversity of interests at work. It is Reeves who provides a very succinct, yet comprehensive, summation of "The Empire Builders and their Realms." His summation is reproduced as an Appendix to this chapter.[21]

Commercial Aviation as an Industry

By the end of the first decade after the Armistice of WWI there was in place a reasoned plan for financial capitalization of aviation considered as a whole industry. Not just an individual airline, but the aviation industry as a complex of interlinked enterprise. Moreover, while it was an industry at a stage only just beyond its early beginnings, it was nonetheless judged to be at a development stage in which it could take advantage of definitely favorable prospects in the years ahead.

It was possible in aviation, between the years 1920-1929, to put together a business entity starting from a single firm—The Curtiss Aeroplane and Motor Company—and culminating in a managerially unified set of transportation related firms. Commercial aviation would be fitted into a more embracing transportation conglomerate. The starting share value of the Curtiss firm was $654,000. By the summer of 1929 their value had risen to $55 million. But the capital value of the companies who made up what Reeves termed an aviation industry "vertical trust" was $175 million at this time. The companies within the "vertical trust" were:

Table 1—The Aviation Industry "Vertical Trust"

Company	Capital at Market Prices (Early Summer, 1929)
Curtiss Aeroplane and Motor Company, Inc.	$55,000,000
Curtiss Flying Service, Inc.	17,000,000
Transcontinental Air Transport, Inc.	12,500,000
National Air Transport, Inc.	13,500,000
Curtiss-Caproni	12,500,000
Curtiss Aeroplane Export Corporation	3,500,000
Curtiss-Robertson Airplane Mfg. Company	1,500,000
Curtiss-Reid Aircraft Company, Ltd.	1,500,000
National Aviation Corporation	15,000,000
North America Aviation, Inc.	35,000,000
Aviation Securities Company	3,000,000
Miscellaneous	5,000,000
	$175,000,000

Source: Reeves, Earl, *Aviation's Place in Tomorrow's Business* (B.C. Forbes Publ. Co., N.Y. City 1930)

The chairman of their finance committee, as well as their President and Board Chairman, was C. M. Keyes, a Canadian teacher of classics who began his business career in the United States as a financial reporter. "I thought I would learn to size up companies and financial issues clearly." His business and industry outlook was by himself expounded in some detail. He took as his guide for the aviation business what he understood to be the policy of General Electric—technological expertise applied to product quality and engineering as the foundation of market domination. Cut wages in critical times? Yes. But! "Never was the engineering budget reduced so much as a nickel. Those of us who could get along without them drew no salaries; but as rapidly as we could we increased the research budget."[22]

Keyes made his choice of securities for financing by reasoning from an historical point of view about how America's successful infant industries had been financed. Equity (stock) rather than debt (bond) financing was preferred. So there were no bonds outstanding for any of the included firms. Moreover, with only two exceptions, there were no preferred shares in the Curtiss companies. The exceptions used preferred stock as the way to provide investors with a guarantee of their investment in the financing of research and development. In sum, common stock financed the plan for the business of aviation. The proceeds from new capital issues were exchanged for the stock of companies brought into the "vertical trust." The aviation industry was to be free of threats from bond holders.

What was the business of aviation? Keyes had a forthright conception of aviation as a business: diversified enterprise, yet capable of both integrated direction and autonomous management; swiftly changing, yet a manageable dynamic; manufacturing elements, but with higher precision, more testing and superior design than that in the automotive industry; foundation for future growth through inventions, development pioneering and acquisitions; market responsive to both military and commercial demands for engines and aircraft; a securities market for aviation financing.

Keyes laid out the separate components of his bundle of building principles for the aviation industry:

" 'Let the best engineering brains design the product. Develop different personnel units for different tasks. Develop a distributor system which is also educational—through schools and through services to the business world. Create an opportunity for the airplane to demonstrate itself. In building air lines, use multiple-engined transports, 2 pilots, provide constant radio communication, to include such a complete meteorological service as will keep the pilot informed of weather conditions over a 100 mile radius. . . . Build a transcontinental trunk line, and let the 'feeders' grow according to traffic demands. And for every part of the industry, provide for constant research, and have ready at hand means of financing a pioneering effort.' "[23]

Clement M. Keyes and his associate, Carl B. Fritsche, had previously organized the Aircraft Development Corporation, an investment group. They had also planned, in 1925, to make Detroit, rather than Chicago, the hub city for aerial transportation and sought to raise one half of a proposed two million dollar fund from Detroit automotive manufacturers to organize an airline between New York and Chicago. This they were unable to do, as "the motorcar men were not too impressed with the prospects of commercial aviation."[24]

Keyes and his associates then turned to Chicago financial sources for the remainder of the two million, which was used to organize the National Air Transport. The authorized capital was a sum then considered extraordinary for the aviation industry— ten million dollars. In May 1926, flying ten Curtiss cargo carrying bi-planes powered by war surplus Liberty engines, National Air Transport began operations. The route was New York- Chicago-Detroit, but Detroit was ignored for a year. Efforts by NAT to get all of the San Francisco-New York route by means of mergers with Western Air Express and with Colonial Air Transport (building a New England Network) were not successful. Since carrying the mail was more profitable (and less of a nuisance) than passenger carrying, NAT resisted the latter until it had to accommodate the passengers delivered at Chicago by Boeing Air Transport for routing on the Chicago-Kansas City link of NAT to Dallas, Texas. The accomodation was done by turning over passenger carrying to another company, Transcontinental Air Transport. This firm was a venture financed by railroad monies—Pennsylvania and Santa Fe and organized by Clement M. Keyes. The actuality of TAT was that "it was a holding company, operating under the cover of an airline while holding blocks of stock in competing airlines."25

The significance of National Air Transport was that by this time, as Whitehouse appraised developments in the aviation industry:

> "Big Business was now crowding out the small-time independent promoter. Pioneer romance had its day. As has been shown, the wartime flier, who had attempted the commercial venture, had risked his life, and to some extent blazed a trail, was not a good businessman—and he seldom had sufficient capital to justify his ambitions. He was soon nudged out when it became evident commercial aviation required a sizeable bank account. Wall Street wizards who seldom left their swivel chairs, stock promoters more skillful in finding investors than boring their way through turbulent skies, and efficient cost analyzers with no interest in shortening the risks between cities, were taking over the business of aviation."26

Pan American Airways was organized in 1927 after the acquisition of Aeromarine Airways which, since 1920, had operated a seasonal 90-mile route between Key West and Havana, Cuba using passenger carrying Fokker planes. The entrepreneurial and organizing brains consisted of a threesome: Juan Trippe and John A. Hambleton and Cornelius Vanderbilt Whitney, the first two of whom were experienced ex-war pilots and had bank connections. A very profitable first-class mail and passenger route, Pan American promptly expanded its terminal facilities—building an international terminal complex in 1928 and extending its routes into the Bahamas. Looking at world air route possibilities for Pan American, Trippe obtained the post office contract for the Seattle to Alaska route.27

By 1934, Pan American had airmail contracts that took it to thirty overseas countries. Its competition was the subsidized European airlines. The competition was for trade routes, as flight routes *were* trade routes. The prize was trade with South America, a two billion dollar prize before WW I. Of that prized commerce, Britain held 30 percent and the United States 16 percent. That war left the European overseas markets open to American penetration. The percentage of South American trade held by American business grew to 26 percent by 1921. However, subsequent to WW I European overseas trade began to make its comeback.

The linkage between aviation and international trade had clearly emerged. Pan American had been building a chain of aviation links to trade throughout the world. It could, by 1936, hook together territorial links to thirty nine countries. Its chains of linkages included a 45 percent interest in China's national airline, the West Indies, Mexico City and feeders to Colombia and Venezuela, the east and west coasts of South America, Alaskan airlines, and a chain of Pacific Islands serviced by its clipper ships. All told, Pan American:

> ". . . ended up owning or leasing 202 air fields, 129 radio stations and the required real estate, necessitating a total investment of more than $5,000,000 and annual rent for leases on operating properties amounting to $300,000.
> Even a cursory consideration will reveal that all this represented an enormous economic market, particularly for American automobile manufacturers, oil companies, international communications companies, and even the motion picture producers in Hollywood. It had become the blood system and nerve network of America's foreign trade. In fact, Pan American now represented a world economic philosophy and became our industrial ambassador, going to any reasonable lengths to promote United States overseas trade. If an American manufacturer wanted to sell shoes in any South American country, Pan Am would collect data on prices, competitors, politics, and the depth of the market. It offered suggestions as to the best way to exploit the market and took all necessary steps when an American salesman got into trouble."[28]

Pan American was now a global firm with global commercial, political and diplomatic presence. It was engaged in competition for transatlantic routes; it had to fight off the competition of German financed and French financed South American and South Atlantic flight routes; it forestalled organized entrepreneurial groups planning to take over the Caribbean market; it had to secure the foreign airmail routes under conditions of competitive bidding; it had to establish and secure a transpacific route; it had to negotiate the operating rights for a North Atlantic route; in all countries it had to obtain the foreign operation rights without which no foreign route could be operated; it had to manage airline operations. All was done under the leadership of Juan Trippe.

The geographic necessities of flight range now required that the technology of advanced plane and engine design be brought into flight planning and execution. For the North Atlantic route, Boeing supplied Pan American with six advanced design Boeing 314 flying boats. These planes had a payload and range that could carry thiry passengers from New York to Southhampton, England. Neither Britain, France nor Germany could match the Boeing 314. In June of 1939, both transatlantic airmail and transatlantic passenger carrying flight were begun. Transpacific passenger flight had been inaugurated in October 1936.

The restructuring of the commercial airline industry, followed upon the hearings (1933) of Senator Hugo Black's Special Committee for Investigation of the Airmail and Ocean Mail Contracts and the enactment of the Air Mail Act of 1934.[29] The legislation mandated separation of the commercial airlines from the manufacturers of aircraft and aircraft engines and components. In the case of United Aircraft and Transport it compelled a reorganization of what was a holding company. The reorganization spun off a manufacturing company, the United Aircraft Company. The reorganization also merged National Air Transport, Boeing Air Transport, Pacific Air Transport and Varney Air Lines. These four were established airlines and they became known as United Air Lines. Finally, there was a transfer of assets for continued operations to the Boeing Airplane Company.[30]

American Airlines also emerged from the reorganization of a nineteen thirties holding company, the $35 million Aviation Corporation. It had bought control of "Braniff, Continental Air Lines, Northern Air Lines, Inc., Universal Airlines, Inc., Air Transportation, Inc., Northrop Air Lines, Inc., Mid-Plane Sales and Transit Company, and Universal Air Lines System Terminal

Company. They were consolidated into American Airways in January 1930, and two years later they were placed under a centralized Operations Department. American Airlines

> ". . . offered the industry's first Curtiss Condo sleeper service, and registered nurses, acting as stewardesses, flitted up and down the aisles, serving first class meals and providing assurance that flying was safe.
> American Airlines made the most of their DC-3 fleet, which, for its day, was the perfect passenger transport. It struck the balance in speed, gross weight, power, pay-load space, and wing area, permitting economies never before obtained."[31]

The history of Eastern Airlines is intertwined with that of the aeronautical complex headed by Clement M. Keyes, North American Aviation, Inc. Its origins were in a New York-to-Atlanta airmail contract route that was expanded to include the Atlanta-to-Miami route. It had the coastal route from New York-to-Miami when it was purchased by NAA. For a number of reasons it was an unprofitable line, but it was saved from extinction when General Motors bought the parent North American Aviation in 1933. It was an airline property that was not sold off by General Motors after the 1934 legislation forced the separation of plane manufacture and airline carriers. "General Motors might have sold Eastern too, if anyone had offered even one million dollars, but the Depression was still a major factor and GM had to hold on."[32]

Captain Eddie Rickenbacker of the 94th Flight Squadron in WW I was working with GM and he was assigned to Eastern as General Manager. With on-hands management, strict economizing, and strenuous around-the-clock maintenance he moved Eastern into profitability and route expansion. Three years of "unprecedented profit" led a Wall Street Syndicate to offer to purchase Eastern for $3,500,000. Rickenbacker obtained a personal option to purchase from Alfred P. Sloan, who was CEO of General Motors. With this option he proceeded to raise sufficient funds to meet the syndicate offer. A period of remarkable growth followed when he became President of Eastern Airlines in 1938.[33]

The year 1938 was the year of the Civil Aeronautics Act of

1938. Competitive price based mail contract routes had long subsidized commercial air transportation. It was a practice that fostered the multiplication of feeder lines, which were short haul lines. Whitehouse lists the period 1920-1928 as the period during which mail contracts were the drivers of growth in commercial aviation. The Board that administered the Civil Aeronautics Act changed the basis for granting airline routes to the public interest.[34]

> "But during the half decade before World War II the American airline industry was far from robust. The network was little more than a hodge-podge of routes established on shoestrings by over-ambitious operators with delusions of wealth, which resulted in an unhealth, weedy growth. There was unnecessary duplication and the acceptance of contracts that promised no future, and many airlines were heading for the same fault of over-extension that the railroads had created for themselves at a comparable stage of development."[35]

REFERENCES

1. Whitehouse, Arch, *The Sky's the Limit: A History of U.S. Airlines* (Macmillan, New York, NY, 1971), p. 112.
2. Ibid., Ch. 5.
3. Ibid., pp. 94-95.
4. Ibid., p. 96.
5. Ibid., p. 117.
6. Ibid., pp. 108-9.
7. Ibid., p. 127.
8. Ibid., p. 103.
9. Ibid., Ch. 12.
10. Ibid., Ch. 9.
11. Ibid., pp. 105-6.
12. Ibid., p. 164.
13. Ibid., pp. 17 et seq. and Ch. 2.
14. Ibid., p. 45.
15. Reeves, Ear, *Aviation's Place in Tomorrow's Business* (B.C. Forbes Publ. Co., (New York, NY, 1930), Appendix p. 310. See, too, Ch. IV, "Building the Air Mail".
16. Whitehouse, p. 107.
17. Ibid., p. 110.

18. Reeves, Ch. VII, provides a laudatory overview of Henry Ford's venture into aircraft production and air transport.
19. Whitehouse, p. 112.
20. Ibid., p. 126. The details are in Chs. 6 and 7 of *The Sky's the Limit*.
21. Reeves, above, n. 15, Ch. VIII.
22. Ibid., p. 93.
23. Ibid., pp. 97-98.
24. Whitehouse, p. 131.
25. Ibid., p. 135.
26. Ibid., p. 132.
27. Whitehouse, pp. 129-30. Aeromarine Airways flew converted twin engine (420 hp. Liberty engines) Navy flying boats that could carry both passengers (eleven) and freight (300 pounds). It operated with both a northern leg ("between New York, Atlantic City, Southhampton, and Newport") and a southern leg ("Miami, Palm Beach, Bimini and Nassau", along with Havana). At its peak in 1924 it operated eleven flying boats, and by then it had flown more than one million miles and carried in excess of 25,000 passengers. According to Whitehouse, it was a well run airline but "it was too early for scheduled airlines to be financially successful." Aeromarine Airways was founded by a successful New York City car dealer.
28. Ibid., p. 207.
29. 48 Stat. L. Pt. II p. 933 (73rd Cong., 2nd Sess. Ch. 466 P.L. 308, 1934) The Airmail Act of 1934.
30. Whitehouse, p. 193.
31. Ibid., p. 197.
32. Ibid., pp. 199-201.
33. Ibid., pp. 201-3.
34. 52 Stat. L. 973, 980 (75th Cong. 3rd Sess. Ch. 601 P.L. 706, 1938). The Civil Aeronautics Act of 1938.
35. Whitehouse, p. 202.

NOTE

U.S. Air had its origins in Adams Air Express, a firm established by Dr. Lytle S. Adams, who was educated as a dental surgeon. His real interest was the invention of an airmail pickup device which would dispense with the necessity of the plane landing. Starting as far back as 1923, and working from Cabot's patented 19th century invention for the pickup of mail bags from speeding trains, Dr. Adams obtained patents for his own device for air pickup of mail. His original financing was his own capital. Through William E. Boeing he was provided with technical assistance by Boeing's engineers. Successful test experiments were conducted in 1928 on Boeing's factory airfield.

There then followed an intense ten year search for financial backing and for airmail contracts. Dr. Adams had established (1929) two companies: The Airways Patent Holding Corporation and Adams Air Express. The purpose of the latter was to interest small towns in a tri-state area to initiate an express or airmail service. It was not until 1938 that he found the critical source of private capital. It was Richard C. duPont. Dr. Adams had been recommended to him by duPont's cousin, who had met Dr. Adams at a dinner meeting given by Mrs. Roosevelt at Hyde Park.

Richard C. duPont was a licensed pilot. He was also experienced as a glider pilot. In his youth he had been enthusiastic about model planes. There was loan agreement between the two men. The loan terms of August 1938 under which duPont provided capital to Dr. Adams specified as collateral the assignment of certain critical patents and a stock purchase option agreement that included both non-voting and voting stock. A shadow corporation of Dr. Adams—All American Aviation—was activated and a further agreement concerning it was entered into with duPont. Three of the five board of directors were duPont controlled. Executive, managerial and financial administration was also controlled. Subsequently a deep and bitter feud developed between Dr. Adams and duPont, who had been elected President of All American Aviation. The latter exercised the stock options that were his under the 1938 loan agreement, the exercise of which invested him with controlling interest in All American Aviation.

See, for the history of the corporation which became U.S. Air, Lewis, W. David and Trimble, William F., *The Airway to Everywhere* (U. of Pitts. Press 1988).

See, for the history of Pan Am, the volume by Bender, Marylin and Altschul, Selig, *The Chosen Instrument: The Rise and Fall of an American Entrepreneur* (Simon and Schuster, NY 1982).

APPENDIX

Aviation's Place in Tomorrow's Business

by Earl Reeves
B.C. Forbes Publishing Company, New York City (1930)

CHAPTER VIII

The Empire Builders and Their Realms

The Harrimans, Hills and Goulds of the aviation industry now are beginning to be discernible.

In the public mind, Wright, Curtiss, and Lindbergh are the names which have stood for aeronautical achievement. But after the pioneer comes always the builder.

Of the "empire builders of the air," three stood head and shoulders above all the others, early in 1929. They were:

C.M. Keys, who was a financial editor.
Richard F. Hoyt, a banker.
W.E. Boeing, a lumber baron of the far Northwest.

Keys headed up the various Curtiss interests. Hoyt was chairman of the Wright Aeronautical Corporation, and partner in the banking house of Hayden, Stone and Company. Boeing had come into aviation through the manufacture, during a dozen years, of airplanes, chiefly for government use.

Around the Curtiss plants at Garden City, Long Island, and

Buffalo, N.Y., the Wright engine unit at Paterson, N.J., and the Boeing airplane factory at Seattle, Wash., these three have built what are in effect "vertical trusts," with units active in many phases of aeronautical industry, commerce and transportation.

The mergers which followed, in the race for continental honors, brought to the fore other units:

W. Averill Harriman, as chairman, and Robert Lehman, as chairman of the executive committee, headed up Aviation Corporation which started with a $40,000,000 issue of an authorized $200,000,000 capital. The chief industrial unit was Fairchild and the major transport company was Universal Aviation Corporation.

A fifth group had moved eastward from the coast. Western Air Express, under the leadership of Harris M. Hanshue, had expanded and assumed control of the Fokker Aircraft Corporation of America. James A. Talbot, of Richfield Oil, became chairman of the board. Later, General Motors acquired a 40 per cent interest in Fokker Aircraft and planned wide expansion. Western Air Express pushed a transcontinental line eastward, while Fokker engineers built a plant at Glendale, W. Va., and designed one for Los Angeles, and the General Motors program was to include plants in many other cities.

In August, 1929, the industrial interests headed by Richard F. Hoyt and C.M. Keys were merged in a 12-company consolidation, the Curtiss-Wright Corporation. In this corporation were units then having an aggregate market value of more than $220,000,000. Transport units were not included.

In the present rapid progress of aviation, no description of alignments can be rated as of lasting value. Nevertheless, a rough delineation of these new business empires becomes significant. A sort of tabloid survey of these big units is attempted in what follows:

BOEING-RENTSCHLER-UNITED—The National City Bank helped to organize and participate in financing of United Aircraft and Transport, for which 1,000,000 shares of $50 par, A stock was authorized; as well as a common stock issue of 2,500,000 shares. Outstanding, in August, 1929, were 240,000 A shares and 1,557,308 shares of no-par common stock.

Chief United units were:

Boeing Airplane Company of Seattle, which had a floor area of 300,000 square feet and additional units under construction. Boeing Air Transport operated air-mail and passenger lines, Seattle to Los Angeles, 1,080 miles, San Francisco to Chicago, 2,018 miles.

Pratt and Whitney Aircraft Company, manufacturer of "Wasp" and "Hornet" air-cooled engines, located at Hartford, Conn.

Chance Vought Corporation, of Long Island City, N.Y., leading manufacturer of military planes.

Hamilton Metal Plane Company, pioneer builder of amphibians.

Stearman Aircraft Corporation, of Wichita, Kan.

Stout Air Services, Incorporated, which was a development of the Ford-Stout plane building and transport operating experiments.

HOYT-WRIGHT.—Richard F. Hoyt, headed it up as chairman.

Wright Aeronautical Corporation, builder of the famous "Whirlwind" engines and of the latest "Cyclone" models.

Aviation Corporation of America, which owns Pan-American Airways, the first big international air transportation system of the Western hemisphere.

Keystone Aircraft Corporation, of Bristol, Pa., lately builder of an overwhelming majority of the army bombers, as well as of the 20-passenger "Patrician" transport.

Travel Air Manufacturing Company, plane builder of Wichita, Kan., which has forged to the front in quantity production of open and closed models.

Moth Aircraft, manufacturer of light sport and training planes.

Aviation Credit Corporation, which underwrites time payments.

New York Air Terminals, Incorporated.

CURTISS-KEYS.—The Keys group includes engine and

plane manufacturing, sales and service, transportation and finance. The central company is the Curtiss Aeroplane and Motor Company, Incorporated.

A subsidiary, Curtiss-Robertson, of St. Louis, manufactures an enclosed model commercial plane.

Curtiss-Reid Aircraft Company, Ltd., operates an airplane factory, an airport, and sales organizations in Canada.

Curtiss-Caproni acquired American rights to and proposed to build seaplane models designed by Gianni Caproni, the Italian designer and constructor.

The Sperry Gyroscope Company produces gyroscopic, mechanical, electrical, and aeronautical equipment.

Curtiss Flying Service operates on 35 fields and sales agencies and schools, selling planes manufactured by Curtiss and other makes as well.

Curtiss Aero Export Company handles foreign sales for the various units.

National Air Transport operates the air mail for New York to Chicago and Dallas. Transcontinental Air Transport operates the New York-Los Angeles air-rail route, of which the rail links are furnished by the Pennsylvania and the Santa Fe railroads.

In this corporation also are finance companies; the biggest of these being North American Aviation, a $30,000,000 concern:

CURTISS-WRIGHT.—Of the foregoing groups the following are included in the Curtiss-Wright Corporation by exchange of stock: Curtiss Airports, Curtiss Flying Service, Curtiss Aeroplane Export Company, Curtiss-Caproni Corporation, Curtiss-Robertson Airplane Manufacturing Company; Wright Aeronautical Corporation; Keystone Aircraft Corporation; Moth Aircraft Corporation; New York Air Terminals and Travel Air Manufacturing Company.

AVIATION CORPORATION.—In this group are the various Fairchild companies, devoted to manufacturing planes, building aero cameras, and operating photographic services, and aerial surveys. Fairchild has built various plane models and for some time was the leading builder of enclosed planes. He is now concentrating on a seven-passenger transport.

A subsidiary, Krieder-Reisner Aircraft Corporation, of Hagerstown, Md., manufactures a line of open cockpit planes.

Aviation Corporation owns a heavy interest in Advance Aircraft Company of Troy, Ohio, builder of "Waco" models, and, in point of numbers, the biggest builder of open planes during the last few years.

Transport units owned by Aviation Corporation include Universal Aviation Corporation, Colonial Airways Corporation, Southern Air Transport, Interstate Air Lines, and Enbry-Riddle Aviation Corporation. These lines include air-mail contracts over 4,675 miles and they operate a combined air-mail-passenger mileage of 9,128 miles, servicing 62 cities. Aviation Corporation owns and operates six airports.

Several western units were consolidated in Detroit Aircraft Corporation, which had an authorized capitalization of 2,000,000 no-par shares of which 887,769 were outstanding.

Several accessory units were grouped in Bendix-Aviation in which General Motors was a heavy owner. This corporation had a 3,000,000 share authorization of which more than 2,000,000 shares had been issued soon after its formation.

A list of leading aviation corporations of the country, or of those which had attained such financial importance that their shares were listed on various exchanges, is given in the following tables.

Public Law Ch. 466, No. 308; 48 statutes at Large Pt. I 933 (June 12, 1934)

p. 936   Sec. 7 (a) After December 31, 1934, it shall be unlawful for any person holding an air-mail contract to buy, acquire, hold, own, or control, directly or indirectly, any shares of stock or other interest in any other partnership, association, or corporation engaged directly or indirectly in any phase of the aviation industry, whether so engaged through air transporation of passengers, express, or mail, facture or sale of airplanes, airplane parts, or other materials or accessories generally used in air transportation, and regardless of whether such buying, acquisition, holding, ownership, or control is done directly, or is accomplished indirectly, through an agent, subsidiary, associate, affiliate, or by any other device whatsoever: *Provided*, That

(*continued on page 168*)

AVIATION COMPANIES, CAPITALIZATION, AUGUST, 1929
(As compiled by B.H. Cram)

Name of company	Capitalization			Listed	Type of company
	Stock authorized	Stock issued	Par		
Aeromarine Klemm	320,000	242,000	$5	O.C.	M
Aeronautical Industries	500,000	100,000	No	N.Y.C.	I
Aero Supply "A"	25,000	25,000	No	N.Y.C.	A
Aero Supply "B"	500,000	379,000	No	N.Y.C.	A
Aero Underwriters	250,000	141,297	No	N.Y.C.	I
Air Investors	1,500,000	158,255	No	N.Y.C.	I
Air Investors (Pfd.)	250,000	90,000	No	N.Y.C.	I
Airstocks, Inc.	250,000	100,000	No	O.C.	I
Alexander Industries	500,000	304,617	No	N.Y.C.	M
Alexander Industries (Pfd.)	6,000	5,850	$100	O.C.	A
Allied Aviation Industries	500,000	110,000	No	O.C.	D
American Aeronautical Corporation "A"	150,000	105,000	No	O.C.	M
American Aeronautical Corporation "B"	500,000	287,000	No		
American Eagle	2,000,000	200,000	No	O.C.	M
Aviation Corporation[4]	10,000,000	3,035,603	No	N.Y.S.E.	M and T
Aviation Corporation of America	1,000,000	228,333	No	N.Y.C.	I
Bach Aircraft	1,000,000	850,00	No	L.A.	M

(*continued*)

AVIATION COMPANIES, CAPITALIZATION, AUGUST, 1929 (Continued)
(As compiled by B.H. Cram)

Name of company	Capitalization			Listed	Type of company
	Stock authorized	Stock issued	Par		
Belianca Aircraft	500,000	175,000	No	N.Y.C.	M
Bendix Aviation	3,000,000	2,250,000	No	N.Y.S.E.	A
Berliner-Joyce Aircraft "A"	50,000	40,000	No	O.C.	M
Berliner-Joyce Aircraft "B"	40,000	37,918	No		
Brunner Winkle Aircraft	250,000	70,000	No	O.C.	M
Central Airport, Inc.	500,000	206,250	No	O.C.	D
Cessna Aircraft[1]	50,000	27,500	No	O.C.	M
Consolidated Aircraft	750,000	550,000	No	N.Y.C.	M
Consolidated Instrument	200,000	192,000	No	N.Y.C.	A
Curtiss Aero Export (Com.)[1]	100,000	75,000	No	N.Y.C.	ES
Curtiss Aero Exprot (PFD.)[1]	50,000	37,000	$10	O.C.	
Curtiss Aero and Motor[1]	600,000	348,896	No	N.Y.S.E.	M
Curtiss Airports Corporation[1]	5,000,000	2,500,000	No	N.Y.C.	D
Curtiss-Caproni Corporation[1]	1,000,000	400,000	No	O.C.	M
Curtiss Flying Service Inc.[1]	2,000,000	750,000	No	N.Y.C.	S
Curtiss-Reid Aircraft (Com.)[1]	300,000	100,000	No	O.C.	M
Curtiss-Reid Aircraft (Pfd.)[1]	50,000	50,000	$30	O.C.	

(continued)

AVIATION COMPANIES, CAPITALIZATION, AUGUST, 1929 (Continued)
(As compiled by B.H. Cram)

Name of company	Capitalization			Listed	Type of company
	Stock authorized	Stock issued	Par		
Curtiss-Robertson Airplane Co.[1]	100,000	60,000	No	O.C.	M
Curtiss-Wright Corporation "A"[1]	2,000,000	1,050,000	No	O.C.	I
Curtiss-Wright Corporation "B"[1]	10,000,000	6,500,000	No		
Dayton Airplane Engine	100,000	100,000	No	N.Y.C.	ME
Detroit Aircraft Corporation[2]	2,000,000	887,769	No	N.Y.C.	D
Douglas Aircraft	1,000,000	345,000	No	N.Y.C.	M
Fairchild Aviation "A"[4]	750,000	700,895	No	N.Y.C.	M
Fokker Aircraft (Com.)	1,000,000	949,900	No	N.Y.C.	M
Fokker Aircraft (1st Pfd.)	40,000	30,144	$25	O.C.	M
Great Lakes Aircraft "A"	500,000	200,000	No	C.S.E.	M
Great Lakes Aircraft "B"	500,000	300,000	No	O.C.	
Inter-Allied Aeronautics	1,200,000	300,000	No	O.C.	I
Irving Air Chute	300,000	200,000	No	N.Y.C.	A
Keystone Aircraft[1]	300,000	287,572	No	N.Y.C.	M
Lincoln Aircraft	125,000	112,500	No	O.C.	M
Lockheed Aircraft[2]	150,000	138,500	No	O.C.	M
Maddux Air Lines[3]	265,000	155,000	No	O.C.	T

(*continued*)

AVIATION COMPANIES, CAPITALIZATION, AUGUST, 1929 (Continued)
(As compiled by B.H. Cram)

Name of company	Capitalization		Par	Listed	Type of company
	Stock authorized	Stock issued			
Mahoney-Ryan Aircraft[1]	100,000	45,000	No	O.C.	M
Moth Aircraft "A"[1]	100,000	30,000	No	O.C.	M
Moth Aircraft "B"[1]	100,000	65,000	No	O.C.	M
National Air Transport	2,000,000	650,000	No	N.Y.S.E.	T
National Aviation	500,000	211,660	No	N.Y.C.	M
New Standard Aircraft	200,000	61,000	No	O.C.	M
North American Aviation	6,000,000	2,000,000	No	N.Y.C.	T
Pollack Manufacturing	100,000	100,000	No	N.Y.C.	A
Sikorsky Aviation[3]	500,000	220,000	No	N.Y.C.	T
Southern Air Transport	1,000,000	300,000	No	O.C.	T
Standard Steel Propeller	300,000	129,000	No	N.Y.C.	A
Stearman Aircraft[5]	100,000	75,000	No	O.C.	M
Stinson Aircraft	150,000	123,905	No	Det.	M
Swallow Airplane Company	100,000	49,000	No	O.C.	M
Transcontinental Air Transport[5]	1,000,000	525,000	No	N.Y.C.	T
Travel Air Company	100,000	97,940	No	N.Y.C.	M

(continued)

AVIATION COMPANIES, CAPITALIZATION, AUGUST, 1929 (Continued)
(As compiled by B.H. Cram)

Name of company	Capitalization		Par	Listed	Type of company
	Stock authorized	Stock issued			
United Aircraft and Transport Corporation[3]	2,500,000	1,557,305	No	N.Y.S.E.	M and T
United Aircraft and Transport "A"[3]	1,000,000	240,000	$70	N.Y.S.E.	M and T
Universal Aviation[4]	500,000	321,564	No	N.Y.C.	I
U.S. Air Transport	150,000	120,000	No	O.C.	T
Waco Aircraft Company	200,000	145,000	No	N.Y.C.	M
Warner Aircraft	500,000	400,000	No	O.C.	ME
Whittelsey Manufacturing "A"	500,000	240,000	No	O.C.	M
Whittelsey Manufacturing "B"	1,000,000	420,000	No	O.C.	
Wright Aeronautical[1]	1,500,000	600,000	No	N.Y.S.E.	ME

Code.—*N.Y.S.E., New York Stock Exchange. N.Y.C., New York Curb Market. O.C., New York Over-the-counter Market. C.S.E., Chicago Stock Exchange. L.A., Los Angeles. Det., Detroit. A, Accessories. D, Development. ES, Export Sales. I, Investment. M, Aircraft Manufacturer. E, Engine Manufacturer. T, Transport. S, Sales.*

[1] Part of Curtiss-Wright group.
[2] Part of Detroit Aircraft group.
[3] Part of United Aircraft and Transportation group.
[4] Part of Aviation Corporation group.
[5] Part of Transcontinental Air Transport group.

The chief air transport "empires" are shown in the following summarizing tables.

THE AVIATION CORPORATION PASSENGER SYSTEM

Route	Mileage	
	Route	Total
Colonial Airways Corporation:		
New York-Boston	191	
New York-Montreal	332	
Albany-Cleveland	443	
Buffalo-Toronto	62	1,028
Universal Aviation Corporation:		
Cleveland-Garden City	1,082	
Cleveland-Louisville	316	
Chicago-St. Louis	287	
Chicago-Kansas City	503	
Kansas City-Omaha	165	
Kansas City-Wichita	191	
Kansas City-Oklahoma City-San Angelo	681	
Wichita-Tulsa-Wewoka-Dallas-Fort Worth	417	
Tulsa-Oklahoma City	100	
Oklahoma City-Wewoka	67	
Oklahoma City-Amarillo	241	4,050
Embry-Riddle Aviation Corporation		
Chicago-Indianapolis-Cincinnati	270	270
Interstate Air Lines:		
Chicago-Evansville-Atlanta	640	
Evansville-St. Louis	145	
Evansville-Louisville	100	885
Southern Air Transport:		
Dallas-Galveston	292	
Waco-San Antonio-Brownsville	435	
Dallas-Fort Worth-Abilene-El Paso	575	1,302
Additional mail only routes		1,593
Harriman total		9,128

CURTISS-KEYS GROUP

Route	Mileage	
	Route	Total
National Air Transport:		
New York-Chicago	718	
Chicago-Dallas	995	
Ponca City-Tulsa	76	
Toledo-Detroit	45	1,834
Transcontinental Air Transport:		1,974
Pitcairn Aviation:		
New York-Atlanta	769	
Atlanta-Miami	622	
Tampa-Daytona Beach	129	1,520
Maddux Air Lines:		
San Francisco-Los Angeles	378	
Los Angeles-Phoenix	414	792
Keys total		6,100

HOYT-PAN AMERICAN

Route	Mileage	
	Route	Total
Miami to Nassau, Miami to Cuba, Haiti, Dominican Republic, Mexico, British Honduras, Honduras, Nicaragua, Costa Rica, Panama, Canal Zone, Colombia, Ecuador, Peru, Chili, Windward and Leeward Isles, Trinidad, Dutch Guiana, British Guiana.		
Operation, September, 1929		12,400
Santiago, Chili, to Buenos Aires, Argentina, and Montevideo, Uruguay		
Optioned and in preparation		950
Hoyt total		13,350
(Under survey, 2,500 miles.)		

BOEING-UNITED AIRCRAFT AND TRANSPORT

Route	Mileage	
	Route	Total
Boeing Air Transport:		
Chicago-San Francisco	2,018	
Seattle-Los Angeles	1,080	3,098
Stout Air Services:		
Detroit-Cleveland	134	
Detroit-Chicago	252	
Detroit-Buffalo	218	604
Boeing total		3,702

HANSHUE-WESTERN AIR EXPRESS

Route	Mileage	
	Route	Total
Los Angeles-Kansas City	1,425	
Los Angeles-Salt Lake City	600	
Los Angeles-San Francisco	365	
Cheyenne-Pueblo	200	
Los Angeles-Tia Juana	120	
Los Angeles-Lake Arrowhead	70	
Los Angeles-Catalina	45	
Hanshue total	2,825	

A detailed table covering all air transport will be found in the Appendix of this volume.

(continued from page 160)

the prohibitions herein contained shall not extend to interests in landing fields, hangars, or other ground facilities necessarily incidental to the performance of the transportation service of such air-mail contractor, nor to shares of stock in corporations whose principal business is the maintenance or operation of such landing fields, hangars, or other ground facilities.

(b) After December 31, 1934, it shall be unlawful (1) for any partnership, association, or corporation, the principal business of which, in purpose or in fact, is the holding of stock in other corporations, or (2) for any partnership, association, or corporation engaged directly or indirectly in any phase of the aviation industry, as specified in subsection (a) of this section, to buy, acquire, hold, own, or control, directly or indirectly, either as specified in such subsection (a) or otherwise, any shares of stock or other interests in any other partnership, association, or corporation which holds an air-mail contract.

(c) No person shall be qualified to enter upon the performance of an air-mail contract, or thereafter to hold an air-mail contract, if at or after the time specified for the commencement of mail transportation under such contract, such person is (or, if a partnership, association, or corporation, has and retains a member, officer, or director that is) a member, officer, director, or stockholder in any other partnership, association, or corporation, whose principal business, in purpose or in fact, is the holding of stock in other corporations, or which is engaged in any phase of the aviation industry, as specified in subsection (a) of this section.

(d) No person shall be qualified to enter upon the performance of, or thereafter to hold an air-mail contract, (1) if at or after the time specified for the commencement of mail transportation under such contract, such person is, (or, if a partnership, association, or corporation, has a member, officer, or director, or an employee performing general managerial duties, that is) an individual who has theretofore entered into any unlawful combination to prevent the making of any bids for carrying the mails: *Provided*, That whenever required by the Postmaster General the bidder submit an affidavit executed by the bidder, or by such of its officers, directors, or general managerial employees as the Postmaster General may designate, swear to before an officer authorized and empowered to administer oaths, stating in such affidavit that the officiant has not entered nor proposed to enter into any combination to prevent the making of any bid for carrying the mails, nor made any agreement, or given or performed, or promised . . . etc. . . . any consideration whatever to induce any other person to bid or not to bid for any mail contract, or (2) or if it pays any officer, director, or ----- employee compensation in any form exceeding $17,500 per year full times.

CHAPTER XI

The Knowledge of Internal Variety: Industrialized Biology

1.
THE INDUSTRIALIZATION OF BIOLOGICAL KNOWLEDGE

The Empty Person of Biology

THE BIOLOGICAL KNOWLEDGE of internal variety is the knowledge of life phenomena. It is the knowledge of life phenomena in both the animate (organic) and inanimate (non-organic) modes of its materiality. It is not the knowledge of human beings *qua* persons. It is the knowledge of humans as a varietal form/type /species/category/evolutional mode of materialized life phenomena. It is knowledge accumulated from investigation into the internal variety of their substance as material entities. The mode of the materiality of human beings is such that, as investigative objects, they can be made to yield up the concealed inwardness of their structure, composition, substances, organs, processes and bio-systems. They yield to application of the techniques, instruments, concepts, methods and procedures of the various fields of scientific investigation—mechanical, chemical, structural, electrical, microscopical, cytological, physical and so on. As investigative objects, they are reducible to the analytic knowledge of physics, chemistry, and mechanics whereby life phenomena are understood, controlled, managed, produced, transformed, generated and modified. In sum, the knowledge of internal variety that is rooted in biology has located humans within the life space of a structured place that is part of the material fundament which, in turn, is the physical ground inseparable from the life phenomena themselves. The human being, because of the focus of the knowledge of biology on life phenomena, remains an empty person.

Materiality and the Knowledge of Life Phenomena

Thus it is that the knowledge of biology parallels the first requisite of the thematic scheme of Braudel with respect to capitalism and civilization—"Material life." But he uses this phrase as a synonym, for "material civilization," which he likens to a primary layer of human activity as an earth cover, functioning as the elementary infrastructure of the market economy.[1] With biology, rather, it is the precondition itself, the inseparable conjoining of life *per se* with materiality; the manifold of materiality through which and within which life phenomena exist.

The applied biological knowledge of internal variety enters into Braudel's "Material civilization" as historical "biological regimes." These are regimes of plague, epidemics and disease. These are also drink, drugs and foodstuffs—the centuries of dietary foods, of seasonings and condiments, of sugar, of alcoholic and non-alcoholic stimulants—tea, coffee and tobacco.[2] There are recorded historical relationships between cultures, production of foodstuffs, food motivated migrations, population growth, social inequalities and diets, food deficiencies and their related illnesses, and cultivated foods and particular civilizations.

There were, however, a variety of market economies for these cultivated products for human consumption. There were food merchants. There were logistical networks. There were food cargoes, modes of traffic, and traffic between geographical areas and between continents. Still, it was pre-scientific; pre-industrial; small scale; risky; low return except in cases of crisis;

low investment; dominated by independent small merchants. In sum, it was micro-capitalist.

It was not until after the discovery of America that Braudel refers to the appearance of "dietary revolutions." He locates them in the eighteenth century and assigns to them a 200 year time frame for their completion.

> "Cultivated food plants are constantly reaching new areas where they can completely alter people's lives. But their natural movements can take centuries or millennia. After the discovery of America, however, such movements became more frequent and faster. The plants of the Old World travelled to the New, and in return New World plants reached the Old: in one direction went rice, wheat, sugar cane and coffee; in the other maize, potatoes, haricot beans, tomatoes, manioc and tobacco."[3]

Industrialized Microbiology and "Real Captialism"

With industrial microbiology the historical stage of "micro-capitalism" is relegated to past history and succeeded by the present stage, which is an historical stage termed by Braudel as that of "real capitalism."[4] Industrial microbiology includes the domains of microbiology, of immunology, of bio-chemistry, of molecular biology, and of microbial genetics. Basic research and applied research are combined; science and technology are synergized; industrial micro-organisms are made to order. The new developments in industrial microbiology refer to an emerging biotechnology, to genetic engineering, and to recombinant DNA. Demain and Solomon have listed the characteristics shared by all micro-organisms:

> First. Small size, and hence, a high surface to volume ratio. High metabolic rate, i.e. a high rate of microbial biosynthesis.
> Second. Adapt to inexpensive nutrients and are capable of a wide variety of metabolic reactions.
> Third. Wide range of support environments, but environmental requirements enable the division of micro-organisms into three groups.[5]

Pharmaceuticals

The production of pharmaceuticals through micro-biology includes antibiotics, vitamins, steroids, hormones, alkaloids, antitumor drugs, synthetic insulin, and interferons (antivirals). The scale to which the commercial market for clinically important pharmaceuticals has risen is indicated in the following:

> "In 1979 the wholesale value of prescription drugs sold in the U.S. was about $7.5 billion. Of this amount some 20 percent, or $1.5 billion, represented sales of drugs in whose production microorganisms played a significant role."
>
> The largest class of pharmaceuticals consist of those in which most or all of the required genetic information is present in the unaltered genome of the cell. The antibiotics are the most important members of this class economically, but also included are viral and bacterial antigens, antifungal agents, certain antitumor drugs, alkeloids and vitamins. In 1978 the worldwide bulk sales of the four most important groups of antibiotics . . . amounted to $4.2 billion [adjusted to 1980 prices] . . . After the antibiotics the pharmaceuticals with the next highest sales were the vitamins; the wholesale value of the six most important vitamins in 1978 [adjusted to 1980 prices] was $670 million."[6] (Brackets are author's)

The foregoing does not include the market for steroids ($300 million world bulk sales of the four major steroids in 1978). Nor does it include the possible market for the bacterially synthesized human (not the animal) insulin. And there is yet the possible market for the synthesized human growth hormone for the remedial treatment of forms of dwarfism. As for the application of recombinant DNA methods to the production of interferons, it "may well represent the next great advance in clinical medicine and in the industrial practices of the pharmaceuticals industry."[7]

Still, the most radical departure of all is marked as that in which the antibiotics were introduced. The drug associated with the start of the antibiotic or "wonder drug" era is penicillin. The roots of its discovery go back to the 1870's, but actual discovery was not until 1928, when, by accident, Fleming observed its bacteria inhibiting qualities and successfully set about growing and separating it as a cell free liquid. But, despite repeated experiments by British chemists, it remained an unstable substance throughout the 1930's. The production of stable penicillin became an acutal reality starting in 1941 with a cooperative research project between British chemists, the U.S. Department of Agiculture and certian American pharmaceutical companies.

Industrial Microorganisms

As between chemical (or non-biological) synthesis and microbiological production of industrial chemicals, the expert judgement is that the combination of economic considerations and recombinant DNA techniques will favor microbiological fermentation as the more attractive choice for the future. The commercial exploitation of enzymes for their catalytic function began in the 1890's. As for the aliphatic organic compounds, the solvent industry has its base in these compounds. Industrial organic acids (acetic acid, citric acid, lactic acid) are also to be found in the second class of industrial chemicals. In their making there is competition between the chemical and the microbiological processes of manufacture. Amino acids (the third class of industrial chemicals) are made both by chemical synthesis and by microbiological production (fermentation). Research in microbiology and recombinant DNA techniques is directed to increasing the efficiency of fermentative production. The prediction is that in time biological methods will dominate the production of all amino acids. "The outlook for the amino acid industry is bright because of new and expanded markets."[8]

The diversity of the product derivatives of micro-organisms is astounding. They are enumerated by Eveleigh as follows:

> "Microorganisms also produce industrial chemicals that can either serve as or be employed to make solvents, lubricants, emollients, demulcents, extractants, adhesives, acidulants, plastics, surface coatings, explosives, propellants, gasoline additives, alternative fuels, pesticides, dyes, cosmetics, antifreeze, brake fluid, meat tenderizers, digestive acids, vitamins and flavorings."[9]

Food, Drink and Microbiological Production

Here scientifically understood and controlled microbial activity enters into a variety of industries—alcoholic beverages (beer, wine and distilled spirits), food preservation (brine treatment and fermentation), food protein enhancement (fish and soybean fermentation), breadmaking, yeast making, and the dairy industry (fermented milk products). The improvement of established empirical technologies is one path of development in the microbiological production of food and drink. Another is the path of genetic manipulation or engineering of strains of microorganisms, either as part of a search for more efficient strains or as programs tailored to achieve specific changes in foods and beverages.[10]

2.
THE KNOWLEDGE OF REGULATION: THE LIFE PHENOMENA MARKET

Regulative Cognition, Biological Knowledge and Varietal Regulation of the Life Phenomena Market

The expanding corpus of modern industrialized biological knowledge is in actuality the economic and technological infrastructure for markets of microbiological product regimes that may appropriately be generally designated as the life phenomena market. In ordinary products it includes the categories of food, drugs and cosmetics. It enters in a determinative way into not just the "biological regimes" as discussed by Braudel, but also into life styles, longevity cultures, biological reproductive practices, dietary beliefs, medical remedies and medicinal habits. Upon these are contructed the market economics of a particular civilization.

Knowledge of the internal variety respecting life phenomena that is biological knowledge is thus the fundament from which emerges an immense and continuing infusion of variety into the structures, the practices, the perspectives, the culture and the economic activity of social, institutional, familial and individual existence itself. As to this varietal infusion, it is a variety that historically has not, and contemporaneously does not, and futuristically will not, endure without regulative constraints. So biological knowledge—the knowledge of internal variety—and varietal regulation are of a piece.

Regulative Cognition

The variety of biological knowledge is the knowledge of the variety internal to organic entities. The utilization of this knowledge emerges as an object of regulative cognition. Regulative cognition transcends positive law.

Regulation exists because of humans, but that is not to say that it necessarily exists in humans at the level of regulative cognition. Biological regulation is present within humans because they are living organisms, and such organisms exhibit biological regulation. There is, in fact, a domain of biological science described as "Regulatory Biology." It is concerned with regulatory processes in biological systems. There is a treatise that deals with "biological regulators" as a set of different and distinctive homeostatic mechanisms of a dynamic character, but which also gives notice that homeostasis is inadequately explanatory of biological regulation. Here the understanding of the regulative within humans as biological regulation is the understanding of humans as the empty persons of biological knowledge.[11]

It is in ordinary experience of humans that there exists, however pragmatic or rudimentary, the ground for the cognitive understanding of the regulative. It is an understanding that provides a platform of reasoning for the design of structures of regulation and control. The cybernetics of Wiener was its first scientific expression. The further clarification of that understanding as an intelligible principle of cognition is the contribution of W. Ross Ashby.

It was he who noted that the regulative is not comprehensible except in relation to the notion of variety.[12] In the face of a tendency towards absolute variety, the regulative will tend to exist at some variety matching level. Implicit in the notion of the regulative is a limitation of variety. Relative variety is the potentiality for variety within a set of possibilities. The regulative functions as a constraint on the potentiality for variety by limiting actual variety to some portion of the relative variety of a set of possibilities. This varietal limiting is control. The relationship between varietal regulation and control is the focus of regulative cognition.

Regulative Capability, Regulative Intelligence and Strategic Knowledge

The regulative surfaces in the *cybernetics* of Ashby is an aspect of the possibilities of mechanism and information. Within the cybernetic frame of reference the regulative is a capability. It is a capability in the sense of being an objective system property. The regulative becomes a system property because it can be made a matter of design of mechanism. These technical solutions to specific design questions can achieve a particular system capability as an objective property of the system. Mechanism and information, functioning with a certain control capability as a consequence of design, would exhibit the attributes of an intelligence like that of regulative cognition.

Nonetheless, regulative cognition in the frame work of cybernetics stops short of strategic knowledge. In the cybernetic frame concern is fixed on what controls varietal regulation in the context of the logic, structure, technology, mechanism, information and processes applicable to the relative variety of a particular system. Design has its own ends and requisites with respect to varietal capability of that particular system.

Strategic Knowledge and the Knowledge of Variety

Strategic knowledge involves the push-the break out- of managed relative variety towards the knowledge of absolute variety. Absolute variety takes the knowledge of strategy beyond the cybernetics of mechanism, information and objective systems capability. The end of the knowledge of strategy becomes the knowledge whereby to multiply the categories of variety itself.

The knowledge of variety is finite at a given stage of time, but unbounded in the progressive accumulation of human knowledge of materiality over time. What takes place as varietal cognition is disclosed by an insightful perception contained in an appraisal of developments about the theory of matter in the light of discoveries in nuclear physics.

> "For ordinary purposes, the world is contained between limits represented by the terrestrial radius of 6,370 km, or 6.3710^8 cm on one hand, and by the dimensions of bacteria, i.e. 0.1u or 10^{-5} cm on the other hand. Within these limits, Euclidian geometry and classical mechanics are in agreement with experiment and thus play a useful role.
>
> But man has carried his experiments well beyond these limits into the realm of the atom and into that of the stars. Now, the radius of the atomic nucleus is 10^{-13} cm, and the distance separating us from the nearest star is 310^{18} cm. The proven everyday tools were found wanting when it came to these dimensions. Other tools had to be forged, of which the old ones were a very good approximation on our normal scale.
>
> Einstein's mechanics and Riemann's geometry were the new tools which allowed men to extend his knowledge well beyond the limits within which he had previously been held prisoner."[13]

The foregoing has its parallels in the invention of the electron microscope (prior to which viruses were not directly observable) and in the invention of the achromatic lens (enabling finely detailed observation of cell structure); in successful organ transplant (Barnard, 1967); in the discovery of the DNA molecule (genetics); in the discovery of intracellular structures (organelles), and so on.

These are all extensions of the material limits of possible cognitions of categories of variety within the manifold of absolute variety. These are all extensions as to which consciousness perceives and arrives at an understanding of their possibilities for varietal innovations that possess attributes of significance for the investment structures of whole economies. So it is that the concern of strategy under the conditions of "real capitalism" is the enlargement of the cognized manifold of absolute variety. Varietal multiplication and extension is rooted in scientific discovery and technological innovation. Its effects on whole economies is traceable as periodic spasms of economic growth and development.[14]

Thus it is that through the managed knowledge of variety the latter becomes the knowledge of strategy, and that this knowledge, in turn, becomes the cognitive understanding for the choices to be made by Braudel's "real capitalism." For Braudel technology is the queen of change, the door that opens to a future different from the present, penetrating the "ceiling of the possible." "Real capitalism," the penthouse level of the hierarchical socio-economic structure of society, chooses because only there is the freedom to move between one opportunity and another, and from one stronghold to another.

> "In a context where other structures were inflexible (those of material life and, no less, those of ordinary economic life) capitalism could choose the areas where it wished and was able to intervene, and the areas it would leave to their fate, rebuilding as it went its own structures from these components, and gradually in the process transforming the structures of others."[15]

3.
FROM EMPTY PERSON TO THE PERSON AS PRODUCT RESERVOIR

The empty person is the empty person of historical biology. It is the person as a deconstituted organic entity. Deconstituted, that is, by progressive biological inquiry into its macro-and micro-materiality. The persistent conflicts with vitalism and vitalist speculation throughout the 19th century was the effort to compel biological science to infuse the person with content *qua* person.

The movement of biological science from micro-biology to molecular biology (see note) established biology as the science of life phenomena, meaning that the intelligibility of the molecular foundation of living organisms as a lawfully coded structure and form of material existence was now both known and knowable. Even more than that: (1) The organic molecular structures could be synthesized-biotic chemistry. (2) Pre-biotic chemistry-non-organic matter could be synthesized molecularly so as to exhibit properties of life phenomena. (3) Organic molecular structures could be modified through synthesis. (4) Genetic synthesis (Recombinant DNA) could be achieved.

An infrastructure for industrialized biology (capital investment in industrial production of life phenomena products)—one from which base technologies could be constructed—had now been created. The deconstituted substances of the person's own materiality are transformable into the domain of life phenomena products. These are products applicable to the modification of organic structures, to modification of the regulatory life processes and mechanisms, and to mitigation or correction of genetic faults.

NOTE

The Path to Recombinant DNA

Watson has singled out advances in the bio-chemistry of living cells as the eventual destroyer of "vitalism", which was a theory that supported the differentiation between living and non-living systems. He has traced the analytic examination of living organisms from its analytic beginning in evolutionary theory, then through cell theory (first convincingly established in 1859), and then to modern inquiry into the precellular (pre-biotic) foundation of systems that both replicate and reproduce themselves (living systems). It was all theory that (1) opened the way to chromosomal and gene discoveries, and (2) that turned out to be a theory applicable to simple as well as higher (more complex) organisms. Biochemistry, as Watson noted, established that the laws of chemistry control cellular behavior, particularly the principles of metabolism and biosynthesis. Through molecular biology (behavior of cellular molecules) a managed knowledge of the gene has been achieved. Technologically that managed knowledge is expressed as Recombinant DNA; that is, an alteration of gene structure or function.[16]

REFERENCES

1. Braudel, Fernand, *The Structured of Everyday Life: Civilization and Capitalism 15th—18th Century* (Eng. Transl., Rev. Transl., Sean Reynolds, Harper and Row 1981 ed.), Vol. 1, Intro., 23-4.
2. Ibid., Vol. 1, Ch. 1, 2, and 3.
3. Ibid., Vol. 1, 163.
4. Ibid., Vol. 1, 562.
5. Domain, Arnold L. and Solomon, Nadine A., "Industrial Microbiology," 245 *Scientific American*, No. 3, September 1981, 66.
6. Aharonowitz, Yair and Cohen, Gerald, "The Microbiological Production of Pharmaceuticals," 245 *Scientific American*, No. 3, September 1981, 141.
7. Ibid., 152.
8. Eveleigh, Douglas E., "The Microbiological Production of Industrial Chemicals," 245 *Scientific American*, No. 3, September 1981, 154-55, 178.
9. Ibid., 155.
10. Rose, Anthony H., "The Microbiological Production of Food and Drink," 245 *Scientific American*, No. 3, September 1981, 126-27.
11. Jones, Richard W., *Principles of Biological Regulation* (Academic Press, N.Y. 1973).
12. Ashby, W. Ross, *An Introduction to Cybernetics* (John Wiley and Sons, Science Editions, N.Y. 1963). The pioneer work is by Wiener, Norbert, *Cybernetics* (Wiley, New York 1948).
13. Duquesne, Maurice, *Matter and Antimatter* (Transl. from French Pomerans, A.J., Hutchinson & Co. 1960), Arrow Books ed., London 1960, 33.
14. Braudel, Vol. 1, Ch. 5 and 6, especially pp. 430-31. Note the statement by Schumpeter: "The boom ends and the depression begins after the passage of the time which must elapse before the products of the new enterprises can appear on the market. And a new boom succeeds the depression when the process of resorption of the innovations is ended." Schumpter, Joseph A., *The Theory of Economic Development*, Ch. VI, p. 213 (Oxford U. Press, Transl. Redvers Opie, 1969 Rep. of 1934 ed.) The leading contemporary study of technology, innovation and cyclical movement is that of Mensch, Gerhard O., *Stalemate in Technology* (Ballinger, Cambridge 1979).
15. Braudel, Vol. 1, 562.
16. Watson, James D., *Molecular Biology of the Gene* (W.A. Benjamin Inc., Menlo Park, CA, 3rd ed. 1976); Watson, James D., Hopkins, Nancy H., Roberts, Jeffrey W., Steitz, Joan A., and Weiner, Alan M., *Molecular Bioloby of the Gene* (Benjamin/Cummings Publ. Co., Menlo Park, CA, two Vols., 4th ed. 1987).

CHAPTER XII

Strategizing Biotechnology

1.
THE BIOTECHNOLOGICAL SCENE

1. The technologies of biotechnology are (a) recombinant DNA technology and (b) monoclonal antibody technology.
2. Strategized biotechnology is focused on the strategy for the commercialization of (a) and (b) above, and the strategy for the commercialization of the combination of (a) and (b).
3. Foreign governments have nationally targeted policies for biotechnology, and targeted policies that differ from the commercialization targets of the American firms.
4. Foreign governments include representation from industrial sectors in the structure and process of nationally coordinated policy targeting for biotechnology.
5. As of March 1983, the conservative estimate was that there were 219 companies commercializing biotechnology in the United States.
6. In the period 1977-1983, there were 68 investments in new biotechnology firms (startups) by established American companies.
7. Venture capital investment in new biotechnology firms is much less favored in foreign countries than in the United States.
8. Pharmaceutical applications, and the pharmaceutical industry, exhibit the most vigorous pursuit of the commercialization of biotechnology.
9. The distribution of biotechnology companies among product markets ranges over pharmaceuticals (62%), animal agriculture (28%), plant agriculture (24%), specialty chemicals and food (20%), commodity chemicals and energy (15%), environment (11%), and electronics (3%).

10. The conclusion (as of 1984) from a world inclusive technology assessment survey was the United States leads Europe in the commercialized applications of biotechnology research.
11. When basic research (open ended knowledge expansion) is taken as one polar extreme, and applied research (product innovation) as the other, then (a) the bridge between the two is defined as "generic applied research," and (b) the rate of movement along this bridge is defined as "the trajectory of innovation." Policy targeting of the commercialization of biotechnology is a targeted commitment to applied (product specific) research.
12. New biotechnology firms exhibit:
    a. A diversity of financial needs, depending upon choice of product market.
    b. Labor costs that constitute a large percentage of their operating costs.
    c. Complex issues of technology transfer, both domestic and international.
13. Biotechnology is adversely altering the foundations of competitive advantage vis-a-vis Japan in world markets of the United States pharmaceutical industry and the United States specialty chemicals industry.
14. The pharmaceutical industry is the preferred industry of entry for 78 biotechnology startup firms and also for 57 established companies manufacturing products for pharmaceutical use.
15. The year 1980 was the peak year for raising venture capital in biotechnology in the United States. In the two following years the valuations of biotechnology startups declined and, contributing to the decline, knowledge of the larger time period required for product commercialization was factored into venture capital investment decisions.
16. A striking difference between the United States and Japan in the thrust and structure of the bioindustry is that the former relies on new biotechnology firms (over 100) while the latter relies on going companies in established industries to exploit the new technology.

2.
THE PATH FROM ANTIBIOTICS TO STRATEGIZED BIOTECHNOLOGY

The passage to strategized biotechnology from the discoveries and investigative technologies of pre-industrialized biology is the modern path of microbiological research. That begins with late 19th century demonstrations of the therapeutic properties of microorganisms, which is antibiotics. It continues through the early isolation and laboratory experiment with penicillin acid (1913); then on through the very significant later discovery of penicillin (1922) and its isolation and the start of clinical testing in 1941. Further research based discoveries of antibiotics continued throughout a period that lasted until about 1960. By this time, programs for systematic selection of antibiotics had been developed, and their clinical use was also well established. The further progress that started in 1970, was in the form of a broadening of research methods, an expanding synthesis of derivatives, more bio-chemically sensitive microorganisms, widening practical applications, and continuation of the use of antibiotics in clinical medicine.

Biotechnology as a modern science/technology knowledge base emerged between the discovery of the structure of the DNA molecule (1953) and the origination of techniques for genetic engineering (1973), which is recombinant DNA. In 1975, Milskin and Kohler, by cell fusion, invented (but did not choose to patent) monoclonal anti-body producing hybridoma. These are hybrid cells that secrete homogeneous anti-bodies in large amounts.[2]

It is this science/technology knowledge base that has served as the cradle from out of which the bioindustry has proliferated. The bioindustry consists of investment capitalized enterprise, which, as a new industry, has been recognized as "a salient example of the dynamism of the capitalist system."[3]

3.
STRATEGIZING BIOTECHNOLOGY

The Dream Knowledge of Strategy: "Bioriches"

At the center of the commercially targeted knowledge of biotechnology are the product dreams. The product dreams are the uncomplicated and optimistic visions of biotechnological products with unobstructed, surprise free, and unlimited markets.

The markets are unlimited because of the attributed qualities of the products. Their attributed qualities are invested with a magic thought to be sourced in biotechnology itself. The magic is the technologically engineered specificity of their powers in relation to a wide array of identified actual and foreseeable market needs. The envisioned needs are identified within categories of opportunity fields for application of biotechnology. Products for the diagnosis and treatment of a variety of ailments and diseases cross the human, the animal and the plant categories of application. So, too, do the applications of the techniques of genetic engineering. There are also applications for the increase of animal and plant productivity. The possible new foods from biotechnology are not necessarily from plants, but from the production of consumable protein structured microbes. Energy constitutes a further category of opportunity fields for biotechnological applications—fuel useful alcohol, alternative fuel sources. To sum it all in terms of industrial impact within a variety of industries—petro-chemical, pharmaceutical, plastics, agri-business, food production, environmental de-toxification—the dream knowledge is the vision of profitable transformation of industrial raw material sources, of industrial processes and technologies, and of preventive and remedial control of environmental pollution.[4]

The Product Knowledge of Strategy

Strategized biotechnology is characterized by a variety of product/market visions. Product visions can be matched with the market visions which they imply. Given a time frame, a structure such as the following suggests a match between projected product visions with projected market visions:

Product Vision	*Market Vision*
Known future products	Known future needs
Known present products	Known future needs
Potentially knowable products	Presently unknown future needs
Unknown present products	Potentially knowable future needs

186 THE KNOWLEDGE OF STRATEGY

In relation to the foregoing matching list, the essential question is: What is product development knowledge as against product/market visions? The response to that question can start with several suppostions. Suppose the following:

1. The research composition of the product is known, but not the stages of product development.
2. The research composition and the product development stages are known, but not the costs of production.
3. Research composition, stages of product development, and production costs are known, but not the outcome of clinical testing.
4. Product development stages, the results of clinical testing, and the market need are known, but do not know the actualities of the structure of market demand.
5. Know product development, clinical testing outcomes, market needs, and demand structure of the market, but do not know the conditions of access to the market.
6. Know product development clinical testing, market needs, market demand and market access, but do not know the results of end-user experience with the product.

THE KNOWLEDGE OF PRODUCT EXPERIENCE

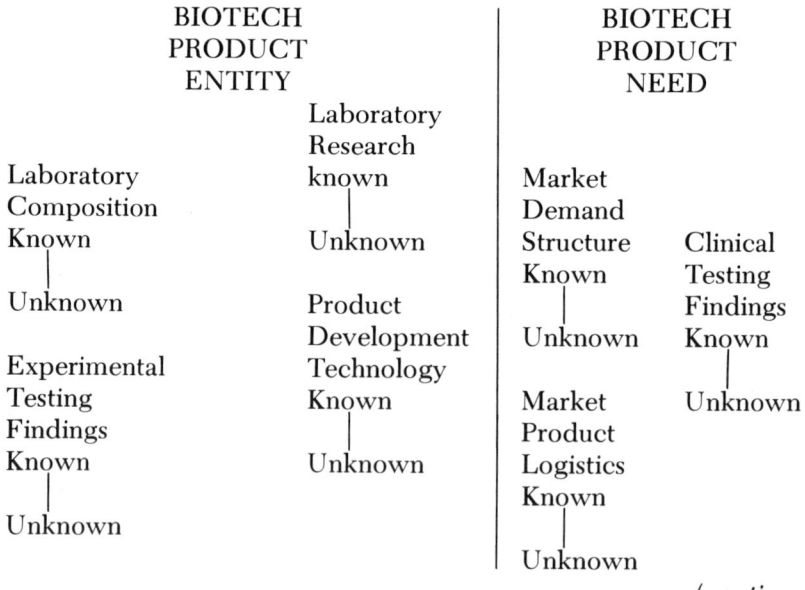

(*continued*)

THE KNOWLEDGE OF PRODUCT EXPERIENCE: (*Continued*)

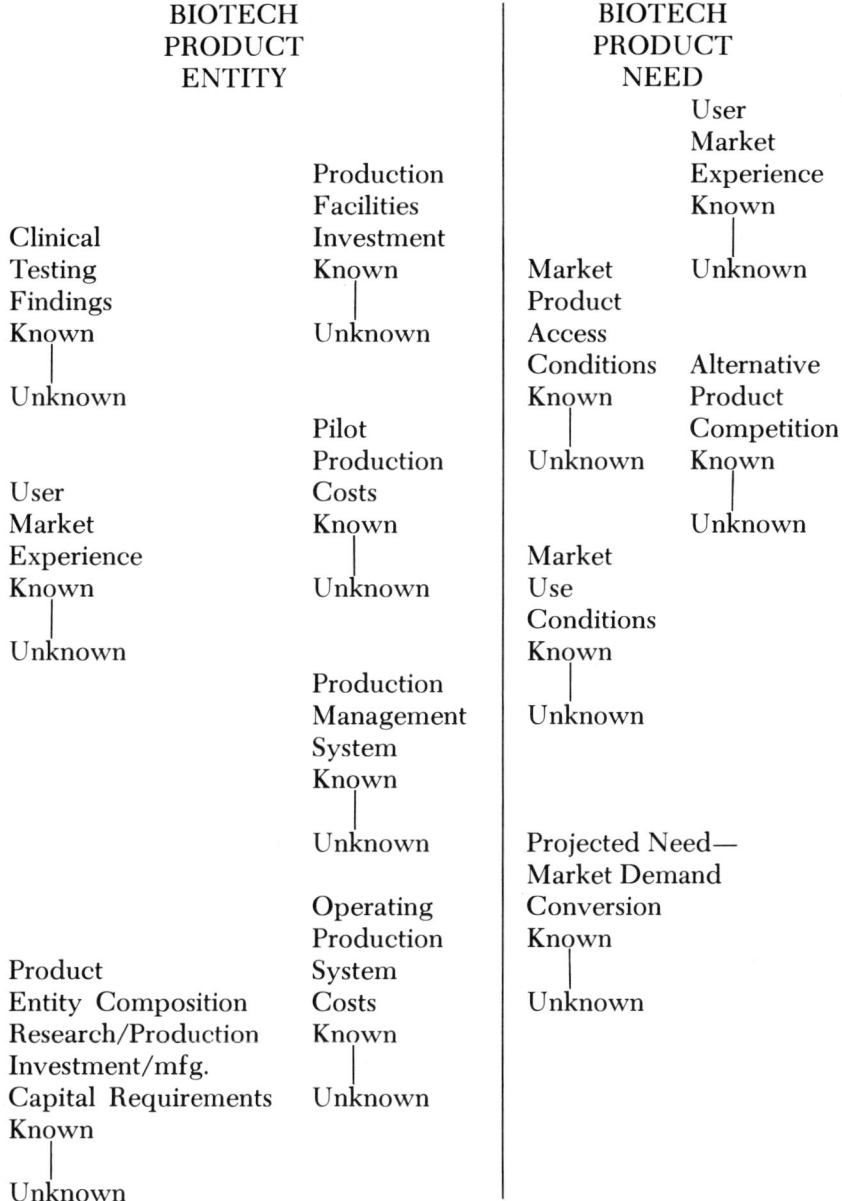

Commercially targeted biotechnology seeks to move across the bridge of generic applied research at a managed trajectory of product innovation. It is a product development and innovation bridge. At one end, the foundation is research based discovery. At the other end, the foundation is delivery of a specific product matched to a commercially relevant market. The bridging is achieved through stages of product development that have been identified as: (1) Selective screening of microorganisms to identify the therapeutically useful antibiotic; (2) Growth, separation and purification of the active substance; (3) Product development—qualitative, technical and engineering (genetic, microbiological, biochemical); (4) Scale production by industrial fermentation; (5) Product improvement.[5] Each of the developmental stages for recombinant DNA technology and for antibody technology present special technical difficulties and possibilities for alternative methods/techniques of preparation.[6]

The Chain of Strategy: The Deterministic Chain

The joinder between command cognition and the power of exercisable choice that is possessed by capital supports both the assumption and the reality of a deterministic chain of strategy. The understated comment by Kenney—"when a startup has a financial crisis, the interaction between its financiers and its corporate founders and managers can become strained"[7]—bares the core of both the directiveness and the determinism of the chain of strategy. The directively deterministic process that has its source in the structure of capital financing is an antecedent quality of the chain of strategy. It is antecedent to those subsequent activities which consist of the performance focused perceptions, logics and actions of strategic management. The latter, encased as they are in originating and integrating intermediate structures for achieving product based commercial success, have their management function adumbrated within an authoritative strategy. The chain of strategy is a directively deterministic set of linkages, one in which each element of the chain is driven by an antecedent element.

The Chain of Strategy

1. The structure of capital market drives capital expectations.
2. Capital expectations drive capital investment.
3. Capital investment terms drive strategies.
4. Strategies drive information systems.
5. Information systems drive strategic management.
6. Short term and/or long term strategic paths drive strategic performance of management.
7. Strategic performance possibilities drive strategic achievement.
8. Stages of strategic achievement drive reformulation of strategy.
9. Reformulation of strategy drives transformation of capital expectations.
10. The transformation of capital expectations drives the remobilization and redirection of strategic commitments between: new research, technological advancements, production improvements, product developments, joint enterprise ventures, geography and scale of markets, distribution arrangements, merges and acquisition.

As to the various elements of the chain of strategy—

1. The major capital market structures are: venture capital, public (shareholder equity) capital, state (subsidy) capital, established corporate capital, and capital from the R&D Limited Partnership.
2. Each capital structure lays down its own ground rules and its own expectations for its own investments.
3. Strategy endeavors to satisfy the terms of investment.
4. Strategy supplies the substantive significance for information system design, and the cardinal reference norms for information based decision inferences.
5. Information systems function as guidance monitors of strategic activity for management.
6. Strategies are not necessarily either/or, but can be mixed strategies, mixed in terms of different parameters and time frames.
7. Technological and process and experimental possibilities abound in biotechnology, but because of problems of feasibility, research costs, clinical requirements, and time, they might be only negatively related to expectations for strategic achievement.
8. The conditions consequent to each expected stage of achievement, or consequent to non-achievement of the business plan, precipitate a reconsideration of strategies by investor capital.

9. The re-matching of capital expectations to re-formulated strategy involves fresh assessment of capital requirements and sources, re-appraisal of asset to debt structures, alteration of equity positions, changes in management, policy with respect to research contracts, and the like.
10. The revision of investment expectation determines the choices for re-strategizing.

The Duality of the Chain of Strategy

In actuality the chain of strategy is a double rather than a single chain. Its duality lies in the fact that the chain consists of an intertwining of (1) an investment expectations chain, and (2) a product expectations chain. The examination of the stages in the strategy of a venture capital investment in biotechnology (following their listing as described by Kenney[8]) will make apparent both their separateness and their interrelation. The sequence of stages is as follows:

1. Joinder of fund linked entrepreneurs with biotech scientist in proposed venture capitalized biotech enterprise.
2. First round financing based on business plan.
3. Work through of the terms for seed money (first round financing) from venture capital funds.
4. Front end outlays ("burn money") to establish the corporate structure of the new entity.
5. Second round financing. Private equity placement to obtain capital after expenditure of seed money.
6. Appointment of scientific advisory board. Networking of academically based scientific talent.
7. New capital through third round financing by registered public stock offering as public corporation.
8. Initiate revenue/cash flow by obtaining research contracts and initiate bridging steps from product research to product commercialization.
9. Meet bridge capital needs through R&D limited partnerships, which tap additional sources of private capital.
10. Restructure for achievement of product commercialization and re-define strategy in relation to multi-national markets and world wide status for the industry.

The Investment Expectations Strand of the Dual Chain of Strategy

The financing of biotech enterprise has its own autonomous objectives. Moreover, they are objectives that are not dependent upon ultimately successful commercialization of market scale production of the biotechnological product.

1. "The venture capitalist's goal is simple: to make an investment for five to seven years that will provide 500 to 1,000 percent capital gains when the company's stock is offered publicly."[9]
2. " 'A lot of people now are making money before they've built their business because people are recognizing that there is potential value in ideas. These firms are being capitalized so that much of the incremental value is being realized before a product is on the market or before it is even very sure there will be one.' "[10]
3. "The public stock offering has proved to be an important source of funds and, simultaneously, has put the venture capitalists and company founders on the road to financial success."[11]

The investment expectations strand is one of a strategy of realizing expected capital gains.

The Product Expectations Strand of the Dual Chain of Strategy

The future of the investor as venture capitalists, then is one strand in the dual chain of strategy. Building the start-up firm itself as a business—bridging from research to market scale production and successful commercialization of the product—is the other strand in the dual chain of strategy. It is a qualitatively different strand. It functions within a different time frame than that which is strategized for the investment pay-off expectations of venture capitalists. Its longer term business building time frame requires a meshing of short term with long term objectives. It enters into, and must effectively deal with, the inescapable and basic business building risks. Without yet having developed a product, it must nevertheless devise modes of financing its operations costs. Research contracts and R&D Limited Partnerships are financial modes for obtaining needed capital.[12]

The R&D Limited Partnerships[13] obtain private investment capital without the sacrifice of equity. The strategic utility of R&D Limited Partnerships is that they "are a financing mechanism that allows businesses to engage in research activities without paying for the activities out of retained earnings or borrowed capital."[14] As of 1984, there were about 30 R&D Limited Partnerships formed or being formed in biotechnology. The startup firm "typically serves as the general partner and assumes liability. The limited partners are the investors whose money buys a share of the partnerships' future profits or losses. The liability of the limited partners is limited to the loss of their investment."[15]

Research contracts also have a specific strategic utility. They are contractual agreements between biotechnology startup firms and established companies to do research and product development. Contract revenues have functioned as a major source of revenue for biotechnology startup firms. Beyond the cost reimbursement and incentive provisions of research contracts:

> "The N(ew) Biotechnology, F(irm), generally retains the patent rights to any technology involved and grants the contracting company an exclusive license to that technology. Thus, such agreements usually provide for royalty payments to the NBF by the established company on the future sales of the product that results from the R&D work; These royalties may range from 2 to 10 percent of total sales, depending on the size of the product market"[16]

While research contracts provide needed operating revenue as well as opportunities for internal learning and knowledge accumulation, they also carry with them relationships in which there are real risks of breach of the security of proprietary technology and product knowledge.

In actuality the product expectations strand of the dual chain of strategy takes on a double structure of risks. One risk structure consists of the risks associated with the uncertainty that can exist with respect to known possibilities. Research contract risks provide the examples in point. The second risk structure consists of the unknown risks associated with the uncertainty that can exist with respect to unknown possibilities. The second risk structure is the structure of lurks. The difference between the two is the difference between uncertainty and the range of known possibilities, and uncertainty and an unknown variety of unknown possibilities. Lurks are the stalking uncertainty of surprise adversity— negative serendipity. The emergence of computer based design of drug compounds as an alternative to complex biotechnological techniques and processes of pharmaceutical innovations provides an apt illustration, of the surfacing of a technological lurk.[17]

4.
COUNTER STRATEGY TO VENTURE CAPITAL STARTUPS

Command Cognition and the Will to Strategize

Biotechnology, in the form of venture capital funded biotechnology startups, both impinges upon and intrudes into the technical processes, the product fields, and the present and future commercial markets of established chemical and pharmaceutical firms. For the management of these firms, the multiplication of biotechnology startups has precipitated a complex of strategic concerns. Not yet the more ultimate and final concerns of strategic choice, but the antecedent and prior concerns of questing for a strategy. The concerns of command cognition, and the concerns underlying the will to strategize. For command cognition, the concern is about the possible loss of dominion over established markets in consequence of the commercialization of biotechnology. For the will to strategize, it is a matter of unease. "The motive for continuing in the same state or action is only the present satisfaction in it; the motive to change is always some uneasiness."[18]

There is a specific content by which to explain the unease of management within the chemical and the pharmaceutical industries. It has been identified as:

A. For the Petro-Chemical Industry
   1. Slow down in the rate of growth.

2. Slow down in the pace of product innovation.
3. Minimization of new product differentiation.
4. Drift to commodity type products.
5. Profit margin declines.
6. New entrants into the industry from the OPEC countries.
7. High dependency on the cost of petroleum.
8. Increasing investment and operating costs of antipollution measures and clean-up activities.
9. Latent liability possibilities in damage suits.

B. For the Petro-Chemical/Pharmaceutical Industries Relationship
1. The latter are specialty product entities.
2. The latter are patented product entities; proprietary rights protect investment returns.
3. The latter are product/market niche focused entities.
4. Biotechnology enables multiplication of patentable new product possibilities for the latter.
5. Possibilities for new drug patentability lower entry barriers into the latter.
6. No fundamental technological barrier exists that would bar entry into the latter.
7. Large market growth opportunities for the latter in different new products.
8. Problems of environmental pollution are not of a major character for the latter.[19]

Yet there is ample ground for the unease of command cognition within the pharmaceutical industry.

1. New entrants into the industry

"Approximately 70 new U.S. companies that have entered the pharmaceutical field just apply biotechnology. Many of these NBFs are wagering their existence on the success of commercial pursuits of biotechnology in nascent pharmaceutical product markets."[20]

2. Decline in world shares

"Since the early 1960's, the U.S. share of world pharmaceutical research, innovation, production, sales, and exports has declined, as has the number of U.S. companies actively participating in the various ethical drug markets compared to the number of foreign firms."[21]

3. Decline in new product innovations

". . . The United States and France were the leaders in 1961-80, with 23.6 and 18.1 percent of new product introductions respectively. . . . The world leader for the years 1981-83 is Japan, with an average of 27 percent of new product introductions." [U.S. Average 1 percent]

4. Rising Japanese Competition in world pharmaceutical markets

"In addition to the pharmaceutical companies, Japanese companies from the food, chemical, textile, and pulp and paper industries have also begun to further exploit their accumulated experience in bioprocessing by diversifying into newly developing pharmaceutical product markets."[22]

Strategizing at the Level of Command Cognition

The construction of a cognitive terrain for strategizing movements is the strategic function of command cognition. Developments in biotechnology—whether entrpreneurial, research or technological in character; and even those altering the patterns or organizational and communication relationships between its scientific and its administrative personnel—generate theaters of strategy. Decisions of entry into particular theaters of strategy are strategizing movements.

The theaters of strategy constitute cognitive terrains. Theaters of strategy introduce strategic variety. The knowledge of strategic variety is the knowledge of strategy. Choice of strategy can be entry, and movement into, a theater of strategy. Thus, to illustrate, the multi-million investment scale of chemical and pharmaceutical companies in biotechnology ranged over four different theaters of strategy.

1. In-house research, by either starting from scratch or by purchase of a startup firm.
2. University contract research, with a licensing option.

3. Contract with a biotechnology startup, with exclusive product marketing rights.
4. Purchase of an equity position in a biotechnology startup.[23]

Command Cognition: The Strategy of Domination

Each theater of strategy constitutes a cognitive terrain of projected possibilities, of expectations of benefits, of exploratory learning, of tactical exploration, of desired intelligence, of likely monetary outlays, and so on. They can each be differentiated in terms of the preferences of the strategic actors with respect to one or the other—or combinations of—these parameters. Can they be understood within some unity of conception? Does strategized biotechnology, despite its varietal expression in a diversity of theaters of strategy, exhibit a unity of strategic conception?

The strategic unity of that varietal expression lies in the conception of the strategy of domination. It is a conception that invests the idea of strategic domination of biotechnology with a dual thrust. There is, first, the thrust of strategizing movements that will achieve, as a necessary strategic end, the domination of the generation, flow and exchange of biotechnological knowledge itself. The knowledge of biotechnology had originated as unprivatized information. It was knowledge that had originated within the scientific minds and laboratories of academic institutions. It was knowledge accessible to and exchangeable between those who were members of the academic community as science researchers in molecular biology. Strategized biotechnology is the strategy of knowledge domination by commercial enterprise. It is a strategy characterized by the transformation of unprivatized information (diffused knowledge) into proprietary knowledge (legally protected property). Proprietary knowledge, as enterprise property, is subject to strategic domination.

It is through that domination of the knowledge of the new biotechnology by which there is secured the technological precondition for protection of future products and future markets against competitors. Kenney has made an informed review of the turbulent debates that took place over the propriety of the new relationships that have been initiated between the bioindustry and the universities/ research scientists with respect to the generation, diffusion, access and ownership of the knowledge of the new biotechnology. He has supplied the details of the decomposition of the university science structure of research and information exchange and its transformation into enterprise structures of proprietary knowledge.[24]

Knowledge domination as a strategy functions as the gateway to subsequent knowledge of future strategic possibilities. The strategizing movements by which the domination of the knowledge itself is secured all focus on priviledged access paths to biotechnological knowledge. This is their common and unifying attribute, even while they take place in different theaters of strategy. While they are priviledged access paths to research and technical knowledge (part and parcel of managing a trajectory of product innovation) there yet remains to be built that further bridge to connect with the knowledge requisite for commercial success.

Strategy and Counter Strategy

Venture capital has, in effect, employed the investment in biotechnology startups as a strategy of assault and penetration of the established bioindustry. A recognized difference exists between the old biotechnology and the new biotechnology. The old biotechnology—the scientific basis of the established bioindustry—is industrialized microbiology. (It is the subject of Chapter 11) Known production technologies with developed products for defined markets and knowledgeable practical relationships with identified distribution networks—all this has been achieved and is maintained by the going firms who make up the established bioindustry that has been built on the foundations of the old biotechnology. Venture capital has subjected it to assault.

Venture capital has aggressively utilized the new biotechnology for its investment strategy. It has also been astute in its inducement, through promises of "bioriches," of surprisingly unresistant lead scientific researchers into entrepreneurial ventures. The firms of the established bioindustry—uneasy about the possible loss of what advantages they do have and possibly their exclusion from expected future advantages—resort to counter strategies. Command cognition intends through these counter strategies to negate or to strip of significance all potential threat of technological transfer of comparative market advantage to the new biotechnology firms. Dominion in a product market of choice is everything. A technological edge may be necessary, but it may still not be sufficient to achieve commercial success. This is the knowledge that underlies the counter strategies.

NOTE 1.

An alternative to the venture capital limited partnership for financing research and development expenditures has been created. The alternative is to establish a separate corporate entity and assign to it all rights to the product undergoing development. The new firm then issues stock and from the proceeds of the sale of the securities it assumes responsibility for the financing of the research, for which it can and does hire the original firm. The latter has reserved the right to buy back the product and its technology. What induces investment in the securities issued by the new corporate entity is their composition as an investment unit.

> "This unit is made up of one share of stock in the new company and one warrant to buy a share of the original company. The new company's stock is an unusual variety called 'callable common,' which gives the original company the right to redeem the stock at fixed prices on certain dated in the future if it likes the outcome of the research.
> "In time—the period varies from deal to deal—the unit breaks into its component parts, which trade separately."[25]

REFERENCES

1. *Commercial Biotechnology: An International Analysis* (Washington, D.C., U.S. Congress, Office of Technology Assessment, OTA-BA-218, January 1984).
2. Antebi, Elizabeth and Fishlock, David, *Biotechnology: Strategies for Life* (MIT Press, Cambridge, Mass, 1986), Intro. p. 7; Pt. 1: Article 1, 20. Florent, Jean, "The Great Turning Point: Antibodies and Secondary Metabolities."; Kenney, Martin, *Biotechnology: The University-Industrial Complex* (Yale U. Press, New Haven, Conn., 1986) Appendix 1, "Biotechnology Briefly Explained."
3. Antebi, 238.
4. Prentice, Steve, *Biotechnology: A New Industrial Revolution* (G. Braziller, Inc., New York 1984).
5. Antebi, Pt. 1: Article 1, 20.
6. *Commercial Biotechnology*, Ch. 3.
7. Antebi, 172.
8. Ibid., Ch. 7.
9. Ibid., 142.
10. Ibid., 146.
11. Ibid., 158.
12. Ibid., 158, 164.
13. Ferguson, M. Carr and Fuller, James P., *Research and Development Limited Partnerships* (N.Y. Practising Law Institute 1989 ed.), Martin, Edwin M. and Martin, Carol H.I., Financing Research and Development (Tax Transactions Library, Commerce Clearing House 1987), Reams, Barnard D. Jr., *University-Industry Research Partnerships* (Quorum Books, Greenwood Press, Westport, Conn. 1986).
14. *Commercial Biotechnology*, 278.
15. Ibid.
16. Ibid., 274.
17. *Wall Street Journal*, August 14, 1990, p B1
18. Locke, John, *An Essay Concerning Human Understanding*, (6th edition, BK II, Ch. XXI, Sec. 29, p. 175), with the notes and illustrations of the author, and an analysis of his doctrine of ideas. Also, Questions on Locke's *Essay*, by A.M., Ethical Moderator in Trinity College, Dublin. (New Edition, The World Library, Ward, Lock & Co., London, undated) The original edition of Locke's *Essay* is 1689.
19. Antebi, 191, 196.
20. *Commercial Biotechnology*, 73.
21. Ibid., 73-4.
22. Ibid., 505-6.
23. Antebi, 199.
24. Ibid., Ch. 2-6.
25. Henriques, Diane B., "Wall Street: Disguising the Risks of Research," *New York Times*, Fegruary 3, 1991, p. 14F.

NOTE 2.

Beyond Venture Capital Strategy in Biotechnology

A surge of interest in the conquest of diseases of the brain was reported to have produced a flow of venture capital large enough to finance six new biotech firms in the years 1982-1987. It was reported that the financing was sufficiently risky for even insiders to raise eyebrows. A judgement of 1988 concluded that new startup and early R&D stage biotechnology companies (a category with 275 firms) could not hope for a product on the market before the mid-1990's. The quest for capital to sustain a company through the stages of research, testing, regulatory approval, and marketing might take the form of going public and, also, of seeking foreign based financing. An estimate of foreign funding of U.S. biotech firms was put at 20 per cent, and growing. By 1991 there would be reference to "a wave" of such acquisitions that was being "driven" by foreign investors.[1]

Japan and Japanese pharmaceutical companies had targeted both biotechnology research and acquisition of U.S. biotechnology firms. Their investment in research could be done by establishing or subsidizing research laboratories at American universities, and also through the purchase of small biotechnology companies. Japanese strategy is not rooted in venture capital motivations. Rather, it is rooted in the drive to transform the domestic pharmaceutical industry, which is deemed an essential if that industry is to become a player in the game of global consolidation by the international pharmaceutical industry. The Japanese strategy can be summarized as:

(a) achieve proficiency in the production of antibiotics;
(b) expand the variety of genetically engineered products;
(c) acquire leading edge capabilities in genetics engineering;
(d) gain access to the international market;
(e) become a global competitor on an industry basis;
(f) individual firms to enter into joint ventures and to engage in mergers and takeovers

—all to achieve economies of scale and to finance product innovations.[2]

The state of Massachusetts made (1989) biotechnology the centerpiece of its technology investment program. It created a Biotechnology Research Park. There is a state biotech council for the 80 to 90 biotech firms operating in Massachusetts in 1989. There were plans, however, for developers within the state to build about 6 million square feet of biotech related space (a $1.6 billion investment) in the decade 1990-2000. The expected demand would consist of: (a) hospital demand for additional space to do biotech research, (b) projected new product manufacturing facilities, (c) transplants from overseas pharmaceutical firms. It is all clouded over by strong doubts: (1) The difficulty of financing speculative biotech projects; (2) What incentives would attract foreign pharmaceutical firms; (3) The reluctance of hospitals to sign 20 year leases; and (4) uncertainty about just how the biotech industry will mature (See "Clouds Gather Over the Biotech Industry," *Wall Street Journal*, January 30, 1989, p. B1).[3]

REFERENCES

1. "The Big Money Chasing Biotech Brainstorms," *Business Week*, May 16, 1988, p. 70; "Biotechnology: Surviving the Adolescent Years," *Scientific American*, June 1988, pp. 112-14.

2. "A Different Kind of Drug Problem," *Forbes*, January 22, 1990, pp. 40-41; "Japan is Buying its Way into U.S. University Labs," *Business Week*, September 24, 1984, pp. 72-73; "Drug Makers in Japan Seek Foreign Firms," *Wall Street Journal*, August 23, 1989, p. A8; "Hitachi to Build Research Lab on U.S. Campus," *Cleveland Plain Dealer*, May 6, 1990, p. 4E; "Lyphomed Inc. Agrees to Sale to Fujusawo," *Wall Street Journal*, September 5, 1989, p. B7 and the related article "Lyphomed's Beryaimen Provides a Cure," *Wall Street Journal*, August 23, 1989, p. B6; La Ganga, Marie, "U.S. Agriculture Biotech Firms Cut Good Deals with Japanese," *Los Angeles Times*, April 9, 1990, p. D3.

Another foreign investor is Switzerland, whose Sandoz Ltd., described as a "Swiss pharmaceutical giant," purchased Systemix, which was founded in 1988, but which had developed new, cutting edge technologies that were important in the medical treatment of "immune disorders, cancers and genetic diseases." *Wall Street Journal*, December 17, 1991, p. B1. The WSJ article also makes reference to the acquisition of 60% interest in Genentech Inc. by Switzerland's Roche Holding Ltd.

3. Gendron, Marie and Callaway, David, "Spontaneous Generation? Business and State Investments in Young Biotech Industry Grow," *The Boston Herald*, June 13, 1989, pp. 23, 28.

PART III

The Foundation Knowledge of Strategic Knowledge

What is the knowledge by which there can be a knowledge of strategy?

1. Knowledge of the Person: The Person as Idea
2. Knowledge of the Person: Pre-Industrial Biology
3. Note: "Fitted Knowledge" and "Possibilities Knowledge"
4. Fitted Knowledge
5. Possibilities Knowledge

CHAPTER XIII

Knowledge of the Person: The Person as Idea

1.
THE PERSON AS MATERIAL ENTITY

Cognitive and Incognitive Existants

LOCKE WAS CONVINCED of the self-evident knowledge that humans had of their "real being." It was "beyond question, that a man has a clear perception of his own being; he knows certainly that he exists, and that he is something." This self-evident knowing could be no more than one's perception of one's own person as an existant. But what kind of existant—"purely material, without sense, perception, or thought?" Such would be an "incogitative" existant. On the contrary, man was a "cogitative" existant, finding himself to be a "sensible, thinking, perceiving" being.[1]

The identity of a cogitative existant did not rest upon the same foundation as that for an incogitative body. As between "a mass of matter and a living body;" wrote Locke, "in the state of living creatures, their identity depends not on a mass of the same particles, but on something else." The identity of matter, regardless of the modes or the relations that it may take, terminates ultimately in identity of substance. It is a mass of the same particles. As to living creatures, however:

> ". . . only as to things existence is in succession such as are the actions of finite beings, e.g., motion and thought, both of which consist in a continued train of succession, concerning their diversity there can be no question: because, each perishing the moment it begins, they cannot exist in different times, or in different places, as permanent beings can at different times exist in distant places; and therefore no motion or thought, considered as at different times, can be the same, each part thereof having a different beginning of existence."[2]

In living bodies there is present a force within "an organization of parts in one coherent body partaking of one common life," making the organized collection of matter an individual life with a unique identity. The two requisites—fitness of organization and an internal life force—are present in the human being. The identity of a human being consisted in "a participation of the same continued life by constantly fleeting particles of matter, in succession vitally united to the same organized body."

Locke had tied the identity to the person to the organized materiality of body, but he had also differentiated it from the machine by the requirement of a motion force within.[3] He took it as generally unacceptable that the idea of a man was of an incorporeal "thinking or rational being."

Consciousness and Identity

What about "personal identity"? What does the term "person" stand for? What is "self"? Locke rooted personal identity in consciousness, not in substance. It was not, for him, a question of whether that which always thinks was always the same identical substance. A person could be a composite of different substances, all partaking in the same consciousness. It was consciousness that transcended change of substances. It was consciousness that preserved personal identity "by the unity of one continued life." It was consciousness that "makes a man be himself to himself . . .

> "For as far as any intelligent being can repeat the idea of any past action with the same consciousness it had of it at first, and with the same consciousness it has of any present action; so far it is

the same personal self. For it is by the consciousness it has of its present thoughts and actions that it is self to itself now, and so will be the same self as far as the same consciousness can extend to actions past or to come; . . ."[4]

Consequently, it is consciousness that individuates that person, and it is in consciousness that there is the repository of "self." It is consciousness that "unites existences and actions," both past and present. There is no existence as a person without consciousness. As to "self," Locke defined it as "that conscious thinking thing" which, because it is, through sensibilization, conscious "of pleasure and pain, capable of happiness or misery," has concern for itself. The individuation of persons is a function of the binding of existence and action in time through consciousness.[5]

It is in this time-binding that are the foundations of personal interests. The self, as person, extends and appropriates past and present actions for itself as a concern for its own happiness. In this time-binding there is, also, "founded all the right and justice of reward and punishment; happiness and misery being that for which everyone is concerned for himself."[6] By this owning of actions and imputing them to itself, the self becomes accountable for them as a conscious, intelligent agent.

"That Conscious Thinking Thing"

"The conscious thinking thing" of Locke's, which was "self" because it could "consider itself as itself" regardless of times and places. What was it? His mind is a "finite mind," yet he understands not either its own operations or "that thinking thing within" him.[7] Of that "thinking thing" Locke wrote:

> "It is past controversy, that we have in us something that thinks; our very doubts about what it is confirm the certainty of its being, though we must content ourselves in the ignorance of what kind of being it is; and it is as vain to go about to be sceptical in this, as it is unreasonable in most other cases to be positive against the being of any thing, because we cannot comprehend its nature."[8]

So man, the person, the human, existed as "some knowing, intelligent being in the world." But what was it within, or of, that material existant of which it could be said that it thought? The judgement of Locke was that no one knew: "Ignorance we are in of the nature of that thinking thing that is in us."[9] Perception is its first intellectual operation, not that which thinks. The latter perceives its own operations: mind perceives its actions with respect to its own objects of thought. But that which thinks still remains an unknown. "We have the ideas of matter and thinking," wrote Locke, "but possibly shall never be able to know whether any mere material being thinks or no."[10] His search for a way out touched on the practice that "we experiment in ourselves thinking," which he took for an activity that could not exist without support in some "substance." So there was, he concluded, a thinking substance within us.

However, he had not thereby found an exit. What barred the exit was the idea of "substance." With substance one always encountered the insuperable obstacle of access to the interior of its materiality. "For I would fain know, what substance exists has not something in it which manifestly baffles our understandings."[11] Locke could only take a position this side of a probable exit gate. He concluded that we cannot prove that "there is an immaterial substance in us that thinks," but it is in the highest degree probable that the thinking substance in us is immaterial.[12]

The Nominal "Person"

Locke had left the person as a "self" where he had left the knowledge of "physica." Knowledge not of a material reality, but a "bare speculative truth." Only the nominal person was there to be known. "Person," the term itself, was described as but "a forensic term," a name for an appropriated "self." As Locke put it, "wherever a man finds what he calls 'himself,' there, I think, another may say is the same person."[13] Everything was annexed to consciousness: "For, whatever substance there is, however framed, without consciousness there is not person,"[14] Still, what is consciousness? In its practical aspect, Locke treated consciousness as an attribute of the subjectness of "intelligent agents." Whatever it might be, however, Locke accepted as "the more probable opinion" that "consciousness is annexed to, and the affection of, one individual immaterial substance."[15] Because of this consciousness, "I am myself to myself," which, when found (acknowledged) by one to be "himself," then the term "person" may be applied by way of "appropriating actions and their merit."

Duration extended beyond the present of existence is at the core of the idea of individual personality as the maintenance of identity; that is, the retention of uniqueness. Consciousness is the fundament of this extension of duration. The extension of duration is the continuation of existence as the same self. It is this continuation of the "very same self" that establishes the retention of identity during its existence.

> "This personality extends itself beyond present existence to what is past, only by consciousness; whereby it becomes concerned and accountable, owns and imputes to itself past actions, just upon the same ground and for the same reason that it does the present. All which is founded in a concern for happiness, the unavoidable concomitant of consciousness; that which is conscious of pleasure and pain desiring that *that* self that is conscious should be happy. And therefore whatever past actions it cannot reconcile or appropriate to that present self by consciousness, it can no more be concerned in, than if they had never been done: . . ."[16]

2.
GENUINE AND FACSIMILE PERSONS

Locke on Understanding Persons

The approach of Locke to persons was not to place them within a cosmological order that is sourced in divine knowledge. Humans, not withstanding that Locke conceded both their origins and their individual after-lives to divine wisdom, were now earth constrained material entities of an unknown and unknowable essence. Persons, as individuals, were in possession of physical faculties adequate to their earthly conditions; had within them a thing that thinks; and were endowed with capabilities susceptible to improvement to where the practical concerns of earthly life might be satisfactorily dealt with. Practical knowledge, in fact, was the second category of Locke's tri-partite division of all that could fall "within the compass of human understanding." Afer the category *Physica*, came the category *Practica*.

> "*Secondly*, Practica.—. . . the skill of right applying our own powers and actions for the attainment of things good and useful. The most considerable under this head is ethics, which is the seeking out those rules and measures of human actions which lead to happiness, and the means to practice them. The end of this is not bare speculation and the knowledge of truth; but right and a conduct suitable to it."[17]

The Natural and the Metaphysical Person

Leibniz was not content to limit the knowledge of persons to Locke's practical concerns of the human understanding, derived from their physical existence as corporeal entities manifesting sensory faculties in relation to their material surroundings. The truth of their essence was the knowledge of the person sought by Leibniz.

> "If the body is a substance and not a mere phenomenon, like a rainbow, . . . its essence cannot consist in extension and we must necessarily conceive of something which is called substantial form and which corresponds in some sort to the soul . . . Nature must always be explained mathematically and mechanically, provided it be kept in mind that the principles or the laws of mechanics and of force do not depend upon mathematical extension alone but have certain metaphysical causes."[18]

Taking the knowledge the person or individual, then, to its most complete and comprehensive level of understanding is to take it to the level of understanding that is the metaphysical. Knowledge of a person is not the knowledge of a particular, determined individual. We can understand that there might be the concept of a person as a conception so complete in its human attributes that the nature of every possible individual derived from it would be complete, determined and unique in its individuality.

Such is the metaphysical concept upon which the facts of a particular, determined person depend—which is the concept of a person in particular and in relation to another particular substance. It provides an explanation independent of and *a prior* to the factual, conditional existence of an individual in particular.

A person as "a real being" cannot be simply a body mass, but must be that which is indivisible in its corporeal substance ("call it soul or form"); and be that which expresses the present state as well as states of the future and of the past; and be that, also, which "always knows itself and continues to exist with self-conscious." Without the concept of souls or forms the person would be understandable only as a body with mass. "I grant," wrote Leibniz, "that the consideration of forms or souls is useless in special physics, it is, nevertheless, important in metaphysics."[19]

Facsimile Being and Genuine Being

While Locke was focused only on human understanding, Leibniz was also focused on understanding humans. Leibniz embarked on a path of thought that takes the understanding of persons beyond the physics of their material being.

A comparison was made by Leibniz between the understanding of genuine being and the understanding of material being; i.e. of an entity in a form that exhibited, as behavior, active power that replicated in its actions what was conventionally associated with human behavior. The issue between facsimile being and genuine being had been precipitated by Locke. At bottom, for Locke, attributes of the active power within persons exist only as the conventions of human form. As conventions, they are both separable and possibly replicable as attributes of other material forms. Locke had left the human without intrinsic uniqueness, merely a conventionally recognized form of material existence. Consciousness invested that conventional form with an internal sense of personal identity, but that did not gainsay that the human being, as an existant, was without an empirical essence.

Leibniz resorted to the automaton as the norm of reference for the comparison of genuine with facsimile being. It was a resort to a then familiar invention. Automatons had entered into the knowledge of the courts of Europe through the inventors of Islam, who in turn, had obtained their knowledge through the inventors of Hellenistic Alexandria.

> "Conspicious in Islamic miniatures are the automatons, all based on Alexandrian principles.
> "The urge to put invention in the service of the miracle survived through Islam down to the eighteenth century. What created a sensation in the late eighteenth century was not the new spinning machines, but the manlike automatons who walked, played instruments, spoke with human voices, wrote or drew. They were shown before the courts of Europe, and finally toured from fair to fair, well into the nineteenth century. The perfecting of automatons in the eighteenth century is related to the high standard of the crafts and especially to the refinement of the clock-making industry. They are based on a minute decomposition and reintegration of movements, which formed the best of disciplines for the invention of spinning machinery.[20]

Leibniz had set the created thing, the components of which were made by man according to mechanical principles, apart from the created thing that owed existence and essence (entelechy) and uniqueness (an internal principle) to a Divine source. No apparently miraculous construction in the form of an automaton could explain the primary activity in the living being that is a created Monad.

> "17. Moreover, it must be confessed that *perception* and that which depends upon it is *inexplicable on mechanical grounds*, that is to say, by means of figures and motions. And supposing there were a machine so constructed as to think, feel, and have perception, it might be conceived as increased in size, while keeping the same proportions, so that one might go into it as into a mill. That being so, we should, on examining its interior, find only parts which work are upon another, and never anything by which to explain a perception. . . ."[21]

The idea of facsimile being is one that is not confined to the frame within which it was put forth by Leibniz. He accepted the frame in which the impulse to invent, and invention itself, was identified with the miraculous. Not until a later century, as Giedion has noted, did the frame of practical utility in the service of production displace the frame of the miraculous. Facsimile being would then take on another significance.

Genuine Being

The point of it all for Leibniz? It was contained within his conclusion that "the organic body of each living being is a kind of divine machine or natural automaton, which infinitely surpasses all artificial automata."[22] The point of it all for Leibniz was that the real unity of things existed in living beings. "Every living thing contains a world of diversity in a real unity," he wrote. "Our experience is in favor of this great number of living things."[23] The point of it all was that the realm of reality lay beyond what he termed Locke's "fictions of the mind." The substantial reality of things is not proved by touch; a machine is conceptualized as a unity because of the relation between its components, but it is only a unity of thought; solids have a "certain degree of fluidity;" a rainbow has visibility, but it is no more than the reality of appearance.

The use by Locke of the sensory faculties as the structural foundation of human understanding was received by Leibniz as leaving thought with a unity of appearances that was not sufficient for the reality back of the phenomena themselves. Appearances were joined in the understanding by the mind, in reflection, finding abstractions and relations from and between modes of things. Thus the names of things that were not the reality of things—"number, time, place, motion, form and sensible quality"—served for their reality.

". . . I say that we only think, and also that we produce only thoughts, and that the phenomena are only thoughts. As, however, all our thoughts are not effective and do not serve to produce for us others of a certain nature, and since it is impossible for us to work out the mystery of the universal connection between phenomena, we must pay attention by means of experience to those which have produced thoughts before, and this is the way the sense do and this is what is called external action outside of us."[24]

Leibniz endeavored to transcend those facts of consciousness that are the contingent facts of experience. He sought to establish a ground for the *a pirori* in the knowledge of humans. The understanding of persons would have to be taken beyond the physics of their coporeality as matter. He was convinced that it could not be done unless there was a recognition of "substances of complete beings and endowed with a true unity in which different states succeed." The rest of knowledge would be considered only as phenomena, abstractions or relations.[25]

Genuine Being and Knowledge of Personal Identity

The knowledge of personal existence is established through intuitive knowledge. On this both Locke and Leibniz are in accord. Nothing by way of a further or mediate knowledge is necessary for the understanding of personal existence.

Something further, something additional, however, is required for knowledge of personal identity. Locke took it that one could be a phenomenon to one's self; that is, that one could establish real identity through only nominal knowledge of one's being as a person. This is the knowledge of consciousness.

Leibniz, like Locke, was of the opinion that consciouness, as perception of the ego, proved personal identity. Consciousness is a knowledge of one's own acts that always accompanies sensations, perceptions and thought. Leibniz, however, made the distinction between the "phenomenon of self" and the self as "identity real and physical." Unlike Locke, therefore, Leibniz did not believe that apparent identity (phenomenon of the self) could be preserved if there were no real identity. To Leibniz, that is to say, every apparent identity to one's self that is perceived by an individual supposes the real identity of that individual. And this simply because such a perception is not capable of deceiving, due to its immediacy and its intimacy.

Leibniz was also convinced that identity was more inclusive than physical and real. There was preserved, within the "soul" of persons, "also identity moral and apparent to ourselves, in order to constitute the same person, capable consequently of feeling chastisements and rewards." The foundation of this "identity moral" was conformity "to the rules of divine providence." Consciousness now also existed as a bond between states of the person—e.g. forgetfulness, loss of memory, mental disease—so as to maintain the moral identity that makes the same person.[26] Leibniz had made of consciousness a qualitative attribute of moral identity.

Consciousness served to transcend changes in the material composition or substances that might constitute the physical identity of individuals. "The thing which thinks at different times and in different places" might have different physical identities or corporalities in those different times and places. Consciousness, nevertheless, is taken to inhere in a certain visible, physical appearance that presents itself to other persons. More fundamentally for Leibniz than alterability and changes in bodies was the physical "organization or configuration without which an existing principle of life, which I call a Monad, would not suffice to cause the continuance of . . . the same individual."[27] The principle of genuine being is incorporated within a Monad.

Genuine Being: The Monad as World Mind

The genuine being of Leibniz is sourced in living things. But the conception of a living thing is itself sourced in a conception by which Leibniz differentiated matter into primary and secondary matter, or substance. While the former is passive mass, the latter contains within itself its own "primitive power" of action, a "moving force," one that is its "first entelechy," and by reason of the constitutive substance of which there exists a perdurable tendency of action. Force and tendency or directionality, which were for Leibniz the two great laws of nature, were manifest within secondary matter, or substance. The creation of a uniquely individuated being (a thing by itself) with perception and desire, though a unified joinder of matter with substance, is the creation of that which Leibniz termed a Monad.

A created Monad exists as a living being with an organic body in which there is a particular order (mechanism or organization) and permeated throughout by an "entelechy." The entelechy is the force of that "soul" which is an "incorporeal automata," containing the virtuality of its own force, and "a certain self-sufficiency" from which source springs its own "internal activities." Leibniz placed the source of the phenomena of the body in the entelechy. Therein were to be found the pre-formation of knowledge as a variety of ideas and the pre-formation of will. They were there as the origins of the faculties of desire (appetite) and perception. They functioned as final causes of action, and hence as the reason for the directionality of activity. Consciousness transformed these inner phenomena into internal experiences. The body responded to the forces of the final causes through its modes of relation, action or movement that functioned as efficient causes for bringing things into existence.

Primary, too, for the principle of genuine being is the location of each created Monad (living being) in relation to all other created Monads. Each is intrinsically different from one another because of the principle of constitutive internal differences (entelechy as universal individuation). Each, moreover, is subject to alteration and continuity in the mode of the particulars of its specific nature. While each thus has its own special point of view of the universe, each also "has relations which express all the others, and, consequently, that it is a perpetual living mirror of the universe."[28] Universal connection is universal adaptation, but with inherent limitations.

> "62. Thus, although each created Monad represents the whole universe, it represents more distinctly the body which especially pertains to it, and of which it is the entelechy; and as the body expresses the whole universe through the connexion of all matter in the *plenum*, the soul also represents the whole universe in representing this body, which belongs to it in a special way."[29]

Leibniz, through the metaphysics of the created Monad, had broken through empirical constraints of the mundane or terrestrial as the limiting condition of attainable human knowledge. With Leibniz, the knowledge of humans is placed within a cosmological context. Absolute variety of individuals, each with its own relational knowledge, each striving in the possibilities of its own tendencies; but each thereby perceptually mirroring the universe in their respective power, knowledge and volition, and in this absolute variety of this striving extending human knowledge to all that happens in the universe through intercommunication.

Genuine Being: The End of Knowledge

Leibniz differed from Locke as to what each put forth as the end of knowledge. Locke had made happiness the pre-eminent end for the acquisition of knowledge. The human understanding could attain to knowledge of "that which man himself ought to do, as a rational and voluntary agent, for attainment of any end, especially happiness."[30]

The end of perfection, rather than that of happiness, was put forth by Leibniz as the end of knowledge. Perfection included power, knowledge and will. It included, in other words, the source of things; the details of ideas, and the production of change in concordance with the greatest good. In their finiteness, as living beings (or created monads) they fall short of perfection, but they may constantly approach it.[31]

Happiness? It was not something to which Leibniz was indifferent. For him, though, it was a question of the relation of knowledge to happiness. It was of their connection that he wrote:

> "It is true, thank God, that in what is of the greatest importance and which concerns the *summum rerum*, happiness and misery, there is no need of so much knowledge, aid and address, as it would be necessary to have in order properly to judge in a council of state or of war . . .; but as recompence mere firmness and habit is necessary, in what concerns this great point of felicity and virtue, in order always to adopt good resolutions and to follow them. In a

word, for true happiness less knowledge suffices with more good will; so that the greatest idiot may attain it as easily as the most learned and most skillful."[32]

REFERENCES

1. Locke, John, *An Essay Concerning Human Understanding*, (6th edition, BK IV, Ch. X, Sec. 2, Sec. 9, pp. 528, 530), with the notes and illustrations of the author, and an analysis of his doctrine of ideas. Also, Questions on Locke's *Essay*, by A.M., Ethical Moderator in Trinity College, Dublin. (New Edition, The World Library, Ward, Lock & Co., London, undated) The original edition of Locke's *Essay* is 1689.
2. Ibid., BK II, Ch. XXVII, Sec. 2-3, pp. 242-43.
3. Ibid., BK II, Ch. XXVII, Sec. 4-5, pp. 243-44.
4. Ibid., BK II, Ch. XXVII, Sec. 9-10, pp. 247-48.
5. Ibid., BK II, Ch. XXVII, Sec. 16, p. 251.
6. Ibid., BK II, Ch. XXVII, Sec. 18, p. 252.
7. Ibid., BK IV, Ch. XI, Sec. 19, p. 536.
8. Ibid., BK IV, Ch. III, Sec. 7, pp. 442-43.
9. Ibid., BK II, Ch. XXVII, Sec. 27, p. 256.
10. Ibid., BK IV, Ch. III, Sec. 6, p. 441.
11. Ibid., BK IV, Ch. III, Sec. 6, p. 443.
12. Ibid., BK IV, Ch. III, Sec. 6, note to p. 441, 458.
13. Ibid., BK II, Ch. XXVII, Sec. 26, p. 256.
14. Ibid., BK II, Ch. XXVII, Sec. 23, p. 254.
15. Ibid., BK II, Ch. XXVII, Sec. 25, p. 255.
16. Ibid., BK II, Ch. XXVII, Sec. 26, p. 256.
17. Ibid., BK IV, Ch. XXI, Sec. 3, p. 608.
18. Leibniz, Gottfried Wilhelm, *Discourse on Metaphysics, Correspondence with Arnould and Monadology* (Intro. by Paul Janet, transl. by George R. Montgomery, Open Court Publishing Co., 1916), Letter, Leibniz to Arnauld, July 14, 1686—Correspondence, p. 135-36.
19. Ibid., Draft of letter to Arnauld, Correspondence, p. 156.
20. Giedion, Sigfried, *Mechanization Takes Command* (New York, Oxford U. Press 1948), p. 34.
21. Leibniz, Gottfried Wilhelm Von, *Monadology and Other Philosophical Essays* (Intro. and notes by Paul Schrecker; transl. Schrecker, Paul and Scrhecker, Anne M., Bobbs-Merrill Co. 1965), p. 228.
22. Ibid., N64, p. 254.
23. Leibniz, *Correspondence*, p. 194.
24. Ibid., p. 152.
25. Ibid., p. 197.
26. Locke, BK II, Ch. XXVII, Sec. 9-11, pp. 245-47.
27. Ibid., BK II, Ch. XXVII, Sec. 4, p. 240.
28. Leibniz, *Monadology*, N55, p. 248.

29. Ibid., N62, p. 253.
30. Locke, BK IV, Ch. XXI, Sec. 1, p. 607.
31. Leibniz, *Monadology*, N48-N55, pp. 261-62.
32. Leibniz, Gottfried Wilhelm, New Essays Concerning Human Understanding: Together with An Appendix Consisting of Some of His Shorter Pieces, (Langley, Alfred G., Transl., with notes). (The Macmillan Co. 1896), (Reprinted 1916, 1949 by Open Court, Chicago. BK II, Ch XXI, Sec. 67, pp. 215-16.

CHAPTER XIV

Knowledge of the Person: Pre-Industrialized Biology

(Internal-Inward-Variety)

1.
THE EMPTY PERSON OF LOCKE

LOCKE, ALTHOUGH EDUCATED as a physician, left the person as an undefined something. The person was not an ineffable something. The person was a something that was there. A something that exhibited consciousness, a precondition of everything else by way of human understanding, but itself inexplicable. A something within which were operative attributes by which understanding was attainable—a that which could think—but in what the operative phenomena of thinking were sourced was itself inexplicable. A something that had duration in time, yet without a chain of unbroken consciousness in the time of its duration. A something that could have an internally induced sense of its own identity and of its own continuity of identity in the time period of its own duration. A something containing within itself, therefore, the ground for the unification of all its actions within a conception of the singleness of its identity over time. A something that existed, that had being but was without essence. A something which was recognized as a person simply by the conventionality of its form as a material entity.

2.
LOCKE'S LEGACY OF BIOLOGICAL VARIETY

The history of biology, as disclosed by Nordenskiold,[1] records that there had been, in England, a period of active research in anatomy that had started in the middle of the 17th Century and had continued until its end. Apart from the works of anatomists such as Glisson (liver, stomach and intestines) and Wharton (glands), the investigation of the anatomy of the brain and the nervous system had been done by Thomas Willis (1621-1675). It was an illustrated work in comparative anatomy, one that included the brain structure and function of vertebrates other than human.

Willis had concluded that it was the penetration into the brain of currents in the nervous system that induced life manifestations. The cortex of "the great brain" was the locus of ideas and memory. Subsequently Willis did "a comprehensive study of the vegetative and sensitive soul," which he considered to be common to animals as well as to humans. The rational soul of the latter was immaterial. The other soul was "that material vital spirit which finds expression in currents in the nervous system" and from which are produced life manifestations that are animal in character. Willis, wrote Nordenskiold, although a scientist of first class rank of his age, had embarked on the absurd "natural-scientific speculation" of his age, and he had drifted into a confused and helpless "psycho-physiological speculation."[2] It was the French anatomist Vieussens, who specialized in the study of the structure of the nervous system, and who, in 1685, published a description of it that "is remarkable for its unprecedented accuracy and completeness in anatomical details."[3]

The question, even then, was whether biology had need of a conception of the soul. Biology could take its function from the conception of nature that was the legacy of Galileo, namely, that the phenomena of biology were like the phenomena of the other physical-mathematical sciences. The pioneer work that did so was the accomplishment of the individual who created experimental biology, Giovanni A. Borelli. It was he who pioneered the experimentally based scientific explanation of muscular movements in animal (Man, mammals, birds, fish, insects) motion. The living body contains within itself mechanical phenomena the analysis of the operations of which can be done solely in terms of mechanical forces.[4]

Microscopical anatomy was founded by Marcello Malpighi (1628-1694), who was an "hitherto unrivalled genius" in the application of microscopical technology. His most important investigation was into the structure of the lungs. It was followed in importance by the investigation of certain glandular organs, and then by microscopical observations of the kidney and the spleen. Inventive and accurately observant microscopical technologists extended the technology of microscopic use and the power of its magnification. They added "facts of fundamental importance" concerning blood, histology, several organs and invertebrate anatomy.[5] It was from the invertebrate findings of Jose Swammerdam (1637-1680) that biological science advanced from Harvey's theory of spontaneous generation (epigenesis) to embryonic preformation.

> "In fact, it resulted in the assertion for the first time of the obedience of ontogenetical evolution to law; it definitely invalidated the old ideas of the spontaneous genesis of lower animals; it established the fact that according to nature the offspring must resemble the parent, whereas in earlier times, practically speaking, anything could arise out of anything . . . and, finally, it satisfied, as far a embryology was concerned, the contemporary demand for a mechanical explanation of nature."[6]

The legacy of the 16th and 17th centuries for the 18th was the triumph of factual knowledge and the demise of purely speculative knowledge in biological investigation. Biology, as a natural science, still had no other ground than the laws of mechanics on which to base a general and inclusive explanation of life phenomena. Life itself—both with respect to its origins and its continuance—was located in an unknown life force. It was from the medical practitioners, nevertheless, that there emerged empirically grounded speculative thought. It was the thought associated with medical treatment of the human body. It was a structure of theoretical ideas that were induced by the facts of the new findings and their medical application.

Friedrick Hoffman (1660-1742) was a professor of medicine, a practicing physician, "a clever chemist," and a knowledgeable anatomist. He put forth a general theory of the functions of the body that was grounded in a juncture of the chemical with the mechanical. But he was also a religious pietist.

> "He began with the principle that matter and motion form the foundation of existence; the body is a machine which is kept going by the circulation of the blood. Life is thus a purely mechanical process, from whose functions the activities of the soul can be excluded, . . . the movement of the blood is caused by the heart; . . . The power of the blood to maintain life is due to the fact that it contains a *'spiritus'* formed of the other constituents of the air and the sulphurous element in the blood.
>
> ". . . supported the Holy Scriptures, he divides man into three *'principia'*—namely, *corpus, spiritus,* and *anima* . . . But besides these man possesses a higher 'substance,' which the ancient—philosphers called mens and which Scripture names the image of the spirit of God; This substance make use of the consciousness's impression of things and forms them into ideas; . . ."[7]

It was Ernst Stahl (1660-1734), (who had originally postulated the substance phlogiston as a "working hypothesis" to support a general conception of conversion processes in inorganic nature) who based a general theory of the human body and its functions on the science of chemistry. He had a keen eye for what was chemically essential in the composition of the organisms. Chemical quality differentiated the different forms of life, and for each individual there was a distinctive chemical quality. What differentiated the organism from mechanism was soul. The body in structure and function and in every manifestation of life was animated and controlled by the soul. His soul theory "cleared up satisfactorily enough the question of the relation of the physical phenomena to the material, a problem on which all previous attempts to explain mechanically the phenomena of life came to grief."[8]

That, from the standpoint of practical medicine, biological investigation should so limit its natural-scientific inquiries as to exclude the ultimate issues of life phenomena—metaphysical and causal—was the position of the influential Hermann Boertraave (1668-1738). Strictly fact analytic, and working from the mass of accumulated information in previous literature, he advanced a conception of body functions that was unqualifiedly mechanical.[9]

It was Swedenborg (born Emanuel Swedberg, 1688-1772), who was educated in the natural sciences, and who wrote extensively in both biology (anatomy and physiology) and the physical sciences, who built a facade of biological speculation as a foundation of biological fact. Eventually, long after his death, he achieved high respect for his valuable anatomical work on the brain. With the data from post-mortem examinations and from extant works on anatomy, he developed the theory for an explanation of the function of the central nervous system. But he also entered into "fantastic speculations," which were theologically based, respecting the brain/soul relation in order to explain why human knowledge is limited.[10]

Nevertheless, descriptive and comparative anatomy continued to flourish in th 18th century. And in that century there also took place large scale developments in experimental biology. All this, moreover, without any cessation of speculative biology. The live animal, experimental research contributions to physiology—anatomy vitalized—of Von Heller (1707-1777) are of this period. Nordenskiold evalutates these investigations and their methods of experiment into body organ sensibility (body organs from contact with which there is induced a mental impression) as those which "must without doubt be regarded as one of those that have led biology into new directions."[11]

It was La Mettrie's (1709-1751) inquiry into the functions of the soul, (rather than of the body, with its mechanistic functions) that led him to investigate the body mechanisms of mental perceptions. His was a "purely natural—scientific view of life," one by which he arrived at firm conclusions about what the soul was not and could not be.[12] It was certainly not the immortal and independent spirit of the theologians. Bonnet (1720-1793), also an experimental biologist, and the discoverer of reproduction by parthenogenesis from his investigations of insects, was a severe critic of the vitalists and their "souls" as explanators of life phenomena.

What was constantly at issue was how to explain the phenomena of life. Both the explanation of these phenomena in machine-like principles of anatomy, and in the biological theory of preformation were explanatory doctrines. So, too, was vitalistic theory. The further doctrine of a life essence or force within the organism as the ultimate cause of what takes place in the living organism (Caspar Friedrich Wolff 1733-1794) was also put forth as an explanatory theory of life phenomena.

The question of a life force or essence in biology, like the question of gravity in physics, raised the issue of whether general explanation of empirical properties could be derived from anything but phenomena themselves. Wolff, however, who had studied the philosophy of Leibniz (who had himself been a critic of Newton's computation of the law of gravitational force) is recognized in the history of biology as the individual who pointed embryology towards new directions of inquiry. As against the prevailing doctrine of preformation, Wolff had advanced the doctrine that the embryo is created as an entirely new organic entity, which is the doctrine of epigenesis. But, as Nordenskiold records, he did "not base his rejection of it on the evidence of the facts he has observed," but on purely theoretical reasons adduced "by a professor of philosophy who was an exponent of the theories of Leibniz."[13]

3.
THE POST-LOCKEAN LEGACY OF BIOLOGICAL VARIETY

The nineteenth century is one in which there continued side by side the dual stands of precise and factual scientific research—the strand of scientific discovery—and system structures of a theoretical kind that were rooted in the strand of speculative natural philosophy. Vicq D'Azyr (who performed detailed studies of the functions of the organs), extended the conceptual and analytic foundation for the scientific development of comparative anatomy. He was a philosopher of natural science inquiry as well as an anatomist. Blumenbach, who was a precise observer, founded comparative physical anthropology, and in so doing laid the foundation for the later anti-Darwinists. Sommering, also an anatomist, did a special anatomical study of the brain. It was a study in which was included the first treatment of the sympathetic nervous system. Gall (whose reputation was discredited after his death by dilletante advocates of phrenology) is judged to be "without doubt one of the most brilliant brain-anatomists of his age," and the ideas he set forth were to be of great future significance for the study of the brain.

> "In his exposition of the nervous system he does not start from the brain, as his contemporaries did, but from the simple nerve-fibre. . . . what is new and of value to the future in this nerve theory is, first of all, the emphasis he lays on the significance of the nerve-tracts; further, and above all, the placing of the soul-functions in the cortex of the great brain; and, finally, the assumption of hereditary intellectual tendencies. In particular, the idea that the cortex of the great brain is the organ of intelligence has been fully verified."[14]

It is to Cuvier (1769-1832), because of the method that he introduced into the study of comparative anatomy, that a position of prominence is assigned to him as one of the founders of modern biology. "He actually created an entirely new view of the connexion of causes in nature, in respect of both the constuction of the separate individual and the mutual relation of the various animal forms."[15] There is a type and system context within which animal structure, habits and organ placement can be determined from the interdependence or correlation between the separate organs in the same animal body. As for the idea of a life essence, Cuvier (in a view reminiscent of that of Newton respecting the essence of gravity) placed the idea of an essence of life in the category of riddles. It could only denote "the summary of the phenomena that have given rise to its formation."[16]

The individual who established organ tissues as a specific

basis for the study of life phenomena was the surgeon-anatomist-organ experimentalist—Bichat (1771-1802). His greatest contribution to the development of biology is listed as "the theory of structure." It was based on precise anatomical knowledge of the relation of tissue structures to the organs in which they were incorporated. The qualities that are associated with life are possessed by the living tissues. Bichat was more interested in the chemical composition of organ tissues than in their histology. The value of his contribution to modern biology "is best realized if we compare his tissue theory with the fantastic ideas of a 'nervous fluid' and 'microscopical life-units,' in which the works of even the most brilliant biologists of the immediately preceding epoch abound."[17]

The nineteenth century, unlike the eighteenth, was one in which there was considerable advance in embryology. The pre-formation theory of embryonic development had dominated the eighteenth century. Pre-formation was a theory that had driven out reliance on embryological observations to explain embryonic development. It was Von Baer (1792-1876) who was the pioneer researcher in mammal embryology. The discovery (published first in 1827) of "the egg of mammals in the ovary," and the first ever explanation of "the conditions obtaining at the earliest stages of development of mammals" was the achievement of Von Baer.[18] Additionally, he did a comprehensive survey of vertebrate embryonic development which, writes Nordenskiold, established modern embryology as both a branch of comparative anatomy and as a separate, self-standing field of research in comparative morphology and morphogenesis.

4.
BIOLOGICAL RESEARCH

Experimental Biological Research

The application of the science of chemistry to the chemical composition of living organisms had the consequence of reducing life phenomena to materialistic processes. The Swedish apothecary-physician "creator of the science of chemistry in general," Berzeluis (1779-1848), in his summing up of his researches on "animal chemistry," wrote that " 'our judgement, our memory, our reflections, as well as other functions of the brain, are organic chemical processes, as well as, for instance, those of the abdomen, the intestines, the lungs, the glands, etc.' "[19] His knowledge of brain structure and of the nervous system is characterized as vague. Nonetheless, he remains a fountainhead from which was disseminated the tradition of experimental investigation on live animals of the functions and life manifestations of their various organs.

Bill (Scotland) in the sphere of nerve physiology; Magendie (France) in the sphere of respiration and blood circulation and nervous processes—but above all in experimental technique; Barnard (France 1813-1878—said to be "the greatest physiologist of the age") in the spheres of nutritive and metabolic processes, and especially discoveries respecting the function of the liver; Purkinje (Czech) in the physiology of the senses, in microscopy and in physiological chemistry; Muller (German) in experimental physiology (sensory organs, motor nerve roots and glandular systems), in microscopy, in subjective sense perceptions, in the functions of the nervous system and in marine zoology. Of the contributions to biology of Johannes Peter Muller, there is the judgment that "he largely created the standard of thought which prevailed in biological circles up to the appearance of the origin-of-species theory, and from which the opposition to that theory largely recruited its forces."[20]

Research in Microscopy and in Cytology

Not until after the construction of the achromatic lens, and not until its utilization in microscopes of gradually improved perfection (following the demonstration of the first achromatic lens system in 1827) were there notable advances in microscopical biology. These advances were in the field of cytoloty, or the scientific study of the formation, structure and function of cells. Actually, it was botonists who led the way in the progress of the knowledge of cells. The cell structure of plants, their cellular contents, cell reproduction, the cell nucleus (cytoblast), the formation of the nucleal body, cellular components, and the relation of cell formation and cell structure to a general theory of life phenomena. As to this last:

> "This conception of the cell [cellular formation and evolution in both animal and plant tissues by Theodor Schwann 1810-1882] as a general unit of life and as a common basis for the vital phenomena in both the animal and the vegetable kingdom was immediately and universally accepted; so self-evident did its truth seem to be . . . , and in fact [it] became the foundation on which since then both animal and vegetable biology have developed. It is thanks to this theory that the present age has been able to work out its conception of life-phenomena as a connected whole, . . ."[21]

The developments in cell research on animals resulted in the early histological handbooks that were based upon cytology; in contributions to the understanding of connective tissue substances; in embryonic neurology; and in the application of microscopical method to a variety of biological researches, such as the structure of nerve fibres. The improvement of histological techniques is linked to advances in microscopical method. "It was not merely that microscopes were rapidly improved, but mechanical and chemical means of a kind hitherto unknown [means of preservtion, coloring and sectioning] were now beginning to be discovered and to become widely used."[22]

Quite apart from method alone, however, the linkages established between cells and health and disease by the research pathologist Virchow (1801-1902) produced the theory of "cellular pathology." The theory establishes the cell as a life unit with a role within the organism as a whole, but also independent of it. Finally, there is in this period the modern conception of the living cell as not a walled space but a space without walls that includes a protoplasmic substance that surrounds the cell as a nucleus. (Schultze 1825-1874)

Organic Chemistry and Experimental Biological Research

Experimental biological research reached out into the separate scientific fields of chemistry, energy and electricity. Within the general field of chemistry, there was a separating out of organic from inorganic chemistry. The distinctiveness attributed to each lay in the differentiation between animate and inanimate nature. It is a differentiation between matter with life (living nature-organic) and lifeless matter (inorganic nature). Researchers following Berzilues had applied chemistry to living entitities and had discovered substances that were not to be found in inanimate natures.

The differentiation between the two branches of chemistry was undermined by researchers who, starting with Wohles (1800-1881), synthesized organic elements out of inorganic ones. Organic chemistry "thus became a chemistry of the carbon compounds, the unique character of which is due to the nature of the elements with which it operates, but which otherwise has recourse entirely to the methods and theories of general chemistry."[23]

The connection between biology and the law of the indestructibility of energy had its origin in the fact that two of the scientist investigators of the phenomenon of heat were also trained in biology—Mayer and Helmholtz. The former had first expounded his theory in 1842, along with a method "of calculating the dynamical equivalent of heat." In 1845, he applied the law to the assimilation of solar energy in the vegetable kingdom and to the relation of energy exertion to muscular action, digestion and metabolism in the animal kingdom.

Helmholtz (1821-1894), like Mayer, was a physician, but he was also a professor of physiology as well as a professor of physics. His great work was in sense physiology—physiological optics, inventor of the opthalmoscope, theory of sensory (including color) perception, and further explanation of the mechanism of lens accomodation. In 1847 he published the empirical basis of the law of the conservation of energy and gave it a precise mathematical formulation. In consequence, physiological experiment with live organisms entered a period of great achievement.

". . . Immediate steps were taken to apply to as many life-phenomena as possible this new conception, which placed all phenomena in existence, both animate and inanimate, in one single simple and clear causal connexion, and which offered the hope of being able to bring all manifestations of life, even the most complex, under the same simple explanatory principles that physics and chemistry had already adopted."[24]

Among these subsequent achievements of experimental physiology were those that were the outcome of study of the phenomena of electric currents in the nervous and muscular systems of animals. Here the most important discovery (of research by Du Bois Raymond whose results were published over the period 1848-1884) was that in an active state muscles and nerves produce electric currents that are measurable with electro-physics apparatus.

Microbiology and Bacteriology

While observational study of micro-organisms (Infusoria, as they were first known) began in the seventeenth centure, with the microscopist Leeuwenhoch, it was the Danish scientist O. F. Muller (1730-1784) who, in the eighteenth century, first did "a systematic description and classification of the Infusoria."[25] The rise of cell research in the third decade of the nineteenth century also gave a new impetus to microbiology, including new researches on the Infusoria. In addition to later advances in their classification and in extending their known number, there were changes in conceptions of the Infusoria put forth by the investigators. It remained for Siebold in 1845 to include them in the definition of Protozoa and to establish them as a simple cell organic form "capable of sustaining a free and independent existence, being reproduced by division without any special sexual organs."[26] In the future development of biology it came to be understood (1) that the Protozoa were living creatures from which a path of derivation to higher organisms was possible, and (2) the cell, as " a true elementary organism," had a significance beyond its basic structural function in more complex organisms.[27]

Bacteria are also single-celled organisms. But they are classified as Schizomycetes; all are the focus of a special field of research. "In connexion with this branch of research there have existed a number of theoretical problems of the greatest significance; the problems of spontaneous generation, fermenting processes, and the origin of various diseases."[28] The theory of spontaneous generation ended with the experiments of Pasteur, who had done considerable research on the chemistry of fermentation processes. The isolation of disease producing micro-organisms was achieved by Koch (1843-1910) in his experiments with the anthrax microbe.

> "The anthrax microbe was at first cultivated in a damp chamber in serum, but Koch soon invented the method of planting bacteria on a gelatin solution; on this substratum, which could be made solid or liquid at will by a slight alteration of temperature, it was easy to isolate the bacteria and produce absolutely pure cultures. The method, which in its simplicity is one of the most brilliant inventions of modern times, has been the foundation on which the whole of present-day microbe-research has since then developed. But, in addition to this, Koch introduced the aniline-dye method into the study of bacteria . . . and, furthermore, he invented the microscopical illuminating apparatus, constructed to his order by the physicist Abbe of Jena . . ."[29]

Researches in fermentation, following Pasteur's experiments, focused on the yeast-fungi. The discoveries of Hansen (1842-1909), a Dane, who devoted his energies to the study of the fermenting process, "reformed the brewing industry and the manufacture of yeast." Hansen developed a controllable technique for the pure cultivation of yeast-fungi.[30]

Biochemistry

The application of chemistry to the search by investigators in biology for the explanation of the phenomena of living substance is biochemistry. Here colloid chemistry and the chemistry of ferments are in close alliance. Ferments can induce both phenomena of disintegration and synthetic processes. Bio-chemistry has also been brought to bear an internal secretions of glands and body organs. Finally, serology (blood, blood serum, toxins and anti-toxins) involves biochemistry.

REFERENCES

1. Nordenskiold, Erik, *The History of Biology* (Transl. from the Swedish, by Leonard B. Eyre, Tudor Publ. Co., N.Y., New Ed. 1936 printing).
2. Ibid., 149-50.
3. Ibid., 150.
4. Ibid., 151-53.
5. Ibid., 164-69.
6. Ibid., 170.
7. Ibid., 177-78.
8. Ibid., 183.
9. Ibid., 184-86.
10. Ibid., 186-88.
11. Ibid., 236.
12. Ibid., 240.
13. Ibid., 249.
14. Ibid., 311.
15. Ibid., 334.
16. Ibid.
17. Ibid., 350.
18. Ibid., 363-64.
19. Ibid., 372-73.
20. Ibid., 386 and Pt. 3, Ch. 6.
21. Ibid., 395 and Pt. 3, Ch. 7.
22. Ibid., 405 and Pt. 3, Ch. 7.
23. Ibid., 407.
24. Ibid., 410.
25. Ibid., 427.
26. Ibid., 429.
27. Ibid., 544-46.
28. Ibid., 430.
29. Ibid., 547-48.
30. Ibid., 549.
31. Ibid., 594-98.

NOTE
THE FOUNDATION OF KNOWLEDGE

"Fitted Knowledge" and "Possibilities Knowledge"

The distinction between "Fitted Knowledge" and "Possibilities Knowledge" goes to the core of the knowledge of knowledge itself. As such, it bears upon the thinking that makes the knowledge of strategy not only a knowledge possibility but also a particular kind of strategic knowledge.

The distinction between the two has its origins in the two treatises that first set out the foundations of modern empirical knowing. One is the treatise of John Locke on human understanding. The other is a critique of that treatise by Gottfried Wilhelm von Leibniz, and in which a different exposition of human understanding is set forth. Locke set himself to strip away all pre-suppositions about how persons know, and to then explain the structure and limits of a human understanding fitted to the practical and ordinary circumstances of human experience. Locke, in other words, had written what became *the* treatise on understanding human understanding. It is a treatise that has dominated and permeated and shaped Western thinking, but its stalking horse has always been the critical treatise of Leibniz, itself a treatise on human understanding. Leibniz introduced the idea of speculative empiricism, thereby providing an escape from only sense experienced knowing and opening a path to possibilities knowledge.

However, the relevance of the distinction to the knowledge of strategy extends beyond its historical origins in the emergence of modern empirical thinking. The distinction has a very contemporary relevance. First, its relevance for comprehending the knowledge of strategy as itself an expression of human understanding. Second, its relevance to the striving for an instrumentalized and technologically expressible knowledge as the output of a facsimile or artificial intelligence of strategy. It is this contemporary relevance that is the concern of this work. And so it has, at the start, gone back into the foundation knowledge of that knowing which, as human understanding, encapsulates and makes derivative the knowledge of strategy.

Even here, at the point of prelude to exposition of the differentiated content of "Fitted Knowledge" and "Possibilities Knowledge" there could be an advantage of understanding to be gained by placing them within a comtemporary frame of reference.

Fitted Knowledge

1. Reducible to operational rules of practice.
2. When operational practices stabilized, reproducible as a programmable protocol of sensory dependent acts.
3. Locatable at appropriate functional/operational niches down the chain of hierarchy in complex organizations.
4. Cognitive invention is excluded in preference to stabilized operational protocol. (concept exhaustion)
5. Becomes part of present behavior. The present is a period of subjective time during which behavioral understanding is coordinated with and adapted to objects and relations that are dependent on sense perception.
6. Procedure and sequence in time are of the essence.

Possibilities Knowledge

1. Remains linked to command cognition.
2. Not reducible to operational rules for present behaviour.
3. Concept independence and invention is preferred to and displaces operations.
4. Future time is both relevant and of the essence. The future is a period of subjective time in which the concepts of possible experiences are not dependent on sense perceived actuality.
5. Judgment is also of the essence.
6. Nominal knowing is not adequate for dealing with futures relevant change.

CHAPTER XV

Knowledge Foundation I: The "Fitted Knowledge" of John Locke

1.
THE FOUNDATION OF "FITTED KNOWLEDGE"

THE KNOWLEDGE OF STRATEGY assumes that individuals are by nature endowed with faculties by which they can acquire knowledge for themselves, by themselves, in the advancement of their own pursuits, as they so choose, guided by the considered judgments of their own minds, and acting on their own volition.

It is an assumption that is an outgrowth of the explication of human understanding that was put forth by John Locke. His contribution is a first knowledge itself; a first knowledge of the empirics of mind's own knowing. The knowledge of strategy is both a confirmation of Locke's human understanding, and an escape from it.

What is surprising about the *Essay Concerning Human Understanding*[1] is the conviction held by Locke about how ill equipped humans are for understanding. He was of definite opinion that humans were not the only "intelligent beings" on earth, but he was not all that certain about their ranking on a comparative basis. Not the lowest, and certainly not the highest, he judged.[2] Yet he also wrote that man, "In all probability is one of the lowest of all intellectual beings."[3] And comparing humans with animals, he assessed the differences of understanding between them to be but a matter of degree. It was a comparison about which he concluded that between "some men and some brutes" the difference would be so negligible that it would be hard to say the understanding "of the man is either clearer or larger."[4]

Though persons have the capabilities for acquiring knowledge by perception, Locke appraised them as "some few and not very acute ways of perception, such as our senses."[5] These supply only "dull and narrow information" for capacities of a "narrow measure." So human beings should not perplex to ourselves "about things to which our understandings are not suited," and persons should not engage in "an affectation of an universal knowledge."[6]

All that, however, was intended by Locke to be no more than precautionary statements. The faculties for knowing with which humans were by nature endowed, invested them with powers of mind capable of finding "out those measures whereby a rational creature, put in that state which man is in this world, may and ought to govern his opinions and actions depending there on."[7] This is the "fitted knowledge" of Locke. "Fitted knowledge," while knowledge that is capable of its own improvement, and capable, too, of making discoveries, is primarily only knowledge sufficient for the practical concerns and useful duties of life.

The reach, the scope, the certainty and the content of fitted knowledge turn the knowledge of strategy to nominal knowledge. The nominal knowledge of nominal man is the knowledge of Locke's human understanding. A knowledge fit enough for the modestly aspirational fitted knowledge of Locke, who believed it useful to begin his *Essay* by disabusing "busy minds" of any and all affectations of unattainable universal knowledge. His explication of the knowledge of materiality—of the world of material things and objects and bodies—illustrates the point of its inadequacy for the knowledge of strategy.

What mind confronts by way of the material world is something that is there in its already constituted material-ness. It does not exist as materiality that mind can reconstitute.

> ". . . The dominion of man in this little world of his own understanding, being much what the same as it is in the great world

of visible things, wherein his power, however managed by art and skill, reaches no farther than to compound and divide the materials that are made to his hand but can do nothing towards the making the least particle of new matter, or destroying one atom of what is already in being."[8]

Even conceding, as Locke did, that "in some other parts of this vast and stupendous universe" there may be "other and different intelligible beings," and bodies with other material qualities, still, the material world that is there before humans is the only one from which they can obtain the ideas of understanding. Therefore, the simple ideas (or "uncompounded appearances") of the mind brought to it only by sensation (external objects), or by reflection (operations of the mind about them) cannot be otherwise invented or received as ideas, or be destroyed.

Suppose, however, there was a reconstruction of the senses; of the sense of sight, for example. What then of knowledge and understanding? The reply of Locke: Not only would a different structure of the senses put a person "in a quite different world from other people; nothing would appear the same to him and others." It would also be absent any practical utility. Locke's illustration has to do with "that most instructive of our senses, seeing . . .

> "And if by the help of such microscopical eyes (if I may so call them), a man could penetrate farther than ordinary into the secret composition and radical texture of bodies, he would not make any great advantage of the change, if such an acute sight would not serve to conduct him to the market and exchange; . . ."[9]

The internal structure of material bodies, down to the smallest particles of matter, are inaccessible to sense. Hence, there is only the idea of solidity of a material body. Solidity is the idea that is most constantly received from sensation. Moreover, material qualities and idea/perceptions are separate and distinguishable. The qualities of matter are in the objects or bodies themselves. Idea/perceptions are in the mind. There is, in consequence of this separation, the phenomenon of material knowledge that

Locke termed "privative cause." It referred to the unknown external cause of an idea/perception that remains separate from the "real positive idea in the understanding."[10] The carry-over of the foregoing to experience means that experience includes idea/perceptions without knowledge of their causal origins.

In sum, the sensory faculties and the understanding allow persons to gain only an imperfect knowledge of things. According to Locke, however, the utility of this knowledge "fits us for the neighborhood of the bodies that surround us, and we have to do with." The explication of the knowledge of human understanding by Locke had fitted what was required by human knowledge by way of its practical utility to what was supplied by that knowledge.

> "We are able by our senses to know and distinguish things, and to examine them so far as to apply them to our uses, and several ways to accomodate the exigencies of this life. . . . We are fitted well enough with abilities to provide for the conveniences of living . . ."[11]

Within the circumscribing frame of the "fitted knowledge," there was an unescapable reciprocality between the "operations of mind" and the knowledge of the material world. Each functioned as an independent limitation on the other. The material world, a surround obtruding on the senses and thus forcing itself upon the mind, offer to it, in the words of Locke, that which "the understanding can no more refuse to have, nor alter when they are imprinted, nor blot them out and make new ones itself, than a mirror can refuse, alter or obliterate the images or ideas, which the objects set before it do therein produce."[12]

2.
THE KNOWLEDGE OF INTELLIGIBILITY

How is the material world made intelligible? No question but that it is there. It is there antecedent to its intelligibility. It exists as a physical surround of things and objects pressing in on the sensibilities of persons. Thus it is at hand and physically present to a consciousness. Further, it communicates itself to a consciousness. It can so communicate as it is, for Locke, the source of those material powers within things and objects from which, through ideas, there takes place "the progress of the mind in its apprehension and knowledge of things."[13]

Still, how is the material world made intelligible? Locke had no architecture of mind by which to explain how matter becomes intelligible. Nor did he have a physiology of the brain. Indeed, as to the latter, he confessed that he was in full ignorance. To explain the intelligibility of the material world, Locke had need of an architecture. He had need of an architecture of intelligilbility, that is, a structure for knowing. He had need, also, of an architecture of knowledge itself, that is, a structure of the knowledge that is the derivative of the structure of intelligibility. Locke, by his disproofs of all innate principles for knowing (stripping all conventional indoctrination from the subject) was in search of a foundation for the intelligibility by which to explain the natural knowledge of humans.

There was yet a prior question, a threshhold question: Were humans at all capable of knowing? Locke rested the capability for human knowing on a triple foundation: (1) on the foundation of intuition; (2) on the foundation of sensation; and (3) on the foundation of human existence as "cogitative matter." The knowledge of one's own existence is intuitive. Each, of his own existence, is beyond doubt. No amount of pain, of pleasure, or of Cartesian doubt could dispel that which is most evident to each person—his own existence. "Experience . . . convinces us that we have an intuitive knowledge of our own existence and an internal infallible perception that we are."[14]

It was in the capacity to sustain demonstrative truths by a line of reasoning, that Locke put the proof of the existence of humans as "cogitative being"—"sensible, thinking, perceiving beings." In this cogitative being of humans they are distinct from "bare incogitative matter," which, as Locke concluded, "could never produce thought."[15] Thought could only begin to be because of its connection with an "external cogitative being."

Neither knowledge of personal existence (intuition), nor knowledge of "external, infinite mind" (the fundament of the chain of finite being), provided the knowledge by which the material world could be made intelligible. That knowledge lay in the "knowledge of the existence of other things," as Locke put it. It is the knowledge that confronts the root question of real existence. It is the knowledge that must confront the absence of all "necessary connection of real existence with any idea a man hath in his "memory" of either objects or other persons. An idea of something, simply as an idea within mind, does not prove the existence of the thing that is the object of the idea.

The source of this knowledge lies in sensation and, Locke further asserted, it could not be otherwise had than by sensation. Less certain than intuitive knowledge. Less certain, even, than the deductions of reason (a property of "cogitative matter") the comparative shortcomings of sensory knowledge not withstanding, "yet it is an assurance—that deserves the name of knowledge." What persuaded Locke to this conclusion? It was that by "different applications" of the sensory faculties "I can produce in myself both pleasure and pain, which is one great concernment of my present state. This is certain, the confidence that our faculties do not herein deceive us is the greatest assurance we are capable of concerning the existence of material beings."[16]

The knowledge of intelligibility thus becomes the knowledge of understanding. It becomes so because of the inter-relations of sensation, idea/perceptions, and the understanding. And because it is sensation that is the source of this knowledge, we know only our ideas. A more ultimate material reality is concededly there, but it necessarily exists only as a supposition of the knowledge of intelligibility.

The architecture of the knowledge by which the material world is made intelligible then becomes the architecture of ideas, both simple and complex. Locke developed an architecture of the knowledge of intelligibility without resorting to an architecture of mind. Nonetheless, he put the operations of finite mind within the ambit of understanding. By doing so he made mind, as understanding, operational thinking. In this way, the understanding, as operational mind, made the material world the intelligible knowledge of things that were other objects and other persons. It was a material world made intelligible by different applications of the sensory faculties. It was also a material world the ultimate reality of which was suppositional, because access to its ultimate materiality was denied to those sensory faculties.

3.
THE KNOWLEDGE OF FINITE INTELLIGENCE FINITE INTELLIGENCE

The theory of mind put forth by Locke set human understanding apart from divine intelligence. The human mind comes to understanding through finite thinking. Human understanding was no more than "finite intelligence."

"Finite intelligences," Locke concluded, are one mode of "the very being of things." Finiteness of thinking and intelligence is present for each existant. It is present because there is a "determinate time and place of beginning to exist and the relation to that time and place will always determine to each of them its identity as long as it exists."[17]

Being in Time and Place

Time and place are taken by Locke as a basis for comparison between things; in particular, for "comparing . . . the very being of things." It is a comparison from which the ideas of identity and diversity are formed. Existence itself fixes a unique time and place for each and everything that has a being. His logic is that there cannot be either two beginnings of existence, or two instances of one beginning in time, in any one place or in different places, for any one thing. Each "finite spirit," has had "its determinate time and place of beginning to exist." Thus existence itself is, for mind, the source of the principle of individuation, or identity, for each of the three classes of substance, of which "finite intelligences" are one.

The World as Idea

How does mind, through its own operational acts, form an initial and primary cognitive structuring of the material world? How does the that within us that thinks, but of which we are in ignorance, know? All that it can know are its own ideas. These ideas are the objects of its thoughts, ideas become knowledge, but how? What is it about its own ideas that mind structures into knowledge? Locke's answer: ". . . Nothing but the perception of the connection and agreement or disagreement and repugnancy of any of our ideas. In this alone it consists."[18]

It was not mere whimsicality or an oddity of thought, that moved John Locke to depict the understanding as a completely darkened room into which, by means of tiny inlets or apertures, there penetrated to the visible images of the "outward objects, that are extrinsical to the mind."[19] At the foundation of this figurative modeling was perception—both "the first operation of all our intellectual faculties, and the inlet of all knowledge into our minds."[20]

The knowledge of finite intelligence as the agreement or disagreement between its own ideas requires a structural ordering of cognition. Knowledge becomes a derivative of this structural ordering. Locke viewed perception as containing the operations by which mind referenced its ideas within a cogitative frame of knowledge categories. His knowledge categories were (1) "Identity or Diversity;" (2) "Relation;" (3) "Co-existence or necessary connection;" and (4) "Real Existence."[21] Locke did not regard these knowledge categories as in any way inventive, nor did he insist on the use of the term "idea," as against a preference for "notion" or "conception."

> ". . . If I have done anything 'new,' it has been to describe to others, more particularly than had been done before, what it is their minds do when they perform that action which they call 'knowing;' . . . Knowledges' an internal perception of their minds' and if, when they reflect on it, they find it is not what I have said it is, my groundless conceit will not be hearkened to, but be exploded by everybody, and die of itself' . . ."[22]

The Knowledge Categories

(1) Identity or Diversity

Every idea is perceived by mind as a something. Mind, by that very perception, which to Locke, engages in "its first act," thereby knows "each what it is, and thereby also to perceive their difference, and that one is not another." Mind knows this identity/diveristy "at first sight." It is knowledge derived from mind exercising "its natural power of perception and distinction." Consequently this knowledge is not a product of deduction or of laborious thought.[23]

(2) Relation

Agreement/disagreement in terms of relation has to do with perception of the "relative" as between any two ideas of whatever kind. Without this capability of mind to perceive the relation between ideas "there could be no room for any positive knowledge at all." The operational activity of mind in determining the relation between ideas is their comparison.[24]

(3) Co-Existence

The idea of substance, particularly, brings to the fore the perception of "co-existence, or non-co-existence in the same subject." Here Locke resorted to his favorite illustration, the material termed "gold." What is signified by the idea of "gold?" No more than it is the term for a "complex idea" of a particular substance with a variety of co-existing qualities that are produced by the powers of its material constituents. A separate and special ground of affirmation or of negation is provided by perception of the idea of co-existence or non-co-existence.[25]

(4) Real Existence

Locke was not indifferent to objections to knowledge defined as the perception of the agreement/disagreement of our own ideas. The general form of the objections was that the real point of knowing was inquiry into the reality of things, and from this alone is it justifiable to prefer one person's ideas to those of another. The response of Locke was that our knowledge does not terminate in our ideas, but reaches out to a further intention. Yet "the mind knows not things immediately, but only by the intervention of the ideas it has of them. Our knowledge therefore is real only so far as there is a conformity between our ideas and the reality of things."[26] What is wanted by mind is a criterion by which to determine agreement/disagreement between its own ideas and things themselves.

The Knowledge of Finite Intelligence

Locke summed up what this four-fold structure of cognitive categories meant for the knowledge of finite intelligence:

> "Within these four sorts . . . is, I suppose, contained all the knowledge we have, or are capable of; for, all the inquiries that we can make concerning any of our ideas, all that we know or can affirm concerning any of them, is, that it is or is not the same with some other; that it does or does not always co-exist with some other idea in the same subject; that it has this or that relation to some other idea; or that it has a real existence without the mind."[27]

It can be a knowledge (a truth of knowing) that may be "actual knowledge," in the sense of the present actuality of the agreement/disagreement of any idea. It can be knowledge that may be "habitual knowledge," in the sense that assurance of its truth is obtained by the elimination of doubt through reflection on the memory of the idea. In the case of the latter, what is remembered ("the reviving of some past knowledge") is the conviction of its truth, the mind retaining "the memory of the conviction without the proofs."[28] As between memory and actual perception, the former loses its clarity because of decay in time. Thus it is that demonstrative knowledge—the knowledge of proofs—has less of a clarity than does the irresistible and immediate "intuitive knowledge" of actual perceptions.

The Knowledge of Materiality ("Physica")

The knowledge of materiality is the knowledge of matter and of substance. Locke, taking his cue from the history of philosophy, designated the knowledge of materiality as "natural philosophy." But, for Locke, it was classified as "physica." He made it one of the three divisions of the sciences that he placed "within the compass of human understanding."[29] Included within the division of the science of "physica" was:

> "The knowledge of things as they are in their own proper beings, their constitutions, properties, and operations, whereby I mean not only matter and body, but spirits also, which have their proper natures, constitutions, and operations, as well as bodies."[30]

Locke came to the conclusion that the end of the knowledge of "physica" was not material reality. Rather, its end was "bare speculative truth."[31]

What was the fundament on which Locke grounded his conclusion that the knowledge of matter and substance could end only in speculative knowing? It had its source in the separation he made between ideas and the qualities of matter. While the former might be caused by the latter, the latter were independent of the former. An idea was that "which the mind perceives in itself, or is the immediate object of perception, thought, or understanding."[32] The qualities of matter are not in the ideas, but are produced by a power in the things of matter. Between that which becomes the object of the idea, and that which is the things of matter, is an unknown something concerning materiality itself.

There was contact with the things of matter, but there was not access to materiality itself. Hence the knowledge of "physica" could only be of a speculative character. The knowledge of "physica", that is to say, was not directly knowable as experiential knowledge. Not surprisingly, then, as between idea/perceptions and the matter of bodies:

> ". . . We may not think (as perhaps usually is done) that they are exactly the images and resemblances of something inherent in

the subject; most of those of sensation being in the mind no more the likeness of something existing without us than the names that stand for them are the alikeness of our ideas, which yet upon hearing they are apt to excite in us."[33]

Still, despite the inability to access materiality itself, the "original or primary qualities" of matter in bodies were known and knowable as the simple ideas of sensation and reflection. These are the simple ideas of solidity, extension, figure, motion/rest, and number. They are, Locke wrote, the "real qualities of bodies, which are always in them," so that as to them ideas are "resemblances of something really existing" in bodies.[34]

Beyond the ideas, however, there is only mediate knowlede of the qualities of matter. Such knowledge is mediate because what appears to be qualities are but the secondary effects of the "powers" of those original or primary qualities, "viz., by the operation of insensible particles on our senses."[35] Here again the inability to access materiality itself prevents direct experiential knowledge of that which affects the sense. And here, too, "the ideas produced in us by these secondary qualities have no resemblances of them at all. There is nothing like our ideas existing in the bodies themselves . . . only a power to produce those sensations in us . . . .[36]

Ideas and Knowledge

Nevertheless, the world of materiality though only mediately known and knowable, is one whose materiality can be made intelligible. It is a world in which there are existants, or things of real existence; things which, as existants, intrude upon human consciousness. It is a world made intelligible by operations of the mind or ideas. Simple ideas enable the understanding to recognize "marks of distinction in things, whereby we may be able to discern one thing from another, and so choose any of them for our uses as we have occasion."[37]

The color blue, for example, as a simple idea. Was it in the mind only (subjective), or in the power of visual texture of the external thing itself to so alter light as to produce that color (objective)? No matter, wrote Locke, it is there, a constant, regular in its operation, discernible by sight, distinguishing itself, and "beyond our capacities distinctly to know." Suppose, however, that this color blue in the mind of one person was, in the mind of another, the yellow color of a marigold? Again no matter, reasoned Locke. Each person would know and understand and regularly "distinguish things for his use by those appearances." To each person they would be marks of distinction, with the assumption by each that in the minds of other persons there would be exactly the same simple ideas of these appearances. At bottom, Locke regarded the foregoing supposition as untenable. "I am," he wrote, "nevertheless very apt to think that the sensible ideas produced by any object in different men's minds are most commonly very near and undiscernibly alike."[38]

The Use Differentiation Between Ideas

In terms of their utility as knowledge, Locke differentiated between ideas that were real and those that were chimerical; between ideas that were adequate and those that were inadequate; between those that were true and those that were false.

Real ideas involve the concept of an archetype, or "the real being and existence of things." The reality of simple ideas is that they conform to or agree with "the reality of things." They agree, that is, with "those powers of things which produce them in our minds." Real ideas are not necessarily "fully imagic or representational" of that which exists in reality. They can only represent the primary qualities of things, the "utterly inseparable" qualities of solidity, extension, figure and mobility. Nonetheless, they are real ideas, because they are ideas of appearances "designed to be the marks whereby we are to know and dinstinguish things which we have to do with." There is a "steady correspondence" with that which is "constantly produced." That the causes or constituent elements underlying the appearances of things remain apart from and inevident to the sensory ideas "matters not."[39]

When an idea is a complete representation of that which the mind takes to be, and fixes upon as the referent archetype, there is an adequate idea. All simple ideas are adequate ideas. The foundation of such ideas is a sensory response to whatever is the power in external things that operates, or excites, the senses. In ordinary speech these powers of things are spoken of as "qualities," a term which Locke assessed as but a "vulgar notion" of common understanding.

However, all ideas of substance as a referent for the real essences of things are inadequate ideas. They are inadequate as to the archetypes of which they purport to stand. Hence, they "cannot be supposed to be any representation of them at all." No known sensible quality (simple idea) can be a basis from which to deduce any other sensible quality of a natural substance. Consequently, the idea of substance is without an archetype of real essence, and therefore inadequate as a copy or representation of it. "For service the powers or qualities that are observable by us are not the real essence of that substance, but depend on it, and flow from it, any collection whatsoever of these qualities cannot be the real essence of that thing."[40]

Ideas *qua* ideas are neither true nor false. They are "but bare appearances or perceptions in our minds" and nothing more. As appearances, they are what they are—the mental phenomena attending perception. What is necessary for any idea to be judged true or false is a referent that is exogenous or "extraneous to" the ideas of mind. "For, truth or falsehood lying always in some affirmation or negation, mental or verbal, our ideas are not capable, any of them, of being false, till the mind passes some judgment on them; that is affirms or denies something of them."[41]

The Way to Knowledge

What were these exogenous referents, and why? Locke enumerated the most frequent as ideas in the minds of others, the assumption of some real existence conforming to the idea itself, and the idea of substance or essence of anything. What interested Locke was an explanation for why the true/false referent selected by mind "is chiefly, if not only, concerning its abstract complex ideas." His explanation followed the path or course that mind "usually takes in its way to knowledge."

Mind comes to know only by reflecting upon the particulars of sensation. But mind has a "natural tendency . . . towards knowledge." There is, in consequence, a drive to know beyond "only particular things," to hasten knowing, "therefore to shorten its way to knowledge." The way of this drive to the enlargement of knowledge is for mind to take its perceptions and "bind them into bundles and rank them so into sorts," thereby transforming perceptions into comprehensive ideas as a way of extending knowledge.

The way to knowledge becomes the way of taking the ideas of nominal qualities and then abstracting a collation of them and assigning a name to the bundled abstraction, thus building a memory bank of nominal essences for purposes of differentiating things. So it is that abstract ideas come to stand mediately between perception/idea and the things of existence, and that the names of identification become confused with actual knowledge. But simple ideas—because they are verifiable by the senses of each person in everyday observation—are most easily rectified and least likely to be judged false.

4.
THE KNOWLEDGE OF KNOWLEDGE ITSELF

Locke put it straightforwardly that "all our knowledge [consists] . . . in the view the mind has of its own ideas."[42] Conscious knowing lies in the ideas about which mind is conscious. The origins of ideas themselves? Ideas are the product of sensation and reflection. An "idea" is a term, wrote Locke by way of explanation, which "serves best to stand for whatsoever is the object of the understanding when a man thinks."[43]

Ideas are both the object of thinking and the path to understanding. External things and objects impinge on the senses, producing perceptions of "sensible qualities." "This great source of most of the ideas we have, depending wholly upon our senses, and derived by them to the understanding, I call sensation."[44] Sensory variety, in terms of contact with external things and objects, introduces variety into the ideas of sensation.

The ideas of reflection, however, are of a quite different

category. Although they, like sensory based ideas, are also traceable to experience, the ideas of reflection are "the perception of the operations of our own minds within us, as it is employed about the ideas it has got."[45] There is thus a source of ideas which, for Locke "every man has wholly in himself" and which he regarded properly as an "internal sense."

Through reflection, Locke had made mind operational. "The term 'operations' here, I use in a large sense, as comprehending not barely the actions of the mind about its ideas, but some sort of passions arising sometimes from them, such as the satisfaction or uneasiness arising from any thought."[46]

Ideas were not knowledge. Ideas were the materials which fed into that whereby they became knowledge, namely, "the understanding." It was not only that knowing, through reflection, involved "operations of the mind," but that the operative product of knowing was understanding. Locke had made thinking operational and operational thinking the power that is "the understanding."[47]

Locke had likened the understanding to "a closet wholly shut from light with only some little opening left to let in external visible resemblances or ideas of things without."[48] What was the opening by which light could enter "into this dark room?" I "confess," he wrote, "that external and internal sensation are the only passages that I can find of knowledge to the understanding."[49]

Locke's analysis of the understanding made perception not only the "inlet" of the materials of knowledge, but also the first step towards knowledge itself. Perception both required and involved an operation of the mind; was one of its two principal actions," the first operation of all our intellectual faculties."[50] Therefore, "to ask, at what time a man has first any ideas, is to ask when he begins to perceive; having ideas and perception being the same thing."[51]

So the perception of Locke's analysis was not mere sensory stimulae. Yet sensations (from observation or otherwise) are a requisite for the ideas of perception—ideas being its operative consequences and the object of thinking. Indeed, sensation is itself an idea.

> "Thus the perception which actually accompanies and is annexed to any impression on the body made by an external object being distinct from all other modifications of thinking, which is, as it were, the actual entrance of any idea into the understanding by the senses."[52]

A sort of transformational conjuction existed between perception and understanding:

> "The power of perception is that which we call 'the understanding.' Perception, which we make the act of understanding, is of three sorts: (1) The perception of ideas in our minds. (2) The perception of the signification of signs. (3) The perception of the connexion or repugnancy, agreement or disagreement, that there is between any of our ideas. All these are attributed to the understanding, or perceptive power, though it be the two latter only that use allows us to say we understand."[53]

Locke did not make it a pre-condition of perception that "the external cause of it be known." Ideas of perception could exist in the understanding without the causes that produced these ideas being understood. Perception was one thing, its causality another. "Two very different things, and carefully to be distinguished," wrote Locke.[54] Nevertheless, "Perception, it is the first faculty of the mind exercised about our ideas, so it is the first and simplest idea we have from reflection, and is by some called 'thinking' in general."[55]

Still, there must be an operation of the mind for thinking to exist. Unless sensory impressions reach the brain, where sensation and idea conjoin, mind is without an actual perception. When this condition is met, then perception functions as "the first operation of all our intellectual faculties, and the inlet of all knowledge into our minds."[56]

Sensation does not, in and of itself, determine the idea produced through the senses. Perception can be an idea formed by judgement. Experience is the foundation of judgement. Judgement based on experiences can alter the idea of the sensory perceptions.

Locke does not assign to reason a singular position in the

structure for knowing. Nor does Locke link or identify reason with thinking. Human understanding requires the "materials of thinking." It is not reason that supplies mind with materials about which to think. These are supplied by "the internal operations of our minds, perceived and reflected on by ourselves."[57] Idea/perception is an operation. Reflection, also, is an operation of mind turning "inward upon itself" and observing its own actions about what the senses have provided as the materials of thought.[58] The common terms of designation—"perception, remembering, consideration, reasoning, etc."—refer to nothing more than operations of the mind.[59] Consciousness there is, but consciousness does not imply reason. "Consciousness is 'the perception' of what passes in "a man's own mind."[60] Nothing about thinking is an essence, only an operation. "Understanding is the outcome of operational knowing.

5.
THE ARCHITECTURE OF KNOWLEDGE

The architecture of ideas is the structure of the ideas by which knowledge is acquired. Locke took ideas to be modes of knowing. He defined a typology of ideas, and within this typology he differentiated between types of ideas for purposes of clarifying their respective knowledge utility. The clarification was done by probing into what differentiated real ideas from chimerical ideas; into what differentiated adequate from inadequate ideas; and into the distinction between true and false ideas. The primary typology upon which these ideas rest is that of simple ideas and complex ideas.

See *The Boundary of Thought*, pp. 90 et seq, and *Ideas and Knowledge*, pp. 253 et seq.

Simple Ideas Queried

As ultimate material reality, because of its inaccessibility to sensory faculties, is unknown, it exists only suppositionally. How then could it be said that "simple ideas" satisfied the condition

Locke laid down for "real ideas," namely, that they "have a foundation in nature?" By this he meant that they conform "with the real being and existence of things, or with their archetypes." The simple ideas are real ideas because mind, being passive with respect to simple ideas, receives in these perceptions the distinctive primary qualities of things as effects of powers that are in the external things themselves. Through the powers of their intrinsic materiality, the things of the material world disclose attributes to the sensory faculties as appearances, thereby producing idea/perceptions in the mind.

> "For these several appearances being designed to be the marks whereby we are to know and distinguish things which we have to do with, our ideas do as well serve us to that purpose, and are as real distinguishing characters, whether they be only constant effects or else exact resemblances of something in the things themselves: The reality lying in that steady correspondence they have with the distinct constitutions of real beings. But whether they answer to those constitutions, as to causes or patterns, it matters not; it suffices that they are constantly produced by them. And thus our simple ideas are all real and true, because they answer and agree to those powers of things which produce them in our minds, that being all that is requisite to make them real and not fiction at pleasure."[61]

Quasi-Autonomous Mind: Complex Ideas

Quasi-autonomous mind stands in contrast—but not in opposition—to non-autonomous mind. The latter is mind passive, "wholly passive" in the reception of the simple ideas received from sensation and reflection. The former is mind, "when it pleases" exerting its power, performing "acts of its own" whereby to consider and unite simple ideas into ideas of its own making, or complex ideas.

> "In this faculty of repeating and joining together its ideas, the mind has great power in varying and multiplying the objects of its thoughts infinitely beyond what sensation or reflection furnished it with; but all this still confined to those simple ideas which it received from those two sources, and which are the ultimate mate-

rials of all its compositions . . . It can have no other ideas of sensible qualities than what came from without by the senses, nor any ideas of other kind of operations of a thinking substance than what it finds in itself: . . ."[62]

Complex Ideas as Real Ideas

Beyond the simple idea are the combinations of simple ideas that constitute "complex ideas." As to these latter mind is not passive. Here "mind uses some kind of liberty" in their formation. Where, then, is their reality? They are real as a subjective mental content (serve as their own archetype). For their reality as material actuality what is required is "that they be so framed that there be a possibility of existing conformable to them." Their reality is in their possibility of becoming an actuality.

Complex Ideas as Inadequate Ideas

Locke held all simple ideas to be adequate, as well as real. They were adequate because they were a full and complete representation of "those archetypes which the mind supposes them taken from; which it intends them to stand for, and to which it refers them."[63] They could not but be adequate because, as sensory perception/ideas, they corresponded to that which could so be produced in persons as "the effects of certain powers in things," and, hence, to the reality of things.

The adequacy of complex ideas, however, was something else. They are not, as ideas, necessarily representational of "real archetypes of standing patterns." They are what the mind, which is at liberty to create them, intends them to be. Therefore, as ideas, and representing only themselves, they have whatever standard of adequacy is satisfactory to mind itself. It is in the social usage and transmission of these complex ideas, when they are then reduced to language and given names for purposes of speech, that they become tainted with inadequacy. The discrepancy between the complex idea as an archetype designed by the mind, and the terms of speech by which the idea is communicated to and comprehended by another, introduces fault and inadequacy.

The idea of substance is a complex idea. Substances, as complex ideas, are inherently inadequate as ideas. As copies of real things, they are ectypes. However, they are inherently inadequate because the real essences which constitute any substance are not known. One cannot proceed deductively from observed nominal qualities of things to their essential properties. A "distinct perception" of "internal constitution" is lacking, noted Locke. Moreover, the qualities attributed to bodies are secondary. Being secondary, they are qualities that depend on the powers of that which constitutes the materiality of the bodies themselves. But powers are not to be known directly. Powers are to be known only by their applications to other substances. In sum, powers are to be known mediately.

6.
THE KNOWLEDGE OF SIMPLE IDEAS
(Real Ideas as Knowledge)

Locke's simple idea is a mode of knowing, a "perfectly different and distinct" mode of the idea as sensation. He described the simple ideas as "the simple modes of the simple ideas of sensation." Being idea, they were grounded in sensation and reflection. They interacted with, and drew upon, the omni-present fundament of physicality, with which—unavoidably and necessarily—the ordinary experience of material existence and action were to be understood.

The Material Surround as Simple Idea

Locke took knowledge of "the things without," the material surround, to be the knowledge of simple ideas. He took these simple ideas to be the realm of thought in which there would be general agreement among persons. There could be little difference about space, figure, place, distance, solidity, duration, extension, number ("the simplest and most universal idea"), expansion, infinity, motion, sound, color, taste. They were the evident, simple ideas of common sensation—the idea of space being a derivative of sight and touch; the idea of figure being a derivative of the inter-relation of extended and circumscribed parts in space; length a mode of space; time a measured duration, and so on. For each of these ideas of "the things without" there was a confirming proof.

The Simple Idea of Thinking

Mind, too, has its own simple ideas about itself. These are the ideas derived from its own thinking about itself. What is Lockean thinking? "When the mind turns its view inwards upon itself, and contemplates its own actions, thinking is the first that occurs."[64] Mind, as it were, observes its own thinking, and thus perceives the "various modes of thinking" by which it has distinct ideas of things. These modes of thinking are sensation ("the actual entry of any idea into the understanding by the senses"); remembrance (what is "sought after by the mind . . . and brought again in view"); attention (notice "of a train of ideas succeeding one another in our minds"); contemplation ("attentive consideration")' and certain other modes of thinking. Was thinking of the essence, queried Locke; that is, the essence of the soul? Not so, concluded Locke, because "the mind can sensibly put on, at several times, several degrees of thinking." Hence, thinking was operative action in a variety of modal forms, rather than an essence.[65]

The Simple Ideas of Pleasure and Pain

The infrastructure of the "passions" are the simple ideas of pleasure and pain. The idea of pleasure and the idea of pain are derivatives of sensation and reflection. The reference base of good and evil are the simple ideas of pleasure and pain. Good and evil, in turn, "are the hinges on which our passions turn"— i.e. love, hatred, desire ("the absence of anything whose present enjoyment carries the idea of delight with it"), fear, hope, anger, envy, and so on. As to anger and envy, however, Locke put them into a special class, because they also involve a mixture of considerations about "ourselves and others." These two passions, therefore, were contingent upon difference in human character.[66]

Power, Volition and Freedom as Simple Ideas

Locke made the simple idea of power—simple because it also was the product of sensation and reflection—the mother lode in which were to be found the ideas of relation, and of volition and liberty. From these simple ideas Locke progressed to the "springs of action," or those motivational grounds of action in which were involved desire, volition and judgement.

The idea of power, being rooted in sensation, is an idea produced by sensibilization as perception of the observable changes in things (see pp. 57, 63). Locke put it straightforwardly:

> "The mind being everyday informed, by the senses, of the alteration of those simple ideas it observes in things without, and taking notice how one comes to an end and ceases to be, and another begins to exist which was not before; reflecting also, on what passes within itself, and observing a constant change of its ideas, sometimes by the impression of outward objects on the senses, and sometimes by the determination of its own choice; and concluding, from what it has so constantly observed to have been, that the like changes will for the future be made in the same things by like agents, and by the like ways; considers in one thing the possibility of having any of its simple ideas changed, and in another the possibility of making that change; and so comes by that idea which we call 'power'."[67]

For Locke, the idea of power included relationality—a relation of some kind to action or to change. It was either a relation to "active power" (make change) or a relation to "passive power" (receive change). As idea, it was less from sensory observation of external things, than from reflection by mind on its own operations, that power, as idea, suggested itself to Locke. He concluded that this was certainly more so for active power. Direct sensory observation of bodies would not yield "any idea in themselves of the power to begin any action, either motion or thought."

Ordinary experience disclosed to humans that they could start or withhold, continue or terminate, mental operations and physical motion "barely by a thought or preference of the mind ordering, or, as it were, commanding the doing or not doing such a particular." This power of mind, wrote Locke, is called "the will," and its exercise is called "volition" or "willing." The power of willing is a power of preferring. That it is such a power is because it is coupled to still another power of mind, namely, the power of perception, and therefore to understanding.

The idea of liberty and the idea of necessity both arise from the consideration of the power of mind that is the will. Liberty as idea is the idea of a power in any agent to do or not to do a particular act in accordance with preferential choices. The preference of an agent could be directed at either performance or forebearance, but a power of that agent equally to follow where preference lies constitutes liberty. "So that liberty is not an idea belonging to volition, or preferring; but to the person having the power of doing, or forebearing to do, according as the mind shall choose or direct. Our idea of liberty reaches as far as that power, and no farther."[68]

Locke, who was without a physiology or neurology of the brain, was troubled by just what language to use in order to provide a clear explanation of "notions of internal actions" of mind. To Locke, both will and liberty were each a separate power or ability of a person as an agent. Neither "ordering, directing, choosing, [or] preferring," were terms sufficiently adequate to explain what Locke meant by volition.

> "Volition, it is plain, is an act of the mind knowingly exerting that dominion it takes itself to have over any part of the man, by employing it in or withholding it from any particular action. And what is the will, but the faculty to do this? And is that faculty anything more in effect than a power, . . . For, can it be denied, that whatever agent has a power to think on its own actions, and to prefer their doing or omission, either to other, has that faculty called will?"[69]

As to liberty, however, which was a power to be separated from volition, Locke put it that: "I think the question is not proper, whether the will be free, but whether a man be free." The transformation of preference into an existing actuality through action was the test of freedom. As between liberty and willing, the former consists "in a power to act, or to forbear acting, and in that only." As to the latter, there are a "vast number of voluntary actions that succeed one another every moment that we are awake in the course of our lives," but that are neither proposed to the will nor, with respect to which, "the mind, in respect of willing, has not a power to act or not to act, wherein consists liberty."[70]

7.
THE KNOWLEDGE OF REASON

The Knowable and Deficiencies in Knowing

Locke, considering the then state of the minds of humans, and weighing ignorance against knowledge in the human mind, concluded that the former was "infinitely larger" than the latter. It was not just that sensation, and reflection on the objects of sensation ("These few and narrow inlets" of ideas) were too limiting. Their limits were such that humans were wanting the ideas by which to conceive of the world as an outcome of either sensation or intellect. It was also that such ideas as humans did have were disconnected, or without discoverable connection. It was, further, that such ideas as humans did have were not so traceable as to be able to find out and compare them one to another. There was, in consequence, ignorance of relationships of agreement/ disagreement between ideas.[71]

Locke had defined knowledge as "nothing but the perception of the connection and agreement, or disagreement and repugnancy, of any of our ideas."[72] Both "outward sense and inward perception," then, were in need of supplementation. The comparison of ideas to which Locke had reference was to (1) identity/diversity, (2) to relation, (3) to co-existence, and (4) to real existence. These four categories are not only categories of inclusion for "all the knowledge we have or are capable of," they are also interrogative categories. They define, said Locke, the inquiries we make into what "we know or can affirm concening" our ideas.

One could attain the certainty of "actual knowledge," but how? Putting aside both memory and habitual knowledge, there remains intuitive knowledge. None of these, however, provides a totally inclusive perception of all that would be known about all the relations between all our ideas. The most narrowly limited is the knowledge of the sense. Intuitive knowledge, while providing an assured immediate comparison of ideas for their agreement/disagreement, is more extensively inclusive, but still too limited. The most inclusive of all is demonstrative knowledge.

The Knowledge of Reason (A)

Demonstrative knowledge is the knowledge of reason. It is put forth by Locke as rational knowledge.

> "Sense and intuition reach but a very little way, the greatest part of our knowledge depends upon deductions and intermediate ideas' and in those cases where we are form to substitute assent instead of knowledge, and to be propositions for true without being certain they are so, we have need to find out examine and compare the ground of their probability. In both these cases the faculty which finds out the means and rightly applies them to discover certainty in this they are said probability in the other, is that which we call 'reason'."[73]

Absent reason, wrote Locke, absent a capability of mind to engage in a step sequence of search and proof in order to discern what connection might exist between ideas, "There men's opinions are not the product of judgment or the consequence of reason, but the effects of change and hazard, or a mind floating at all adventures, without choice and without direction."[74]

Demonstrative knowledge, as Locke's rational knowledge, is a knowledge of connection. It functions by the introduction of "intervening" or "intermediate" ideas. Demonstration is by these "intervening proofs," which serve ("not without pains and attention") to discover agreement or repugnancy between the ideas under consideration.

The operational aspect of reason is reasoning, not syllogizing, the rules for which do not teach understanding to reason. The syllogism is an inferior approach to reasoning. It is also not the best way to reason for the attainment of knowledge. The way of reason was the "four degrees," as put by Locke:

> "The first and highest is the discovering and finding out of proofs; the second, the regular and methodical disposition of them, and laying them in 'clear and fit order,' to make their connexion and force be plainly and easily perceived; the third is the perceiving their connexion; and the fourth, a making a right conclusion."[75]

Locke rejected the general belief that only the quantitative ("ideas of number, extension, and figure alone") was capable of demonstrative certainty. Rather, "it may possibly be the want of due method and application in us, and not of sufficient evidence in things; that demonstration has been thought to have too little to do" with qualitative knowledge. Demonstrative knowledge (proof requiring) is one of three degrees of knowledge, the other two being the intuitive (which contains known clarity of perception) and the sensibilized or "sensitive knowledge" (i.e. only of things present to the senses).[76]

The Limits of Rational Knowledge

The foundation of demonstrative knowledge is not the idea, but the ensuing perception. Clarity or abscurity of the perception determines knowledge, not the ideas themselves. Knowledge then consists of the perception of the agreement/disagreement of two ideas by the application of "intervening proofs." Reason, consists of the sagacity by which one "finds out the means" and the ordering of the connection between ideas in the steps of reasoning that is inference.[77] Knowledge results in that perception which removes the doubt that was precedent to the proofs produced by demonstration. Hence the link between demonstrative knowledge and assent, which is a link to either certainty or probability.

As between rational knowledge and knowledge without reasoning—"intuitive knowledge"—Locke took the latter as providing the highest degree of certainty. The certainty was the "clear light" of ideas that are so "in the mind" that immediate comparison of them is perceived "barely one simple intuition, wherein there is no room for any the least mistake or doubt; the truth is seen all perfectly at one."[78] Here Locke is on the edge of innate ideas, putting forth a knowledge that "every man" not only asserts to, but the truth of which is known to him "as soon as even they are proposed to his understanding."

The Knowledge of Reason (B)

Nonetheless, demonstrative knowledge extended beyond that of sense and intuition. Discoveries are dependent on reasoning. "The greatest part of our knowledge depends upon deductions and intermediate ideas." Still, there are limitations on reason, and therein lay its failures. Reason fails where ideas fail. Reason fails where it is applied to obscure, imperfect or confused ideas. Reason fails when the "intermediate ideas" employed as "intervening proofs" by which to subject the connection of ideas to a chain of inference cannot be discovered. Reason fails when it is based on "wrong principles," and when it is subjected to dubious and confusing languages. In and of itself, demonstrative reasoning can be long, perplexing, taxing, confusing, intricate, and "in need of more than one review before they can arrive at certainty."[79]

Rational knowledge could not penetrate beyond that by which Locke limited the extent of human knowledge itself. Particularly as to the agreement/disagreement of the co-existence of simple ideas as complex ideas of material substances (e.g. man, gold), "our knowledge is very short." Underlying these ideas of substances are the secondary, not "the primary qualities of their minute and insensible parts." The connections between primary and secondary qualities are undiscoverable, because the connections with the human sensations produced by primary qualities are beyond discovery. "Our knowledge in all these inquiries reaches very little farther than our experience."[80]

8.
THE KNOWLEDGE OF CHOICE AND ACTION

The Idea of Power

Locke established knowledge of choice and action on the idea of power as its infrastructure. The idea of power served as general explanation of observable changes "in the things without" that mind could not but take notice of because of what was brought to it by the senses. Perception (understanding) of change, and preference (volition) in time, by agents of change supplied Locke with the idea of power, both active and passive.

All choice and all action presupposed the presence of understanding and will (a power of volitional choice). All choice and all action, furthermore, were reducible to thinking and motion. These are powers the operation and exercise of which are manifestations of mind. Action is that which an agent is able to do, or to forbear from doing. Actions produce effects. As for volition, to will "is an act of the mind directing its thought to the production of any action, and thereby exerting its power to produce it."[81]

The Voltional Determinant

"What is it that determines the will?" queried Locke. His answer was, "the mind." He meant whatever it is in every particular instance that moves the mind to direct this or that particular action. What was that determinant? His answer:

> "The motive for continuing in the same state or action is only the present satisfaction in it; the motive to change is always some uneasiness; nothing setting us upon the change in state, or upon any

new action, but some uneasiness. This is the great motive that works on the mind to put it upon action, . . ."[82]

Not desire for some greater good in view, but present "uneasiness" determined the will, motivated to action. Locke, in fact, put it "that desire is a state of uneasiness," and that "the uneasiness of desire fixed on some absent good, either negative . . . or positive" determined the will to voluntary action. He had put forth an individualized psychology of motivation, which was a psychology of contingently motivated individuals. Good and evil were not irrelevant; were, in fact, influences that "work upon the mind." But "good, the greater good" as as generalized motivator? "I am forced to conclude," explained Locke, "that good, the greater good, though apprehended and acknowleged to be so, does not determine the will until our desire, raised proportionately to it, makes us uneasy in the want of it."[83]

Time and the Volitional Determinant

He justified his conclusion by a line of argument that stressed the determinative significance for action of the present in time, regardless of a more ultimate aim (happiness) of all actions. The relation of present uneasiness to present action is fixed by the will being able to direct "only our action at once." The next present act, therefore, is the first necessary act for removing whatever present uneasiness mars the happiness that is the more ultimate aim of all action. Experience makes happiness knowledge of a sequence of future actions.

However, the future is a time of things not yet existing. It may exist in the mind as idea, but as idea it is "the object of unactive speculation." That which is absent cannot, by contemplation, be made "able to counterbalance the removal" of a present and volitionally operative uneasiness. The "topping uneasiness" that steadfastly holds the will prevents the understanding from removing the object of its unease from the thoughts of the mind. Thus it is that the will is held both to a succession of voluntary actions and to its choice of the next action. "Whereby it comes to pass, that as long as any uneasiness, any desire, remains in our mind, there is no room for good, barely as such, to come at the will, or at all to determine it."[84]

Judgement: The Interrogative State of Command Cognition

Judgement as a state of inquiry consists of the interrogative operations of mind in cognizing a structure of choice and action. That sensibilized "uneasiness" of Locke precludes anything and everything that is in any way pre-cognitive. It is also an "uneasiness" that precludes prescience, as only an experienced sequence of future actions can disclose things not yet existing. What remains for cognition is only an interrogative state by which to structure choice and action. It is a command cognition because Locke merged the infrastructure of power into the "intellectual liberty" of free agent. The interrogative operations of mind judging become a directive knowing. Locke made the acquisition of the foresight to choose and to act without either pre-cognition or prescience the function of judgement.

The Knowledge of Choice

The reasoning of Locke put the question: Is there, then, only the volitional determinism of an incessant and omni-present "succession of uneasinesses out of that stack which natural wants or acquired habits have heaped up?" Almost, yet not always. Experience makes it evident that the individual mind is at liberty to subject its wants and desires to consideration—"opportunity to examine, view, and judge of the good or evil of what we are going to do," Knowledge of choice becomes the knowledge of choosing ("the will supposes knowledge to guide its choice"); the knowledge of choosing becomes the final result of the knowledge of judgement. Judgement is the power of a free agent to determine his will as inquiry may direct. Indeed, stressed Locke, for the volition of an intelligent being to be determined by anything other than the thought and judgement of one's own mind is the negation of the "intellectual liberty" to do "what is best for him to do."[85]

The Pursuit of Happiness

That best, according to Locke, was "a careful and constant pursuit of true and solid happiness." Happiness was the "utmost pleasure" of which humans were capable. Misery was the "utmost pain." Good and evil were sensibilized functions of happiness and misery. It was to avoid being misled in the pursuit of happiness that the expected satisfaction of particular desires was subjected to the inquiry of judment for guidance in choosing. Still, how is it that men make wrong judgments of their future good and evil, are misled in matters of their happiness? At bottom it is due to the separation in time of the conjuction between the apparent and the real that characterizes things in the present. Here is the pit for error that is too large for "the weak and narrow constitution of our minds," especially in the judgement of the consequences of actions.[86]

9.
THE LANGUAGE OF KNOWLEDGE

Locke did not separate language from knowledge. He listed as one of the ends of language the conveyance of "the knowledge of things." In the relation of language to knowledge, the point of inquiry for Locke was both what knowledge is communicable by language and what was communicable by language that was knowledge.

> "There is no knowledge of things conveyed by men's words, when their ideas agree not to the reality of things. Though it be a defect that it has its original in our ideas . . . yet it fails not to extend itself to our words, too, when we use them as signs of real beings which yet never had any reality or existence."[87]

Language and Simple Ideas

How is it that an erroneous semblance of knowledge enters into language? The explanation of Locke is in terms of the relation of language to the peculiar differences between his classes of ideas. The immediate significance of all spoken words has to do with "the ideas in the mind of the speaker;" yet they "intimate also some real existence from which was derived their original pattern." The names of simple ideas (light, motion) signify both the nominal and the real of that extent to which they refer. However, Locke put it that the names of simple ideas are undefinable. Using the simple idea of light as an example, Locke goes on to separate an explication of the idea of the cause of light from "the idea of light itself as it is such a particular perception in us." Locke's simple idea, in sum, cloaks two separate ideas. One is the idea of the cause of a sensation. The second is the idea of the sensation itself. It is the idea produced by the latter that Locke took to be "properly light." As he summed it up:

> "Simple ideas, as has been shown, are only to be got by those impressions objects themselves make on our minds by the proper inlets appointed to each sort. If they are not received this way, all the words in the world made use of to explain or define any of their names, will never be able to produce in us the idea it stands for. For words, being sounds, can produce in us no other simple ideas than of those very sounds; nor excite any in us but by that voluntary connection which is known to be between them and those simple ideas which common use has made them signs of . . . In light and colours, and all other simple ideas, it is the same thing: For the signification of sounds is not natural, but only imposed and arbitrary . . . For to hope to produce an idea of light or colour by a sound, however formed, is to expect that sounds should be visible, or colours audible; and to make the ears do the office of all the other senses."[88]

Language and the Idea of Substance

What about substance, the abstract idea of an essence of things? What knowledge of the nature of things can be conveyed by that abstract idea of essence? It is a complex idea (a bundling of simple ideas) by which a single name is used so as to comprehend (or cognitively enclose) a set of particular things within "one common conception;" that of *genera* and species. There is thereby conveyed not the real nature of things, not the real essence, wrote Locke; only the dependent qualities and properties of its nominal essence.

> "So that 'essential' and 'not essential' relate only to our abstract ideas, and the name annexed to them; which amounts to no more but this, that whatever particular thing has not in it those qualities which are contained in the abstract idea which any general term stands for, cannot be ranked under that species, nor be called by that name, since that abstract idea is the very essence of that species."[89]

Language and the Idea of "Man"

Taking the idea of that which is named "man," the complex idea of individual man, as his example, Locke delved at length into the difference between the nominal and the real essence. What is but nominal in the definitional language of the species man?

> "For though, perhaps, voluntary motion, with sense and reason, joined to a body of a certain shape, be the complex idea to which I and others annex the name 'man,' and so be the nominal essence of the species so called; yet nobody will say that that complex idea is the real essence and source of all those operations which are to be found in any individual of that sort."[90]

What is real or foundational knowledge "of that constitution of man from which his faculties of moving, sensation, and reasoning, and other powers flow, and on which his so regular shape depends?" Nothing that can be gleaned from common names. Colour? No. Shape? No. Reason? No. Memory? No. Sense? No. Understanding? No. Once the pattern and standards contained in an abstract idea are put to one side, "particular beings, considered barely in themselves, will be found to have all their qualities equally essential; and everything in each individual will be essential to it, or, which is more, nothing at all."[91]

There is real essence in substances. It consists of their foundation constitutions, which, as to each substance, is "within itself and without any relation to anything without it." From these foundational constitutions are generated the combination of properties co-existing with the nominal essence. Still, as to these real essences of substances, Locke made two assertions. First, that "we only suppose their being, without precisely knowing what they are." Second, that knowledge of them does not extend beyond what is supplied by sensibilized ideas.[92]

Nor can an essence "within itself" be said to be real for an individual. Even in this sense of the term, Locke wrote of essence that it "relates to a sort, and supposes a species: for, being that real constitution on which the properties depend, it necessarily supposes a sort of things, properties belonging only to species, not to individuals."[93]

Comprehensive classes of things, extending over numbers of qualities and particulars, are characterized by incompleteness and partialness. They are "designedly imperfect" because of their deliberate ommissions. Thus, as applied to "man" as a *genera*, which Locke chose to do, "however some men seem to prize their definition of *animal rationale*, yet should there a creature be found that had language and reason but partook not of the usual shape of man, I believe it would hardly pass for a man, how much soever it were *animal rationale*."[94]

The utility of nominal essences is that they serve the common, ordinary language of speech well enough as an approximation of what is intended to be conveyed in discourse with others. Mind borrows from the nature what it supposes to co-exist. It puts them together as a complex idea of substance. But knowledge of the real essence of man?

> ". . . Had we such a knowledge of that constitution of man from which his faculties of moving, sensation, and reasoning, and other powers flow, and on which his so regular shape depends, as it is possible angels have, and it is certain his maker has, we should

have a quite other idea of his essence that what now is contained in our definition of the species . . ."95

REFERENCES

1. Locke, John, *An Essay Concerning Human Understanding*, (6th edition), with the notes and illustrations of the author, and an analysis of his doctrine of ideas. Also, Questions on Locke's Essay, by A. M., Ethical Moderator in Trinity College, Dublin. (New Edition, The World Library, Ward, Lock & Co., London, undated) The original edition of Locke's *Essay* is 1689.
2. Ibid., Bk. IV, Ch. XVI, Sec. 12, 565.
3. Ibid., Bk. IV, Ch. III, Sec. 23, 451.
4. Ibid., Bk. IV, Ch. XVI, Sec. 12, 565.
5. Ibid., Bk. IV, Ch. III, Sec. 6, 440.
6. Ibid., Bk. I, Ch. I, Sec. 3, 2.
7. Ibid., Sec. 6, 4.
8. Ibid., Bk. II, Ch. II, Sec. 2, 71.
9. Ibid., Bk. II, Ch. XXIII, Sec. 12, 214.
10. Ibid., Bk. II, Ch. VII, Sec. 1-7, 83-85.
11. Ibid., Bk. II, Ch. XXIII, Sec. 12-13, 213-14, 215.
12. Ibid., Bk. II, Ch. I, Sec. 25, 70.
13. Ibid., Bk. II, Ch. XXIX, Sec. 1, 289.
14. Ibid., Bk. IV, Ch. IX, Sec. 3, 527.
15. Ibid., Bk. IV, Ch. X, Sec. 8-10, 530-32.
16. Ibid., Bk. IV, Ch. XI, Sec. 3, 537.
17. Ibid., Bk. II, Ch. XXVII, Sec. 1-2, 241-42.
18. Ibid., Bk. IV, Ch. I, Sec. 1-2, 424.
19. Ibid., Bk. I, Ch. I, Sec. 24, 70.
20. Ibid., Bk. II, Ch. IX, Sec. 15, 96.
21. Ibid., Bk. IV, Ch. I.
22. Ibid., note to p. 424, at p. 420.
23. Ibid., Sec. 4, 424-25.
24. Ibid., Sec. 5, 425.
25. Ibid., Sec. 6, 425.
26. Ibid., Bk. IV, Ch. IV, Sec. 3, 483.
27. Ibid., Bk. IV, Ch. I, Sec. 7, 425-26.
28. Ibid., Secs. 8, 9, pp. 426-27.
29. Ibid., Bk. IV, Ch. XXI, Sec. 1-2, 607.
30. Ibid.
31. Ibid.
32. Ibid., Bk. II, Ch. VIII, Sec. 9, 85.
33. Ibid., Bk. II, Ch. VIII, Sec. 7, 85.
34. Ibid., Sec. 22, 89.
35. Ibid., Sec. 13, 86.

36. Ibid., Sec. 15, 87.
37. Ibid., Bk. II, Ch. XXXII, Sec. 14, 310.
38. Ibid., Bk. II, Ch. XXXII, Sec. 15, 310-11.
39. Ibid., Bk. II, Ch. XXX, Secs. 1, 2, pp. 296-97.
40. Ibid., Bk. II, Ch. XXXI, Sec. 13, 306.
41. Ibid., Bk. II, Ch. XXXII, Sec. 3, 307.
42. Ibid., Bk. IV, Ch. II, Sec. 1, 433.
43. Ibid., Bk. I, Ch. I, Sec. 7, 4.
44. Ibid., Bk. II, Ch. I, Sec. 4, 60.
45. Ibid., Bk. II, Ch. II, Sec. 4, 60.
46. Ibid.
47. Ibid., Bk. II, Ch. VI, Sec. 2, 80.
48. Ibid., Bk. II, Ch. XI, Sec. 17, 107.
49. Ibid.
50. Ibid., Bk. II, Ch. IX, Sec. 15, 96.
51. Ibid., Bk. II, Ch. I, Sec. 9, 62.
52. Ibid., Bk. II, Ch. XIX, Sec. 1, 158.
53. Ibid., Bk. II, Ch. XXI, Sec. 5, 166.
54. Ibid., Bk. II, Ch. VIII, Sec. 1-2, 83-4.
55. Ibid., Bk. II, Ch. IX, Sec. 1, 92.
56. Ibid., Bk. II, Ch. IX, Sec. 15, 96.
57. Ibid., Bk. II, Ch. I, Sec. 2, 59.
58. Ibid., Bk. II, Ch. V, Sec. 1, 80.
59. Ibid., Sec. 20, 69.
60. Ibid., Sec. 19, 68.
61. Ibid., Bk. II, Ch. XXX, Sec. 2, 297.
62. Ibid., Bk. II, Ch. XII, Sec. 2, 108-9.
63. Ibid., Bk. II, Ch. XXXI, Sec. 1-2, 299.
64. Ibid., Bk. II, Ch. XIX, Sec. 1, 158.
65. Ibid., 158-60.
66. Ibid., Bk. II, Ch. XX, 160-63.
67. Ibid., Bk. II, Ch. XXI, Sec. 1, 163-64.
68. Ibid.
69. Ibid., Sec. 15, 169.
70. Ibid., Sec. 21-24, 172-73.
71. Ibid., Bk. IV, Ch. III, Sec. 22, 450-51.
72. Ibid., Bk. IV, Ch. I, Sec. 2, 424.
73. Ibid., Bk. IV, Ch. XVIII, Sec. 2, 567.
74. Ibid., 568.
75. Ibid., Sec. 3, 568.
76. Ibid., Bk. IV, Ch. II, pp 433 et seq.
77. Ibid., Sec. 2, 567.
78. Ibid., Bk. IV, Ch. XVII, Sec. 13, 579.
79. Ibid., Bk. IV, Ch. XVII, Sec. 8-16, 577-80.
80. Ibid., Bk. IV, Ch. III, Sec. 9-14, 443-45.
81. Ibid., Bk. II, Ch. XXI, Sec. 28, 174.
82. Ibid., Sec. 29, 175.
83. Ibid., Sec. 35, 177.

84. Ibid., Sec. 46, 184.
85. Ibid., Sec. 47-48, 184-86.
86. Ibid., Sec. 64-67, 194-96.
87. Ibid., Bk. III, Sec. 25, 409.
88. Ibid., Bk. III, Ch. IV, Sec. 11, 344.
89. Ibid., Bk. III, Ch. VI, Sec. 3, 357.
90. Ibid., Bk. III, Ch. VI. Sec. 3, 356.
91. Ibid., Sec. 6, 358.
92. Ibid., Sec. 7-11, 359-61.
93. Ibid., Sec. 6, 358.
94. Ibid., Sec. 29, 370.
95. Ibid., Sec. 3, 356.

"This relationship between the infinite and the finite is what I was coming to. Our minds are finite, and yet even in these circumstances of finitude we are surrounded by possibilities that are infinite, and the purpose of human life is to grasp as much as we can out of the infinitude."

Price, Lucien (Recorder)
Dialogues of Alfred North Whitehead
(Little Brown & Co., Boston, Mass, 1954), p. 153

CHAPTER XVI

Knowledge Foundation II: The Knowledge Possibilities of Gottfried Wilhelm Von Leibniz

"Yet although we are very inferior to so many intelligent beings, we have the advantage of not being visibly controlled upon this globe where we hold indisputably the first rank; and with all their ignorance in which we are immersed we have always had the pleasure of seeing nothing which surpasses us."[1]

It was, thought Leibniz, an unnecessary degradation of humans to place them, as did Locke, in "the lowest rank among intellectual beings." Given the location of the earth within the planetary system of the universe, Leibniz was of the opinion that the earth "appears well chosen for a comtemplative animal who should inhabit it." As for the deficiencies of human knowledge enumerated by Locke, these were mainly traceable to a failure to make fuller use of given human capabilities for knowing. Looking at the data already beginning to accumulate from the spread of physical experiments, Leibniz was optimistic about future progress in the explication of physical phenomena.[2] The mind of Leibniz expressed an investigative curiosity that ranged from the phenomena of physical nature, on the one hand, to "abstract thoughts" in both metaphysics and mathematics, on the other hand.

Humans: Not at the center of the universe, but at a place of dominion. Not only an understanding suited to the practical. Beyond the understanding of practical knowledge, they had a power of cognitive domination. Humans! Existing with a power of domination within themselves, and therefore commanding the source of dominion as to all that was external to themselves. Embodying in their existence what Leibniz advanced as the two cardinal principles of nature itself—the power to create, which is the power to bring forth into existence in the world; and the power to give directionality to events, which is the power to infuse the world with tendencies of human endeavor in time.

Human understanding becomes intelligible only within the larger frame of understanding humans. Humans *qua* humans exist as a part of a choice by an infinite intelligence from among infinite possibilities with respect to the creation of the world itself. Human understanding as a finite intelligence incorporates a like power of cognitive domination. It is by reason of this power that humans can choose from finite possibilities of alternative creation with respect to the world. It is also by reason of this power that they can over time, approximate that infinite intelligence of which they are themselves but a possible cognition. Reason lies in the knowledge of possibilities emanating from consciousness of the power within of cognitive domination. It is by reason of the joinder of the two—possibilities as knowledge and dominion as the expression of an inherent power within—that knowledge foundation II adumbrates the knowledge of strategy as the possibility for event creation through human understanding as the possibilities of cosmological knowledge.

Knowledge as idea is thereby linked to knowledge of possibility. It could now be said, as did Leibniz, "that the criterion of a true idea is that its possibility can be proved, whether *a priori* in conceiving its cause or reason, or *a posteriori* when experience enables us to know that it is actually found in nature."[3] That *a priori* knowledge was in and of itself a possible knowledge released human understanding from the confines of the pen of *a posteriori* knowing within which Locke had staked it out. The pre-operative knowing of Leibniz could now be conjoined with the post-operative knowing of Locke. Finite intelligence had an internal structure of knowledge as well as a sensory contingent internal structure for knowing.

It was this internal knowledge structure of finite intelligence that Leibniz singled out as the repository of virtual knowledge. Virtual knowledge is both pre-informational and pre-operative. It is, nonetheless, knowledge. But, as knowledge, it is a pre-formative knowledge. As a pre-formative knowledge, virtual knowledge is a knowledge-in-waiting, so to speak. Virtual knowledge is a knowledge-in-waiting for its emergence within human consciousness under the conditions of sensiblized experience.

There was still another liberation of human understanding that needed doing, and which was done by Leibniz. It was liberation from the additional constraint that Locke had imposed on human understanding. Locke had deliberately chosen to tie his explanation of human understanding to the experience with things in their macrostructures. Leibniz, however, tied human understanding to knowledge of themselves, as well as of external things, in their microstructures. The understanding of humans would have its fundament within the microstructure of the person as a class or type of material entity. The microstructure of physicality extends to the things of nature that are not human, as well as to humans. It is in these physical microstructures that there are the mechanisms of bodies and the forces indigenous to each, and by reason of which their inherent efficacy is expressed as the acts and powers of individual substances. So it is that nature, as the aggregate of things, contours a preformation of events. So it is, too, that the minds of persons as created monads or living things produce acts immanent within the internal and inherent force of the microstructures that constitute their physical being.

Here it is that mind, inherently capable of forming its own intelligible world, engages in cognitive dominion. Rather than forming a derivative conception of power (Locke), mind contains within itself its own inherent and active power. It is a power of domination—domination of the reasons for the acts that constitute the expression of its own intelligible world. The domination of this rational expression is domination of the connection between thinking, choice of action, and the consequences of choice. Leibniz established cognitive dominion as "The Art of Consequences." He also invested it with operative accoutrements that have since become the empirical attributes of decision management.

It is, in fact, decision management that is the nub of "The Art of Consequences." What Leibniz did was to delineate how the understanding makes space for the management of volitional choice. At the same time, Leibniz brought moral choices within "The Art of Consequences." Moral decision management was possible because the moral could be given a knowledge content and thus be included within a frame of knowledge like that which reason brought to bear on motivated actions themselves.

In no event, however, was the moral to be conceptualized as the practice of virtue. Rather, the moral emerged as a part of the growth of practical benefits brought about through the enlargement of scientific knowledge. Moral knowledge took form as a methodical knowledge of the values of what was good and what was evil in the benefits of scientific achievement. It is a knowledge separate from the probable future consequence of a decision, having, as Leibniz put it, its own "consequent." Yet it can enter into the balance of reasons that is part of "The Art of Consequences."

Still, what emerges in the analysis by Leibniz is the impotence of the ethical/the moral as a determinant of volition and choice of action. It was not that there were known and specific motivations that might be accounted as more determinative. Given the complexity and the variety of the microstructure of human physicality, no universal about "sufficient reason for" and its linkage to motivational determination was sustainable. It was that for purposes of volition and choice, present perceptions of the moral and images of the future that are associated with the moral yield a "too feeble representation of the future."

His metaphysics notwithstanding, it was a tenet of Leibniz that "in three-fourths of our actions we are nothing but empirics."[4] Yet practice without theory left knowledge to expectations rooted in the empirics of habit and memory. It was a kind of provisional knowledge that often took its verification from custom and convention. Mind, however, sought another and different kind of knowledge. Leibniz had reference to a particular kind of reflective knowledge. Mind sought those truths in which reason itself and the sciences brought human thinking to reflective knowledge of the principles of that which is within them, and also within the universe represented by the human mind.

Leibniz was familiar with the scientific experiments of his time—the experiments in optics, in pneumatics, in physics, and in medicine. For him the improvement of the sciences was based on inventions of reason as well as on "The art of inventing experiments." His primary interest was in a new art of general analysis. It was a new art that may be likened to the interest in a new art of general problem solving of a later century. This new art of Leibniz was one in which method would make analytical use of symbols and signs, and also one in which logic of probability and of proof and suppositional and conjectural weights would be applied. As for his "Art of Consequences," it is the first (and still relevant) inquiry into what enters into rational decision analysis and the application of these factors as rational choice.

1.
FINITE INTELLIGENCE

Post and Pre-Operative Knowing

Both Locke and his critic, Leibniz, were intent on providing an explanation of human understanding. Locke took his stand on post-operative knowing.

The finite intelligence that is the human understanding, as exposited by Locke, acquires knowledge by operative knowing. Knowledge is a product of operations of mind on prior sensory data. It is an operative knowing in which mind is both passive with respect to what the senses provide it (perception/idea) and quasi-autonomous (reflection). Understanding is the culmination of post-operative knowing.

Neither a structure for knowing nor a structure of knowledge pre-exists the information of sensory data. Nothing in the way of either information or knowledge is pre-operative. Consciousness is a necessary pre-condition for human knowing. Certain ideas of the understanding are traceable to consciousness, but it is not "that which thinks" or that which structures the understanding.

The sensibilized materialism of Locke had brought him to a point where he was baffled to explain how the non-materiality of the understanding—of the intelligence of mind—commanded the materiality of the actions of the body. How, in other words, the cogitative moved and directed the non-cogitative, since matter (by his own argument) could produce neither "real being," nor perception, nor knowledge. "For it is as impossible to conceive that ever bare incogitative matter should produce a thinking intelligent being, as that nothing should of itself produce matter."[5]

Moreover, the explanation of Locke effected a certain separation of information from thinking. The "that which thinks" could not be explained through the operative knowing of sensory information. There were also some non-factual conceptions of thought that could not be accounted for by post-operative knowing.

Critique of Post-Operative Knowing

Locke, stripping away all conventional knowledge, had thereby established the ground for his adamant contention that there could be no pre-operative knowing. True enough, there could be no knowledge in terms of Locke's idea/perception, but that was not the conception of knowledge to which Leibniz had reference. True enough, moreover, there could be no matter that thinks in terms of Locke's conception of matter, but that was neither the conception of matter nor the conception of thinking to which Leibniz had reference. The foundation for the introduction of pre-operative knowing into the structure of finite intelligence by Leibniz provides the critique of the exclusivity of post-operative knowing.

The Material Fundament of Thinking

The error of trying to extract an explication of thinking from the notion of immaterial substance is that no substance can be separated from matter. Persons are substances in corporeal form. Hence, they are inseparable from their materiality. Through reflection they discover the important idea of substance within themselves. It is because persons are existants as substances, that the supposition of the human mind as a *tabula rasa*, without an idea and devoid of everything, was rejected by Leibniz as a fiction inadmissible even to nature itself.

> "Uniform things and those which contain no variety are never anything by abstractions, like time, space, and the other entities of pure mathematics. There is no body whatever whose parts are at rest, and there is no substance whatever that has nothing by which to distinguish it from every other. Human souls differ, not only from other souls, but also among themselves, although the difference is not at all of the kind called specific. And, according to the proofs which I believe we have, every substantial thing, be it soul or body, has its own characteristic relation to every other; and the one must always differ from the other by *intrisic connotations* . . . You may perhaps reply that this *tabula rasa* of the philosophers means that the soul has by nature and originally only bare faculties. But faculties without some act, . . . The pure powers . . . are also only fictions, which nature knows not, and which are obtained only by the process of abstraction. For where in the world will you ever find a faculty which stuck itself up on the power alone without performing any act?"[6]

An Internal Knowledge Structure

A structure of knowledge exists prior to the data of the senses. The data of the senses are but subjective phenomena.

These phenomena provide very little certainty of knowledge about the reality of things. What knows is more primary than what the senses initiate as ideas. Knowing requires something more basic than the operations of mind on the simple ideas of the senses. Leibniz continues on in refutation of the spokesperson for Locke:

> "Have you forgotten, sir, how I have shown that ideas are originally in our mind, and that indeed our thoughts came to us from the depths of our own nature. . . . Besides the ground of our certitude in regard to universal and eternal truths is in the ideas themselves, independently of the sense, just as ideas pure and intelligible do not depend on the senses, for example, that of being, unity, identity, etc. But the ideas of sensible qualities, as color, savor, etc. (which in reality are only phantoms), come to us from the senses, i.e. from our confused perceptions. And the basis of the truth of contingent and singular things is in the succession which causes these phenomena of the senses to be rightly united as the intelligible truths demand . . . all intelligible ideas have their archetypes in the eternal possibility of things."[7]

The Function of the Senses

What then, was the function of the senses in relation to thoughts? What was the contribution of the senses to the furtherance of understanding? Leibniz contended that in "understanding is the origin of things," meaning that in understanding (not in the senses) is their very ground.[8] "It seems that the senses cannot convince us of *the existence* of sensible things without the aid of reason."[9] So, too, of the idea of power and unity; they also had their origins in reason. The function of the senses, then, in relation to thoughts? Not the impossible one of investing a person with thoughts. Rather, as Leibniz wrote:

> ". . . One can say in a certain sense that the external senses are in part causes of our thoughts, . . [but] . . . there are some ideas and some principles which do not come to us from the senses, and which we find in ourselves without forming them, although the senses give us occasion to perceive them."[10]

Necessary Truths and Truths of Fact

Leibniz had introduced a knowledge structure for pre-operative knowing into the finite intelligence of persons. A knowledge structure is in existence prior to mental operations. By his statement that the senses function as "causes of our thoughts" Leibniz had meant that the senses give the occasion for one to perceive those ideas that one finds in one's self without one having actually formed them from the data of the senses. He had made a distinction between "the origin of the necessary truths, whose source is in the understanding, from that of the truths of fact drawn from the experiences of the senses."[11] He had thereby both linked *a priori* (pre-operative) knowledge to knowledge *a posteriori* (post-operative), and established a separate ground for the structure of pre-operative knowing.

The dual capability of mind is that of both knowing these "necessary truths" and also of "finding them in itself." Its capability, then, was decidedly more than a passive one, indeterminate in content and directionality, but receiving knowledge from the senses. This dual capability, wrote Leibniz, is not "a naked faculty which consists in the mere possibility of understanding them; it is a disposition, an aptitude, a preformation, which determines our soul and makes it possible for them to be derived from it."[12]

The Black Box of Human Understanding

Locke had depicted the human understanding as the equivalent of an impenetrable black box. Was it a black box without any content? There was no objection to the black box equivalence on the part of Leibniz. However, in his *New Essays* he gave it a certain content so as to make what he considered to be a greater resemblance between it and the human understanding.

> ". . . You should suppose that in this room there was a canvas to receive the images, not even, but diversified by folds, representing the (kinds of) innate knowledge; further, that this canvas or membrane being stretched would have a kind of elasticity of power of action, and also an action and reaction accomodated as much to the past folds as to the newly arrived kinds of impressions. And this

action would consist in certain vibrations or oscillations, such as are seen in a stretched string so touched that it gives forth a kind musical sound. For not only do we receive images or outlines in the brain; but we form besides new ones, when we look at *complex ideas.* Thus the canvas that represents our brain is necessarily active and elastic."[13]

Virtual (Pre-Formative) Knowledge

Leibniz had placed the origins of cognition in virtual knowledge. It was because of virtual knowledge that finite intelligence had inherent within it a structure of knowledge that enabled human understanding to transcend and to impose unity on factual (sensory based) knowledge.

Leibniz had also set forth a basis for cognitive variety as between persons. He had thereby introduced the element of variety into the nature of finite intelligence. Locke, by way of comparison, had recognized a variety of experientially acquired knowledge, but not the variety of finite intelligence itself. It was, however, Leibniz who had recognized that there was, in individual tendencies and dispositions to action, and in individual preferences between actions, a non-sensiblized preformation of action. "I believe even," he wrote, "that all the thoughts and acts of our soul came from its own depths, with no possibility of their being given to it by the senses."[14]

He had reference by this belief of his to the conclusions that he had come to with respect to innate ideas. Virtual knowledge was sourced in innate ideas. Without this innate knowledge "there would be no means of attaining actual knowledge of the truths necessary in the demonstrative sciences, and the reasons of facts." Innate ideas were not innate thoughts. There were no innate truths of thought. Thoughts were acts, expressions of the activity of substance, whether material or immaterial. There were truths within persons as habits, dispositions, aptitudes—both natural and acquired—and these could exist within persons apart from, and even undiscovered by, their thoughts.

"The ideas of *being,* of *possibility* of *identity,* are so completely innate that they enter into all our thoughts and reasonings, and I regard them as essential to our mind; . . . we are, so to speak, innate into ourselves, and since we are beings, the being is innate; and the knowledge of being is wrapped in that knowledge which we have of ourselves."[15]

"Now the soul comprises being, substance, unity, identity, cause, perception, reason, and many other notions which the senses cannot give."[16]

In that dialogue between Philalethes (the fictitous protagonist of Locke) and Theoplilus (who expounds the views of Leibniz), the dialogue that forms the content of the *New Essays*, the response to Lockean type queries about innate ideas is distributed among a number of statements of their exchanges. Thus the distributed utterances of Leibniz (Theophilus) state the following:

p. 70 1. The propostions of arithmetic and geometry originate in innate ideas.
p. 93 2. "Not every innate idea is known always and by all."
p. 100 3. "What is natural to us is not known to us as such from the cradle."
p. 100 4. The proposition: "it is impossible for a thing to be and not to be at the same time" illustrates the innate ideas of being, of possibility, and of identity.
p. 94 5. "What is innate is not at first known clearly and distinctly as such."
p. 98 6. "Innate ideas and truths cannot be effaced, but they are obscured in all men (as they are now) by their inclination toward the needs of the body, and often are stilled by the occurence of bad customs."
p. 104 7. "Not virtue, but the idea of virtue, is innate."

". . . It is incontestable that the senses do not suffice to show their [the neccessary truths] necessity, and . . . thus the mind has a disposition (action as well as passive) to draw them itself from its own depths; although the senses are necessary to give it the occasion and attention for this, and to carry it to some rather than to others. . . . The original proof of the necessary truths comes from the understanding alone, and the other truths come from experience or from the observation of the senses. Our mind is capable of knowing both; but it is the source of the former, and, whatever number of particular experiences we may have of a universal truth, we could not be assured of it forever by indirection without knowing its necessity through the reason." [17]

Cognitive Variety

Mind as "more than *tabula rasa.*" The pre-formation of knowledge. Ideas or truths as active and passive habitudes natural to persons. Excepting "the soul and its affections" from coming through the senses. By all this Leibiz introduced a pre-sensory cognitive variety between persons. Moreover, he bridged a connection between cognitive variety and the principle of individuation among persons. Cognitive variety becomes part of "an internal principle of distinction," providing an "internal basis" for differentiating persons.[18]

2.
COMMAND COGNITION (See Ch. II, Pt. I)

The coupling of command to cogntion infuses thought with attributes of dominion, domination and directive control. Cognitive dominion? Cognitive Domination? Directive control through cognition? Of what?

It is a question that Leibniz addressed on two fronts. The first was the connection between mind and power. The second was the connection between thinking, choice of action, and the consequences of choice. The first brought Leibniz to a non-phenomenal exploration of the tie between thought and action. The second brought him to an explanation of thought and decision, one that delineates the modern frame of empirical decision making.

Thought and Action

Power and Action: Locke

Leibniz had put it as Locke's position that mind reflecting provides us with the idea of thought. Locke had also put it that mind reflecting on the phenomena of things observed to be coming into existence and ceasing to be, and reflecting, then, on the possibility of producing the changes that mind has observed, mind thinks the idea of power itself. Thus it is that the materiality of action is dominated and controlled by the non-materiality of thinking. The volition—the will—that determines action itself is itself determined by the "that which thinks."

Power and Action: Leibniz

Locke's explanation of power and action was not one that Leibniz would accept as adequate. Locke had explained the idea of power as a derivative of the sensory faculties and the phenomena of the senses. For Leibniz, however, the faculties are only "modes of being" in the world. More basic than the faculties are substances, matter which contains within its own material interiority a unity that constitues its own intelligible world, that world, as an intelligible world, may be capable of rational expression. Substances, though matter, are complete beings, not machine-like mechanisms. "It is not within the power of mere mechanism to produce perception, sensation, reason. They must then spring from some other substantial thing."[19]

In sum, something more primary than observed changes in external things gave rise to the idea of power. It is mind itself, wrote Leibniz, that provides us with "the clearest idea of active power."[20] Mind could not be analogized to matter as such because the passivity of the latter provides no idea of active power. Mind could be analogized only to that which was like itself, namely, to entelechies. Leibniz had drawn upon the Aristotelian conception of entelechy to introduce dynamic considerations into the conception of power.

His dynamics came from a uniting of tendency with faculty (of doing) to explain active power as a force. An entelechy is a primitive acting force. "Entelechies, i.e., primitive or substantial tendencies, where accompanied by perception, are souls."[21] Humans, existed, therefore, as a force with a power of doing that which was within themselves.

Leibniz was addressing a question that was again addressed

in a subsequent inquiry by Hume into human understanding. The quuestion had to do with how to connect the knowledge of matter to the knowledge of a desired event. Locke had left it as an unanswerable question in terms of the nominal knowledge of matter. Hume was later to write that no necessary connection could be established from the data of sensible perception. Locke had concluded that material cause existed as an unknown within the primary properties of matter. He had, in consequence, gone to the ideas derived by reflection from observable phenomena of matter in time for the understanding of power. Mind, therefore, reflected an extrinsic power, but was itself not empowered.

Leibniz invested power with another meaning, in addition to establishing that mind was intrinsically empowered. By referring back to the Latin term *potentia* for its equivalent, he separated the act from power and defined *change* as the passage from power to act. The actuation of power is the act. In its most general significance, the idea of power becomes "the possibility of change." The differentiation between active and passive power was treated by Leibniz as more than the reciprocal differentiation between subjects in terms of the faculty of action and receptivity to the act. There was more than the "simple faculty" to act. There was "tendency," or the dynamic aspects of action. The "*dynamical* consideration" extended the idea of power even further:

> "The word *force* might be appropriated to it in particular; and force would be either entelechy or effort; for entelechy . . . appears to me more appropriate to *primitive acting forces*, and that of *effort* to the *derivative*. There is even also a kind of *passive power* more particular and more endowed with reality; namely, that which is in matter in which there is not only mobility, which is the capacity of receptivity for motion, but also resistance, which includes *impenetrability* and *inertia*."[22]

Thought and Action

Again referring back to the Latins for the equivalent, Leibniz viewed the *understanding* as corresponding to the term *intellectus*. Intellectual activity, or thinking, consisted of uniting perceptions with reflection. Each such union is a thought. Being the object, rather than the form, of thought, it expresses "the qualities of things . . . [and] . . . may exist previous to and after the thoughts."[23] As to the relation between sensation, ideas and thoughts:

> ". . . I believe that we are never without thought, and also never without sensation. I distinguish only between ideas and thoughts; for we always have all pure or distinct ideas independently of senses; but thoughts always correspond to some sensation."[24]

An explanation of will as the power of mind to determine or command that an action be done or not done by a thought or choice of mind left out too much. There was tendency (entelechy); there were the insensible perceptions (apperceptions); there was conscious perception—all precede voluntary actions. As to volition:

> ". . . Volition is the effort or tendency (*conatus*) towards what is considered good and against that considered bad, so that this tendency results immediately from the consciousness one has of them. And the corollary of this definition is this celebrated axiom: that will and power united, action follows, since from all tendency action follows when it is not hindered. Thus not only the internal voluntary actions of our minds follow from this *conatus*, but also the external. . . ."[25]

Action as Command Cognition
Perceptions and Action

What Locke had put forth to explain the initiation of action by a subject was the sensory state of "uneasiness." The ambiguousness of what was indicated by the use of that term brought Leibniz to its reconsideration. Leibniz advanced the "doctrine of perceptions too small to be perceived." No perceptions "are wholly indifferent to us," but not all perceptions are consciously notable. "Uneasiness" remains, but as a sensory condition of a body "which can never be perfectly at ease" because of the relation of incessant perceptions to alterations of internal organs. Leibniz made uneasiness refer

> ". . . to the little imperceptible solicitations which keep us always in suspense; these are confused determinations, so that often we do not know what we lack, while in the case of the *inclinations and passions* we at least know what we ask for, although confused perceptions enter also into their methods of acting, and the passions themselves also cause this uneasiness or longing. These impulses are like so many little springs which try to release themselves, and which make our machine go."[26]

What was the function of this doctrine of perception? It was a doctrine put forth in recognition "that we should often be in ignorance and among confused perceptions, in order to act more promptly by instinct, and in order not to be disturbed by too distinct sensations of a multitude of objects. . . ."[27]

Action to effect some change can be initiated under a state of uneasiness. But what is the relation of such action to reason? It will not be action that is divorced from reason. It will not be unreasoned action. What it will be is action, the supporting inclination to do which—because of unrecognized and indistinguishable perceptions—is "without our being able to give a reason for so doing."[28]

Thought and Decision

Decision as Command Cognition

Cognition commands because of its power of domination over understanding, action and decision. The spokesman for Locke (Pilalethes) states the following belief regarding the necessary joinder of freedom to will and doing that which is willed.

> "Concerning which I believe that man cannot be free in reference to this particular act of willing an action which is in his power, when this action has been once proposed to his mind. The reason therein is wholly manifest, for the action depending upon his will, must unavoidably exist or not exist and its existence or non-existence

following without fail exactly the determination and choice of his will, he cannot avoid willing the existence or non-existence of this action."[29]

The response for Leibniz is simple and direct: "I should think he could suspend his choice, and that this happens very often." Deliberation about action is not necessarily followed by a decision to act.

Cognitive domination over understanding, action and decision lies in the domination over possibilities of choice. As to action, there is a separation in terms of connected decisions and acts. It is not only that those prior in time may contribute to those later in time. It is also that a person can "so act in advance that he judges or wills at the time what he would wish to be able to will or judge today."[30]

The possibilities of choice themselves have their foundation in the modes of thinking. These are modes of perception and reflection.

1. *Sensation*: The perception of an external object.
2. *Remembrance*: Repetition of the perception without the reappearance of the object.
3. *Memory*: Knowledge that one has had the sensation of the perception.
4. *Recollection*: (Lockean—finding the original sensory idea and bringing it to the view in the mind.)
    (Leibnizean—disengagement from things in order to engage in meditative thought.)
5. *Attention*: (Lockean—registering and reflecting upon ideas which present themselves to mind.)
    (Leibnizean—distinguishing and preferring some objects to others.)
6. *Consideration*: (Lockean—study. Fixed attention and examination of an idea.)
    (Leibnizean—continued attention, independently of the presence of the external object.)
7. *Contemplation*: Consideration tending to knowledge without reference to action.
8. *Study*: Attention whose aim is to attain and to retain knowledge.
9. *Meditate*: "To consider in order to form a plan."

10. *Vision*: "A dream which passes for a sensation just as if it acquainted us with the truth of objects."[31]

Choice itself, however, emerges as a matter of fitting the act of thinking to the employment of the art of consequences in the coming to determinative decision about voluntary actions.

Decision As
"The Art of Consequences"

The topic is nested within an infrastructure of ideas concerning the relation of mind to freedom, of mind to necessity and of mind to contingency. The topic is further linked through them to ideas of volition, to ideas of understanding, to ideas of reason and to ideas of the determinative aspect of thinking. It was, then, not at all astonishing to Leibniz that "a matter which has so many concealed windings" would be so perplexing.

Suppose one took an ideal case. It would be the case of a person who had perfect knowledge of all the circumstances, both external and within himself, that a perfect mind could foresee. Would, then, the thoughts or determinations of his mind produce free acts or necessary acts?

It was taken as a "fundamental axiom" by Leibniz "that *nothing happens without reason.*" He also linked volition to contingency, put necessity into opposition with contingency, and emphasized that necessity should not be confused with determination. Putting all this into a connected pattern of thoughts for application to volitional choice, Leibniz wrote:

> ". . . necessity should not be confounded with determination, for there is no less connection or determination in thoughts than in movements (to be determined being a wholly different thing from being pushed or forced by compulsion). And if we do not always notice the reason which determines us or by which we determine ourselves, it is because we are as little capable ourselves of perceiving the entire play of our mind and its thoughts, very often imperceptible and confused, as we are of recognizing all machinery which nature causes to play in the body. . . . But necessity must

be distinguished from contingency although determined; and not only are contingent truths not at all necessary, but further, their connections are not always of an absolutely necessary character; for it must be admitted that there is some difference in the manner of determining between consequences which take place in necessary matter and those which take place in contingent matter."[32]

That thoughts were determined and determinable ruled out the conception that freedom was the power of a person to do or not do as may be willed. A person could not have "the freedom of willing against all the impressions which can come from the understanding."[33] The improvement of volitional choice depended on improvement of the understanding. There was also the factor of "vigor of will" by which choice focused and regulated thought, maintaining their order and connection, "instead of being determined and carried away by involuntary perceptions." Nevertheless, there remains to persons, if not freedom, then an actual power to act in obstinant contrariness to all that may have been taken into consideration for action. While not gainsaying this bit of human caprice, Leibniz evaluates it as something that "enters into the balance and makes that please them which would otherwise not do so, so that choice is always determined by perception."[34]

In addition to the determinable thoughts with which volitional choice was connected, there were two other types of thoughts: (1) There were "involuntary thoughts, partly from outside by means of objects which strike our senses, and partly from within by reason of the impressions (often insensible) which remain from preceding perceptions whose action continues and which mingle with those which appear for the first time." (2) Mind "enters, and seems good to itself, into certain *trains of thought*, which lead it on to others. But this is true only when internal or external impressions do not at all prevail."[35]

Decision: "The Final Determination"

A will that is determined by perception and understanding is a will determined by intelligence. But how is it brought to final determination? It is possible for volition never to be determined. There is concurrence of many conflicting "perceptions and inclination" in volition. Mind, in its thinking about them, may become irresolute, and never be brought to final determination. Yet determination, the judgement that is a final result, is a requisite of effective choice.

A final determination has been made when there has been a determination of that which is to prevail as the final result in the determination of the will. It is not mind only, but desire also, that can determine the will, for desire (and its opposite, aversion) give force to volition. There is this duality of volitional determinators. What is the question thereby posed? Not one of either/or; not either desire and the will to act, or reason and the will to act. Absent desires, mind would remain irresolute and never be determined for action. Yet there is at times need to suspend or stop or prevent the execution of desire.

The Determinative Reason of Command Cognition

It can be done through mind "in a free and voluntary way in which the reason can share." Not always, however, and not directly. Leibniz recognized in mind only a certain indirect and partial power to stop desire. For mind to do so, however, it must itself be prepared for opposition and resistance to the execution of desires in time of need to do so. The preparation is mind determining itself in preparation for the determination of the will by intelligence.

> "It is then necessary for the mind to be prepared in advance, and to find itself in process of going from thought to thought, in order not to hesitate too much at a slippery and dangerous step. . . . It is better to accustom ourselves to proceed methodically, and to fasten ourselves to a train of thought whose connection reason and not chance (i.e. insensible and causal impressions) makes. And for this purpose it is well from time to time . . . to say to ourselves: . . . 'where are we then? Or let us come to the purpose; let us come to the point.' . . . Now being once in a condition to stop the effect of our desires and passions, i.e. to suspend (their) action we can find means to combat them. . . . It is by these methods

and artifices that we become as it were masters of ourselves, and can make ourselves think and do at the time what we should wish to will and what reason command."[36]

The reason of command cognition lies in the course of the examination taken by a mind that is itself determined by preparation for the final determination. It is a course proceeding always "through determined paths," and always with those explicable means of thinking that invest it with a reason.

Decision: The Final Determination As Judgement

Substantively, the final determination is a judgement of prevalence, so much enters into the making of that choice. There is a mass of "imperceptibles." They can impel the will, but they do so blindly, for no cause is seen. There are joinders of perceptions and inclination, which also impel the will to follow; but as a tendency and with an unformed feeling state. There are new sensations and the renewal of ideas arising from past sensations. There are clearly perceived pleasures, pains, displeasures. There is desire, as well as the state produced by uneasiness itself. "Uneasiness exists not only in the troublesome passions, as hatred, fear, anger, envy, shame, but further in their opposites, as love, hope, favor, and glory."[37] There is the future as imagined expectations and there is the present as the time of sensory appearances presented to perceptions. What will prevail? At the moment when the final determination must be made, there will be that which bears particularly on the balance, forming something which Leibniz likened to "a *compound direction* almost like that in mechanics."

Inescapably, the final determination involves a general reckoning. Leibniz put it that it would be one in which there would be a final judgement as a balancing of reasons and taking many things into account.

> "Thus we should still need the art of thinking and that of estimating probabilities, and besides the knowledge of the value of

goods and evils in order properly to employ the art of consequences; and furthermore, attention and patience would be necessary after all that, in order to push to the conclusion. Finally, a firm and constant resolution to execute the conclusion arrived at is necessary; and address, method, particular laws, and habits entirely formed in order to maintain the course in the future, when the consideration, which have caused it to be taken, are no longer present to the mind."[38]

Freedom and Command Cognition: Volition and the Understanding

For Leibniz, the resolution of the question of freedom lies in command cognition. Action follows from a union of will and power. Despite the presence of non-conscious elements (the appetitions of the insensible perceptions), voluntary actions are conscious actions. The question has to do with the tie between freedom and voluntary actions.

That tie is a double one. The first is the tie to freedom to act. The second is the tie to freedom of will. The power to will concerns the will to do, and not the will to will. "If we willed to will, we should will to will to will, and thus would go on to infinity."[39] Freedom to act, therefore, does not consist in the power to will as we ought, but in the power to do whatever it is that one wills to do.

As to the second tie—freedom of will—it concerns the relation between "the naked will," understanding, and necessity. Can the understanding determine the will yet leave an act of the will contingent rather than subject to absolute necessity? "And it is in this sense," wrote Leibniz, that I am accustomed to say that the understanding can determine the will, according to the prevalence of perceptions and reasons, in a manner which, even where it is certain and infallible, inclines without compelling."[40]

For the will to be determined by mind, that is, by the connection of thoughts, is not to subject the former to necessity. Volition remains contingent. Leibniz has here staked out the real within which command cognition, by its directive control of the art of consequence, can manage the art of thinking through to the final determination.

> "But necessity must be distinguished from contingency although determined; and not only are contingent truths not at all necessary, but further, their connections are not always of an absolutely necessary character; for it must be admitted that there is some difference in the manner of determining between consequences which take place in necessary matter and those which take place in contingent matter. Geometrical and metaphysical consequences necessitate, but physical and more incline without necessitating."[41]

Reason and freedom thus co-exist where the will can be determined, without being compelled, by the understanding, and where there is enough independence in the will itself. In this latter respect, Leibniz took notice that "one intelligence might be freer than another."

NOTE

If one were to envision parties engaged in working out deals, rather than moving through a formal sequence of decision steps, one could fully appreciate the subtleties of the explanation by Leibniz of command cognition. Real life empirics that illustrate the foregoing are to be found in the following:

1) Bruck, Connie, "Leap of Faith," *The New Yorker*, September 9, 1991, pp. 38-74. (The acquisition of MCA Inc. by Matsushita Electric Industrial Company). The acquisition is the subject of lead articles in the business section of the *New York Times*, November 27, 1990. For comparison with formal analytic considerations, see Rock, Milton L. (ed.), *The Mergers and Acquisitions Handbook* (McGraw Hill 1987).
2) Lardner, James, *Fast Forward*: Hollywood, The Japanese and the VCR Wars (Norton, NY 1987).
3) A "done deal" is another matter. There is a charge of a done deal and of failure to exercise fiduciary responsibilities on the part of the directors of Time Inc. in the case of the merger of Time Inc., and Warner Communications, Inc. See the review of *To the End of Time*, authored by Richard M. Clurmon (Simon and Schuster, NY 1992), which is subtitled "The Seduction and Conquest of a Media Empire" (*The Wall Street Journal*, March 12, 1992, p. A10).

3.
THE FIELD OF KNOWLEDGE

The Idea Itself

With Locke we do not know what an idea itself is. "Clear and distinct ideas" is the hallmark phrase of Locke. But this is a reference not to ideas *qua* ideas, but to attributes which mind assigns to ideas for its own purposes. An idea is that which has a particular and special significance for the understanding. Idea becomes defined as an object of mind engaged in the operations of thinking. We know what a mental operation is with respect to an idea, but we do not know what an idea itself is.

Locke himself made special note in the fourth edition of his *Essay* that "clear and distinct ideas" was inadequately precise for what he intended them to mean. His meaning would be better served by substituting "determinate" or "determined" for "clear" and "distinct," whether it be a simple or a complex idea.

> "By those denominations, I mean some object in the mind, and consequently determined, i.e., such as it is there seen and perceived to be. This, I think, may fitly be called a "determinate" or "determined" idea, when such as it is at any time objectively in the mind, and so determined there, it is annexed, and without variation determined, to a name or articulate sound which is to be steadily the sign of that very same object of the mind, or determinate idea."[42]

For Leibniz, too, an idea was also something that was in the mind. Where he differed from Locke, however, is that he did not place ideas in the context provided by the frame of mental operations. The idea for Leibniz *"consists not in a certain act of thought, but in a power. . . ."*[43] It is a power of mind that can be exercised on the occasion for its exercise as thinking acts.

Even to Leibniz himself, idea as a mental power was not completely satisfactory. It was possible to think of things without having any idea of what they were or might be. Further, adherence to method itself could lead to the attainment of things without having any idea of them. The function of ideas is their relation to that which is in a person—"There must necessarily . . . be something in me, *which not only leads to the thing, but also expresses it.*"[44]

To "express" a thing? What is that as a power of mind? It is a power such "that out of its own workings it can draw those things which perfectly correspond to those which follow from things. And so, although the idea of a circle is not like the circle, yet from it truths can be drawn which in the true circle experience would no doubt confirm."[45] An idea thus becomes the power within mind ("something else than the brain, or a more sutble part of the brain substance") by which "a certain analogy of conditions" with those of the thing to be expressed is maintained (e.g. a model).

Beyond Idea as Knowledge

Leibniz released the conception of knowledge from that place of confinement where Locke had placed it. It was much too limited a confinement for Leibniz. Knowledge was not just the truth of an idea; not just the final determination of agreement/disagreement between two ideas. Knowledge of the truths of particular ideas did not occupy the entire field of knowledge *qua* knowledge. As a term of general significance, knowledge was more inclusive than ideas. Leibniz had it include variety and diversity of information; one who had been exposed to information variety "I say, will have more knowledge than another, even though there should not be a word of truth in all that which was portrayed or related to him."[46] The comparative advantage in knowledge would consist in being "more fit to conceive what is placed before him." Discernment of the "sense and force" of thematic expositions also constitutes knowledge, quite apart from their proofs.

No truth, therefore no knowledge, was rejected as unacceptable. It was a proposition that demanded too much of personal consciousness about the knowledge of the agreement/disagreement of ideas. For Leibniz, it was not generally true that knowing empirically from having had the experience of a truth, and conscious perception of the reason of it went hand in hand. As to knowledge resting upon part proofs, it was a question of what reliance could be placed upon these proofs. Here it was not a matter of memory simply, but of remembrance of accuracy, without which there could be no certitude. "And this accuracy consists in an orderly procedure, the observance of which in each part is an assurance as regards the whole."[47]

Intuitive knowledge consisted of "primitive truths." As to those that are truths of reason, Leibniz concluded that "you can say in general that all primitive truths of reason are immediate with respect to an *immediateness of ideas*. They do not require proof. The primitive truths of fact (e.g. *"I am a thing which thinks"*) "are the immediate internal experiences of an *immediateness of feeling*." It, too, "cannot be proved by anything more certain."[48]

Demonstrative knowledge involved two difficulties. The first had to do with the extent to which there is a "parallelism of reason and experience." There were fields of knowledge as to which (metaphysics and ethics) Leibniz concluded that experience could not guarantee reasoning. As to demonstrative knowledge in physics, the experiments of physics "demand labor and expense."[49]

The second difficulty of demonstrative knowledge is the discovery of the "mediate ideas" by which proof is established. The art of finding mediate ideas is the art of analysis. Given the requisite sagacity for analysis, the question of demonstrative knowledge then becomes: "Proof of What?" Something is or is not? By whom and how? Form and manner? "And it is these questions alone, which have a part of the proposition blank, which the mathematicians call *problems*." The nature of certain questions makes it necessary that analysis generate and employ method as a thread in a groping labyrinth of search for demonstrative proofs.[50]

Leibniz subordinated opinion to probability. It is only in this subordination context that the accepted opinion is knowledge. "*Opinion*, based on probability, deserves perhaps the name of knowledge also." It could function as knowledge for those questions that could not be decided absolutely. But where a degree of factual "resemblance" could be determined, and hence a reasonable judgement to be made the estimation of probabilities as an established knowledge might, so he thought, "be not less useful than a majority of our demonstrative sciences." Investigation of "the probable or the likely" was thought by Leibniz to have been greatly neglected, to the detriment of logic itself.

> ". . . it must be drawn from the nature of things; and the opinion of persons whose authority has weight is one of the things which may contribute to render an opinion probable, but not what completes the entire verisimilitude. At the time when Copernicus was almost alone in his opinion, it was still incomparably more *probable* than that of all the rest of the human race."[51]

Sensibilized Knowledge

Locke had concluded that an idea of an external object drawn from the data of the senses about it established only the certainty of the mind having the idea. What he had left inconclusive was whether from this knowledge "we can certainly infer the existence of anything without us corresponding to this idea." Still, there was an evidentary basis in the data of the senses themselves that took belief in certainty "beyond doubt." Leibniz thought knowledge of the probable would confirm the certitude of actually experienced sensory knowledge, but that imagination might sometime prove stronger than feelings. There was, however, a more basic criterion by which to establish the truth of sensible things."

> ". . . I think the true *criterion* concerning the objects of the senses is the connection of the phenomena, i.e. the connection of that which takes places in different places and times, and in the experience of different men who are themselves, each to the others, very important phenomena in this respect. And the connection of the phenomena which guarantees the *truths of fact* in respect to sensible things ourside of us, is verified by means of the *truths of reason*; as the phenomena of optics are explained by geometry. . . . Experience's shows that we are not deceived in the measures

we take concerning phenomena when they are understood according to the truths of reason."[52]

4.
THE KNOWLEDGE OF REASON

Reason and its Knowledge

The "reason of" and the knowledge of reason were differentiated by Leibniz. As to the former:

> "The *reason* is the known truth whose connection with another less known makes us give our assent to the latter. But in particular and pre-eminently we call it reason. If it is the cause not only of our judgement, but also of the truth itself, which we also call *reason a priori*, and the *cause* in things corresponds to the *reason* in truths. This is why cause indeed is often called reason, and particularly final cause."[53]

As to the latter, the knowledge of reason, which is the faculty of reasoning, there is empirical reasoning and a level beyond the empirical. The knowledge of strictly empirical reasoning "is only the expectation of a similar event in a case apparently similar to the past, without knowing whether the same reason holds good."[54] The limitation of empirical reasoning is that it cannot reach a perception of

> ". . . The connections of truths, the connections, I say, which themselves indeed constitute the necessary and universal truths. These connections are indeed necessary although they produce only an opinion, when after an exact research the prevalence of probability, so far as may be judged, may be demonstrated, so that then there is *demonstration*, not of the truth of the thing, but of the side prudence requires us to take."[55]

The Knowledge of Truth

A truth, in and of itself, what is it? It has reference to the objects of ideas and to the relation of one to the other. A truth goes to that which is independent of subjective desire and is distinguishable from the language of nominal indication.

> "Let us content ourselves with seeking truth in the correspondence of the propositions in the mind with the things in question. It is true that I have also attributed truth to ideas in saying that ideas are true or false; but then I mean, in reality, the truth of propositions affirming the possibility of the object of the idea."[56]

The truths of fact, as contingent truths, have only a relative certainty and are learned by observation and experience. Here there can be certainty of knowledge. There can be, that is, a perfect knowledge of ideas and their objects. But with contingent truths there can be no assured knowledge of necessity and only an imperfect knowledge of universality.

Leibniz agrees that with respect to these truths of fact, judgement may go further than knowledge. There may, in other words, be speculative conjectures about that which has not yet been discovered by experience. The truths of reason can be learned by analysis. They are thus grounded "in the necessities of thought. For these truths of reason there can be a metaphysical certainty of 'the truth itself.' Facts, as the experiences of the senses, do not give truths that are absolutely certain."[57]

There are both primitive truths of fact and primitive truths of reason. The Cartesian "I think, therefore I am," is an illustration of the former. The reason for this is that "for the *primitive truths of fact*, they are the immediate internal experiences of an *immediateness of feeling*." No more certain proof is possible. The same can be asserted with respect to primitive truths of reason, the ideas of which can be known intuitively.

> "*Two* is one plus one, *three* is two plus one, *four* is three plus one, etc. It is true that there is therein a concealed statement, which I have already spoken of, viz. that these ideas are possible: and this is here known *intuitively* so that it may be said, that an intuitive knowledge is comprised in definitions when their possibility appears at once. And in this way all *adequate* definitions contain primitive truths of reason and consequently intuitive knowledge. In short, you can say in general that all primitive truths of reason are immediate with respect to an immediateness of ideas."[58]

Reason and Analysis

The function of analysis is to introduce both method and instrumentation into reasoning. Non-analyzed sensory information produces confused ideas of sensible qualities. It is because of this confusion that the connections of these ideas cannot be known otherwise than by experience—unless by analysis the confusion is eliminated. Referring to what had been done with the use of prisms to analyze light, and to what had been done to eliminate the confusion of ideas with respect to the colors of the rainbow, Leibniz wrote:

> "And this method presents a beginning in analysis which is of great use in physics; and by following it I doubt not that medicine in time will find itself considerably more advanced, especially if the public is a little better interested than hitherto."[59]

The plentitude of sensory images, colors, impressions, tastes and so on, and of which there is not always a distinct consciousness, do yield a knowledge, but it is a knowledge defective in its inability to uncover that which is concealed within the confusion of sensory impressions. Their utility is "to give rise to the *instincts* and to establish the observations of experience than to furnish matter to the reason, except so far as they are accompanied by distinct perceptions."[60] Their very multiplicity may require resort to "the science of numbers."

Reason and Knowledge of the Possible

Leibniz ventured into aspects of human knowledge that Locke not only refused to venture into, but thought it pointless to do so. Locke restricted his inquiry to the world in its physicality and to the physical things of the world. It is not that Leibniz put to one side the matter of "the aggregate of finite things," his phrase of designation for the world. It is that he raised questions about it that Locke would not and could not. The assumption buttressing the empirical theory of the understanding by Locke is the assumption that because of its physicality the posterior states of the world are determined from the prior states. "In fact, having assumed that it is which it is, it follows that things must be what they are."[61] Moreover, it is imaginable under such an assumption that the world will be eternal as an endless succession of states, persisting as a series of changing things that "proceeds from a prior series eternally."

The query of Leibniz was: What is it that is at "the ultimate root" of an assumption of the physical necessity of the temporal existence of the world? He was convinced that the answer lay in the connection between existence and possibilities.

> ". . . We must first know, that, by the very fact itself that something rather than nothing exists, there is some demand for existence in possible things or in possibility itself or essence, or (so to speak) a stretching forth to existence, and, to sum it up in a word, that essence *per se* tends to existence. Whence it hereafter follows, that all possible things, or those expressing essence or possible reality, with equal right tend to essence. . . .
>
> "But from this we see most clearly that from the infinite combinations of possible things and possible series there stands forth one through which the greatest quantity of essence or possibility is brought through to existence."[62]

Leibniz had introduced ideas of knowledge of the possible through the employment of what he termed a certain "metaphysical mechanics." He had used the metaphysical to provide an understanding of physical necessity, without contradicting that the world was physically determined. He had, as he intended to, introduced reason into the assumption of the temporal world existing as an eternal series of successive states. It was a truth for Leibniz that "actually in the world we observe that all things take place . . . not only according to material necessities, but also according to formal reasons."[63]

The inclination or tendency of possibilities to existence made understandable the existing, the non-existing, and the rather than otherwise existing world as knowledge of the ultimate reason of things, which was a knowledge of them as both essences and existences. "We see, by a wonderful plan in all nature, the metaphysical laws of cause, power, action, have place, and these prevail over the purely geometrical laws themselves of matter."[64]

As the reality of essences, and therefore of existences (or existants) is anterior to their presence in the mode of the phenomena of sensibility, possibilities have a reality that is part of the mechanism of the world as constituted. Every existant in its present state has within it an essence or force "which carries with itself a change for the future. The rest is only phenomena and relations."[65]

Reason and the Knowledge of Matter

There is an interlinking of the deterministic meta-physical mechanism and the deterministic physical mechanism in his critique of Locke's reasoning about the substance of matter. Locke regarded "substance" as merely a name (e.g. gold) for a complex idea of observed co-existing qualities of an unknown substratum within some particular matter. The question was then whether this nominal knowledge would mark the limit of the knowledge of matter. Could there be certain knowledge of still other coexisting qualities without knowledge of the internal composition/structure of the substance of matter?

Suppose, however, that internal composition/structure were known (the primary qualities). Would one then know the experienced secondary or sensible qualities (color, taste, etc.) of matter? Leibniz enters into a distinction between what each is as knowledge. The one (knowledge of sensible qualities) will not be known as a recognizable sensory derivative of the other.

> ". . . If we had reached the internal constitution of some bodies, we should see also how they must have these qualities, which would themselves be reduced to their intelligible reasons; although it would never be in our power to recognize them sensibly in those sensitive ideas which are a confused resultant of the actions of bodies upon us, as, now that are have the perfect analysis of *green* into blue and yellow in our sensitive idea of green, for the very same reason that it is a confused idea."[66]

So there are two separate realms of knowledge with respect to matter. The one, the realm of commonly sensed qualities, lacks the knowledge of the other, which is the knowledge of the "intelligible reasons" for the necessity of their material qualities. Leibniz had here disclosed the reason for the possibility of two cultures of knowledge.

REFERENCES

1. Leibniz, Gottfried Wilhelm, *New Essays Concerning Human Understanding*: Together with an Appendiz Consisting of Some of His Shorter Pieces (Langley, Alfred G., transl., with notes). (The Macmillan Co. 1896, reprinted 1916, 1949 by Open Court, Chicago). Bk. IV, Ch. XVII, 575.
2. Ibid., Bk. IV, Ch. III, Sec. 22-28, 439-44.
3. Leibniz, Gottfried Wilhelm von, *Discourse on Metaphysics: Correspondence with Arnould and Monadology*, (Intro. Paul Janet; transl. George R. Montgomery, (Open Court, Chicago, 1916). Correspondence, Leibniz to Arnould, July 14, 1686, p. 141.
4. Ibid., Monadology, N28, p. 233.
5. Ibid., Bk. IV, Ch. X, Sec. 10, 531.
6. Ibid., Bk. II, Ch. I, 110.
7. Ibid., Bk. IV, Ch. IV, Sec. 4, 445-46.
8. Ibid., Bk. II, Ch. XII, Sec. 3, 148.
9. Ibid., Bk. II, Ch. VII, 130.
10. Ibid., Bk. I, Ch. I, 70.
11. Ibid., Bk. I, Ch. I, Sec. 1, 70-71.
12. Ibid., Sec. 2, 81.
13. Ibid., Bk. II, Ch. XII, 147.
14. Ibid., Bk. I, Ch. I, 70.
15. Ibid., Bk. I, Ch. II, 100.
16. Ibid., Bk. II, Ch. I, 111.
17. Ibid., Bk. I, Ch. I, Sec. 10, 81.
18. Ibid., Bk. II, Ch. XXVII, 238-39.
19. Ibid., Bk. IV, Ch. III, Sec. 1, 428.
20. Ibid., Bk. II, Ch. XXI, Sec. 4, 177.
21. Ibid., Bk. II, Ch. XXI, Sec. 2, 175.
22. Ibid., Bk. II, Ch. XXI, Sec. 1, 174-75.
23. Ibid., Bk. II, Ch. 1, Sec. 1, 109.
24. Ibid., Bk. II, Ch. 1, 119.
25. Ibid., Bk. II, Ch. XXI, Sec. 5, 177.
26. Ibid., Bk. II, Ch. XX, Sec. 5, 171.
27. Ibid., 170.
28. Ibid., Bk II, Ch. XXI, 188.
29. Ibid., Bk. II, Ch. XXI, Sec. 11, 186.

30. Ibid., Sec. 25, 187.
31. Ibid., Bk. II, Ch. XIX, 164-66.
32. Ibid., Bk. II, Ch. XXI, 183.
33. Ibid., 184.
34. Ibid., 187.
35. Ibid., 182.
36. Ibid., Bk. II, Ch. XXI, 203.
37. Ibid., Ibid., 199.
38. Ibid., Bk. II, Ch. XXI, 215.
39. Ibid., 187.
40. Ibid., 180.
41. Ibid., 183.
42. Locke, John, *An Essay Concerning Human Understanding*, (6th edition), with the notes and illustrations of the author, and an analysis of his doctrine of ideas. Also, Questions on Locke's Essay, by A. M., Ethical Moderator in Trinity College, Dublin. (New Edition, The World Library, Ward, Lock & Co., London, undated) The original edition of Locke's *Essay* is 1689. Locke's Epistle to the Reader, p. XV.
43. Leibniz, *New Essays*, Appendix, p. 716, italics in original.
44. Ibid.
45. Ibid., 717.
46. Ibid., Bk. IV, Ch. I, Sec. 1, 397.
47. Ibid., Bk. IV, Ch. I, Sec. 9, 403.
48. Ibid., Bk. IV, Ch. II, Sec. 1, 410.
49. Ibid., Sec. 13, 416-17.
50. Ibid., Sec. 7, 411-13.
51. Ibid., Sec. 14, 419.
52. Ibid., Sec. 14, 422.
53. Ibid., Bk. IV, Ch. XVII., Sec. 1, 555-56.
54. Ibid., 556.
55. *Loc. cit*
56. Ibid., Bk. IV, Ch. V, Sec. 2, 452.
57. Ibid., Bk. IV, Ch. VI, Sec. 13 and note, 461-62.
58. Ibid., Bk. IV, Ch. II, Sec. 1, 410.
59. Ibid., Bk. IV, Ch. III, Sec. 17, 432.
60. Ibid., Bk. IV, Ch. XVII, Sec. 9, 570.
61. Ibid., Appendix, 693.
62. Ibid.
63. Ibid., 695.
64. Ibid.
65. Ibid., 711-12.
66. Ibid., Bk. IV, Ch. VI, Sec. 7, 458-59.

CHAPTER XVII

Foundation Knowledge III: Moral Knowledge Motivational Knowledge and the Knowledge of Morality

Strategy and the Knowledge of Morality

1. Motivational Knowledge and the Knowledge of Morality
2. Moral Knowledge and the Art of Consequences

"Beati Possidentes"
"Quaerenda pecunia primum est,
virtus post nummos"

NOTE

Moral Knowledge and the Knowledge of Strategy

Three questions have been put forward about what constitutes the knowledge of strategy. They are questions that can also serve for inquiry directed to ascertaining the moral knowledge of the knowledge of strategy.

1. What is the knowledge by reason of which it may be asserted that there can be a moral knowledge content of strategic knowledge?

2. Considered by itself, what is moral knowledge?
3. The knowledge of moral knowledge exists as a knowledge for whom?

Starting points are elusive. The idea of social responsibility as the moral knowledge has been effectively exposed as non-knowledge.[1] There is the idea of virtue, which is the idea of moral goodness. But it was long ago noted that because of the loss of its religious foundation, virtue had exited from the belief structure of human preference in secular matters.[2]

The ethical—is it, perhaps, the ethical that constitutes the moral knowledge of strategy? Sometimes the moral and the ethical are coalesced into one, so that there is no differentiation between the two. Sometimes the moral and the ethical are used as interchangeable language equivalents. Sometimes the idea of the ethical is taken to occupy the whole field of discourse.[3]

Within the frame of the knowledge of strategy, the ethical will be differentiated and set apart from the moral. Strategy is focused on generating action fields of opportunity for capital from the discriminant possibilities presented by economic, technological and societal (cultural, demographics, and political) developments or changes. This is a focus outside of the ambit of the ethical. Ethics is focused on ascertaining the obligations adhering to the relationships between parties who are engaged in the performance of expected roles. It is well illustrated by the classic Texas Gulf insider trading (inside information about a mother lode) case.[4] Ethics is also illustrated by the famous Lockheed Aircraft Corporation case (bribery of foreign officials)[5] and the once notorious 3M case (concealed slush fund of laundered corporate funds for secret political contributions).[6] The obligations of normative relationships *inter se* among the respective corporate constituencies of national and multi-national corporations is applied ethical knowledge. The non-ethical is a falling away from rectitude.[7]

Ethical knowledge is the knowledge of rectitude. But it is not the moral knowledge of the knowledge of strategy. It is not such because relational rectitude is not a knowledge that presents itself as an imposition of limits on strategy. The moral knowledge of the knowledge of strategy appears in the mind of the strategist as a cognition limiting strategic freedom. Stated thus, the position can now be argumentatively put:

1. Morality presents itself as cognition of an idea limiting strategic freedom.
2. An idea limiting strategic freedom is knowledge of limits on strategic possibilities.
3. Therefore, limits on strategic possibilities are limits confronting command cognition.
4. Morality thus presents itself—is thrust into—the cognition of the strategist.

The argumentative theme is straightforward: No morality without limitations on strategic freedom. The moral knowledge of the knowledge of strategy begins here with cognition of the emergence of limits on strategy that are sourced in moral justification. With respect to these limits:

1. They can be limits that are sourced within entities and on grounds extrinsic to those of the strategizing entity and its ground of strategic reasoning.
2. Extrinsic entities and their justificatory grounds impose the judgements of others than the strategists on the strategic preferences of the strategists themselves.
3. They can be limits that are sourced within the processes of strategic cognition internal to the enterprise entity.
4. Instrinsic limits emerge from self-imposed grounds of judgement generated by the entity strategists.
5. The two limit categories—extrinsic and intrinsic—have their respective foundations in two separate cognitive frames.
   a) Extrinsic limits are outcomes of interactions between societal liberty (the liberty of the social contract undergirding civil government) and the market questing strategic freedom of the enterprise entity.
   b) Intrinsic limits are traceable to the foundations of those considerations judged determinative for strategic decision, considerations which function within the structure and processes of the enterprise entity in cognizing strategy.

6. In sum, extrinsic limits and intrinsic limits represent two cognitive frames for understanding the moral knowledge of the knowledge of strategy:
   a) The liberty based cognitive frame and
   b) The judgement preference based cognitive frame

The Moral as Idea

There yet remains the central question: The what and the where of the moral that constitutes this moral knowledge. It is to Locke that one is indebted for the liberty (societal) based cognitive framework, which is set forth in Chapter 17.

Locke differentiated the religious "true ground" of morality from the secular or positive knowledge of moral obligation. As to the former, he postulated a visible hand. As to the latter, he advocated that there be an adequate method for acquisition of the knowledge of moral understanding. Moral knowledge is the knowledge consequent upon examining actions. This is to say that the idea of the moral—morality itself—remains without substance; that as idea only it is absent understanding and not knowledge. There is, however, a knowledge of actions. As actions draw good and evil after them, there is a knowledge of actions as the precedent causes of what follows afterwards. Moral knowledge is thus a later knowing which understanding endeavors to make a prior knowing.[8]

Locke was optimistic that "a right method" would yield for morality demonstrable propositions of a clarity and truth equal to those of mathematics. Yet Locke could not supply that "right method." What could not be solved were the dilemmas precipitated by time. Motivation is the uneasiness of desire about an absent good. An absent good is a future good; between the present state and the desired future state lies time. Despite the power (liberty) to choose a future state in preference to a present state, judgements about the future are knowledge deficient. Not the absence of data, but the weaknesses of human mental capacity account for these deficiencies of judgement.

So Locke put the knowledge of the moral as knowledge of that which was put forward as moral, and the rules by which it was applied to action, and to which it was compared as a reference so as to judge its morality. The positive character of moral rules was that they were law-like; that is, that they were vehicles through which punishment and reward were justified. Morality was the dominating restraint on desire in the mechanism of action, and it defined the liberty of a free agent. As to the application of rule based moral relations, they were applied as an outcome of public temper, of custom and social judgements, of political preferences, of differences in education, class and interests. Moreover, being law-like, they were vehicles for the expression of whatever passions or whatever reason might sway the populace.

The Moral as Judgement

At this point exposition turns away from moral rules and their use as a form of positive law. It departs the socio-political context in which they are shaped and within which they are applied. It leaves them absent a "true ground" of morality and absent a knowledge of moral understanding.

At this point exposition turns toward judgement. But there is still no getting away from the root conundrum, which is time—the time of the future that is the object of present understanding and present desire. To select a religious foundation as the "true ground" of the moral is to obliterate time as conundrum of understanding and knowing. The time of religiosity is the time of final things, of eschatology, when all is known because all is revealed. In secularly experienced time—non-eschatological time—the to-be and not-yet experienced stand unrevealed to the strategist.

Locke had concluded that the unexperienced was beyond human ken, presenting the mind with occasions for wrong judgement in the pursuit of satisfactions and pleasures. However, his contemporary and critic, Leibniz, inquired into what humans do when engaged in processes of judgement. Why was there false thinking about the future? His answer was that the future presents itself too feebly to the present. What dominates judgement are present perceptions. The future appears not as an actuality but only as an image.

Even so, all this would be nothing more than judgemental error; where is the morality of all this? There was a certain code of honor introduced by Locke that was by him asserted to be binding on all who exercised their individual freedom of desire and judgement: Not to be precipitant in judgement, and, according to the importance of the matter at hand, to "open the eyes, look about, and take a view of the consequences" of intended acts (see p. 325).

Only that? Nothing more? Where was a knowledge of morality? Nothing more than enormous expectations despite a conscientious judgement? Without derogating either a requisite quality of thinking or the necessary estimation of probabilities, Leibniz introduced a moral content into judgemental reasoning. Moral knowledge was the "knowledge of the value of the goods and evils" of the consequences of that by which human will was determined (see p. 336).

The strategist is not thereby brought to a simple value calculus. He is brought to the necessity of preparing in advance for proceeding methodically in a course of thinking. Human thought was not conceptualized by Leibniz as being directed straightways to action by a psychological mechanism of desire, motivation; sensibilization, perception, and so on. Rather, there was to be taken into account a mass of imperceptibles and indistinct impulses, with perhaps a hovering unease about present enjoyments, and even the intrusion of habits, feelings, and temperaments. Nor was personal character (with the variety of its propensities) to be excluded. These are considerations of psychology and of personal character, not of organizational processes.

Prudence as the Morality of Strategy

In truth, though, within the perspective put forth by Leibniz, what were values to moral judgement? In truth, at the time, advancement in the knowledge of the physical world, and its utilization in human affairs, seemed to foreshadow unknown promises of unknown benefits. Not the morality of the known, but a moral path to discern the knowledge of the yet unknown as an emergent known. Something more than the physical outcome or consequences of actions adhered to the acts of humans. Acts of motivational desire are subject to appraisal by other standards that are also indigenous to humans. Values serve as a reaching knowledge for these other standards.

Why characterize it as a reaching knowledge? Because what needs to be known in its normativeness is wanting firmness in the knowledge for so knowing it. Topics of large significance for physical existence—such as species extinction, atmospheric ozone, rain forests, toxic pollutants—want bases for judgement that are directive regarding strategic courses of preference.[9]

Values are not moral equivalents. They are like reflexive markers for a path of understanding whereby to formulate moral knowledge for inclusion in judgement.[10] Such a path is one of prudential knowing; a path whereby the understanding is disciplined for prudential judgement regarding the preference limits to be imposed on strategy in the making.

Strategy takes place within the context of a liberty which society also reserves to itself through its powers of policy, but which does not exclude freedom for commercial entities in the prudent exercise of their own strategic capabilities.[11] Prudence is the practical virtue of strategic knowing. For Aristotle, prudence implied the presence of all the moral virtues. In this sense, the limits of prudence on strategic purpose (desire) establish a reasoned pschological space for the moral. The sagacious, the wise, the circumspect, and the discreet are all practical virtues that are associated with prudential thought, judgement and conduct.

Prudence, then, is the umbrella morality that presents itself as cognition of an idea limiting strategic freedom. Prudential knowledge, with its content of moral virtues, provides the frame for the moral knowledge of the knowledge of strategy. What is it that this moral knowledge purports to limit? It purports to limit the effects of the other knowledge as determinants of strategic judgement. Both knowledges—moral (prudential) and other than moral—should be knowledges of causalities significant for strategic outcomes. If moral knowledge were only a knowledge of agents and relationships that were without causal significance, it would be pointless because it would be without causal consequences. It is a knowledge that should be of causal significance when present in the judgement process, and also of causal significance when not so present.

The query: "In Financial Scandals, Is Blind Greed Meeting Sightless Watchdogs" introduces a different twist in the response; namely, in finance why limit "financial high rollers" at all, whether by prudence or by regulation?[12] The argument is that by introducing moralities of denial and regulation the non-conformist is justifiably motivated to find loopholes, corrupt the system, and take "wild risks"—all for the private purposes of large gains in financial markets; particularly, so the argument goes, because the moralities of regulating financial strategies are without causal significance (out of the know, too late in knowing, stupid as against smart traders). Managing briefer catch-up times to accomplished frauds is what would constitute moral knowledge. The foregoing states not only a position that has its defenders, but it is also strengthened by a money culture apparently more tolerant of private than of public fraud.[13] Suppose this morality were to be applied to foods, to medical devices, to pharmaceuticals (proprietary and non-proprietary), and to cosmetics. Not likely, given firmly established moral beliefs about the value of human life. But one is apt to forget that historically (prior to 1906) it was once otherwise.[13a]

For market strategies within the financial industry, however, what is the moral knowledge of the knowledge of strategy? Reintroduce rectitude in behavior, at a very high standard—"exemplary behavior"—?; more than legality?, excluding all behavior "that we, as citizens, would find offensive"? The absence of rectitude has its direct and secondary costs; still, more than an ethically indifferent monetary calculus should be at stake. What is at stake has been put as "First-class business . . . in a first-class way." Here rectitude is conceptualized as that which would establish the criterion of what strategy we would accept as defining qualitatively the business of the firm.[14]

Beyond the recommendation for a single firm (for such it was) what about the whole financial industry as exemplified by the term Wall Street? Knowledge consists of the cognitions which enable the structuring of phenomena or surrogates of phenomena (i.e. data) into explanatory (connectedness), or relational (causal), or analytical (hypothesized), or specualtive (imagined), or replicative, or teleological comprehension. Moral knowledge should be fitted within these cognitions. It should, in short, be thought of as part of the knowledge design applicable to the entities constituting an industry. Still, as in the case of the financial industry, all of that knowledge might be in disarray and also in an incessant flux as respects financial institutions.[15]

Applicable though it is as an umbrella morality, prudence cannot evade the conundrum of time. That conundrum compels prudence to be expressed in terms of cognized particulars and patterns and dynamics of understanding as perceived and generated within the flow of events and affairs of the time of their unfolding. The conundrum of time is what lawyers term "ripening" (of the issues to be litigated), which is akin to what medical and genetic researchers term "epigenetic." It refers to the mechanism and process in time by which the structure and substance of change or development makes itself apparent in form and functions. In practical terms, the response to the epigenetics of change is characterized as adaptive, which expresses the capability of the understanding to regulate the directiveness of response to change.[16]

Epigenetic change unfolds, revealing itself to perception and understanding. Whatever unease may be generated by the unfolding drives the search for another knowledge base for strategizing. Wherein would morality present itself to strategic cognitions? Take, for example, the circumstances of widespread layoffs occurring in the computer industry and threatening in the automotive industry. A strategic mix of downsizing, restructuring, plant closings and massive layoffs are put forth as knowledge justified.[17] Put to one side labor contract terms, severance pay arrangements, outplacement assistance (the ethics of rectitude, see p. 309). Beyond this, could there yet be cognition of a moral knowledge limiting strategic freedom?

There could, and the morality of the knowledge in support of the cognition is as follows:[18] In terms of economic analysis, there is a crucial difference between future costs and future revenues. The difference is one that is significant for management. It is that future revenues are less predictable than future costs. The managerial significance of this difference is its effect on risks. Managers tend to be risk aversive. Risk aversiveness will favor the more certain as against the more uncertain. Therefore the value significance of future costs will be higher than that for future revenues in the knowledge of strategy. Layoffs introduce a measure of known certainty about future costs. Analytically, then, layoffs do not confront management with a tough judgement about strategy.

However, a strategy of massive layoffs may also be understood in its actuality as a normative attitude toward present costs as a measure of future risk. Prudence would not of itself prevent management from accepting that risk. All would hinge on management thinking its way through to generating credible expectations of the desired higher future revenues from those presently on the payrolls. Restructuring, to be sure, but a restructuring not premised on the layoffs. More risky? Sure. How would prudence come to judgement? What enters into judgements of this kind, meaning judgements about moral consequents put up against the strategy itself (e.g. no drift net fishing, no carcinogens, no chlorofluorocarbons (CFCs), etc)?

It was the philosopher Leibniz who provided the first modern conspectus of judgement. He did not confine it to cognition (see Ch. XVI). Contemporary evaluation of research into the topic of judgement confirms that understanding, particularly when involved in significant social concerns. While explications of processes and preference structures were now said to have an acceptable technological foundation, a full review of the topic of judgement and decision (theory and application) concluded that prescriptive rules for guidance of their preferences were still outside the possibility of definitions.[19]

REFERENCES

1. Friedman, Milton, "Profit Business' Prime Purpose," *Cleveland Plain Dealer*, October 16, 1970, p. 14A. Perhaps it is the universities that are burdened with the "social mission," which may not be the synonym for "social responsibility." The President of Harvard University (Derek C. Bok) was reported as suggesting that universities redefine their social mission, even though the present be a time of "eerie indifference" on the part of the nation's leaders to social ills. "Departing Harvard President Decries 'Eerie Indifference,' " *New York Times*, June 7, 1991, p. D16.

2. See p. 338; "Low Marks in Ethics," *Business Week*, September 28, 1968, p. 64. For current proof of belief in holiness and in moral goodness as a religious counterweight to secular norms, see "Pizza Tycoon Considers Selling Empire," *Cleveland Plain Dealer*, November 19, 1991 (Billionaire owner of Domino's Pizza and the Detroit Tigers spiritually bothered by his accumulation of wealth). Reconsidered: Doron P. Levin, "Domino Founder Seizes Command," *New York Times*, December 10, 1991, p. C1. (He had read C.S. Lewis, *Mere Christianity*, and had experienced a large spiritual awakening. The return to executive command over Domino's Pizza, Inc. was explained as a response to signs of Divine Guidance that he so do.)

There is a review of the state of contemporary belief in the idea of Hell in *U.S. News and World Report*, "The Rekindling of Hell," March 25, 1991, the cover story.

3. Gert, Bernard, *The Moral Rules* (Harper and Row, New York, Torchbook ed. 1973); Gustafson, James M., "Ethics: An American Growth Industry," 56 *The Key Reporter*, No. 3, Spring 1991.

4. Chernow, Ron, *The House of Morgan*, Pt. 3 "The Casino Age," pp. 562 *et seq.* (origins of the Texas Gulf Sulphur case and the basis for the early rumblings of unease about insider trading).

5. Hougan, Jim, "The Business of Buying Friends," *Harpers* (Vol. 253, No. 1519, December 1976); Hearing, *The Foreign Corrupt Practices and Domestic and Foreign Investment Disclosure* (Senate Committee on Banking, Housing, and Urban Affairs, 95th Cong., 1st Sess., Senate Bill 305, March 16, 1977). Singer, Andrew W., "Ethics: Are Standards Lower Overseas?," *Across the Board*, September 1991, pp. 31-34.

There is a variant of the more inclusive dilemma, which is the local politics of enforcing compliance by domestic firms with the MacBride Principles, which are intended to secure equal employment opportunities for Northern Irish Catholics in Northern Ireland. BP America, which has operations there, ran afoul of a Cleveland ordinance that barred the city from doing business with the firm because it refused to sign a document of adherence to the MacBride Principles: "Changes Sought on 'MacBride City Ordinance,' " *Cleveland Plain Dealer*, December 13, 1991, p. 1B; "An Irish Question for Cleveland," Editorial, *Ibid.*, p. 18C; "O'Malley Toughens Stance as BP Gets More Time," *Cleveland Plain Dealer*, December 17, 1991, p. 1B.

6. "How 3M Got Tangled Up In Politics," *New York Times*, March 9, 1975, Section 3.

7. Bartlett, Sarah, "A Straight Arrow's Inexplicable Fall," *New York Times*, March 24, 1991, Section 3-1.

8. Tate, Cassandra, "In the 1800s, Antismoking Was a Burning Issue," *Smithsonian*, Vol. 20, No. 4, P. 107 (July 1989).

9. El-Sayed, Sayed Z., "Fragile Life Under the Ozone Hole," *Natural History*, Vol. 97, No. 10, p. 73 (October 1988); "Of Time and the Forest" (Tongass National Forest of Alaska), *Natural History*, Vol. 97, No. 8, p. 41 (August 1988); "Costs Could Slow Lakes Cleanup Effort," *Cleveland Plain Dealer*, December 10, 1991, 5A; "Global Warming Has No Quick or Easy Fixes," *Cleveland Plain Dealer*, December 10, 1991, p. 4A; "Proposed Space Plane May Hurt Ozone," *Burlington Free Press*, June 1, 1991, p. 14A.

10. Hayes, James L., "Modern Values or Just Values?", Beta Gamma Sigma (From the Podium), November 1980; Norton, Bryan G., "What is a Whooping Crane Worth?", Natural History, Vol. 96 No. 6, p. 64 (June 1987); Stigler, George J., "What an Oil Spill is Worth," *Wall Street Journal*, April 17, 1990, p. A22; Singer, S. Fred, "No Scientific Consensus on Greenhouse Warming," *Wall Street Journal*, September 23, 1991, p. A16; Imperato, Pascal V. and Mitchell, Greg, *Acceptable Risks* (Viking, N.Y. 1985); Nash, Roderick F., *The Rights of Nature* (U. Wisc. Press 1989).

As to the "value" of corporate takeover activity, see Labaton, Stephen, "$200 Million in Wall Street Fees Seen From Federated Deal," *New York Times*, April 5, 1988, p. 25.

11. Buchholz, Rogene A., "An Alternative to Social Responsibility," 25 Michigan State University Business Topics 12 (Summer 1977). Sawyer, George C., "Social Issues and Social Change: Impact on Strategic Decisions," 21 Michigan State University Business Topics 15 (Summer 1973); *Growth and Preservation*, No. 42 Resources For The Future, Inc., September 1972.

12. Rosenbaum, David E., "Ideas and Trends," *New York Times*, September 15, 1991, p. 4E. And see, too, Henriques, Dearia B., "Wall Street: Treasury's Troubled Auctions," *Ibid.*, at p. F13.

13. Epstein, Edward Jay, "Offshore Reporting," *The New Yorker*, January 22, 1972, p. 89. (A review and commentary on the Investors Overseas Services (I.O.S.) financial scandal, comparing reporting by the domestic press and a book by three British authors: Raw, Charles, Bruce, Page, and Godfrey Hodgson, *Do You Sincerely Want to Be Rich?*)

13a. Nonetheless, the morality of (1) post-injury regulation, and (2) no, or relatively defective, public accessibility to pre-testing data regarding possibly injurious consequences of product use, has again surfaced with respect to: (a) genetically altered foods, (b) irradiated foods, (c) steroid implants, and (d) the sleeping pill, Halcion.

As to Halcion, see Gina Kolata, "Maker of Sleeping Pill Hid Data on Side Effects, Researchers Say," *New York Times*, November 20, 1992, p. A1.

As to silicone breast implants, see Philip J. Hilts, "Maker Is Depicted as Fighting Tests on Implant Safety," *New York Times*, January 13, 1992, p. A1; "Strange History of Silicone Held Many Warning Signs," *New York Times*, January 18, 1992, p. A1; and "F.D.A. Seeks Halt in Breast Implants Made of Silicone," *New York Times*, January 7, 1992.

As to genetically altered foods, see Warren E. Leary, "Gene-Altered Food Held by the F.D.A. to Pose Little Risk," *New York Times*, May 26, 1992, p. A1.

As to regulative capability, see Gina Kolata, "Questions Raised on Ability of F.D.A. to Protect Public," *New York Times*, January 26, 1992, p. A1.

The response of the leading breast implant manufacturer? See "Top Manufacturer of Breast Implant Replaces Its Chief," *New York Times*, February 11, 1992, p. A1.

14. "Salomon Inc.: A Report by the Chairman on the Company's Standing and Outlooks" (Warren E. Buffett, Interim Chairman), *Wall Street Journal*, October 29, 1991, p. C12. Compare the report by Kurt Eichenwald, "Wall Street Sees a Serious Threat to Salomon Bros.," *New York Times*, August 16, 1991, p. 1A; and the report by Siconolfi, Michael and Cohen, Laurie P., "How Salomon's Hubris and a U.S. Trap Led to Leaders' Downfall," *Wall Street Journal*, August 19, 1991, p. A1; Hansell, Saul, Beth Selby and Henny Sender, "Who Should Run Salomon Brothers?," *Institutional Investor*, September 1991, pp. 11-14 (Command character, command cognition and changes in the culture of institutional ethics).

15 "Insider Trading and Stock Market Realities," Editorial, Fortune, May 1973, p. 178; Crudele, John, "Drexel 'Junk Bond' Wizard," *New York Times*, November 21, 1986, p. 29; the several articles on Boesky, inside trading and SEC proceedings, also in the *New York Times*, November 21, 1986, pp. 1, 34; the varity of articles on the theme "Collapse on Wall Street: A Different World in its Wake," *The New York Times*, October 24, 1987, pp. 17 *et. seq.*; the long lead article by Uchitelle, Louis, "The Uncertain Legacy of the Crash," *New York Times*, April 3, 1988, Sec. 3 (and its supplementary articles).

16. The complex of industry transformations, new competition, and innovations in trading and portfolio management that compelled an all-encompassing changeover at Morgan Stanley (starting in the 1960's) is traced in detail that is enlightening and fascinating: Chernow, Ron, *The House of Morgan* (Atlantic Monthly Press, New York 1990) "Part Three: The Casino Age." Here is the stuff of another knowledge design, a break with traditions, entry of non-traditional personnel, new standards of character, a reconceptualization of the business and of the style of doing business, a deliberate meshing with the newly dominant personalities, values, culture and practices of Wall Street.

A more generalized review of changes in Wall Street and the redesign of the knowledge base underlying the structure, personnel and business of the firm of Merrill Lynch, in order to build on the new understanding of opportunity, supplies the materials for a two part cover story by *Insight*, September 19, 1988 (Vol. 4, No. 38): Pt. I "Wall Street Stares Hard at Revision," Pt. II "Securities House Divided is a Secure House Indeed."

17. Two articles by John Markoff in the *New York Times*: "I.B.M. Announces a Sweeping Shift in its Structure," November 27, 1991, p. A1 and "At I.B.M., Refocusing Yet Again," November 25, 1991, p. C1. In the *Wall Street Journal*, Paul B. Carroll, "How an IBM Attempt To Regain PC Lead Has Slid Into Trouble," December 2, 1991, p. A1. With reference to General Motors, "New GM Leadership Flails For Ways To Halt the Car Maker's Slide," Doron P. Levin, *New York Times*, December 15, 1991, Sec. 3-5; and also this article by

the same author, "G.M. Hints Deep Cuts Are Ahead," *New York Times*, December 12, 1991, p. C1.

18. Pye, Gordon B., "More Layoffs? Hold the Applause," *New York Times*, Forum, December 1, 1991, p. 13. Relevant to the argument advanced by Mr. Pye is the article by John Markoff, "Abe Pelid's Secret Start-up at I.B.M.," *New York Times*, December 8, 1991, Sec. 3-1 (Internal, autonomous commercial hi-tech product start-up entity that builds quickly on basic research to pioneer new markets and business).

19. Pitz, Gordon and Sachs, Natalie J., "Judgment and Decision: Theory and Application," 35 *Ann. Rev. Psychol.*, 139-63 (1984).

A suggested guide to the development of moral judgement among managers is provided by Carroll, Archie B.—"In Search of the Moral Manager," 30 Business Horizons No. 2 (March—April 1987) 7 (Indiana U. Grad. School of Bus.). The author expounds the differences between immoral, amoral and moral management actions in organization context.

1.
THE KNOWLEDGE OF MOTIVATION

"Nature, I confess, has put into man a desire of happiness, and an aversion to misery; these, indeed, are innate principles, which, as practical principles ought, do continue constantly to operate and influence all our actions without ceasing; . . ."[1]

The Separation of Motivation from Morality

Locke separated motivation as knowledge from morality as knowledge. Why? Why did he not, rather, unite the two in a synthesized and unified explanation of action?

Locke was committed to disclosing precisely of what the act of knowing consisted. He took knowing to be, like willing and believing, a distinguishable action of the mind. But what does mind do which performs the actions termed "knowing"? He took it that individuals have a conscious and particular sense of knowing when they know something. Yet nowhere, as Locke took pains to note, had it been set down with particularity—a protocol—what mind does when acts of knowing are performed.

Motivation presents questions of knowledge and of knowing. Morality, too, presents questions of knowledge and of knowing. To differentiate each as to its knowledge. To be consistent in the analysis of each as knowledge with his explanation of knowledge itself. To determine whether the knowledge of one can also be the knowledge of the other. These are the concerns behind the separation, by Locke, of motivation as knowledge from morality as knowledge.

Motivation, Desire and Volition

The fundament of motivation, nature itself in the materiality of persons, is independent of and anterior to knowledge. Thus the fundament of motivation is independent of and anterior to the ideas that enter into the understanding. "Natural tendencies imprinted on the mind," wrote Locke; "inclinations of the appetite." They are at the very threshhold of sense and perception, but still not knowledge. Certainly not innate truths impressed on the understanding.²

Motivations as inclinations and no more, being nothing innate, leaves unresolved the question of what precisely determines volition as "a power in the mind to direct the operative faculties of a man." What is volition? It "is an act of the mind directing its thought to the production of any action, and thereby exerting its power to produce it."³

Human motivation is encapsulated by Locke within the more general ideas of power and liberty. Motivation provides the natural ground for preferential choice. In the making of this choice, however, Locke separated out volition, desire, and "several acts of the mind." The reference standard for any preferential choice is the preference for either the continuation or the termination of a present action state. The choice is always between "the present satisfaction in it" and "some uneasiness" about it. In either case, motivation is there, working on the mind to determine volition.

How does desire enter into the choice? Desire may exist in "a quite contrary tendency" to volition, thus demonstrating a distinctness from will. It exists as "an uneasiness of the mind for want of some absent good." Consequently both desiring and willing co-exist as "two distinct acts of the mind." Nonetheless, it is uneasiness that "immediately determines the will" to a succession of voluntary actions.⁴

Motivational Knowledge

Locke has now established the basis for a generalized, abstract idea whereby to explain the motivation of individual persons. It is an idea of motivation rooted in sensibility and reflection. It is also general enough both to encompass all individual motivation and to allow for motivational differentiation between individuals. Volition is "immediately determined" by whatever uneasiness of desire exists with respect to an absent good. "That absent good, or, which is the same thing, future pleasure, is a positive individual or personal good."⁵

The knowledge of motivation is the knowledge by which to attain the desire for happiness and the avoidance of misery. The core knowledge difficulty involves the issue of time. Motivation, as the uneasiness of desire for an absent good, functions as an immediate or present determinative of volition. Present happiness or misery, being in their present enjoyment what they seem to be, and known and judged solely in this light, do not introduce possibility of error into the preferential choice of action.

> "But since our voluntary actions carry not all the happiness and misery that depend on them alone with them in their present performance, but are the precedent causes of good and evil, which they draw after them, and bring upon us when they themselves are past and cease to be; our desires look beyond our present enjoyments, and carry the mind out to absent good, according to the necessity which we think there is of it to the making or increase of our happiness."[6]

Motivational Judgement

Necessity in time with reference to an absent good compels resort to motivational judgement. What is involved in judgement is the critical appraisal of the knowledge of motivation. It was the opinion of Locke that humans, because of their very materiality, had only a "narrow scantling of capacity" about absent good; being apt therefore "to conclude that they can be happy without it." The comparison between present and future pleasure or pain was more than likely to be the occasion for wrong judgement because of "the weak and narrow constitution of our minds." It is "the pursuit of nearer satisfactions" that will dominate motivational judgement.[7]

Locke, by having brought motivational judgement within the ken of understanding, thereby linked the knowledge of motivation to liberty. Locke had made human liberty of a piece with "the thought and judgement of the understanding."[8] Moreover, he had reduced human desire to a desire "only to be happy." Individual desire guided by individual judgement establishes that "the satisfaction of any particular desire can be suspended from determining the will to any subservient action, till we have maturely examined whether the particular apparent good, which we then desire, makes a part of our real happiness, or be consistent or inconsistent with it."[9] For those choices by which, through the judgements of one's understanding, the individual is mislead in the pursuit of the happiness by which he is motivated, he is himself responsible.

> "The first, therefore, and great use of liberty is, to hinder blind precipitancy; the principal exercise of freedom is, to stand still, open the eyes, look about, and take a view of the consequence of what we are going to do, as much as the weight of the matter requires."[10]

Locke established motivation as an "is," but left morality as an "ought." Motivation was an "is" because it was part of liberty, and thus it was intertwined in the pursuit of happiness. The one cannot be extricated from the other. The "ought" of morality, however, was set apart from liberty. It was made part of divinely established final things, of eschatology, and existed in the shadows of piety. Was there a way by which morality could be rescued from its subordination to eschatology?

2.
MORALITY AND MOTIVATION

> "Nothing can be so dangerous as principles thus taken up without questioning or examination; especially if they be such as concern morality, which influences men's lives, and gives a bias to all their actions."[11]
>
> "Hence I think I may conclude, that morality is the proper science and business of mankind in general (who are both concerned and fitted to search out their *summum bonum*)."[12]

Morality as Knowledge

What has motivational knowledge to do with morality? "We do not fix our desires on every apparent greater good, unless it be judged to be necessary to our happiness; if we think we can be happy without it, it moves us not."[13] Does the desire for happiness, that ceaseless and universal motivator of Locke's, contain within itself that which contradicts morality? Why had morality as knowledge been separated from motivation as knowledge?

The threshhold question to which Locke addressed himself was whether morality consisted of knowledge. Was it defensible to ascribe a substance to morality? If so, what was the nature of moral ideas? Do the ideas of morality satisfy the conditions for knowledge? Locke took knowledge to be an internal perception of the mind. It "consists in the perception of the agreement of disagreement of the immediate objects of the mind in thinking, which I call 'ideas'."[14]

Locke did not place the main analysis of morality within the chapter on *Power*. He placed it, instead, within that chapter both titled and concerned with *"The Improvement of Our Knowledge."* True enough, Locke, in his *Essay Concerning The Human Understanding*, did include an extended treatment of morality, but only as "moral relations." There his real concern was to clarify for the understanding the idea of relation. Morality then becomes understood as those ideas that mind has of things through the comparison of one with another. The idea of the moral—morality itself—still remains without understanding. In "moral relations" there is a true notion of relation, but not, as Locke takes pains to point out, of the moral as an idea of the understanding. The moral still remains without substance. It is without a determinate foundation. Hence it is not knowledge.

Morality Not Innate Knowledge

Locke rejects outright, in a direct and detailed argument, that the moral might become knowledge anterior to perception and reflection. If that were so, then morality would consist of innate ideas. Morality would then be pre-cognitive, which, for Locke, meant more than just pre-sensory. It would be innate knowledge in the form of innate principles of the mind. As such knowledge, morality "must be [within] constant impressions which the souls of men receive in their first beings, and which they bring into the world with them, as necessarily and really as they do any of their inherent faculties."[15]

Locke, in refutation of the above, demonstrated innate knowledge to be an impossibility. There could be no by-passing of the understanding in the acquisition of knowledge. And certainly no principle, no maxim, no general proposition, no self-evident and established general truth could be innately in the mind. The point of the line of proof taken by Locke was not his evidentiary refutation of the criterion of universal agreement by all mankind to establish the existence of innate principles.

The thesis of the proof developed by Locke was two-fold: First, that human faculties for the acquisition of knowledge must be separated from the knowledge that could be acquired, "Men, barely by the use of their natural faculties, may attain to all the knowledge they have, without the help of any innate impressions, and may arrive at certainty without any such original notions or principles."[16] Second, while it is possible for a number of moral rules to be generally approved by mankind, "without either knowing or admitting the true ground of morality," there was need for a method by which to progress in the discovery or "rational and contemplative knowledge" of the moral.[17]

Virtue and Conscience Non-motivational

It was recognized by Locke that that which was designated moral—that to which the name "moral" was nominally attributed—existed in human affairs. He did not doubt, however, that virtue was not the "internal principle" of the actions of men. The rule of virtue was without "internal veneration," without persuasion of obligation, and without certainty of content. Nothing about moral rules was proved by conscience. "Conscience is nothing else but our own opinion or judgement of the moral rectitude or pravity of our own actions." Outwardly there might be a seeming approbation of rules of moral obligation, but such as it was, it was based on self-interest and utilitarian conveniences, rather than an "inward assent."[18]

3.
MORAL KNOWLEDGE

The "True Ground" of Morality

All this and more than that not withstanding, Locke professed no doubt about there being a "true ground" of morality. It was a religious ground, a divine ground, a necessary and indispensable ground. It was God, who had, "by an inseparable connection, joined virtue and public happiness together, and made the practice thereof necessary to the preservation of society, and visibly beneficial to all with whom the virtuous man has to do."[19] Consequently not an invisible, but a visible hand of moral obligation; one that meted out reward and punishment; one that had power to call offenders to account; a morality that was the instrument of one who saw "men in the dark."

Positive Moral Knowledge

Positive moral knowledge, however, was another matter. The knowledge of moral understanding was what was lacking. What was requisite was the improvement of knowledge about moral obligation. It was the method for so doing that was the concern of Locke. It could not be the method for the discovery of the knowledge of nature. Why not? What supported his advocacy of a different method for moral knowledge?

In the main, it was because of the repudiation by Locke of a resort to general proposition, maxims and principles as the method of building moral knowledge. It was also because of the difference in the subject matter of the moral as compared with the subject matter of physical things. "We must therefore, if we will proceed as reason advises, adapt our methods of inquiry to the nature of the ideas we examine, and the truth we search after."[20] Thus physical substances are not to be known through general knowledge and the relations of abstract ideas. "Here we are to take a quite contrary course; the want of ideas of their real essences sends us from our own thoughts to the things themselves as they exist. Experience here must teach me what reason cannot."[21] Locke doubted that natural philosphy was capable of becoming a science. It was the inaccessibility of the internal nature of bodies—and hence the unknowability of their properties—to human faculties for discovery and improvement of this knowledge.

What human faculties for the acquisition of knowledge were most suited to was to:

". . . plainly discover to us the being of a God, and the knowledge of ourselves, enough to lead us into a full and clear discovery of our duty and great concernment, it will become us, as rational creatures, to employ those faculties we have about what they are most adapted to, and follow the direction of nature, where it seems to point us out the way. For it is rational to conclude that our proper employment lies in those inquiries, and capacities, and carries in it our greatest interest, i.e., the condition of eternal estate."[22]

Accessible Inwardness For Moral Knowledge

The difficulty that limited natural philosophy to nominal particulars of knowledge was the inability to access the material composition of external bodies. But the difficulty of inaccessibility was not there for moral knowledge. Persons could access themselves. Their own inwardness was accessible to their own faculties for the acquisition of moral understanding. There, within this inwardness, there could be and was a coalescence both of nominal ideas and ideas of essence in the knowledge of morality. All this persuaded Locke to advance a "conjecture." It was:

". . . that morality is capable of demonstration as well as mathematics. For the ideas that ethics are conversant about, being all real essences, and such as, I imagine, have discoverable connection and agreement one with another; so far as we can find their habitudes and relations, so far we shall be possessed of certain, real, and general truths; and I doubt not but, if a right method were taken, a great part of morality might be made out with that clearness that could leave, to a considering man, no more reason to doubt than he could have to doubt of the truth of propositions in mathematics, which have been demonstrated to him."[23]

Moral Relations

Absent the discoveries of proofs and orderly demonstrations of moral knowledge by "a continued chain of reasonings," as in the method of the mathematical (algebra and geometry) schools, what was left as knowledge? Only the knowledge of relations, of which "moral relations" was an illustration. Locke's moral relations consist of relations between that which was put forth as moral and the rules by which it was compared so as to judge its morality. Locke's "moral relations" denominate morality in terms of the relation of the actions of persons to these rules. These are relations, the moral good and evil of the actions of which, consist in "only the conformity or disagreement of our voluntary actions to some law, whereby good and evil is drawn on us from the will and power of the lawmaker; which good and evil, pleasure or pain, attending our observance or breach of the law . . . is that we call 'reward' and 'punishment.' "[24]

Rule Basis of Moral Relations

Moral rules emerge as enforceable, law-like constraints on the motivators of the "free actions of man." Their object is to reward and punish through that which "is not the natural product and consequence of the action itself."[25] Locke set out three classes of law-like moral rules.

1. *The Divine Law*—"The only true touchstones of moral rectitude." Establishes the relation for judging whether actions be sins or duties.
2. *The Civil Law*—The law of the commonwealth, and by which the criminality of actions is established in order to "protect the lives, liberties and possessions" of the law abiding.
3. *Philosophical Law*—"The law of opinion or reputation." It stands for the inherent "virtue" and "vice" of actions. In this respect, Philosophical Law is a mirror of the Divine Law as universals of rectitude. It is also the space left by civil law for political man to exercise "the power of thinking well or ill, approving or disapproving, of the actions of those whom they live amongst, and converse with."[26]

In application, therefore, in its positive aspect as actual opinion or reputation, the measure of applied Philosophical Law is an outcome of the public temper; of customary approbation; of difference in education, fashion and interest; of social judgements, and the preferences/dislikes of political society.

> "Virtue is everywhere that which is thought praise- worthy; and nothing else but that which has the allowance of public esteem is called virtue!"[27]

The rule to which the action is related is the touchstone of morality; the mark of the value of the examined action.

> "The mind is easily able to observe the relation any action hath to it, and to judge whether the action agrees or disagrees with the rule; and so hath a notion of moral goodness or evil, which is either conformity or not conformity of any action to that rule; and therefore is often called 'moral rectitude.' "[28]

Morality As Relation

By placing morality in the context of relation (a category of the understanding), Locke had succeeded in establishing a foundation of sensation (perception and action) and relfection (operations of mind) for ideas of the moral. These are a mixed mode of ideas about moral purpose, moral beings, and moral actions with respect to another. It was also placement in a context that made all actions morally "relative." Locke was very specific about separating out "the positive idea" of any action (e.g. murder, lying, etc.) from its moral relation (rectitude or pravity).[29] There was no moral idea *per se*. There was only "the positive idea" of an action. There was no moral action *per se*. There was only a rule applied to the action. There was only the relations between the rule and the action, and by which moral relations were to be comprehended and judged.

The reasoning of Locke established the co-existence of motivation and morality; the one indigenous to the individual and the other exogenous to him. But the former was a vehicle of the power of the person in the exercise of liberty. The latter could be a vehicle of constraint on that liberty. Would the individual, in reflection, be likely to presume in favor of the one as against the other? It is not a question capable of general resolution within the logic employed by Locke. He left morality not an absolute, but a "relative." It was a moral relative made so by relations much too varied to be reduced to rules whereby to judge the moral rectitude or pravity of actions. As for the law—likeness of "the relation of human actions to a law, which therefore I call 'moral relations,' " that lies not in rule generality but in the punishment and the reward consequent to moral actions rightly conceived. As Locke put it, "no man escapes the punishment of their censure and dislike who offends against the fashion and opinion of the company he keeps, and would recommend himself to."[30]

REFERENCES

1. Locke, John, *An Essay Concerning Human Understanding* (6th edition), with the notes and illustrations of the author, and an analysis of his doctrine of ideas. Also, Questions on Locke's Essay, by A. M., Ethical Moderator in Trinity College, Dublin. (New Edition, The World Library, Ward, Lock & Co., London, undated) The original edition of Locke's *Essay* is 1689. Bk. I, Ch. III, Sec. 3, 27-28.
   2. Ibid., 28.
   3. Ibid., Bk. II, Ch. XXI, Sec. 28, 174.
   4. Ibid., Sec. 30-34, 175-77.
   5. Ibid., Sec. 65, 194.
   6. Ibid., Sec. 59, 191.
   7. Ibid., Sec. 60, 192, Sec. 64, 194.
   8. Ibid., 199.
   9. Ibid., Sec. 71, 199.
   10. Ibid., Sec. 68, 196.
   11. Ibid., Bk. IV, Ch. XII, Sec. 4, 546.
   12. Ibid., Sec. 11, 549.
   13. Ibid., Bk. II, Ch. XXI, Sec. 69, 196.
   14. Ibid., Bk. IV, Ch. I, note, 428.
   15. Ibid., Bk. I, Ch. II, Sec. 2, 12.
   16. Ibid., Sec. 1.
   17. Ibid., Bk. I, Ch. III, Sec. 6, 29; Bk. I, Ch. IV, Sec. 23, 55.
   18. Ibid., Bk. I, Ch. III, Sec. 4, 28; Sec. 8, 30.
   19. Ibid., Bk. I, Ch. III, Sec. 6, 29.
   20. Ibid., Bk. IV, Ch. XII, Sec. 7, 546.

21. Ibid., Sec. 9, 547.
22. Ibid., Sec. 11, 549.
23. Ibid., Sec. 8, 547.
24. Ibid., Bk. II, Ch. XXVIII, Sec. 5, 279.
25. Ibid., Sec. 6, 280.
26. Ibid., Sec. 10, 281.
27. Ibid., Sec. 11, 281.
28. Ibid., Sec. 14, 283.
29. Ibid., Sec. 16, 284-85.
30. Ibid., Sec. 12, 282.

CHAPTER XVIII

Moral Knowledge
and the Art of Consequences

"If geometry were as much opposed to our passions and present interests as is ethics, we should contest it and violate it but little less, notwithstanding all the demonstrations of Euclid and of Archimedes, which you would call dreams and believe full of paralogisms."[1]

"When I consider how much ambition or avarice can accomplish in all those who once place themselves in this course of life, almost destitute of sensible and present attractions, I despair of nothing, and I hold that virtue would be infinitely more effective accompanied as it is by so many solid goods, if some happy revolution of the human race brought it for a day into demand and made it as it were fashionable."[2]

Locke and Leibniz

LOCKE HAD LEFT IT that rule generating social units of political society, through the intimacies of their associative existence, establish the comparative norms of reference by which to judge the morality of the actions of another. Those others whose "moral relations" the individual so judged would, in their turn, do likewise for his own acts. But what of the acting person's own decision about the consequences of those of his own actions, those actions motivated by the pursuit of one's own liberty and happiness? For Locke, an autonomous rule of reference by which to judge of moral relation was always there to be appropriated by the individual for application to his own actions. For Leibniz, however, the moral could be given a knowledge content and be included within a frame of knowledge that reason brought to bear on motivated actions themselves.

Comparative Impotence of the Moral

The impotence of the ethical/the moral as a determinant of volition and action emerges in the analysis by Leibniz of its place in the human understanding. Not an absolute, but a comparative impotence. Comparatively impotent because of its subordination. A subordination to other, comparatively more potent, desires and aversions; and a subordination to their concurring perceptions, impulses and inclinations, all of which enter into volition. The ethical in action, the moral as "the practice of virtue," is assigned only a possibility for becoming a dominant that would prevail in the final determination of volition.

It is not that thoughts of good and evil are not present in the mind. The point at hand is why do they have such "little application to true goods." Leibniz explained, first of all, that thoughts of good and evil are cogitations with respect to which "the senses act but little." In consequence, they are like empty conceptions, lacking an established object content. Further, knowledge of good and evil is not, of itself, enough to determine volition. "Now this knowledge cannot move; something living is necessary in order to arouse us." Like thoughts of virtue and happiness, about which persons frequently think, they are ideas without definiteness. Ideas of "an absent good or evil" have the quality of feebleness, and scarcely affect the considerations persuading to preference.

Leibniz concluded that there was an opposition of tendencies, which, absent time and through negligence, is reduced to an opposition of "too feeble images to living feelings." As between the bad and the good, therefore, the preference for the bad "is because we perceive the good which it includes without perceiving either the bad therein or the good in the contrary consideration."

Beyond Desire

A good that is "almost destitute of sensible and present attractions is an absent good." How, then, does it enter into desire? Locke had coupled "uneasiness" to desire. Through this coupling he introduced anticipation of the future as an uneasiness that could be even more pressing to the mind than present enjoyment. The correction introduced by Leibniz was to take into account the influence of "imperceptibles" on volition, and also to separate uneasiness as a state from "full grown desire, or want for a known something." There is, then, the influence of imperceptibles as a mass, and impulses that are unaccompanied by distinct pleasures or pains.

The Art of Consequences

By infusing the moral with knowledge, Leibniz could link it to the special function of reason in the determination of volition. Moral knowledge was "knowledge of the value of the goods and evils." The taking into account of moral knowledge is a part of the balance of reasons that is to be done in the employment of the "art of consequences." Leibniz had put it that without desires mind would remain irresolute and undetermined. It would remain so "whatever examination it might make, and whatever good reasons or efficacious sentiments it might have."[4] Yet how was the execution of desire to be restricted, suspended or stopped "in case of need"? This, for Leibniz, was the real point. What Leibniz advocated to deal with it was a mind "prepared in advance" for proceeding methodically "from thought to thought" in a "train of thoughts."[5] In this way reason entered to command inclinations, propensities and desires over whose presence "in the soul" it had no power.

> "Thus we should still need the art of thinking and that of estimating probabilities, and besides the knowledge of the value of goods and evils in order properly to employ the art of consequences; and furthermore, attention and patience would be necessary after all that, in order to push to the conclusion. Finally, a firm and con-

stant resolution to execute the conclusion arrived at is necessary; and address, method, particular laws, and habits entirely formed in order to maintain the course in the future, when the considerations, which have caused it to be taken, are no longer present to the mind."[6]

False Judgements of Morality

There can be false judgements in the choice of good and evil. A present judgement, says Philatethes in the dialogue of the *New Essays*, with all consequences wholly put aside, is always right in its estimate of good and evil. The comment of Theophilus agrees that "if everything were limited to the present moment, it would not be right to refuse the pleasure which presents itself." But, he goes on, the present puts forth seeming perfections (pleasures) in which are contained "greater imperfections" (pains). The course of true judgement would be to proceed from perfection to perfection—from pleasure to pleasure.

> "Thus the perfection which is found in certain present pleasure should yield especially to the regard for the perfections which are necessary; in order that we be not plunged into misery, which is the state in which we go from imperfection to imperfection, from pain to pain."[7]

So there is always a future to be set against a present judgement of good and evil. A false judgement is one that is a derivative of false thinking about that future. As to this false thinking, Leibniz had more in mind than expectations denied because of erroneous judgement about that which could not be. He had in mind how thought of the future is itself annihilated by "a too feeble representation of the future, which is considered only a little or not at all."[8] Habits, feelings, temperaments, in all their human variety, all enter into thinking about the future. "But whatever variety is found among men, it is always true that they act only according to present perceptions, and when the future impresses them, it is always by means of an image they have of it, or by resolution and habit which they have contracted. . . ."[9]

True Judgements of Morality

It was that "too feeble representation of the future" that most concerned Leibniz. He stressed a distinction between consequence and consequent for true judgements of good and evil. They were not to be understood as the equivalent of one another. "It seems to me that if by the importance of the consequence we understand that of the consequent, i.e. the greatness of the good or evil that may follow, we must fall into the preceding kind of false judgement, in which future good or evil is poorly represented."[10] They were not comparable because of their heterogenity. The consequence of judgements would yield to estimates of probability, whether experiential or mathematical. Not so the consequent, the good or evil that may attend a probable consequence.

> "As these are two *heterogeneous* considerations (i.e. considerations which cannot be compared with each other), that of the greatness of the consequence and that of the greatness of the consequent, moralists in desiring to compare them are much perplexed, as appears in the case of those who have treated of probability. The truth is that there as in other estimates *disparate* and heterogeneous and, so to speak, of more than one dimension, the greatness of that which discussed is in reason composed of both estimates, and is like a rectangle, in which there are two considerations, viz., that of length and that of breadth."[11]

The Foundation of Virtue

For Leibniz, virtue entered into the "art of consequences" as virtue deposed from its once held place of domination in the structure of human preference. He attributed this to the loss of its religious foundation, lost through the evaporation of belief in the doctrine of the future life. "The future and reason rarely make so strong an impression as the present and the senses."[12] The separation of virtue from piety lodged virtue as an uncertain preference in the complicated context of things secular that must be thought about and be taken into account in the determination of volition.

Given what Leibniz took as a fact—"That a hidden unbelief reigns in the depths of their [person's] souls"—what was there besides "the art of thinking in time of need of what we know" to regain for virtue its place of domination? There was firm resolve "to look upon the true good and the true evil with the purpose of following or shunning them." There was personal character, for moral precepts and "the best rules of prudence take effect only in a soul which is *sensible*" either directly or indirectly to them. There was education designed to inculcate the "habit of acting according to reason, which makes virtue pleasant, and as it were natural."[13]

The Advancement of Moral Knowledge

Yet there was more than just the attributes of personal character to sustain morality. Leibniz, like Locke, not only included morality within the obligation to improve knowledge, but also tied that improvement to the actual benefits to be derived from the advancement of the science of nature.

> "True morality or piety, very far from favoring the inactivity of certain idle quietists, must impel us to cultivate the arts. And as I said not long since, a better police would be able to bring us some day a much better medical science than that we have at present. We cannot preach this doctrine enough, next to the care for virtue."[14]

The knowledge of ehtics was assigned by Leibniz to the "*analytical* and *practical*, commencing with the end of men, i.e. with the goods whose consummation is happiness and seeking in order the means available for acquiring these goods or avoiding the contrary evils."[15] Given the practical character of its knowledge, the tie between ethics and those arts in which "knowledge has been very much bound up with performance" is not surprising.[16]

"Moral Relations" and the Judgement of Others

In the exposition of moral relations by Locke, without an extrinsic rule of belief against which an action would be compared there could be no idea of the moral. Further, there would be no such rule of belief without a basis in the judgement of others. The judgement of others implies that certain views have prevailed in the minds of others. The query of Leibniz was the following: What is the assent to be given to the judgement by which the rule exists?

The spokesperson (Philalethes) for Locke's view discloses a variety of judgement formulations, each supporting a different degree of assent of belief. These range from assurance (the highest degree of factual probability), through confidence (confirmed custom), firm belief (vouched testimony of "unsuspected people"), to conjecture, doubt, uncertainty, distrust (contradictory/conflicting information). Assent, in sum, would be proportioned to the degrees of probability. The spokesperson was intent upon establishing the sensory grounds for "right judgement" concerning things capable of proof with degrees of certainty of knowledge as to their probability.[17]

Such an intent, in itself, would not dispose of the question: Who are those others who judge and what is the basis of the views on which they do so? Locke accepted that the associated others do not necessarily have to establish the rule of morality on the basis of knowledge. If there is no such acceptance, what shall guide the judgement of the judged about those who have incorporated their judgements in the rule by which moral rectitude or pravity will be decided? Locke had neither selected out nor placed restrictions on the assent quality of that from which the rule of relation was formulated —"a power of thinking well or ill" of actions. Here Locke's basic concern was set forth as the maintenance of peace between persons amid a diversity of opinions and viewpoints. But when should the individual not yield in the interest of peace within the commonwealth? Particularly where private motives of interest or ambition are in play, "rooted opinion" should not yield to objections. Such was the stated position of Philalethes.[18]

Moral Judgements and Motivated Actions

The power of motivation is indigenous to the individual. The relational power of morality lies within a social aggregate. Each, as Locke noted, carries within itself its own special consequence. A notably distinctive attribute of morality is that it will result in consequences different from those of motivation. Leibniz, too, separated the consequences of acts of motivation from those of moral acts, terming the latter the consequent (see p. 338).

Motivation, therefore, must function within a certain penumbra of "unease" about morality. It is because of the latter that acts rooted in motivation will be subjected to appraisal by other than motivational standards. Leibniz endeavored to synthesize the two in a recommended analytical method of decision whereby to apply the "Art of Consequence" in choosing and judging. There would be something akin to a "balancing of accounts" by prepared and disciplined minds.

Just what the data base might be for assigning values to moral factors was neither dealt with nor segregrated out from the data base underlying motivation. The nub of the matter in arriving at a balance of accounts is the influence or force of the data base of each in the determination of volition. One might expect, in the frame of Locke, that the force of relational morality in the total data base of individual motivation would tend to be more tenuous than determinant. One might also expect that the force of motivation in the total data base of aggregate (relational) morality would tend to be more tenuous than determinate.

Leibniz took his stand on character and mind. The first because it would make morality a determinate factor in the individual. The second because an impasse between morality and motivation could be avoided by method and by disciplined capability to judge. His response to relation was one of psychological insight and attitude.

> "Not that there is not, in truth, reason very often for censuring the opinions of others, but it must be done in a spirit of fairness, and sympathy with human weakness. It is true that we are right in taking precautions against bad doctrines, which are influential upon

manners and upon practical piety; but we must not attribute them to people to their prejudice without having good proofs of the same. If fairness wishes to spare persons, piety demands the representation, where it is fitting, of the bad effects of their dogmas when they are imperious. . . ."[19]

For Locke, however, the ultimate response was the civil law. Morality would thereby become an imposed determinant of volition. It would be the power of the commonwealth forcibly constraining motivation with the punishments of positive law. Relational (aggregate) morality could not elude a political solution. Individual motivation could not withdraw morality into its own preserves of preference in the pursuit of happiness. Too, individual motivation was left with the fuzzy dilemma of discovering just what relations or social aggregates, might be generated by its motivated acts.

REFERENCES

1. Leibniz, Gottfried Wilhelm, New Essays Concerning Human Understanding: Together with An Appendix Consisting of Some of His Shorter Pieces, (Langley, Alfred G., Transl., with notes). (The Macmillan Co 1896), (Reprinted 1916, 1949 by Open Court, Chicago). Bk. I, Ch. II, 93.
2. Ibid., Bk. II, Ch. XXI, 198.
3. Ibid., Bk. II, Ch. XXI, 191.
4. Ibid., 204.
5. Ibid., 202-203.
6. Ibid., 215.
7. Ibid., 209.
8. Ibid., 210.
9. Ibid., 211.
10. Ibid., 212.
11. Ibid., 213.
12. Ibid., Bk. I, Ch. II, 92.
13. Ibid., Bk. I, Ch. II, 92, Bk. II, Ch. XXI, 192, 193, 196, 215.
14. Ibid., Bk. IV, Ch. XII, Sec. 12, 526.
15. Ibid., Sec. 1, 624.
16. Ibid., 628.
17. Ibid., Bk. IV, Ch. XVI, Sec. 5, 537-38.
18. Ibid., Sec. 5, 534.
19. Ibid., Sec. 4, 535.

BIBLIOGRAPHY

Periodicals/Articles

Booth, William. "NIH Scientists Agonize Over Technology Transfer," Vol. 243 Science, January 5, 1989, p. 20.

Brooks, John. "The Go-Go Years," The New Yorker Magazine, June 23, 1970, p. 40.

Bruck, Connie. "Undoing the Eighties," The New Yorker Magazine, July 23, 1990, p. 56.

Churbuck, David. "The Ultimate Computer Game," 145 Forbes No. 3, February 5, 1990, p. 154.

Cross, Michael. "Do Computers Dream of Intelligent Humans?," New Scientist, November 26, 1988, p. 42.

Cullison, A.E. "How New Technologies Will Change Society," 36 Sumitomo Quarterly 8 (Spring 1989, Tokyo, Japan)

Duffy, M.C. "Techmorphology and the Stephenson Traction System," 54 Newcomen Society Transactions (1982-83) 55, 56.

Eisenstodt, Gale. "A Different Kind of Drug Problem," Forbes, January 22, 1990, p. 40.

Hinterhuber, Hans and Wolfgang, Papp. "Strategy as a System of Expedients," 21 Long Range Planning No. 4 (1988)

Institutional Investor. "The Way It Was: An Oral History," Vol. 21, No. 6, June 1987 (20th Anniversary Issue)

"Japan's Quest for the Brainy Computer," New Scientist, January 26, 1991, p. 51.

"Japan Shares It's Fifth Generation Dream," New Scientist, December 10, 1988, p. 26.

Lessing, Laurence. "Into the Core of Life and Self," Fortune, March 1966, p. 146.
  "Inside the Molecules of the Mind," Fortune, July 1966, p. 100.
  "The Life-Saving Promise of Enzymes," Fortune, March 1969, p. 119.

Metal Working News, "AT&T Bell Lab Scientist Cite New Form of Matter," February 6, 1989, p. 10.

Monnmane, Terence. "Complex Window on Life's Most Basic Molecules (Molecular Graphics)," 16 Smithsonian No. 4, July 1985.

Scientific American, Vol. 245, No. 3, September 1981, Domain, Arnold L. and Solomon, Nadine A. "Industrial Microbiology, p. 66.
Aharonowitz, Yair and Cohen, Gerald. "The Microbiological Production of Pharmaceuticals," p. 140.
Eveleigh, Douglas E. "The Microbiological Production of Industrial Chemicals," p. 154.
Rose, Anthony H. "The Microbiological Production of Food and Drink," p. 126.
Seikman, Philip. "In Electronics, The Big Stakes Ride on Tiny Chips," Fortune, June 1966, p. 120.

Newspaper/Articles

Angier, Natalie. "Biologists Unravel Key Link of Cell Division," New York Times, November 6, 1990, p. B5.
Browne, Malcolm. "Chemists Make Synthetic Molecules with a Hint of Life," New York Times, October 30, 1990, pp. 1, 35.
Carnevale, Mary Lu. "Bell Ruling Seen Touching Off Legal, Legislative Battles," Wall Street Journal, July 29, 1991, p. B1.
"Eight Will Spend Next Two Years In Big Terrarium," Cleveland Plain Dealer, September 13, 1990, P. B5.
Fries, Peter. "Neoreality Comes to High Tech World," Cleveland Plain Dealer, February 18, 1990.
"Here's What's Involved in Biosphere Venture," Cleveland Plain Dealer, September 29, 1991, p. 21A; and "Living in an Artificial World," Ibid., at p. 20A.
"Hitachi to build biotechnology laboratory on campus of the University of California, Irvine," Cleveland Plain Dealer, May 6, 1990, p. 4E.
"Laboratory Synthesis of Self-Replicating Molecules," New York Times, October 30, 1990, p. B5.
Ono, Yumiko and Brauchi, Marcos W. "Drug Makers in Japan Seek Foreign Firms," Wall Street Journal, August 23, 1989, p. 8A.
Rifkin, Glenn. "Keeping Track of a Hermetic Universe," New York Times, February 10, 1991, Sec. 3-8.
Sandberg-Dirment, Erik. "The Executive Computer," New York Times, November 23, 1986, p. 18F.
Shulins, Nancy. "What in Creation (Producing Artificial Life)," Cleveland Plain Dealer, January 13, 1991, p. 1G.
Shellenbarger, Sue. "Lilly's New Supercomputer Spurs a Race For Hardware to Quicken Drug Research," Wall Street Journal, August 14, 1990, p. B1.

Stevens, William K. "Evolving Theory Views Earth as a Living Organism," New York Times, August 29, 1989.
"The Theater of High Tech," New York Times, February 10, 1991, Sec. 3-1.

Books

Angyal, Andras. Foundations for a Science of Personality (Viking, New York, 1972)
Antebi, Elizabeth and Fishlock, David. Biotechnology: Strategies for Life (MIT Press, Cambridge, MA, 1986)
Florent, Jean. "The Great Turning Point: Antibiotics and Secondary Metabolities," Pt. 1, Article 1, p. 20.
Beppu, Teruhiko. "Microbiological Engineering," Pt. 5, Article 13, p. 176.
Ashby, W. Ross. An Introduction to Cybernetics (Wiley and Sons, Science Editions, New York, 1963)
Auw, Alvin von. Heritage and Destiny: Reflections on the Bell System in Transition (Praeger, New York, 1983)
Barry, J.M. Molecular Biology: Genes and the Chemical Control of Living Cells (Prentice Hall, 1964)
Beasley, W.S. The Modern History of Japan (Praeger, New York, 2nd ed., 1974)
Braudel, Fernand. Civilization and Capitalism: 15th-18th Century
    Vol. I—The Structures of Everyday Life (Miriam Kochan, transl., rev. transl., Sian Reynolds, Harper & Row, New York, 1981)
    Vol. II—The Wheels of Commerce (Sian Reynolds, transl., Harper and Row, New York, 1982)
    Vol. III—The Perspective of the World (Sian Reynolds, transl., Harper and Row, New York, 1982)
Clark, Ronald W. Einstein: The Life and Times (World Publ. Co., New York, 1971)
Commercial Biotechnology: An International Analysis (Office of Technology Assessment, U.S. Congress, Washington D.C., OTA-BA-218, January 1984)
David, Lewis W. and Trimble, William F. The Airway to Everywhere (U. of Pittsburgh Press, 1988)
Duquesne, Maurice. Matter and Antimatter (Transl. from French by Pomerans, A.J., Hutchinson and Co., 1960; Arrow Books ed., London, 1960)
Einstein, Albert. Ideas and Opinions (Sanja Bargmann, transl., Crown Publrs., Inc., New York, 1954)

Einstein, Albert. Out of My Later Years (Philosophical Library, The Wisdom Library, New York, 1950)
The Encyclopedia Britannica (11th ed., Vol. 16, 1911 (The Encyclopedia Britannica Co., New York)
Fagan, M.D. (ed.). A History of Engineering and Science in the Bell System: The Early Years (1875-1925) (Bell Telephone Laboratories, Inc., 1975)
Feigenbaum, Edward A. and McCorduck, Pamela. The Fifth Generation: Artificial Intelligence and Japan's Computer Challenge to the World (Signet ed., 1984, New American Library, New York)
Ferguson, M.C. and Fuller, J.P. Research and Development Limited Partnerships (Practicing Law Institute, Handbook No. 230, 1985 ed.)
Freedman, Paul. The Principles of Scientific Research (Public Affairs Press, Washington D.C., 1950)
Fuller, J.F.C. (Major General). A Military History of the Western World, Vol. III (Minerva Press, Funk and Wagnalls, New York, 1967 ed.)
Gregory, Gene. Japanese Electronics Technology: Enterprise and Innovation (John Wiley and Sons, 2nd ed., 1986, New York)
Grundstein, Nathan D. The Futures of Prudence: Pure Strategy and Aristotelian and Hobbesian Strategists (EAA, Hudson, Ohio, 1984)
Guillemin, Victor. The Story of Quantum Mechanics (Scribners Sons, New York, 1968)
Howard, Frank and Gunston, Bill. The Conquest of the Air (Random House, New York, 1st Amer. ed. 1972)
Jones, Richard W. Principles of Biological Regulation (Academic Press, New York, 1973)
Kahn, Alfred E. Great Britain in the World Economy (Columbia U. Press, New York, 1946)
Kenney, Martin. Biotechnology: The University Industrial Complex (Yale U. Press, New Haven, CT, 1986)
Kimble, Daniel P. Psychology as a Biological Science (Goodyear Publ. Co., Pacific Palisades, CA, 1973)
Leibniz, Gottfried Wilhelm. New Essays Concerning Human Understanding: Together with an Appendix Consisting of Some of His Shorter Pieces (Langley, Alfred G., transl., with notes) (The MacMillan Co., 1896, reprinted 1916, 1949 by Open Court, Chicago)
Leibniz, Gottfried Wilhelm. Discourse on Metaphysics, Correspondence with Arnould and Monadology (Intro. by Paul Janet, transl. by George R. Montgomery, Open Court Publishing Co., 1916)
Leibniz, Gottfried Wilhelm von. Monadology and Other Philosophical Essays (Intro. and notes by Paul Schrecker, transl. Schrecker, Paul and Schrecker, Anne M., Bobbs-Merrill Co., 1965)
Leibniz, Gottfried Wilhelm. The Monadology and Other Philosophical

Writings (Intro. and notes by Robert Latta, Oxford U. Press, 1898, rep. ed. 1945)

Locke, John. An Essay Concerning Human Understanding (6th ed.), with the notes and illustrations of the author, and an analysis of his doctrine of ideas. Also, questions on Locke's Essay, by A.M., Ethical Moderator in Trinity College, Dublin (New Edition, The World Library, Ward, Lock & Co., London, undated). The original edition of Locke's Essay is 1689.

Lodge, Sir Oliver. Pioneers of Science (MacMillan and Co., Ltd., London, 1926)

Luttwak, Edward N. Strategy: The Logic of War and Peace (Harvard, The Belknap Press, Cambridge, MA, 1987)

Lwoff, Andre. Biological Order (MIT Press, Cambridge, MA, 1962)

Mantoux, Paul. The Industrial Revolution in the Eighteenth Century (Rev. ed. 1928, Harcourt, Brace & Co., New York)

Marshall, Alfred. Elements of Economics of Industry, Vol. I (MacMillan and Co., New York, 1892)

Mason, Stephen F. A History of the Sciences (Rev. 1962, Collier Books, New York)

Mensch, Gerhard O. Stalemate in Technology (Ballinger, Cambridge, MA, 1979)

Mumford, Lewis. Technics and Civilization (Harcourt, Brace & Co., New York, 1934)

Muramatsu, Teijiro. Industrial Technology in Japan: A Historical Review (Hitachi, Ltd., Tokyo, Japan, 1968)

Nordenskiold, Erik. The History of Biology (Transl. from Swedish by Leonard B. Eyre, Tudor Publ. Co., New York, New ed., 1936 printing)

Oglivie, John (ed.). Imperial Dictionary (New Edition, Annandole, Charles (ed.), London, The Century Co., New York, 1883)

Pais, Abraham. Inward Bound: Of Matter and Forces in the Physical World (Oxford, New York, 1986)

Prentice, Steve. Biotechnology: A New Industrial Revolution (G. Braziller, Inc., New York, 1984)

Reeves, Earl. Aviation's Place in Tomorrow's Business (B.C. Forbes Publ. Co., New York, 1930)

Roobeek, Anne and Mieke, J.M. Beyond the Technology Race (Elsevier, New York, 1990)

Sagan, Carl. The Cosmic Connection: An Extraterrestrial Perspective (Anchor Press, Doubleday, Garden City, New York, 1973)

Sarton, George. Six Wings: Men of Science in the Renaissance (Meridian ed. 1966, World Publ. Co., Cleveland, Ohio)

Sobel, Robert. The Entrepreneurs: Explorations Within the American Business Tradition (Weybright and Talley, New York, 1974)

Schumpeter, Joseph A. The Theory of Economic Development (Oxford U. Press, New York, R. Opie, transl. 1961 reprint of 1934 ed.)

Space Science Board. Space Research: Directions for the Future, Part Three (National Academy of Sciences, National Research Council, Washington D.C., 1950)

Usher, Abbott Payson. A History of Mechanical Inventions (McGraw-Hill, New York, 1929)

Utter, James M. and Kim. Invasion of a Stable Business By Radical Innovation, Ch. 10 of Kleindoryer, Paul R. (ed.). The Management of Productivity and Technology in Manufacturing (Plenum Press, New York, 1985)

Watson, James D. Molecular Biology of the Gene (W.A. Benjamin, Inc., Menlo Park, CA, 3rd ed. 1976)

White, John T. The White Latin Dictionary (Follett Publ. Co., Follett Foreign Language Series, Chicago, Il., 1958)

Whitehouse, Arch. The Sky's the Limit: A History of U.S. Airlines (MacMillan, New York, 1971)

Weiner, Norbert. Cybernetics (Wiley, New York, 1948)

INDEX

ACTION
And choice, 264 *et seq.*; and power (Locke), 57, 63; and power (Leibniz), 286; person as agent of, 58.

BASE TECHNOLOGY
Centrality of, 6 *et seq.*; mechatronics as, 40; and hegemonic industrialization, 42-43.

BIOLOGY (PRE-INDUSTRIALIZED)
Pre-Lockean, 221-225; post-Lockean, 225-233; modes of biological knowing —factual, speculative, natural science, theoretical, empirical, and experimental, Ch. XIV.

BIOLOGY (INDUSTRIALIZED LIFE PHENOMENA)
empty person of, 170, 179; biological regimes, 171; industrial microbiology, scope of, 172-175; strategic knowledge regarding, 177-179; variety of and regulation, 175-177.

BIOTECHNOLOGY
The scene, 182-184; product strategizing, 184-188; venture capital and chain of strategy, 188-193; command cognition and strategic concerns, 193-198; alternative to venture capital, 198; Japanese strategy, 200-201; public funds investment, 201.

CAPITAL
Conception of, 3-4; as superior force, 2-3; and command cognition, 61; as time, 10; and industrialization, 102.

CAPITALISM
Strategic freedom of, 59-62; real and micro-capitalism compared, 59-62, 172; Real capitalism and industrialized microbiology, 173-175; entrepreneurial capitalism, 26 *et seq.*; knowledge rules of, 67 *et seq.*; negative sector experiences, 69 *et seq.*; disciplined cognitive competence, 66-67; finance capitalism transformed, 29 *et seq.*; real capitalism, 45-46; understanding of external variety, 104-106.

CAPITALIST
As disciplined agent of action, 65-67.

COGNITION
As power, 57, 63; Rule cognition, 64; as domination, 277, 285-289; cognitive variety, 285.

COMMAND COGNITION
As knowing and thinking, 15-16; Leibniz and, 285 *et seq.*; and possibilities knowledge, 28; as strategic knowledge, Ch.II; rule categories of, 67-69; as knowledge, 285 *et seq.*; and strategizing biotechnology, 193 *et seq.*; and judgment, 266; more than practical knowledge, 275; freedom and, 295.

COMPUTERIZATION (of strategic knowledge)
Sixth (Japan) Generation Computer-knowledge frame-Prologue, xxix *et seq.*

CONSCIOUSNESS
As pre-condition of knowing, 240; and personal identity, 206 *et seq.*; 214-215.

CREATION
I knowledge of, 121-123; II knowledge of, 123-128.

DECISION
And command cognition, 289; and Art of consequences, 291-293; decision managment, 277; as judgment, 294.

ELECTRONICS
And strategic knowledge, Ch. II, 3, 34 *et seq.*

ENTELECHY
As an internal force, 216.

EXPERT SYSTEMS
Appraisal of and separation from artificial intelligence, Prologue, Note, xxxvi-xxxviii.

FITTED KNOWLEDGE
Contrasted with possibilities knowledge, Note, 234; Applied to finance and capitalism, 26 et seq.

FREEDOM (LIBERTY)
Motivation, liberty and choice, 259-260; 323, 331-332; and command cognition (Leibniz), 295 et seq.

HUMANS
Estimated intelligence (Locke), 236-238; Estimate of intelligence (Leibniz), 274-275; inherent power of, 286.

IDEA
Truth or falsity, of 94; moral as idea, 311; Locke/Leibniz compared, 297 et seq.; related to knowledge (Locke), 243 et seq.; ideas and finite intelligence, 242-243; 90; ideas and the physical world, 87 et seq.; innate ideas (Leibniz), 283; and knowledge, 92.

INDUSTRIALIZATION
Focused industrialization, 47-49; institutionalized industrialization, 45-47; Hegemonic industrialization, 41 et seq.; pre-industrialization, 71 et seq.; capitalism and, 102-106; pre-industry, 71-73.

INFORMATION
Sensory information, 47; perception, 47.

INTELLIGENCE
Meanings of (Prologue), xxxi-xxxii; human understanding and artificial intelligence, xxxii et seq.; expert systems and artificial intelligence, Note, xxxvi-xxxviii; finite intelligence (Locke), 242; and (Leibniz), 278.

JUDGMENT
As interrogated command cognition, 266; As decision, 294; motivational judgment, 324; and morality, 337-338.

KNOWLEDGE
Fitted and possibilities knowledge, Note, 234; possibilities knowledge and knowledge possibilities, 34-35; possibilities knowledge and strategic knowledge, 28; knowledge of variety (Pt. 2A), 75; and (Pt. 2B), 115; knowledge of reason, 260-264; post and pre-operative knowing, 278 et seq.; pre-formative knowledge, 283. See Knowledge Foundations I, II and III; of engagement, 58-59; and matter, 246 et seq., 305; physics as strategic knowledge, Ch. VII; domain knowledge, 123-125; Pre-strategic (inventions), 99.

KNOWING AND THINKING
Ch. XV (Locke); Ch. XVI (Leibniz); Boundary of thought, 87, 90.

MIND
And relational knowledge, 118 et seq.

MONAD
Person as, 215-217.

MORAL
As idea and judgment, 311-313; comparative impotence of, 335; true and false judgments of, 337-338; as relation, 330-331; and motivation, 322 et seq.; as a foundation knowledge, Ch. XVII and Ch. XVIII; Note, Moral Knowledge and Knowledge of Strategy, 308 et seq.

PERSON
As idea, Ch. XIII; consciousness and, 206; genuine and facsimile persons, 209 et seq.; being and, 211-217; as empty person, 170 and 220; finite intelligence of, 242 et seq. (Locke); and 278 et seq. (Leibniz); and agency, 58-59; natural and metaphysical, 210. See Monad.

POWER
Idea of, 63; and cognition, 57; as simple idea, 258, 264; Leibniz/Locke compared, 285-287, 292; and agency, 58.

REASON
Knowledge of, 301 et seq. and 260 et seq.; as command cognition, 293.

RULE
Rule cognition and rule categories, 62 et seq.

STRATEGY
Re Sixth Generation (Japan) Computer Project (Prologue), xxix et seq.; not task specifics, xxxiii-xxxiv; three questions regarding, 1 et seq.; knowledge focus of, 10-12; and the business of telephony, 16 et seq.; as possibilities knowledge, 267 et seq., 34 et seq., 130 et seq.; as globalized strategy, 35; as knowledge of variety; Pt IIA (75) and Pt IIB (115); and venture capital, 188 et seq.; as grand strategy, 44 et seq.; capitalism and strategic freedom, 102 et seq.; as domain knowledge, 123-125; focus of, 309.

TELEINFORMATICS
As the business of information, 24-25.

INDEX 351

THINKING
As mind active, xxviii; as making intelligible, 239 *et seq.*; as conscious knowing, 250-253; as quasi-autonomous mind, 253; as the power of mind with respect to a knowledge structure internal to the knower, 276-285; as quasi-autonomous mind, 119 *et seq.*

UNDERSTANDING
As operational Thinking (idea, perception, reflection), 250-253.

VARIETY
Categories of (relational, internal, external, invisible), Pt. 2A and Pt. 2B; and strategic knowledge, 75, 79-85.